C000242762

COLIN CHAPMAN'S LOTUS

COLIN CHAPMAN'S LOTUS

Robin Read

Foulis

Haynes

Dedication

To the Unsung Heroes of Sales Team Lotus 1959-62

Ian McLeod, Ron Richardson and Peter Warr

without whose particular dedication and effort the story of Lotus would have
followed a shorter and less favourable course . . . and to the memory of the
Driving Force behind us all

Anthony Colin Bruce Chapman
CBE, RDI, Hon Dr (RCA), BSc Eng, FRSA
(1928–82)

whose talents and unusual energies transformed the course of motor racing
so forcefully and profoundly.

A FOULIS Motoring Book

First published 1989

© Robin Read

All rights reserved. No part of this book may be reproduced or transmitted in any
form or by any means, electronic or mechanical, including photocopying,
recording or by any information storage or retrieval system, without permission
of the publisher.

Published by:
Haynes Publishing Group
Sparkford, Nr. Yeovil,
Somerset BA22 7JJ, England

Haynes Publications Inc.
861 Lawrence Drive, Newbury Park,
California 91320 USA

British Library Cataloguing in Publication Data
Read, Robin F.
Colin Chapman's Lotus, the early years; the Elite and origins of the Elan
1. Lotus cars to 1981
I. Title
629.2'222
ISBN 8-85429-703-0
Library of Congress Catalog Card No.
88-82691

Editor: Robert Iles
Design: Tim Rose
Printed in England by: J.H. Haynes & Co. Ltd

Contents

Acknowledgements

Because I wished to keep this very personal book just so, I have mainly relied on my own archive and memories for inspiration. However, at a reunion of old Lotus employees organised by my successor Graham Arnold at Cheshunt in November 1986, I met again after a quarter of a century my former colleague Ron Hickman. When the time came I consulted Ron in my search for information about the technical development of the Elite and the Elan – a subject shrouded in mystery and not a little official secrecy. My curiosity (coupled with the inadequate and inaccurate information on this particular subject contained in my early drafts) stimulated Ron to help me by drawing on his recollection of events. Later he was able to cull from John Frayling, now in retirement, even more information from the interval when Ron was not directly involved in the Elite project. This invaluable assistance has made it possible to clarify many hitherto obscure aspects of the origin of these two Lotus road cars and I am deeply indebted to Ron for his generously-given advice and encouragement.

Thanks are due to Sy Kaback of New York – long suffering Lotus Distributor and friend – who generously sent over his collection of documents and photographs. I have drawn gratefully on this mine of information.

I count myself particularly fortunate to have persuaded Mike Costin to read the text and contribute a Foreword. He "was there" long before my time and his role at Cosworth kept him in contact with Colin Chapman and the Lotus World throughout the succeeding years. Mike is as much Lotus as anyone other than the Founder himself and his unobtrusive support during the early years at Hornsey and Cheshunt was essential to Colin's success.

I also have to thank my former colleague Ian McLeod (the only member of my Lotus sales team whom I appointed, rather than inherited) for unrestricted access to his private collection of photographs and other Lotus memorabilia.

Throughout the extended birth pangs of this book I have been greatly aided by the dedication of my secretarial assistant Dorothy Abel and the encouragement of Rod Grainger's patient and enthusiastic team at GT Foulis. To them all I extend my heartfelt gratitude.

Robin Read
Olney

Foreword

by Mike Costin

Chairman, Cosworth Engineering Limited
(Formerly Director of Engineering Development, Lotus Group of Companies)

By the time that Robin Read arrived at Cheshunt in 1959, it seemed to me that I had already given the best years of my life to Lotus. Like most of the early band of enthusiasts who spent all hours at Hornsey working with Colin to build up his business and racing activities, I never counted the cost. However, the Chapman Experience was one that I shall not forget and although I often had doubts about its benefit to health and sanity, I enjoyed it.

When Robin joined the company we were in transition from a small band of dedicated enthusiasts, to fledgling managers of a growing industrial enterprise. We needed to bring into the company outside skills from the established Motor Industry and this was why Robin was recruited. Until I read his book I thought of him as our unfortunate Sales Manager, but I see now that he studied what was going on further afield. It is interesting to be reminded of those early years and to read Robin's effort to place the Elite and Elan in technical and historical context. I am also intrigued that he has attempted to pass judgement on Colin's achievements as a designer.

There are many books about Lotus cars but not much has appeared in print about my old friend Colin Chapman himself. I welcome this new book for the way in which it sheds light on his character, the people round him and the way in which he operated, as much as on the cars themselves.

Mike Costin

Chapter One

Introduction

When I left Lotus as a result of a gentle (by Chapman standards) sacking, I turned my back on a six year period of devotion to very different sectors of the Motor Industry. I had no further contact with Colin Chapman or any of my erstwhile colleagues until late 1986 when I had the pleasure of attending the launch of "Jabby" Crombac's authorised biography of Chapman. The one exception to this was my old friend Mike Costin who left Lotus (entirely of his own free will!) in that same year – 1962. Whereas Mike has remained active in the world of high performance motoring at Cosworth, I ventured into pastures new in conventional commerce.

From time to time as a result of a continuing interest in motoring matters I observed and noted the development of Lotus, which although at a much more advanced level than in "my" years still seemed to have the erratic but often brilliant qualities of a Chapman-controlled endeavour. Nevertheless Chapman was making money for himself and occasionally the shareholders, while continuing his oustandingly successful career in Grand Prix motor racing. My memories of the company had been encapsulated by the subsequent overlay of totally different experience. When therefore I decided to record my memories of time spent in the shadow of Colin Chapman I was not distracted by subsequent events or confused by the jumble of an extended period of recollection.

What was apparent to me was that the short time (1959 – 1962) in which I was based at Cheshunt encompassed the most important series of events in the life of Colin Chapman the designer. This was the time when Chapman had experienced a period of defeat – even ignominy – before casting off the mantle of failure by a two year sequence of brilliant designs which totally restored the prestige of Lotus and shored up its battered financial strength for the future. Chapman's sudden embrace of the rear engined racing car configuration – forced finally by the success of his arch rival Cooper – marked a decisive turning point in Lotus fortunes which continued almost unabated in the immediately succeeding years. I was there; overheard many of the vital conversations and saw subsequent developments with my own eyes. My work at Lotus would perhaps have been easier – although much less absorbing – if I had not had an overwhelming interest in automotive technicalities. Like all Special builders and amateur designers of the period I had aspired to the levels of success enjoyed by Chapman. It was therefore fascinating to find myself at the centre of the Chapman power house, able to see how the man worked, to make my own contribution to the regularisation of Lotus commercial activities and to begin the establishment of the present day distribution network.

What began as a series of recollections of events past developed into an assessment of Lotus technical development; a study of Chapman the designer and the influences on him during his climb to maturity. At a crucial stage in this process Ron Hickman whose role in the Lotus story is more important than widely understood, made a vital contribution to the process by generously shedding new light on the origins of the Elite and Elan, thus in many ways making my task easier but forcing considerable revision of what had so far been written.

This book is my personal homage to the late Colin Chapman; a man occupying a unique position in automotive history and without whose brightly burning presence we should all have been infinitely the poorer. Much has been written about Lotus racing successes and cars but I hope that these words will to some extent restore the balance by revealing obscure personal qualities and commercial history inextricably linked to the Lotus design and development story. Never forget that Chapman was first and foremost a super-salesman, promoting himself, his products and services for financial gain.

(ii) Meeting Colin Chapman

In 1959 I found myself at a loose end after the closure of the Dante Engineering Company which since 1956 had manufactured and distributed speed equipment, chassis conversions and aluminium bodies for Austin Seven and Ford Ten owners and Special builders. This was the very field in which Colin Chapman had established Lotus, but by the end of the Fifties the once booming 750/1172 market was beginning to level off. There was a bewildering array of suppliers and products but a lack of customers to support them all.

I continued to freelance during the Spring of 1959 but it soon became obvious that I would need permanent employment to support myself and family. I therefore responded with enthusiasm to an advertisement issued by a recruitment consultancy seeking a sales manager for an unnamed (but easily identified) car manufacturer. At that time the reputation of Lotus was at an extremely low ebb and I had mixed feelings about the prospect of joining. On attending the interview I made it clear that I was aware of the identity of the company and this certainly intrigued the consultant interviewing me. The fact that earlier in my career I had been employed by the Standard-Triumph Motor Company in export sales and that my experience with Dante gave me an understanding of the specialised car production world helped to obtain the preliminary interview and later to be recommended to Chapman, whom I had never met.

In July I made my way to the Lotus works in Hornsey Lane, North London, where a tiny factory with offices and showroom had been built by Colin behind his father's pub, The Railway Hotel. Present at my first meeting with Colin Chapman was N J (Nobby) Clark (the company's first employee) who at that stage was Works Director. This was a time in Chapman's life when the excitement of the new factory nearing completion at Cheshunt was tempered by the disappointing performance of Team Lotus in Grand Prix racing and the disastrous showing of the Seventeen sports racing car intended to meet competition from Lola.

My future boss was nevertheless in remarkably good humour and obviously enjoyed the prospect of giving me a thoroughly difficult interview. It became

A portrait of Colin Chapman by John Cowan taken at the time when I met him – well before the stresses of taking Lotus into the realms of high finance resulted in premature ageing and death from a heart attack at the age of 54.

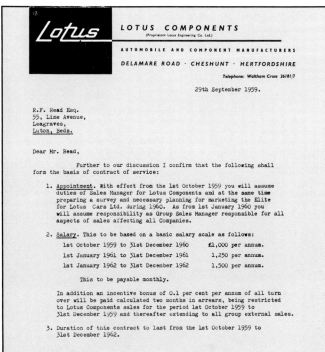

LOTUS COMPONENTS
(Proprietors Lotus Engineering Co. Ltd.)

AUTOMOBILE AND COMPONENT MANUFACTURERS

DELAMARE ROAD · CHESHUNT · HERTFORDSHIRE

Telephone: Waltham Cross 26181/7

29th September 1959.

R.F. Read Esq.
55, Lime Avenue,
Leagraves,
Luton, Beds.

Dear Mr. Read,

Further to our discussion I confirm that the following shall form the basis of contract of service:

1. Appointment. With effect from the 1st October 1959 you will assume duties of Sales Manager for Lotus Components and at the same time preparing a survey and necessary planning for marketing the Elite for Lotus Cars Ltd. during 1960. As from 1st January 1960 you will assume responsibility as Group Sales Manager responsible for all aspects of sales affecting all Companies.

2. Salary. This to be based on a basic salary scale as follows:

1st October 1959 to 31st December 1960   £1,000 per annum.
1st January 1961 to 31st December 1961   1,250 per annum.
1st January 1962 to 31st December 1962   1,500 per annum.

This to be payable monthly.

In addition an incentive bonus of 0.1 per cent per annum of all turn over will be paid calculated two months in arrears, being restricted to Lotus Components sales for the period 1st October 1959 to 31st December 1959 and thereafter extending to all group external sales.

3. Duration of this contract to last from the 1st October 1959 to 31st December 1962.

manufacturing or design methods, process and data as may come to your knowledge during the term of this Agreement and upon its completion, or if called upon to do so, hand over to the Company all drawings, paper and data whatsoever which may have been entrusted to you and which may have been prepared by you or any other person on behalf of the Company.

10. Within three months prior to the expiration of this Agreement the Company will re-consider the whole question of your future employment with the Company and at this time, subject to satisfactory completion of your services during the period of this Agreement, will most actively consider inviting you to join the Board of Directors of Lotus Cars Ltd.

Yours faithfully,
p.p. LOTUS COMPONENTS.

A.C.B. Chapman
Managing Director.

After an initial trial period at £750 per annum, a contract of service was issued by Chapman to the author. This was the time when all senior members of the company were at last put on a formal footing and I was treated in the manner used for Fred Bushell, Mike Costin, John Standen and Nobby Clark who up to that time had been employed on an informal basis. Acting with caution, Chapman gradually moved me towards overall sales responsibility from 1 January 1960 after the preliminary period in which I concentrated on the needs of Lotus Components. At the time the terms of this contract were generous and the incentive bonus (0.1% per annum *(sic)*) provided very welcome gilt on the gingerbread.

evident that I had to sell myself to him and eventually we did a characteristically-Lotus deal. I told him that he would not find anyone better suited than me and therefore I was prepared to give him three months at £15 per week in which to decide whether he wanted to keep me on. From 1st. October my basic salary would be increased by a third to £1000 per annum and thereafter by £250 per annum until 31st December 1962. On the basis that Chapman had achieved the initial victory, my triumph was to negotiate an overall commission on all sales of 0.1%. Before the completion of the last year, Lotus would "actively consider inviting me" to join the Board. Both parties considered this to be a thoroughly satisfactory arrangement and in fact it worked well while it lasted.

Although interviewed at Hornsey I never worked there and took up my appointment at Cheshunt which was occupied from June 1959 onwards. Despite earlier misgivings about Colin Chapman and his company, my initial meeting with him persuaded me that I should risk exposing myself to Lotus. In fact, despite the vicissitudes of those early years at Cheshunt my experience was overall enjoyable and certainly interesting. I saw my responsibilities clearly and Chapman let me get on with things in my way until he felt that he knew exactly what I was up to. Even then, although he would occasionally interfere, he gave me a remarkably free hand.

(iii) Names and Numbers for Lotus Cars and People

Confusion reigns when it comes to determining the correct name and number for the earlier models. I have therefore made an arbitrary choice of terminology based as closely as possible on what applied at the time – at **Lotus.** Almost every book on Lotus follows a distinctive and different line in this important area, but mine is thus:

Mk. 1 – Mk. 6	Fifteen	Twentyone (sic)
Seven	Sixteen	Twentytwo
Mk. 8 – Mk. 10	Seventeen	Twentythree
Eleven	Eighteen	Twentyfour
Twelve	Nineteen	Twentyfive
Elite (Lotus Type 14)	Twenty	Elan (Lotus Type 26)

Where people are concerned, I try to refer by their given name only to those whom I addressed so at the time. I find that I have a natural tendency to switch to the family name of my subjects when the going gets a little technical – when referring to the giants of automotive achievement I prefer formality to familiarity. And what on earth is "Team"? "Team What"? The Factory Teams of my time were always Team **Lotus** or Team **Elite.**

Chapter Two

The Early
"Specials" and Hornsey Cars

Colin Chapman was nurtured in the British Special building tradition and his earliest designs spring directly from the humble pre-war Austin Seven and later Ford Ten cars. To understand this influence it is necessary to examine a tradition which stretches back almost to the dawn of motorsporting history and of which the leading characteristic is the triumph of ingenuity over lack of financial and technical resources. The earliest significant Chapman achievement in this tradition was his Mk. 3A 750 Formula car of 1951 which clearly established his design philosophy.

The evolution of his early spaceframe cars beginning with the Mk. 6 and enjoying uninterrupted success up to 1957 is traced in this section. Also revealed is the faltering of 1958 and 1959 by which time others had learned from Chapman's example and challenged his supremacy. In the earliest years of this first period of Chapman's development as a designer may be traced the origins of the Elite road car which although a commercial disaster was beyond dispute a technical and aesthetic masterpiece.

(i) Colin Chapman and the British "Special" building tradition

No account of Chapman's life and work can disregard the tremendous two-way traffic in ideas between the world of the small home-built sporting car and his early achievements. By a happy chance Chapman discovered circuit motor racing in 1950 when he achieved instant fame by his quite unexpected victory at Silverstone Eight Clubs' meeting against Dudley Gahagan in his fast Bugatti Type 37, while driving the Lotus Mk. 2 car powered by an absolutely standard and rather tired Ford 10 sidevalve engine. Chapman thereupon decided that he preferred racing on a hard surface to competition in muddy trials and although he had cleverly designed the Mk. 2 for use on the road as well as off it, it was frankly not intended for circuit racing in the grand manner.

From the very earliest times enthusiasts rich and poor have created individual cars by joining together chassis and engines of separate provenance. But it was the case however that the British tradition of building such "one-off" or "Special" cars became a highly developed art most notably as a means of enabling the keen enthusiast or gifted engineer of limited means to engage in motor sport when unable to purchase a factory-fresh production competition car.

Brooklands was the cradle of a particular type of overpowered monster sometimes created from the amalgamation of an aircraft engine with large road car chassis (e.g. Chitty-Chitty-Bang-Bang). A separate tradition grew up in the Twenties and Thirties around the Sprint and Hill Climb venues such as Brighton and Shelsley Walsh still in use today. These short events were doubly attractive to the enthusiast of limited means in that most homebuilt, often over-tuned cars would survive long enough at least for the thirty or forty seconds taken to reach the finish line. Equally, the less material used in the construction of the car, the lighter it was and hence potentially more successful. The pre-war Sprint car Special building tradition was largely founded on the basis of the GN chassis and its later very similar successor the Frazer Nash, both of which came from the same designer – Archie Frazer-Nash – himself an expert Sprinter. The GN/Frazer Nash chassis was simplicity itself with front suspension by forward-facing quarter elliptic leaf springs and tubular axle while at the rear similar springs pointing in the reverse direction located a remarkable arrangement of a narrow differential-less tubular axle carrying a series of sprockets linked by chains to a countershaft on the chassis. This transmission was connected to engine and clutch by a short propeller shaft and bevel box. This arrangement had the great advantage for Sprinting of no differential effect, which reduced the tendency to wheelspin while encouraging the "tail out" cornering technique beloved of hill-climbers. Its two parallel chassis members were so sited that a wide variety of power units could be substituted for the originals. Generally speaking the earlier GN chassis ended up with powerful motorcycle V-twin engines by JAP or Blackburne etc., while the later Frazer Nash cars would appear with anything up to and even beyond a 2-litre 6-cylinder AC engine. Many of these cars (and some of the really original home-brewed vehicles such as John Bolster's "Bloody Mary" and the wonderfully sophisticated Issigonis-Dowson Lightweight Special) were quite capable of giving "real" racing cars a run for their money.

Even in pre-war years there were very successful Austin 7 and Ford 10 based Specials to be seen. "Bill" Williams of Cambridge Engineering built a series of competition cars based on sporting Austin 7 components while Leslie Ballamy was already to be seen in competition at Brooklands and elsewhere in small Specials based on Ford and Austin parts. But the war of 1939 – 1945 was the great turning point in the history of British Special building after which an activity which hitherto had been the preserve of a relatively small number of enthusiasts blossomed and flourished. After 1945 nothing was ever the same again. Servants were hard to come by, complained the wealthy and aristocratic. New cars were restricted by the iniquitous Covenant Scheme of the first post-war Labour Government. Servicemen returning to "Civvy Street" had money to spend and rushed to buy anything on four wheels that could drag itself along. Naturally the cost of cars rocketed and by 1950 pent-up interest in motor sport fostered by the early airfield races of the late Forties at Silverstone, Goodwood and elsewhere was creating strong demand for a source of sporting cars at modest cost. This demand was met by the rapid development of interest in the home-built or "Special" car.

Although formed in 1938, the 750 Motor Club really got into its stride after the War. As its name suggests it was a Club founded to foster use of the Austin Seven (750 cc) car in sporting events. Production of the Seven finished in the year of the Club's formation when 400,000 examples of Lord Austin's quaint little car for the masses had been produced at the Longbridge, Birmingham works together with thousands manufactured under licence in France, Germany, the USA, Japan and

Australia. The Austin Seven was already antiquated at its birth in 1922 – being almost Edwardian in concept. It was an appalling design but very well executed. The engine in standard form was so inefficient that no part of the car was highly stressed and the many defects of handling and braking were partially concealed by the inability of the standard car to go much faster than 45 mph. However, the Austin Works in parallel with production of the Seven family car had evolved a series of sporting models for sale and a much rarer sequence of pure competition cars with origins in the humble road-going Seven but intended for racing and record breaking on an international scale; particularly with the object of defeating the rising MG star of the rival Nuffield Organisation.

From 1945 onwards the real "sporting" Austins – the Ulster, Speedy and Nippy, were much sought after and commanded high prices. These little cars had lowered suspension (but retained the same awful braking system of the saloons) and were fitted with slightly more durable and noticeably more powerful versions of the basic Seven engine. The Works-designed cars clearly pointed the way to what could be done by the skilled and patient amateur using standard components and carrying out similar modifications. A great spur to the development of the 750 Motor Club came in 1950 with the introduction of the "Unblown 750 Formula". This was largely inspired by Holland Birkett who penned a remarkable article in *Motor Sport* (May 1950) describing the development of the sporting Seven and arousing much interest at the time (Just try to trace a copy of that issue!). The 750 Formula was intended to foster the construction of very simple Austin Seven-based cars for Club racing and in that same year Chapman decided that his next car should be constructed to run under the rules of the Formula. If one accepts the view commonly held, that this new car – the Mk. 3A – was the first to really demonstrate the qualities for which Chapman later became famous we must be eternally grateful to the 750 MC for its inspiration to Chapman at the point when an enthusiasm for circuit racing had been kindled in him. Up to that point during the winter of 1950/51 when he began to construct the Mk. 3A (and its two belated sisters) Chapman had been just another enthusiastic home-builder producing fairly ordinary examples of the contemporary Special building art. His success at Silverstone against Gahagan may be largely ascribed to Chapman's remarkable driving talent rather than the intrinsic qualities of the Mk. 2 Austin-Ford Lotus.

The British post-war Special building revolution was of kaleidoscopic complexity. Based principally around the pre-war Austin Seven and the pre- and post-war Ford 8 and 10 hp cars the movement reached its peak in advanced competition cars such as the Lotus Eleven, the products of Derek Buckler, Elva, Dellow and many others with a commercial interest in the movement. The great mass of Austin Seven and Ford Special builders however were pure amateurs with perhaps one or two cars only to their credit and including such famous names as Arthur Mallock, Jack French and Eric Broadley (Lola). The 750 Formula of 1950 continues (with updates of course) to this day and currently is modelled around the power unit of the Reliant three wheeled car – a logical choice since it was Reliant who took over the manufacturing rights in Britain of the pre-war Austin Seven who continued in desultory fashion to develop the original power unit until replacing it with a completely new overhead valve engine of their own design. Later Formulae such as the 1172 Formula for cars using the sidevalve Ford 10 engine "grew up" as the old E93A sidevalve engine became obsolete and interest focussed on the later 100E sidevalve, ohv 105E and its successors. Nevertheless the 750 MC flourishes today as never before and manages the successful operation of a number of other Club Racing Formulae that it has taken under its wing over the years. Many of these classes can trace their roots to the original 750 Formula of 1950 and the spirit in which it was conceived. The influence of Colin Chapman's thinking, apparent in the seminal

Mk. 3A, can be observed on all sides at a 750 MC race meeting today.

The Mainstream Post War British sporting (as distinct from the "cosmetic", poseur's wing of the movement) Special building tradition in the form developed and refined by Chapman and his contemporaries may be summarised as follows:

> The "Special" competition car is based on the skilful use of modified road-car chassis and/or welded tubular steel structures with simple, single plane (sometimes stress-bearing) aluminium rivetted panels. Compound curvature body sections achieved by expensive panel beating are to be avoided wherever possible. Appearance is subordinate to function. Light weight is essential. The engine, gearbox and other transmission components are taken in basic form from mass production cars and modified appropriately.

Following these precepts it was possible for a brilliant amateur like Chapman in his early years to take on and beat the established conventional automotive design wisdom. As a Civil Engineer skilled in structural design Chapman had the edge on many contemporaries but his principal assets were the steep rate of climb of his learning curve coupled with the urge to win in all fields (he regarded authority and the rule book as a challenge rather than a constraining influence) and his brilliance as a racing driver. So successful was he at the wheel that natural skill may have allowed him to tolerate design deficiencies while he remained Lotus' principal Works driver and thus able to conceal or overcome roadholding shortcomings on the race track.

The Mk. 3A drew heavily on contemporary sports racing car practice. It was of course closely governed by the rules of the original 750 Formula. In a very Chapmanesque way it is typical of his later creations in that it incorporates a multitude of the ideas of others to which a few special "tweaks" have been added to make it instantly superior. The direct Special building tradition adopted by Chapman for the Mk. 3A car and then for the Mk. 6 of 1952 in which the entire chassis frame was for the first time his own concept, continued with one interruption only – the Elite – until the advent of the Lotus Twentyfive monocoque. Whereas the Elite unquestionably was a *serious production car* – albeit of very unusual kind – all Chapman's other creations up to the Twentyfive were of a type that could be understood and largely reproduced by an advanced Special builder. The only exceptions to this rule are the unique Lotus transmission introduced on the Twelve and perhaps the Chapman Strut; the former designed substantially by the consultant Richard Ansdale and the latter used by Chapman *en passant* from Twelve to Seventeen. Even the Twentyfive embraced no technology beyond the abilities of a skilled modern workshop and cars of this era and general concept are today regularly reproduced by businessmen of the welding torch/pop rivet gun/panel-bashing breed which had its roots in the post-war Special building movement. Close comparison of one of the *ci-devant* Lotus Sixteen Formula cars still in use in Historic racing circles with contemporary photographs and technical descriptions will reveal a subtle divergence from the original specification with discrepancies including wheel track, transmission specification, (and see those Rzeppa joints that came too late for Team Lotus) leading to the conclusion that perhaps as much as 100% of some of those Sixteens might never have emanated from Hornsey or Cheshunt. As a very elaborate Special the Sixteen is easy to reproduce but we still await the first "new" Alfa Romeo Tipo 158.

Chapman was elected President of the 750 MC and later under pressure of work became its Patron. In the period up to early 1955 he made a considerable input to the Club by addressing meetings and writing a series of fascinating articles and letters of absorbing interest to all of us who admired him and his work. Apart from his direct encouragement of the Austin and Ford Special building movement there was the natural and continuous spin-off of ideas which competitors incorporated in their own cars. It is interesting and a tribute to his remarkable talents that he was able to maintain pre-eminence in this peculiarly British field of Special building with its roots in the world of the "IE" (the Impecunious Enthusiast so beloved of the 750 MC) for the eight years from 1950 before the Broadley Brothers finally and comprehensively beat him with the Lola Climax.

There was a second, subordinate British tradition of competition Special building co-existing with the Austin Seven/Ford 10 inspired movement to which Chapman belonged. Eventually he permeated both fields of endeavour when Lotus subsequently "crossed over" and proceeded to dominate both streams.

The subordinate wing of the British Special building tradition was led by Cooper. Cooper *Père* had worked for Kaye Don among others before the War and understood the world of the wealthy motor racing amateur. After the War, encouraged by his son John and the latter's friends, most notably Eric Brandon, Charles built a series of Specials for what later became yet another outstanding new Formula (International Formula 3) initially using suspension and chassis components derived from the Fiat Topolino miniature family car and powered by a rear mounted 500 cc single cylinder JAP Speedway engine driving the rear wheels via a motorcycle gearbox. Coopers were always sold as complete cars and although Formula 3 had a slightly "down market" aura it attracted many serious mainstream drivers and formed a vital nursery class for the emerging team of British Grand Prix drivers including Moss and Collins together with such present-day racing industry notables as Ken Tyrrell and Bernie Ecclestone. Later, as Cooper extended their activity into the larger capacity classes they attracted buyers who pre-War might have gone to ERA or Maserati. By 1955, with the advent of the Kamm-tailed Cooper Climax sports racing cars, the products of Surbiton and Hornsey were well and truly locked in international combat as their paths merged. It took Chapman another six years to gain the ascendancy over Cooper who had had a start of roughly the same length by beginning serious production almost immediately after the cessation of hostilities in 1945.

Today, the Special building philosophy is almost universally adopted in the motor racing field (Ferrari and Porsche excepted) and every car competing in all classes right up to Grand Prix owes a clearly distinguishable debt to the Chapman influence and the humble Special building movement which fostered it.

(ii) Swing Axle Independent Front Suspension

If there is one common technical feature of early Lotus designs which deserves special mention it is the use by Chapman on all models from the Mk. 3A to the 1956 Eleven Series One of swing axle independent front suspension.

The origins of this simple suspension system may be traced to 1933 when Leslie M. Ballamy (LMB) applied for a provisional patent for a system of *front* wheel suspension based on centrally pivoted swinging half axles. Ballamy was concerned to improve the roadholding of a small Austin Seven Special which, as with the small Fords of the time and post-war up to the ending of production in 1959 of the 103E Popular, featured front suspension of a particularly archaic type popularised by Henry Ford on the immortal Model T. It is not surprising that as a farmer's son Henry should have devised such an agricultural solution for suspension (both front and rear) on the cars that made his reputation; in fact, so enamoured was he of the system that he continued it until well after the second World War on cars of his manufacture on both sides of the Atlantic. The Austin Seven, although perpetuating the errors of Henry Ford at the front, used a different but equally archaic positive camber quarter elliptic suspension system at the rear.

The Ford/Austin front suspension utilised a transverse leafspring with free shackles at both ends attached to an "I" section forged axle beam held by torque arms joining at their rear a crossmember-mounted ball joint. Because of the free shackle system there was no absolute control of axle movement in a lateral sense and sloppiness after wear had intruded affected not only the general roadholding qualities of the car and its directional stability in particular, but also in the case of all Austin Sevens and Fords before 1938, had an adverse effect on braking. At the time of Ballamy's provisional patent application Austin Seven and Ford retardation was by brake arms so positioned on the drum backplate that as the applied torque increased so the natural "wind up" tendency of the axle threw off the brakes. Those of us familiar with these dreadful cars in pre-MOT Test days will remember the regular halting of the vehicle by contact with the car in front regardless of herculean efforts with footbrake, handbrake and brutalized gearbox.

Leslie Ballamy, designer of the LMB Ford-based swing axle IFS conversion always insisted on perfect geometry for both the swinging half-axles and accompanying steering and mechanical braking arrangements. This line drawing shows the final form of the LMB conversion in which the mounting points for the radius arms are exactly on the centre line of the chassis in perfect alignment with the pivot points of the severed axle halves. The brake actuating mechanism is equally perfectly positioned beneath and in front of the axle pivots and the track rod is likewise correctly bisected with a specially constructed drag link extended beyond the centre line to engage with an adapted lever type shock absorber to reduce steering "kick back" on irregular surfaces and under fast cornering conditions. A conical bump stop is provided above each end of the transverse leafspring which is designed to replace the standard Ford component. If this is the perfect manifestation of swing axle IFS we can appreciate how the version used on Lotus up to the Eleven Series One broke many of the Ballamy rules (not however doing too badly in the process).

Ballamy calculated that if the good features of the transverse leafspring system – wide spring base and minimal encroachment on mechanics and accommodation – could be retained while at the same time adapting it to acquire new, more desirable properties, he would achieve a light, good handling and low cost sports car. His solution was like all good ideas, simple. He divided the axle, and pivoted it centrally beneath the nose of the chassis to provide simultaneously independent front suspension, strict lateral control of wheel movement, abolition of the old braking problem, improved comfort, security and cornering power. After resolving one or two initial difficulties – including recognition of the need to divide the steering track rod, too – Ballamy knew that he had made a discovery of great importance. At this point it is amusing to recall that Chapman at the age of seven (1935) made his first "car" based on perambulator components and a wooden crate, and here too he chose a divided front axle. History does not tell us whether he appreciated that his Soap Box Derby Model encroached on the Ballamy patents or whether its influence on him was greater than that of LMB himself.

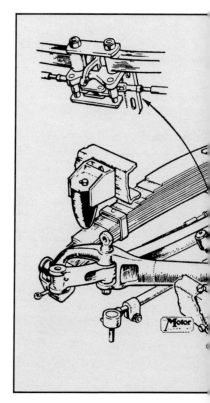

Interestingly, despite efforts made by Ballamy to promote his new suspension in the corridors of power of the motor industry the system was not taken up pre-war by any regular manufacturer. However, a number of notable private individuals including the Chairman of the Ford Motor Company commissioned conversions to their car. Thus Sir Malcolm Campbell, Richard Seaman and Peter Berthon among others drove cars with the LMB system which was freely available to the general public as a conversion before 1939. Early Allard cars were fitted with suspension conversions built from components made by Ballamy but subsequently Allard "pirated" the swing axle IFS for his post-war production with outstanding success. The wide publicity gained by Leslie Ballamy as a result of campaigning his own cars and drawing attention to other LMB conversions (including, amazingly, a Bugatti Type 37 and Bentley 3-litre) aroused considerable interest. The LMB version of swing axle IFS was never cheap because by nature Ballamy is a perfectionist and *his* swing axle IFS was the only application of the principle which consistently over the years demonstrated the desirable qualities of accurate geometry and high quality execution absent elsewhere. To Ballamy, swing axle IFS was an intrinsically perfect system whereas to others it was a low cost means of achieving good road holding and if you could make it a bit cheaper, so much the better.

By 1950 when Chapman was laying out the design of the Lotus Mk.3A, swing axle IFS was well and truly accepted and nowhere more so than in the upper echelons of the 750 Motor Club. Arthur Mallock and Holland Birkett himself – not to forget Jack French the great 750 propagandist – were all advocates of the swing axle system. The LMB conversion could be based on Austin Seven or Ford parts which were freely available at low cost. Generally speaking, if one could afford a Ford axle beam and radius arms they were to be preferred in view of the greater strength and durability of the highly-stressed kingpin arrangement; important in racing. Furthermore, although Austin Sevens were frequently converted to (Morris Minor based) hydraulic brake actuation for racing, the standard Girling mechanical braking system of the Ford was more than adequate for Club racing in these lightweight, relatively low powered specials. Chapman chose a Ford axle as the basis of his IFS on the 750 Formula Mk. 3A and although he disobeyed the cardinal LMB rule of mounting the inner pivot point of the radius arms in line with the pivots of the divided beam, the results were adequate enough to sweep all before, influence the course of 750 Formula racing and more beyond that.

So good is the inherent stability of a car with swing axle IFS and either conventional or de Dion rear axle combined with a rigid chassis structure that Chapman was able to leave the suspension specification of his cars fundamentally unchanged from 1950 until the announcement in October 1956 of wishbone IFS and the Chapman Strut in April 1957. This remarkable continuity enabled him to concentrate on the structural design of the spaceframe and general aerodynamics of his new cars. Chapman has left for posterity a short piece written towards the end of 1954 which summarises his attitude to swing-axle IFS after it had been used on Lotus cars for several years:

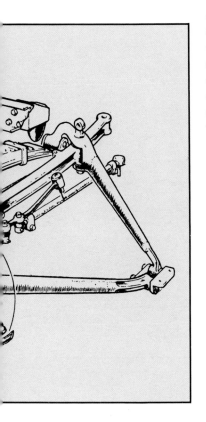

. . . People ask me why I used divided axle IFS. It was not arranged specifically to fit in with the use of Ford axle components although it was very convenient. The reason for using a "swing axle" is because I think that with a small relatively low powered car it is absolutely essential to keep your wheels as vertical as possible whilst cornering. As soon as your wheels start to lean out on a corner they develop camber thrust away from the direction in which you wish to travel. This camber thrust has to be resisted by an increase in cornering force and to provide this the wheel must run at a greater slip angle. Now as the slip angle is increased so does the drag or rolling resistance and this means that as a car with "leaning out wheels" goes through a corner, it suffers a considerable retarding force which slows it down appreciably.

This effect is quite noticeable and once or twice I have nearly been caught out when following one of these cars through a flat out corner as it gives the impression that the driver in front has applied his brakes although his stop lights have not come on at all. Also it must be borne in mind that a tyre under any given set of conditions can only generate a certain amount of cornering force and if some of this is being used up to offset camber thrust then there is less available to counteract centripetal acceleration – so the cornering speed must suffer.

This wheel "lean out" is tolerable when there is tremendous power on tap to accelerate away from the corner but when the engine is a small capacity and relatively low power it is imperative that "way" is not lost through the fast corners. The finest way to achieve cornering with upright wheels is with a beam front axle but this type of axle has several inherent defects in "shimmy" and "tramp" when used in conjunction with currently desirable soft suspension.

A "swing axle" front end will give you an almost upright wheel angle if a low enough roll centre is used and it will also provide the desirable soft ride in conjunction with ample suspension movement. This type of front suspension coupled with a "live" rear axle has gained Lotus cars the reputation for fast cornering . . .

Throughout the entire piece there is no acknowledgement that the system was invented by Ballamy although on occasions and in fairly restricted circumstances Chapman was known to have admitted his debt to the originator who generally speaking never seemed to wish or to be able to make his patent "stick". The LMB swing axle influence on Chapman went beyond his actual use of such a system when during later design periods he still attempted to achieve the desirable attribute conferred naturally by the swing axle system of "keeping your wheels as vertical as possible whilst cornering". As late as 1961 great interest was aroused in Chapman by the study of action photographs of Grand Prix cars to observe whether their suspension was achieving this goal. If you study some mid-Fifties shots of Coopers at speed you will see exactly what Chapman was trying to avoid.

By 1961 Ballamy himself had abandoned his single minded promotion of the LMB swing axle system and had moved on to a variation of it which sounded the death knell of his business and a return to other things for this remarkable original thinker. Swing axles continued to appear in front engined low cost Club racing cars well into the Sixties for the same good reasons that had recommended them since 1933. Chapman is generally considered to be *the* suspension system designer and in later years he certainly was. But in his early period during the 1950s there is no doubt that he was – as he had been trained to be – a structural engineer (and I quote him again verbatim):

. . . a car is but a structure, as amenable as a building to stress calculation – if only one knows what stresses it must sustain and what safety factors are required . . .

By employing the simple, well-tried and reliable swing axle IFS system in conjunction with conventional rear suspension, Chapman was able to concentrate on developing the structure connecting the two systems to the point where he could keep ahead of the opposition. When he at last began to make fundamental changes in suspension design policy in 1956 he had brought chassis frame design to such a peak of development that he was able to provide a superior base for his new suspension while continuing to retain a competitive lead. This therefore is the importance to the Lotus story of swing axle IFS and the man, Leslie Ballamy (b. 1904), who conceived it.

(iii) Learning Curve – The Mk. 3A 750 Formula Car 1951

Chapman's earliest creations, appearing in the late Forties were simple 'Specials' constructed from Austin Seven and Ford Ten components. They were fitted with crude, angular bodywork and were designed for both on- and off-road competitive use, following the practice of the time.

Although Chapman had attracted much favourable comment with his Mark 2 Lotus, a high, dual purpose trials and sports racing car in which he had beaten Dudley Gahagan's Type 37 Bugatti at Silverstone in a thrilling race, the first significant Lotus design (Mk. 3A) appeared in 1951. It was a car built for use in Formula racing events organised by the 750 Motor Club. At that time the 750 MC was primarily concerned with the organisation of motoring events for the impecunious enthusiast. Initially activities were centred around cars built with components from the Austin Seven (1922 – 1939) and until Chapman burst on the scene with the Mark 3A the regulations were fairly loose. In a manner which was later to prove characteristic, Colin sat down and studied the regulations as had not been done since the 1934 – 1937 750 kg. Grand Prix Formula but which he now firmly re-established as the norm. The 1950 750 Formula stipulated that cars should be based on the side rails of the Austin 7 chassis, using the original rear axle and springs, basic engine and gear box. A standard Seven crankcase assembly and cylinder block had to be employed but beyond that there were at that time no

The first important Chapman design was the Lotus Mk.3A hill climbing here in the hands of Pamela Slade, shortly after the Chapman ownership period. The two features of the Mk.3A which made it outstandingly different from all other 750 Formula cars were the powerful engine (the result of a daring "de-siamesing" of the inlet ports) together with the supplementary, detachable, tubular stiffening super-structure fitted to the front of the chassis. The third and final success factor was Chapman's driving ability.

further restrictions. One important rule allowed the Club the right to reject any car which did not meet 'the spirit of the Formula'.

Chapman's Mk. 3A was the ultimate Austin Seven Special and demonstrated subsequently unequalled performance. It was so successful that certain elements of the rules had quickly to be re-written in order to preserve 'the spirit of the Formula'. Chapman laid out the chassis with a Ford-based swing-axle IFS system with hydraulic brakes and wire wheels, and later built a complex superstructure of small diameter tubes around the engine and front suspension mountings in order to stiffen the notoriously flexible Austin Seven chassis. It was in the engine modification that the "win or bust" Chapman philosophy was best seen. Because the Formula was intended for the impecunious enthusiast it may have escaped the minds of the 750 MC Racing Committee that there might be just one Club member who would break with tradition and attempt the impossible. Chapman decided that his engine was going to rev. faster than any other and therefore chose the post-1936 three bearing engine as the basis of his racing power unit. Those familiar with 750 thinking of the time will know that this standard engine was regarded with universal contempt in racing circles. The reason for this was that although theoretically superior, the Austin three bearing crankshaft in practice was an unmitigated disaster. The earlier two bearing Seven crankshaft was mounted on a self-aligning double row ballbearing at the nose and a sliding roller bearing at the rear. At high rotational speeds, the crankshaft would flex sufficiently to allow the pistons of numbers two and three cylinders to strike the head of a highly tuned engine and in road versions the car was unacceptably rough and vibratory even by the standards of the mid 1930s. So, for 1937 Austin fitted a plain centre main bearing and hoped for the best. They had overlooked that by squeezing into the small space available a third bearing without fundamental re-design and by retaining the original two bearing system, they had created a monster. The crankshaft now flexed about the centre main bearing which in consequence received a monumental hammering.

Three bearing cranks broke with monotonous regularity. Chapman knew about this but he was prepared to win races at all costs and therefore accepted the need for a large stock of brand new crankshafts and limitless quantities of lubricant which would now have to be changed between each race. The three bearing crankshafts would also require to be changed at about the same frequency. But the Chapman engine would now rev. to unprecedented speeds.

In order to benefit fully from the use of a three bearing crankshaft Chapman had to radically improve the inherently poor breathing qualities of this sidevalve engine with two "siamesed" (two inlet valves of adjacent cylinders sharing the same external port) inlet ports.

His solution was to design an inlet manifold with dividing tongues projecting into each of the inlet ports to "de-siamese" them. Instead of fitting the car with two SU carburettors in the classical British sporting tradition he linked within his special manifold the now separate inlet ports two and three and then quite independently one and four. Each pairing was then fed by one of the two chokes of a Ford V8 Stromberg carburettor.

The body of this car was of lightweight aluminium with two tiny headlights mounted above the air intake and a huge rubber radiator hose "snorkel" pointing rearwards from the carburettor inlet to exclude bumblebees and dust. The results were devastating and even on an off-day with only three cylinders functioning, the Mk. 3A was impressive. I only saw it race once (at Castle Combe on 22nd May 1951) but the Lotus' performance was hardly eclipsed by the remarkable achievements of the young Mike Hawthorn in his first season at the wheel of his father's TT Rileys. The Mk. 3A was driven to and from the circuit and I

remember returning to school by coach and looking down as Hazel Williams (as she then was) drove by on her way home. Shortly afterwards the 750 MC committee banned "de-siamesing" or the equally heretical reversal of port function, much to the relief of the other impecunious enthusiasts . . .

(iv) The Mk. 6 – 1952–55

The Mk. 3 cars (three were to be laid down) were originally created by Colin and his friends the Allen Brothers for their private amusement. Their success as Special builders had attracted the attention of like-minded enthusiasts and led them to subsidise their own cars by producing modified parts for others. The type-numbering system applied to his creations at this early stage indicated that Chapman was already looking to the future and almost certainly already had in mind the ultimate intention of becoming a "full time" car manufacturer. There was only one Lotus Mk. 4 – a Ford Ten engined trials car built for Mike Lawson

The Lotus Six in its diversely engined forms was a mainstay of Club racing during the early Fifties. Powered by anything from the humble Ford E93A 1172 cc sidevalve engine upwards, the Six was hard to beat in any class and here H.P. Deschamps is seen in his Climax engined car winning at Snetterton on 15 April 1956 and looking as though he had just given up motorcycle racing (Deschamps rode a Norton in the Senior TT of 1939). He would have enjoyed the wind in his face and the instant responses of the "four-wheeled motorcycle" Mk.6.

and Mk. 5 in the Lotus numbering system was reserved for the proposed "100 mph sidevalve Austin 7" which Colin was known to have in mind after his initial successes with the "de-siamesed" 3-bearing engine of the Mk. 3A. However a new design was in preparation and this was the first series-produced Lotus type which appeared in prototype form in 1952 as the Mk. 6.

The Mk. 6 was a typical "boxy" Chapman design of the period. So much of an "ugly duckling" was it that two notable owners Peter Kirwan-Taylor and "Jabby" Crombac designed special bodies for their own cars; thus missing the point that the Mk. 6 was intended as a strictly practical "minimal" motor car with no pretensions to elegance.

It was constructed on a simple round and square section steel tubular ("space") frame to which were directly riveted the main internal and external body panels. The front suspension was independent by Chapman's now standard LMB-inspired swing-axle system in which the Ford 8/10 hp axle beam was divided and pivoted centrally. Suspension was by combined coilspring/damper units replacing the original Ford transverse leaf spring. The radius arms which on the Ford design joined the chassis at the centre line were in the Lotus Mk. 6 installation cut and bent to locate on the chassis side rails in order to clear the

My Club Lotus badge No. 431 issued in 1960 and showing a Mk. 6, inaccurately drawn with immense built-in positive camber on the front swing axle, mounted far too low and with exaggerated angles of inclination of the suspension units. Even at this stage, Chapman resisted external use of the Lotus motif. There is no link between the graphic design of this badge and any other design or lettering associated with the marque. Only the colours (green and yellow) are related.

That intrepid driver Peter Gammon campaigned a successful and highly modified MG during 1953 but made a wise investment by buying one of the original batch of eight Mk.6 Lotus. This was put on one side but during 1954, sensing that the competition was becoming sharper, he transferred his MG engine and gearbox to the Hornsey car seen here at Goodwood for the Easter Monday meeting complete with blanking plate to shield it from the harsh winds characteristic of these early season meetings at the Sussex track. UPE9 became a legend in its own time in Gammon's hands and was regularly seen taking on and pulverising the most unexpected opposition. Gammon's career continued to the end of the decade in a variety of cars but he is chiefly remembered for his remarkable performances in his Lotus Mk.6-MG.

low-mounted power unit. The geometry of the Lotus independent front suspension was therefore imperfect in that the wheels were subject to toe-in and out on bump and rebound. The merits of the system include low cost and adequate performance measured against the speeds and general standards of the day. Many purists have had difficulty in accepting the simple swing axle types IFS but it is typical of Chapman that he was able to make a pragmatic assessment of the system and recognise the benefits conferred including reduced chassis frame weight (because of the simpler mounting methods required) and low cost of manufacture.

Although the Mk. 6 was originally conceived to accept the Ford 1172 cc E93A engine, gearbox and transmission, examples of the type were made with an amazing variety of power units including MG, Ford Consul and the tall six-cylinder Bristol engine. The basic design of the car assumed that a Ford E93A torque tube rear axle assembly would be fitted and this governed the rear suspension system and hence the whole of the rear chassis frame. The Ford 10 axle at that time was of almost obsolete type – of full length (gearbox to axle) torque tube construction. The Ford torque tube axle was not greatly heavier in construction than any other type of "live" rear axle with open propeller shaft combined but the torque tube (a light, large diameter steel tube surrounding the propeller shaft and running from the rear of the gearbox to the nose of the axle final drive assembly) transmitted all driving and braking forces to a hemispherical mounting at the rear of the gearbox.

By incorporating the torque tube assembly Chapman was able to restrict lateral

Faster than you think!

Build yourself a replica of the outstandingly successful LOTUS cars seen racing at all the principal circuits last season.

By using a LOTUS semi-monocoque multi-tubular lightweight chassis frame as the basis of a LOTUS replica the customer is ensured trouble-free assembly and guaranteed high standards of finish and performance; no welding equipment, specialised tools or technical knowledge are required, and the use of Ford 8/10 axle assemblies and other components makes original equipment and spare parts readily available.

Chassis are supplied complete with stressed panels, all brackets and standard engine mountings (made for either Ford 8/10, Ford Consul, or TC/TD MG engines) to choice for £110. It is possible to complete the panelling as illustrated for an additional £75 (approx.).

Other essential components, such as I.F.S. conversion, suspension units, pedals, brake linkages, radiators, steering columns, etc., are available from our Hornsey works to provide the customer with a stage by stage service until completion.

Photo " AUTOSPORT "

Photo " AUTOCAR "

★ During their first production year the first four cars to race collected no less than 50 —1st, 2nd and 3rd—awards during only half a season's racing.

★ " The Autocar " said : " A run in a Ford 10-powered Lotus showed that the handling qualities of the car are of a very high order indeed . . . the car is extremely well balanced . . . wheel adhesion is quite outstanding . . . there can be few cars, if any, which are quicker through sharp S-bends."—J. A. Cooper.

★ " Autosport " said : " I feel that the Lotus is the best attempt yet to provide the enthusiast with a competition car at the price he can afford to pay. . . . It is just as sound an engineering job as the most expensive sports car, and the economy is only brought about by the clever adaptation of mass-produced components."— John V. Bolster.

★ A service of specialised racing components is also available for LOTUS builders, such as lightweight 15-in. wheels, special CW & Pin., engine tuning, manifolds and hydraulic brake conversion.

★ Medium-tuned Ford 10 engine gives : Max. speed 93 m.p.h., standing ¼-mile 19.0 secs., 45 m.p.g.

LOTUS Engineering Co. Ltd.

SPORTS AND RACING CAR DESIGN and DEVELOPMENT

7 TOTTENHAM LANE, HORNSEY, LONDON, N.8.
TEL.: MOUntview 8353

Lotus advertising began in the early Fifties with simple, small panels in *Motor Sport* and other magazines. At that time a variety of conversion services were available to the Special builder and the Mk.6 was the first complete Lotus available in kit form from 1953. Following a successful opening season Lotus were advertising successes and won the approbation of the Press in this half-page advertisement from *Motor Racing* of February 1954. The upper photograph shows John Bolster demonstrating the light weight of the Mk.6 CBU and the second photograph of 1611H appeared regularly in advertising and promotional material during the lifetime of the Mk.6. The advertisements of this period were written by Colin himself with assistance later from Colin Bennett.

axle movement by that most simple expedient, the Panhard rod; again using the same suspension medium as at the front – combined coil spring/telescopic damper units. Provided the Ford front torque tube mounting was retained any modest output engine could be adapted to this system. For more powerful installations however, it became necessary to use an open propeller shaft axle and more complicated location by parallel radius arms left and right in conjunction with the same Panhard rod for lateral location.

The Mk. 6 chassis/body unit was advertised in basic aluminium panelled form at £110 and for a further £75 could be equipped with hand beaten aluminium mudguards front and rear together with all the miscellaneous bits and pieces required to fit them. The body panels were produced by Williams & Pritchard; two highly skilled panel beaters with a magnificent eye for line, used by Lotus (and latterly by many others) to produce prototype and small series production bodies. Like John Teychenne who built the early Lotus chassis, Williams & Pritchard started their business in and around the Hornsey site behind Stan Chapman's Railway Hotel. Their workmanship was as good as the best from Italy and the W & P influence may be detected on all Lotus products of the Fifties and some even later.

The Mk. 6 was an instant success on the race track and thereby, commercially. By August 1954 Lotus were able to advertise the sale of "over 70" examples and to catalogue a remarkable list of successes in races at Club and National level. It was the Mk. 6 that put Lotus on the map as a commercial force in the specialist sporting car world and provided a sound financial footing for Chapman's next, infinitely more ambitious designs.

(v) Going International – Mks. 8, 9 and 10 Sports Racing Cars 1954 – 1955

Chapman understood the limitations of the Mk. 6 as a vehicle for winning major international events and therefore gave thought to a development of this basic concept which would enable him to achieve success on a broader front. Reserving for the moment for other things Type No. 7 he began work on his Mk. 8 car which represented the first collaboration with the aerodynamicist Frank Costin, brother of Mike (later responsible for technical development at Lotus but now the 'Cos' of Cosworth).

The Frank Costin influence meant that the simple body form of the Mk. 6 and earlier Lotuses was to be replaced by an all-enveloping aluminium shell designed to reduce drag and lift and thereby release power previously wasted in forcing the brick-shaped Mk. 6 through ever-increasing air resistance. The contrast was remarkable and the prototype Mk. 8 (registered SAR 5) sparked controversy on all sides. The characteristic tail fins intended by Costin to aid directional stability (which Chapman feared might suffer above 120 mph from the incorporation of swing-axle IFS) were progressively reduced in size on later models with wishbone or strut-type front suspension. However, on the Mk. 8 every aspect of airflow was considered by Costin and there are photographs of him strapped to the car to study the behaviour of tufts of wool attached to reveal airflow patterns at speed on test.

Although the Lotus Mk. 8 retained the familiar Ford 8/10 based swing-axle IFS (now with dropped pivot points to lower the roll centre) it used a very different chassis frame. This was formed of 1.25″ steel tube in a complex pattern over a basic floor structure and weighed only 35 lbs. In order to achieve

The 1500 cc Mk.8 Lotus of 1954 was a gigantic stride forward for the company. The result of a collaboration between Chapman and the brothers Costin the Mk.8 was based on a delicate steel tube space frame with highly modified MG 1500 cc engine and gearbox. This photograph taken by the author's father at the Easter Monday meeting at Goodwood 1954 shows the car on its second appearance (so new is it that the chalk guidelines on the registration number SAR5 can still be seen on the original negative). The 26 year old Chapman appears thoughtful and this was not to be a successful outing for the car which misfired during its race despite having lapped promisingly. Shortly afterwards, the car achieved its first victory at Silverstone when Colin won the 1500 cc class of the 17 lap sports car race, resoundingly beating John Coombs and Peter Gammon in the Mk.6 Lotus MG. The complex Mk.8 with Frank Costin aerodynamic body set new standards of sports racing car design and established a line of Lotus front-engined lightweight world-class competition cars ending with the only disappointment in the series – the Seventeen of 1959.

Splendid car that it was, the Mk.6 was really intended for the British "Club" market. Examples were used abroad with success but Chapman knew that an expensive car incorporating his and Frank Costin's latest ideas was necessary to bring the name Lotus to international competition. This advertisement from *Motor Racing* of October 1954 appeared at the end of the Mk.8's first season showing Chapman's own car, SAR5.

LOTUS

SPORTS CARS ARE

WINNERS

THE MK VI LOTUS

THE MK VIII LOTUS

SINCE the beginning of the 1954 Season to the end of August, Lotus Sports Cars in the hands of private owners have been placed

1ST -33 TIMES

2ND - 26 TIMES

3RD - 20 TIMES

and have won numerous awards in sprints and hill climbs.

✻ We are now able to offer either Mark VI or VIII Lotus chassis to accommodate the outstanding 1,100-c.c. Coventry Climax sports engine. This engine is also available through the Lotus Engineering Co. Ltd.

Write for Illustrated Brochure
LOTUS ENGINEERING CO. LTD.
7, Tottenham Lane, Hornsey, N.8
MOUntview 8353

The Mark IX LOTUS

THE ULTRA HIGH PERFORMANCE 2-SEATER SPORTS CAR.

LOTUS ENGINEERING CO. LTD., are pleased to announce that chassis frames and components are now available to construct Mk. IX Lotus replicas.

Various alternative axle specifications can be used as follows:

- Ford 10 with Girling cable brakes and pressed steel wheels.

- Hydraulic brakes and knock-on wire wheels.

- De Dion axle using 11 in. × 2¼ in. turbo - finned drum brakes, 2 L/S front and leading/trailing inboard rear.

The chassis is made to accomodate either Ford 10, Coventry Climax, or 1½ litre M.G. (special dry sump modification is required for this unit).

PRICE of Lotus Mk. IX exclusive of power unit varies from £590 for basic Ford spec. to £850 for full racing specification.

PERFORMANCE:
Maximum speed 130 m.p.h. plus.

LE MANS, 1955
The Lotus Mk. IX with Coventry-Climax engine was the fastest 1100 c.c. car and lapped at over 97 m.p.h.

Write for further details to
LOTUS ENGINEERING CO. LTD.
7, Tottenham Lane, Hornsey, N.8
MOUntview 8353.

The relatively few Mk.8s manufactured at Hornsey were operated either by the Works or experienced competition drivers able to cope with its complexities. For more general appeal a simpler car was necessary and this was announced for the 1955 season as the Mk.9, a machine nearer to its successor the Eleven in character and practicability than its predecessor. The advertisement offers a range of versions of the Mk.9 from the very simplest with mechanical Ford-Girling brakes and pressed steel wheels to "state of the art" international versions using de Dion axle, Climax engine etc. Restrained use is made of the 97 mph fastest lap at Le Mans 1955 achieved by the Mk.9 in that most disastrous year of all on the Sarthe circuit, when no competitor wished to dwell on the memory of that hateful day (and when Chapman was disqualified).

maximum frame stiffness, tubes and riveted aluminium panels encircled the modified MG T-type engine as closely as possible and this feature created a nightmare of removal and replacement in the prototype Mk. 8 leading to a local redesign in the production version. Power was transmitted via a BMC 4-speed gearbox and open propeller shaft to a Lotus aluminium casting specially designed to hold a BMC crownwheel and pinion unit; the whole being bolted firmly to the frame. Gone was the simplicity of the Ford torque tube axle used in the Mk. 6. Chapman evolved a de Dion rear axle with the light, large diameter tube itself so shaped as to allow the long articulated driveshafts to pass through it to the hubs mounted on bearings in separate aluminium castings in order to achieve minimum angularity change under suspension loading. By mounting the final drive unit and drum brakes on the chassis frame as required by the de Dion system unsprung weight was greatly reduced and all driving and braking loads transmitted directly to the frame. The de Dion tube was located laterally by a ballrace sliding within a curved groove cast and machined on the rear of the final drive unit and fore and aft movement was contained by light parallel trailing radius arms at each side. The rear springing of the Mk. 8 was unique among Lotus designs in using a transverse tension spring actuated by extensions of reinforced damper levers; the whole mounted ahead of the final drive unit.

Although suitable for use under the control of the Works, the Mk. 8 was a complex design of limited appeal as a private owner car. For 1955 Chapman therefore designed a "cleaned up" version with a less extreme body shape than the Mk. 8 but still showing strong Frank Costin influence. The body of the new car – the Mk. 9 – featured lower but still prominent tailfins. The Mk. 9 was intended for the new Coventry Climax FWA 1100 cc engine whereas the Mk. 10 announced at the same time was in effect merely a variant of the Mk. 8 (with Mk. 9 rear suspension) to accommodate the 2-litre in-line six-cylinder Bristol engine, notably in three cars ordered by leading drivers of the day – Mike Anthony, Cliff Davis and Peter Lumsden.

Apart from its "cleaned-up" rear suspension the Mk.10 closely resembled the Mk.8 of 1954. Several owners expressed interest in running a Lotus in the 2 litre class for which the standard choice at that time was the Bristol engine. Accordingly a small batch of these Mk.10s was laid down with revised engine bay arrangements to accept the tall, long, six-cylinder power unit. An early example was purchased by Cliff Davis (later to be associated with Cheshunt as the "part exchange man" for Elite kit sales). Cliff ran the car at Brands Hatch and then a week later on 16 July 1955 entered his Lotus for one of the supporting races to the British Grand Prix won by Stirling Moss and Fangio, both in W196 Mercedes Benz. The author travelled by train from Euston to Liverpool and thence to Aintree to witness this memorable day of racing in blazing sunshine. The four German cars in the Grand Prix event were the main memory but this is a snapshot (taken without telephoto lens) of Cliff pressing on regardless in his new Mk.10.

Note – The FWA Coventry Climax Engine

Before 1954 there was no competitive small (below 1500 cc) power unit available to the British producer which would enable him to match the continental opposition. The FWA engine was therefore a godsend to all concerned and did a great deal to foster the development of the British specialist sports racing car industry in the Fifties. The design of this engine had been carried out by Wally Hassan and Harry Mundy; both engineers with a racing background. Hassan – the older – had been active at Brooklands (e.g. the Barnato-Hassan Special – a highly modified Bentley still running today) and Mundy's experience had included periods with ERA and BRM. Stories exist to explain the intriguing design of the Coventry Climax FWP Fire Pump engine which with gentle modification was transformed into the FWA sports racing power unit. The MOD (Ministry of Defence) Fire Pump specification required that the entire unit including engine, water pump and frame could be carried by two men. Therefore the engine had to be extremely light and of necessity was based on aluminium

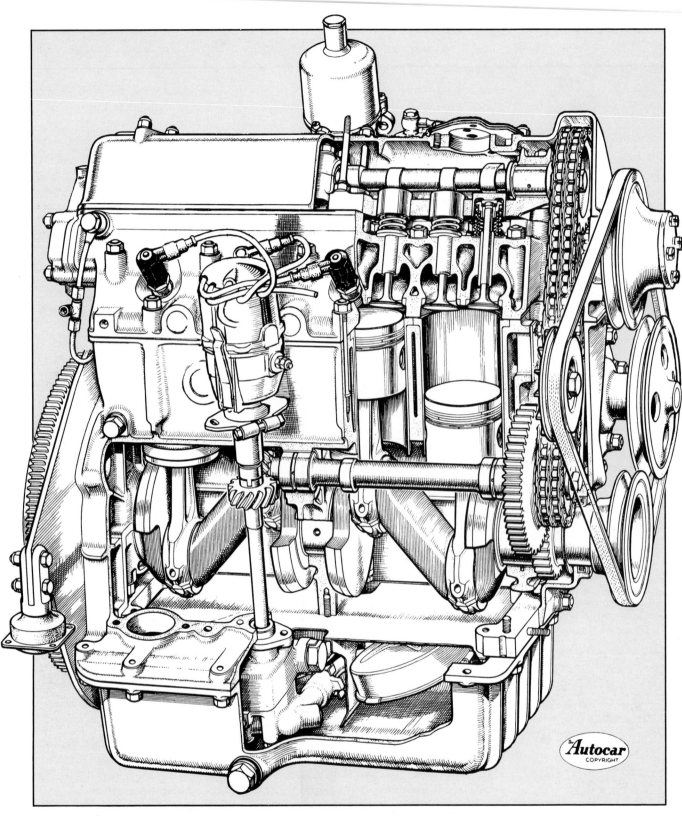

Rather like the improbable pre-war Austin Seven and Ford Ten engines which provided an introduction to competitive motoring for countless enthusiasts, the Coventry Climax FWA engine virtually transformed the British sports racing scene in the mid-Fifties. This FWE cut-away drawing reveals its salient features including the highly efficient valve gear involving direct actuation of the valves via bucket tappets, the aluminium block with dry iron liners, simple three-bearing crankshaft with oil pumps and ignition distributor driven by a short jack shaft, also serving via a two-row chain to drive the overhead camshaft. Initially the engine was modified by Coventry Climax themselves with two SU carburettors and later a number of specialists including one Keith Duckworth developed advanced versions of the engine yielding over 100 bhp from a capacity of 1098 cc. Later the FWA was enlarged to 1½ litres (FWB) and as a half way stage 1216 cc (FWE) for the Elite.

block and head castings. The power output required for the Fire Pump application was modest and the most desirable characteristic after light weight would be reliability. We can therefore assume that Hassan and Mundy specified a single overhead camshaft with tongue firmly in cheek; knowing full well that they were giving the engine a development capability well beyond the original intention. It was also gratifying that they should equip their Fire Pump engine with eight separate ports and had they not taken a racing designer's view of the project there is no doubt that the course of British small car motor sport might have taken a totally different turn and failed to achieve the outstanding international stature of the Fifties and early Sixties.

The little FWP engine was issued to eager British sports car constructors as the FWA with its potential liberated by the substitution of suitable camshaft, valve gear and other "internals". Two large-bore SU carburettors were generally fitted and with a freeflow exhaust manifold the engine (now FWA) in basic form developed 75 bhp at 6250 rpm. Cooper introduced their immediately successful Kamm-tailed central seater sports car and the main Lotus contribution was the Mk. 9.

As soon as FWA Coventry Climax 1100 cc engine became generally available in 1955, the leading manufacturers of sports racing cars rushed to adopt it. Here is a Climax installed in a T39 Kamm-tail Cooper central seater sports racing car entered by Gilby Engineering and driven by Keith Greene, son of the Gilby boss. Note the characteristic Cooper use of curved chassis frame tubes and the rear suspension in which the main leaves of the spring are free to move laterally within two pairs of rollers subject to the restraint of the curious bowed upper leaf. Chapman abandoned the use of "old fashioned" leaf springs after the 1951 Mk. 3A but Cooper soldiered on to the end of the decade. However, Cooper understood the benefits of a mid-engine installation before Chapman and the T39 frequently gave the Eleven a run for its money.

(vi) The Eleven Series One Sports Racing Car 1956 – 57

If the Mk. 6 was the first major landmark in series production Lotus then the
Eleven was undoubtedly the second and became the greatest single commercial
success of any of the pre-Cheshunt designs. In series One and Two versions it was
in production from 1956 to 1960 (yes!) and more than 300 examples were made.
Together with the Seven it is still available in replica form.

The Eleven (Series One) announced in February 1956 in two versions – the
"Le Mans" with de Dion axle and "Club" live-axle car – was clearly derived from
the previous year's Mk. 9 but with substantial improvements including stiffer
multi-tubular chassis, revised rear suspension linkages and de Dion tube, subtly
improved IFS and lower-profile bodywork panels. It had to be practical for the
amateur owner driver perhaps carrying out his own maintenance or at best calling
on the services of a single mechanic. The by now traditional Lotus frame was
therefore carefully designed to allow easy installation and removal of the power
unit which (Le Mans) was a FWA 1100 cc or FWB 1470 cc Climax engine with
BMC (MG type) gearbox with four-speed close-ratio option driving by open
propeller shaft to a chassis-mounted differential unit (with ZF LSD option) and

**The distinguished artist Cavendish Morton, RI, ROI, is well known as the designer of the more attractive bodies
seen on the racing cars of John Tojeiro, including several Le Mans entries. Living in Eye and Aldeburgh, Suffolk
during the Fifties he was Chairman of the Snetterton Motor Racing Club and designed a poster for their 1957 Six
Hour race. Cavendish Morton was attracted by the beautiful Frank Costin body of the Lotus Eleven Series One
and used it as the centre-piece of his poster. Cavendish Morton maintains a strong interest in all motor sporting
matters and it is fitting that this tribute to his fellow artists Chapman and Costin should appear in these pages to
evoke the wonderful atmosphere of the "real" sports car races of that epoch . . .**

de Dion axle. The "Club" and later "Sports" models were progressively cheaper alternatives fitted respectively with the FWA Climax or Ford 100E sidevalve engine which had by that date supplanted the earlier E93A. The method of suspending both live axle and de Dion tube was identical on all Eleven variants and different from the system used on previous types. Whereas the Mk. 9 de Dion tube lateral location was by a sliding ballrace engaging a slot on the rear of the final drive unit, lateral location on the Eleven was achieved by triangulation of the lower offside rear radius arm. This method could be criticized in that it forced the rear axle/de Dion tube to follow a short-radius arc on bump and rebound compared with the better geometry possible with a Panhard rod as used on the Mk. 6. The Lotus Eleven de Dion tube was a work of art; of 3.25″ diameter extremely light gauge tubing manipulated to curve round the final drive unit and provided with neatly welded brackets to locate the radius arms at the outer ends which themselves were cleverly designed to house the large hub bearings within the tube itself. It was Nobby Clark, Lotus' first weekly-paid employee who was responsible for establishing the high standard of welding used on components manufactured by Lotus itself. Nobby would chuckle as he claimed "It might be flimsy but at least it's well made".

The front suspension of the Eleven was again by the time-honoured swing axle IFS system using a simple Ford axle beam divided and pivoted even lower below

Few would argue that the most beautiful sports racing Lotus was the Eleven Series One of 1956 with elegant Frank Costin-designed all-enveloping body here shown in full Le Mans version with aerodynamic windscreen and head fairing. This is Keith Hall's car YTN 444 seen in the August Bank Holiday Monday 1956 meeting at Crystal Palace, where his very highly developed (Weber carburettor) FWA Climax engine took him to a win over Team Lotus driver Cliff Allison in the August Trophy race. Keith Hall's racing activities were managed by Ron Richardson who had joined Lotus shortly before the author and who continued efficiently to handle export business during succeeding years.

the frame than before in an effort to reduce the often chronic understeer of earlier Lotuses. Again, modified Ford radius arms attached well away from the centre line of the car resulted in imperfect front suspension geometry.

As was the practice of the day all major suspension joints were equipped with Silentbloc bushes which hid a multitude of sins of misalignment by internal and external steel bushes sandwiching a hard rubber sleeve. Today of course the self-respecting high performance car designer insists on metal-to-metal joints throughout the suspension system. Concentric coil spring damper units were used front and rear as in the Mk. 9 and 10 cars and the Eleven was equipped with drum brakes as standard although Lockheed discs were an expensive option. Rear brakes were mounted immediately outboard of the final drive unit and therefore formed part of the sprung weight of the car. Brake and drive torque was entirely absorbed through the final drive mounting bolts.

The body of the Eleven was of outstanding beauty and showed the aerodynamic influence of Frank Costin. Its principal features included partial enclosure of the 15 in wire wheels (with "knock-off" eared nuts) front and rear; fully (upward) opening bonnet and front wing panel allowing complete access to engine and front suspension, balanced by a similar rear panel pivoted at the tail. Single curvature panels covered the lower flanks of the car and joined a stressed, riveted undertray. The doors were hinged at the lower edge and opened to comply with current sports-racing regulations. The principal fuel tank was mounted in the near side of the body immediately behind the front wheel and reached by a filler projecting through the bodywork. A long range supplementary matching tank could be fitted on the offside. The spare wheel and battery were mounted behind the driver. Air for the small low mounted water radiator was admitted via a tiny slot at the front of the car and exhausted through the under surface. The radiator was fully ducted and the header tank was mounted on the bulkhead behind the engine at the highest point available. In order to comply with varying regulations a full width wrap-round screen to permit the carrying of a passenger or a metal tonneau cover and a wrap-round screen for the driver alone (usually incorporating a faired headrest blending into the rear form of the car) could be specified.

The Eleven looked absolutely right and its early performance demonstrated that it was highly competitive. Orders flowed in and with 150 Elevens in 1956 it could be said that Lotus was now established as a serious constructor of small sports cars suitable for national and international competition. The successes of the Eleven are well chronicled and it is without question the classic early sports racing Lotus. At Club level it was eventually banned from 750 MC 1172 Formula events for being so successful as to be "outside the spirit of the Formula".

(vii) The Eleven Series Two Sports Racing Car 1957 – 60

With the development of the FWA and FWB power units which could be tuned to provide over 100 bhp, the shortcomings of IFS by swing axle were becoming increasingly obvious. For the 1957 season Chapman had presented in October 1956 his first single seater racing car – the Twelve F2 model with FPF Climax engine incorporating a simple IFS system by wishbones. This now became standardised on the entire 1957 range including the Eleven which thus equipped was known henceforth as the Series Two.

The new suspension required major redesign of the front of the chassis frame to provide suitable mounting points for upper and lower wishbones. The lower wishbone was fabricated from steel tube and provided a pick-up point with a coil spring damper unit angled at approximately 45 degrees. An Alford and Alder upright of the type developed for the Triumph Herald car supplied wheel hub and steering in place of the antiquated kingpin system inherent in swing axle IFS. It was the upper location of the upright which was achieved with particular ingenuity in the Chapman tradition. The Ford 100E Prefect/Anglia family cars introduced in 1953 used a MacPherson Strut front suspension of which the lower link was provided by a tubular member engaging the end of the anti-roll bar.

THE LOTUS ELEVEN 1957

THE LOTUS ELEVEN SPORTS AND THE LOTUS ELEVEN LE MANS

SEE IT AT THE MOTOR SHOW
on
STAND 161

LOTUS ENGINEERING Co. Ltd.

7, TOTTENHAM LANE

HORNSEY

MO Untview 8353   LONDON, N.8

Chapman had greatly advanced the "growing up" process of Lotus Engineering by joining the principal motor trade body – The Society of Motor Manufacturers and Traders (SMM&T) – thus becoming eligible to exhibit at the annual London Motor Show for the first time in 1955. At a period when this annual show was the only occasion when the products of the then great British Motor Industry could be seen together this was an unrivalled opportunity to arrest attention and further the Company's commercial success. The Lotus Stand became a Mecca for the enthusiast and in 1956 I remember well the impact of the Twelve Formula Two car which made its bow in that year. This advertisement from *Motor Racing* magazine draws attention to the 1957 Eleven range shown on the same Stand. These were heady times for Colin; he had achieved his first great success at Le Mans, was now entering the world of Formula racing and the disasters of 1958 and 1959 were far ahead..

Colin liked this and calculated that he could design a 'cut-and-shut' version of the Ford lower link so that (inverted) it would form a suitable upper wishbone for his new Lotus front suspension. The new main upper members were located fore and aft by the anti-roll bar which passed across the front of the car in the Lotus application, mounted positively in machined aluminium blocks. The new suspension was as before used in conjunction with a modified Morris Minor rack and pinion steering unit which had established outstanding standards of control on many small British sporting cars. In the Lotus application a shortened rack was used (the heat treatment of the teeth often leaving something to be desired)and the whole was much lighter than the original BMC arrangement.

(viii) Strutting Ahead – The Twelve F2 Car – 1956–57

Among the sensations of the 1956 Earls Court Show was the new Formula Two
Lotus Twelve single seater racing car, designed for the equally new Coventry
Climax FPF 1¹/₂ litre engine. This car and the Formula Two Lister announced at
about the same time were "minimalist" designs and both unsuccessful in their
original form. The Lister disappeared almost immediately, displaying insurmoun-
table deficiencies of traction but similar problems arose from the use on the Lotus
Twelve of a de Dion rear axle which in so light a car incurred an unacceptable
unsprung to sprung weight ratio despite featuring every Chapman "trick" de
Dion feature in the pursuit of lightness. The de Dion system of the prototype was
almost immediately replaced by what came to be known as the Chapman Strut
before the car was used in anger.

**A happy Chapman at the wheel of the 1956 Earls Court Show model of the Twelve single seater car, differing in
certain respects to the definitive version of April 1957 in which the rear suspension was totally revamped from
Chapman's original plan. Here a de Dion system is used with very short lateral radius arms (longer arms were
later used before the de Dion system was finally abandoned for the Chapman Strut) and rear suspension units
having enclosed springs reminiscent of motorcycle practice. Mike Costin remembers it as a car with fragility
inbuilt in the pursuit of lightness so that the chassis constantly broke while vibration often caused fuel tank
splitting and other infuriating hazards which usually prevented it from achieving the success promised by its
ingenious design.**

The Chapman Strut rear suspension system was used – with detail modification
– on all new high performance Lotus designs from 1957 – 59. It was the subject of
a patent application and as a result of this and increasingly obvious shortcomings
leading to its eclipse by the Eighteen's Lola-inspired rear suspension, was not
adopted by the competition. In essence, the Chapman Strut was typical of the
man in the way it sought to derive all the functions of the rear suspension system
from the smallest possible number of individual components. The Strut itself was
an aluminium casting supporting the rear hub and its bearings and forming a
rigid mounting for the coil spring and damper unit. The fixed length tubular
drive shaft was articulated by Hook-type universal joints at each end and
therefore located the wheel laterally. Fore and aft location was by single tubular

radius rod and during its lifetime it was only the design and geometry of the radius rod which changed significantly.

The Twelve was not a particularly lovely car nor was it very successful. A slender space frame was used; just sufficiently wide to accommodate engine and driver and using the new* wishbone front suspension with disc brakes and magnesium "wobbly" wheels inspired by the Convair aircraft wheel. The Twelve marked the appearance for the first time of a new transmission system which if it had worked reliably would have represented a distinct advance. This transmission was designed by Harry Mundy and Richard Ansdale and its novelty included a method of gear selection similar to that used on early motorcycles. This involved passing through all gears up or down the box when changing speed. There was a zigzag gate; the gear lever being pushed progressively forward to change up and backwards to change down gear. The theoretical advantages of the layout included compactness, light weight and reduced power loss. The gearbox and selectors were enclosed within a neat magnesium alloy casing incorporating the final drive unit and bolted to the rear chassis frame. Lotus persisted with this system in various forms on all subsequent "Works" single seaters up to and including the Eighteen but during its currency it was

The Lotus Twelve, while not particularly successful in the role for which it was intended – Formula Two (1½ litre) and Formula One (anything over that capacity and not more than 2½ litres) – plays an important part in the Lotus story. Appearing in 1956, it was the first Lotus single seater racing car; was the first example of the Marque to bear the characteristic IFS system used on the entire product range into the early Sixties (and even today on the Caterham Seven) and also marks the introduction of the so called Chapman strut; fitted to the Twelve in a frantic move to overcome the failure of the cherished de Dion system to perform on this very light little car. The tubular brace for the unsupported outer end of the Strut radius arm pick-up point conveniently ran to the (second) – definitive – mount for the de Dion tube radius arm, but never quite looked as though it was intended to be that way. Chapman (bending in light coloured flat hat) appears to be looking for trouble while the overalled headless figure behind him is probably Cliff Allison.

* see Section (vii) above

never really made to perform as intended despite the presence in the Factory of a small group headed by Steve Sanville (and at one stage including Keith Duckworth) specifically to develop and maintain a collection of these later-improved transmissions which were still causing frustration when I joined the company during the 1959 racing season.

Note: The Chapman Strut

To the 1957 onlooker the Chapman Strut design was striking. We assumed that – as a Chapman design – it would work effectively and therefore its simplicity was arresting to say the least. "Why had no one thought of it before?". Chapman must have engaged in a brainstorming session after the failure to perform of the Twelve's original de Dion system and returned to first principles. As already before and again after this episode he demonstrated his ability to sit down and reject all but bare essentials in order to create a technical solution of beauty and simplicity.

Starting with a normal chassis-mounted final drive unit with inboard brakes an articulated drive shaft was required to transmit power to each wheel. By omitting the normal sliding splined element of the drive shafts and using them as the lateral locating link, the Chapman "at least two birds with one stone" dictum was observed. Wheel hub taper roller bearings were mounted in an aluminium casting supporting a hollow steel splined hub carrying wire spoked or cast magnesium "wobbly" wheels. The upper part of the hub casting was shrunk over the lower extremity of a combined spring and damper unit similar in general concept to a MacPherson Strut and the upper end of this was located on the chassis or monocoque well above the outer diameter of the tyre and towards the centre of the car at a steep angle from the vertical. Projecting forwards and pivoted on the aluminium hub casting was a tubular steel radius arm to restrain the suspension in the fore and aft plane. The early (pre 1959) arrangement of the radius arm was, as in the case of the radius arms used on the earlier Lotus swing axle IFS system, a little short of geometrical perfection, but the system had as its principal theoretical advantage uniform handling characteristics under wide variations of load.

The Chapman Strut was first seen in early 1957 on the Twelve Formula Two car which had originally appeared in October 1956 with a simplified de Dion rear suspension system. The disappointing performance of the car in its original form forced Chapman to rethink this area of the car rapidly and with commendable economy he continued to use the basic Strut solution until the Eighteen rear-engined car designed in late 1959. A tie-bar from the original pick-up point for the de Dion radius arm was used to support the outrigged pick-up for the Strut's fabricated radius arm. The original upper suspension unit mounting of the de Dion system was also retained.

Note: Coventry Climax Engine Development 1956 – 59

The $1\frac{1}{2}$ litre FWB Coventry Climax single cam engine had been developed from the FWA by stretching both bore and stroke of the basic 1100 cc power unit to 76.2 x 80 mm. The result was a loss of traditional FWA reliability. The FWB was increasingly thrashed during 1956 pending arrival of the "proper" racing FPF intended for the new 1957 $1\frac{1}{2}$ litre Formula Two class.

The FPF was a totally new four-cylinder design incorporating twin-overhead camshafts driven by spur gears, a five-bearing crankshaft and dry sump lubrication system. Lotus, Lister and Cooper all ran Formula Two cars fitted with the new engine in 1957 and although Chapman insisted that the Twelve – and even the Sixteen – were intended as Formula Two cars, he and John Cooper soon began to apply pressure on Leonard Lee and Wally Hassan to increase the capacity of the FPF for use in sports car and Formula One racing. Coventry Climax responded by introducing a 2-litre version for the 1958 season (later stretched to 2.2 litres) and during 1959 a full 2 1/2 litre FPF based on new cylinder block and head castings was introduced. On Avgas (120 octane) in Formula One guise these engines produced almost 100 bhp per litre and not much less on pump fuel for sports car events.

Coventry Climax developed the twin overhead camshaft FPF 1.5 litre engine specifically for Formula Two racing in the 1957 Season although early versions of the engines were seen towards the end of 1956 as in this photograph of the Type Twelve Lotus (October). Enthusiastic racers had been using the FWB single cam Climax engine of 1460 cc in Formula Two racing with frequently disastrous results and the new FPF was intended to act as a more powerful, robust alternative to the little fire pump engine-derived FWB. This photograph shows clearly the new Chapman IFS based partly on a cunningly-modified Ford 100E saloon suspension link.

Coventry Climax automotive engines 1954-61

Type	Dimensions	Capacity (cc)	Application	Note
FW (Fire-pump) 4-cylinder single overhead camshaft				
FWA (1954 on)	72.4 mm x 66.7 mm	1098	Sports racing	Direct development from fire-pump engine
FWB (1956)	76.2 mm x 80.0 mm	1460	Sports racing/F2	A fragile engine used in Eleven
FWC (1957)	76.2 mm x 45.2 mm	744	Le Mans	One built for Chapman
FWE (1957 on)	76.2 mm x 66.7 mm	1216	Lotus Elite	Only "production" Climax type
FPF Series 4-cylinder twin overhead camshaft				
FPF (1957 on)	81.2 mm x 71.1 mm	1475	Formula Two/ sports racing	Derived from 1953 FPE V8
(1957)	86.4 mm x 83.8 mm	1960	F1/sports racing	Interim type
(1958)	87.5 mm x 83.8 mm	2015	Formula One	Interim type
(1958)	88.9 mm x 88.9 mm	2207	Formula One	Interim type
(1959 on)	94.0 mm x 89.9 mm	2495	Formula One/ sports car racing	Definitive 2 1/2 litre Formula engine
(1961)	81.8 mm x 71.1 mm	1498	1 1/2 litre Formula One	Interim "panic" engine
FWM Series 4-cylinder single/twin overhead camshaft and V8 twin cam				
FWMA (1958)	4-cylinders 64.3 mm x 57.2 mm SOHC	745	Le Mans	Exclusively for Lotus
FWMC (1961)	4-cylinder 64.3 mm x 57.2 mm DOHC	745	Le Mans	Exclusively for UDT-entered Elite
FWMV (1961 on)	V8 63.0 mm x 60.0 mm DOHC	1495	Formula One	'Over-the-Counter' GP engine

(ix) The Seven Series One – 1957 – 60

Although production of the simple Mk. 6 continued during the lifetime of the Mks 8, 9 and 10 full width bodied cars, it was becoming increasingly obsolescent even for Club level racing. Chapman considered that there was a market for a more up to date version of the simple cycle wing narrow bodied concept. Accordingly a car to be known by the side-stepped number Seven was designed during 1957 and based on the elements of the Eleven Series Two but with a simplified aluminium-panelled space frame. The bodywork of the Seven was entirely of aluminium; only the nose cone, front and rear wings requiring Williams and Pritchard's compound curvature panel beaten art. The front suspension was identical to that of the Eleven Series Two "standardized" wishbone system and the rear axle was a BMC-sourced unit located in exactly the same way as on the Sport/Club model Eleven by three trailing plain radius arms and one triangulated arm to provide lateral location.

This frequently published photograph shows the prototype Seven Series One with its proud designer taken before or immediately after the 1957 Earls Court Motor Show at which the Seven and the Elite in the background were revealed for the first time. The prototype was fitted with the Ford 100E sidevalve engine of 1172 cc equipped with two SU carburettors and a 4-branch exhaust manifold to give a top speed of a little over 80 mph under favourable conditions. The gear lever for the Ford 3-speed transmission (fitted with Buckler close ratio gears) was linked to the gearbox by a crude extension. Also evident is the way in which Chapman adopted the old trick of ballasting a show car to make it show its lines to advantage. Note that the rear wings of the prototype differ from the production version. The prototype Elite in the background has not yet acquired the Hillman-derived door catches and the fit of the driver's door leaves a great deal to be desired, the show car having been assembled in furious haste. It was not a runner and spent the rest of its useful life as a static exhibit in the Hornsey showroom. Note that here too Chapman has added ballast resulting in pronounced negative rear wheel camber.

The reduction in weight over even the Eleven gave this new car a more than useful power-to-weight ratio for Club racing and sprints and it achieved instant success. In its more exotic forms the Seven enjoyed a vogue abroad particularly in the United States to which a number of cars (Super Sevens) fitted with the FWA Coventry Climax engine were supplied. The prototype Super Seven 7TMT was fitted with a FWA engine at a reasonable level of tune and Graham Hill while a member of the Lotus Grand Prix team entered the car for the Boxing Day 1958 Brands Hatch meeting. The manoeuvrability and acceleration of this car coupled with Hill's driving ability resulted in a number of red faces among the owners of more exotic machinery.

The Seven was principally fitted with the Ford 100E sidevalve engine for 1172 Formula racing and later at my instigation the BMC A series 948 cc engine of the type used in the Austin-Healey Sprite sports car was offered as an option while we waited for the Series Two car to appear. This Hornsey designed Seven was known in retrospect as the Seven Series One. Not many were made and with the exception of "knock-off" hub wire wheels very few variations from standard specification were officially permitted, although a few de Dion axle cars slipped out from time to time.

The "Graham Hill" Super Seven 7TMT was used for road test purposes by the Press and subsequently became the Works demonstrator. We had the most enjoyable time subjecting it to regular checks to ensure that the engine was running nicely, etc. Its acceleration at that point in history was of a very high order indeed for a road car and apart from being impressively fast on the circuits it was also an extremely well mannered and tractable fun car for the road, preferably in dry weather.

(x) The Fifteen Sports Racing Car 1958 – 59

Although the Eleven was competitive when fitted with engines from 750 cc (the FWC, specially developed for a successful assault on the 1957 Le Mans Index of Performance award) up to 2-litres (privately installed FPF Coventry Climax, Maserati and Bristol in 1956–57) it became increasingly desirable to consider a new production sports racing car for 1958 with the availability of the 1960 cc variant of the FPF 4-cylinder twin-overhead camshaft power unit. The Fifteen as this car was to be known was in no sense a replacement for the Eleven (the Seventeen was later intended for that purpose) but was Lotus' large capacity offering to extend the range upwards from the Eleven. In fact the Fifteen was little larger overall than the Eleven and looked very much like it with body panels in position. There were however a number of significant design differences under the skin. Whereas the Fifteen front suspension was similar to that used on the Lotus Eleven Series Two, the rear suspension was the new Chapman Strut type used on the definitive Twelve and Sixteen Formula cars and the Elite.

The Coventry Climax FPF 1½- and 2-litre engines were canted over to the right at an angle of 60° from vertical and carburation was either by (in early days) two twin-choke SU carburettors or later by the preferred twin-choke Webers. The standard transmission was by the same inherently tricky but tantalisingly promising Lotus system first seen on the Twelve Formula car. The later (1959) Series Two Fifteen was available with engine canted 17° to the left, BMC four-speed conventional gearbox with separate chassis-mounted final drive unit and this was a reliable combination.

The ultimate Fifteen, a remarkable "Works" 2-litre (later 2½-litre) FPF

A semi-naked photograph of a Works Fifteen campaigned during 1959. This car has Series Two transmission with conventional gearbox and final drive unit. The Fifteen would accept the FPF from $1\frac{1}{2}$ litre to $2\frac{1}{2}$ litre capacity.

This car is well worn but probably went on to do several seasons in the hands of private owners. Note the magnesium "wobbly" wheel mounted vertically in the spare position within the streamlined headrest. The Seventeen was the first sports racing Lotus to use fibreglass body panels and the large unsupported areas of aluminium sheet seen here on the Fifteen made a splendid resonator, vibrating in sympathy with every buzz and rumble.

Climax powered car was built principally for the 1959 Le Mans race where it was driven by Derek Jolly (the owner) and Graham Hill. This car incorporated a Grand Prix Lotus final drive unit with integral five-speed positive-stop gearbox. Unfortunately although astonishingly fast it failed to complete more than a few

Not many really original Lotus remain from the spaceframe period. It is temptingly easy to "recreate" such simple, hand-built structures. This however is a very original restoration of the 1959 Le Mans Hill/Jolly Fifteen ($2/2\frac{1}{2}$ litre Climax), now the property of Grant Gibson. It retains the original Lotus 5-speed transmission and every effort is made to use the original elements of the car. This photograph shows the ignition switch on the right-hand body sill where it was obscured by the concussed Roy Badcock in the notorious "flying schoolgirl" test accident in a similar car.

laps of the 24 hour race and later one or two British short circuit events in the hands of Graham Hill. But it does represent the ultimate Fifteen and therefore the ultimate front engined Lotus sports racing car. The Jolly Fifteen lay under Tony Caldersmith's eye in the Cheshunt service department at the time of my arrival but was soon shipped to the long-suffering owner in Adelaide. It is now under restoration in the UK.

(xi) The Sixteen F1 – F2 Cars 1958 – 59

During 1956 Chapman and Frank Costin were retained by Tony Vandervell to rework the Vanwall Grand Prix car intended to challenge the all-conquering Maserati and Ferrari – those "Red Cars". Vandervell was a passionate patriot and devoted his last years to the task (in which of course he succeeded so well) of developing a British World Championship winner. Having been associated with the abortive BRM V16 project he had a hearty contempt for design by committee and was well known for his autocratic approach and for using the ideas and skills of others to achieve his personal objectives.

In the period immediately preceding the intervention of Chapman in the Vanwall design process, Vandervell was running a car with a chassis showing strong Ferrari influence. This was hardly surprising since he had owned a succession of three Grand Prix Ferraris of up-to-date type raced as "Vanwall Specials" as a result of his close personal contact with Enzo Ferrari and the business connection between Ferrari and Vandervell Products as suppliers of Thinwall bearing shells to the Italian marque. Vandervell was a major shareholder in the British Norton Motorcycle Company and had drawn heavily on that company's technology in development of his 2½-litre Grand Prix engine which is often likened to a watercooled set of four Manx Norton single-cylinder units mounted on one crankcase.

Although the earlier British Vanwalls had failed to achieve their owner's long term objective, performance was sufficiently promising to justify retaining the major mechanical elements of the design including the rear mounted gearbox/final drive unit and engine. Vandervell was also addicted to the Ferrari-inspired forged wishbone independent front suspension and de Dion system rear. However he was quite prepared for Chapman and Costin to have a go at updating the chassis and bodywork of the vehicle (and even allowing a comprehensive redesign of the de Dion rear suspension). The result of this collaboration is now history and with very little development the "new" Vanwall with its light Lotus-type tubular steel spaceframe and strange, tall low-drag aerodynamic body went on to win the Manufacturers' World Championship in 1958. At the outset it was even considered that Chapman should be a member of the Vanwall Works Team but he positively retired from Grand Prix racing after a coming-together with Hawthorn's sister-Vanwall at the 1956 French Grand Prix at Reims. I suspect that his life insurance company, wife and future financial backers also had a hand in that decision.

While the Vanwall redesign and return to the fray was in progress (making a large lump of welcome capital available in the form of a fee to Chapman) the Lotus Twelve single seater Formula Two car was being readied for launch at the October 1956 Earls Court Show. The Twelve was very different in overall concept from Vanwall. Whereas the Vanwall was a "no expense spared" Grand Prix car very much in the classical Italian tradition of elaborate design and execution, the Twelve was a "minimal" racing car. One can only assume that experience with the successful Vanwall project, the disappointment of the Twelve's performance during 1957 and continual doses of Frank Costin indoctrination eventually rubbed off on Colin because his single seater to follow the Twelve for 1958 resembled a miniature Vanwall but with none of the restrictions imposed on Chapman in the earlier project by retention of the existing Vanwall mechanical and suspension components.

Whereas the Vanwall was unusually tall (because the driver sat over the massive gearbox) the new Lotus Sixteen single seater was unusually low because in this case the driver reclined on the undertray. This was achieved by turning the front mounted Coventry Climax FPF engine almost completely on its side (as in the contemporary Fifteen Series One) and at a marked angle to the centre line of the car. In this way it was possible to run the propeller shaft to the left of the

Alan Stacey finished eighth in the 1959 British Grand Prix at Aintree and is here seen leading Brookes driving the penultimate front engined Vanwall – a smaller, lighter car than the 1958 version. The direct comparison allowed by this photograph shows that the redesigned Vanwall is still substantially higher than the Sixteen although heavily influenced by it. Neither of these two cars achieved fame and within two years the front engined Grand Prix car would be totally eclipsed.

driver where it joined a modified version of the original Lotus positive stop gearbox used in conjunction with the now-familiar Chapman Strut rear suspension. The front of the car was supported on the "normal" Lotus wishbone front suspension and the design later (1959) incorporated a feature reputed to have been conceived by Len Terry during his first Lotus period – an oval fabricated scuttle bulkhead of steel tube and thin sheet steel pierced for lightness and intended to provide additional torsional rigidity in the cigar shaped structure which was – as ever – undesirably interrupted to provide access for engine and driver.

A study of Frank Costin's work demonstrates that from time to time the quest for theoretical perfection has led to certain impracticalities. In the case of the Sixteen I suspect that he was fully supported by Chapman in allowing the exhaust system initially to be enclosed within the bodywork in the pursuit of minimum aerodynamic drag. It was said that Graham Hill threatened to withdraw his services until the pipes were rearranged to exit the bodywork in the conventional manner, although Chapman may well have considered asbestos racing overalls the technically preferable alternative. Both the Vanwall and Lotus Sixteen seemed to include arrangements to pass cooling air from the rear inboard disc brakes through the cockpit and past the driver's face (remember the photographs of Moss after Vanwall victories?) There was at this time a regular conflict of interest between driver welfare and the achievement of Chapman's technical objectives.

In its original form the Sixteen was less than a triumph. The severely angled transmission line resulted in considerable power loss as did the near horizontal installation of the FPF engine, which was certainly not foreseen by designers Hassan and Mundy. Two major problems arose from the positioning of the engine; one was that oil would accumulate in the crankcase and create power loss arising from "churning" of the lubricant by the crankshaft assembly. The scavenge pumps mounted under the main bearings were now badly positioned to drain the crankcase adequately to avoid accumulation. Secondly the standard coolant exit points in the cylinder head were in the new installation no longer in the optimum position and pockets of steam were trapped within the head; restricting circulation and causing overheating. The latter problem was overcome by the use of a repositioned water offtake manifold glued into the head with Araldite. Having seen the modification at first hand and observed the total reliability under adverse operating conditions of this remarkable adhesive developed for aircraft construction I have always been a regular user of it myself for the repair of anything from spectacles to castings.

The Grand Prix performance of Team Lotus became a standing joke reminiscent of the original V16 BRM racing team. Much of 1958 and early 1959 was devoted to frenzied attempts to improve results but the overwhelming success of the rear engined Cooper using the same power unit mounted in what Chapman regarded as a "joke" chassis further underlined the Lotus Sixteen's overall failure. By the time that the type was abandoned by Chapman at the end of the 1959 season the Sixteen incorporated several substantial modifications from the original concept. These included a revised engine installation in which the cylinder head was now inclined at a much reduced angle to the offside of the car. In order to reduce mechanical losses in the transmission arising from the enforced use of crude Hook-type universal joints an order had been placed with Hardy-Spicer (now GKN Birfield) for Rzeppa constant velocity universal joints similar to the type evolved by that company for use on the driveshafts of the Issigonis Mini launched in August 1959. In fact the Rzeppa joints were not delivered until the end of the season and so were never fitted to Team Lotus cars when raced. This and many other modifications which might well have been incorporated by the Works had time and other circumstances permitted are seen

Occasionally we failed to sell ex-Works cars out of the country and this specimen went to David Piper (centre) with backer Bob Bodle and wife. Piper had raced Lotus for several years and knew the ropes, not expecting more of the car than was reasonable. His was a true "shoestring" operation, the car transported on an ancient home-made trailer of dubious strength behind a tiny Fiat 1100 car. Note the offset rim of the rear "wobbly" wheel with large section tyre and the prominent filler for the dry sump oil tank placed as far back as possible to improve weight distribution and fed by external pipes on the nearside of the car doubling as additional heat exchangers.

on the surviving Sixteens which race with brilliant success in VSCC events in which they are able to realise their full potential. Most remarkable improvement at the time of writing results from the increase in the rear track of the "modern" Sixteens which has helped to reduce the original understeering tendency and enhance cornering power. Major reworking of the Lotus gearbox too has overcome the inherent unreliability of the original.

As tyre and brake technology advanced, the front suspension braking load on Grand Prix cars was such that the simple 1956-type Lotus wishbone suspension system had to be strengthened. The upper wishbone was now fabricated as a separate unit with the rollbar independently installed as an "accessory" which could be rapidly changed to provide different handling characteristics. The performance of the suspension of the Sixteen was a fundamental disappointment; the worst aspect being pronounced understeer effect (the tendency to go straight ahead rather than round the bend). In an attempt to overcome this Chapman improved the geometric alignment under bump and rebound of the rear Strut suspension by replacing the original side mounted single-tube radius arm with a wide based centrally-pivoted reversed wishbone-like alternative which picked up on either side of a new cast aluminium hub assembly. This modification avoided the excessive variations in toe-in and resultant "bump-steer" effect of the original layout without affecting the constant-camber characteristics of the Chapman Strut under wide variations of load as the fuel tanks emptied from start to finish of a race.

(xii) The Seventeen Sports Racing Car 1959

The two most prolific manufacturers of Coventry Climax engined sports cars during the late Fifties were Lotus and Cooper (with their T39 rear engined cars). Many drivers drove both although they represented diametrically opposed solutions to the same design challenge. Because the power available was identical one could make direct comparisons and the Lotus Mk. 9 and Eleven usually demonstrated superiority over the Surbiton product. However, the situation was about to change with the arrival on the scene of a third Climax-powered challenger.

In the same way that the 750/1172 Formulae of 1950-on provided a hothouse to nurture Chapman's budding skills, 1957 saw the first flowering of another remarkable talent; that of the Broadley brothers, Eric and John. In that year they appeared in 1172 Formula races with a car of their own design and construction bearing the cheeky name Lola, to indicate adequately enough the target of their ambition. The 1957 1172 Lola swept all before it and won the Championship. It was a car which borrowed heavily from Lotus design principles but beat fairly and squarely the Elevens and Sevens against which it competed in that class.

For 1958 the Broadleys struck at the heart of the cosy Lotus 1100 cc sports racing market by introducing a FWA Climax-engined car of such dazzling superiority as to cause all to sit up and take immediate notice. The Lola Mk. 2 Climax was even more beautifully shaped than the Lotus Eleven – its sleek form following very closely the minimum dimensions allowed by enclosure of wheels and chassis. There were no fins and protruding headrests to create turbulence or controversy. Apart from this the basic chassis design inevitably resembled the Lotus with a tubular spaceframe and wishbone front suspension on coil spring/damper units. It was at the rear that matters were dramatically different. Like Frank Nicholls of Elva a little before them the Broadleys had studied the Chapman Strut principle and decided that it could be improved. That they were right was consistently demonstrated by the superior performance of their identically powered car over the Seventeen and the fact that Chapman later paid them the compliment of adopting Lola Mk. 2 rear end geometry on the Eighteen Series.

Where the Lola Mk. 2 rear suspension differed from the Chapman Strut most significantly was in its deletion of the Strut itself . . . The Broadleys used the fixed length articulated drive shafts of the Lotus system but instead of a coil spring/damper unit mounted rigidly at its lower end in the hub casting the rear suspension unit was pivoted at both upper and lower extremities. The hub casting continued below the wheel centre line to a point just above the wheel rim and a wishbone then extended to the centre line of the car to complete the parallelogram geometry of the rear suspension. Upper and lower radius arms on either side of the chassis supported the hub casting in the fore and aft plane. The idea was so simple, so successful and so obviously "right". It was surrounded by none of the "scientific" mystery of the Chapman Strut and it was so much better than a de Dion layout with that system's (for a very light car) excessive unsprung weight that we could appreciate why Lola was so superior to Lotus and the rest.

Chapman was undismayed by this newcomer and by late 1958 had responded with a new 1100 cc FWA Climax sports racing car design under serial number Seventeen. At first glance the Seventeen resembled the Eleven but was very much smaller overall; smaller in fact than the Lola Climax. Its diminutive size resulting in reduced track and straight line stability may have been one of the factors that prevented it from becoming a success. Chapman still believed implicitly in the virtues of his Strut and the Seventeen was equipped with the familiar rear end

Chapman was so occupied during 1958 that he was happy to leave to Len Terry much of the detailed design work on the Seventeen – a new 1100 cc sports racing car to supersede the Eleven and respond to the Lola threat. Terry later claimed that he was obliged to use short MacPherson struts for the front suspension of this car against his better judgement but it is interesting that the first car of which the design was thoroughly delegated by Chapman turned out to be an unmitigated disaster. This brand new specimen is fitted with Cosworth-prepared, Weber carburettor FWA Climax engine. What was to have been the ultimate Lotus Strut car (Chapman at the rear and MacPherson at the front) became a rod for Chapman's back. The tiny front struts and their equally fragile looking wishbones failed to perform to plan and eventually the entire front section of the chassis was discarded and replaced with a conventional wishbone system. Alas, this was too late for the 1959 season and the Seventeen vanished into obscurity as Formula Junior took over from 1100 cc sports racing as the Nursery Class.

layout but now most intriguingly complemented at the front by a miniature MacPherson Strut arrangement incorporating a hub casting with integral coil spring/damper unit swivelling on a knuckle at the outboard end of a lower wishbone to provide articulation for springing and freedom of rotation for steering.

Under test by Alan Stacey the car was initially unmanageable and required much personal attention from the designer to achieve reasonable lap times. The difficulties of sorting out the prototype and preoccupation with the move to

Cheshunt meant that the car was late in arriving at the circuits in the hands of private owners loyal to the Lotus marque and Lola were able to take commercial advantage of this. Those Seventeens that did appear in 1959 caused serious headaches to their drivers and I can remember frenzied activity and headscratching to resolve the mystery of the evil handling. It is ironical that the ultimate unravelling of the problem revealed the same elusive "gremlin" that had bedevilled the BRM P25 Grand Prix car until Chapman, called in by Raymond Mays and Peter Berthon as consultant, spotted it.

The MacPherson strut front suspension would lock as a result of the springing unit spindle bowing between the upper and lower guides within the damper unit. The harder the cornering effort the less easily would the suspension travel and generally the luckless owner spun or slid off the track complaining of chronic understeer.

Eventually the problem was solved by the radical but commercially disastrous step of replacing the front struts with a conventional wishbone system. This required the whole of the front of the spaceframe to be altered. In order to quieten the outraged and demoralised owners of the new "Lola-beater" Chapman offered free of charge conversion. Even so, most were by now thoroughly fed up with the small Lotus which had become an object of derision and not too many of them were converted at the time. Of course none of the several examples exported were included in the modification programme!

The disastrous Seventeen episode meant that until 1962 and the advent of the Twentythree, Lotus enjoyed little further success in the small sports racing car class. It was sad that the traditional preserve of the marque was left to the domination of others but just as Chapman had established himself with the Mk. 6 at an opportune moment so the Broadleys profited from the chance to introduce an updated version of the Eleven concept at a time when no immediate Lotus replacement was on the horizon.

When the Eleven replacement model did at last appear, Lola continued to enjoy good fortune created by the poor-performing and belated follow-on Seventeen model from their main competitor. The rest of the Lola achievement is of course well known, but in 1960 Chapman had a short-lived sweet revenge when *he* got the Formula Junior Lotus Eighteen right, while the Broadleys miscalculated with their lovely, Lotus Sixteen-influenced Junior, and lost out in the first year of the Formula in Britain before they recovered with their own rear-engined car.

Chapter Three
Cheshunt Organisation and Operation

Moving to Cheshunt was the Coming of Age of Lotus. From its situation behind the pub at Hornsey the company moved into a purpose built factory for manufacture of the Elite and intended to generate profits to secure future development as a major component of the British Motor Industry.

The organisation at Cheshunt was very closely derived from patterns established at Hornsey but now able to "breathe" in more spacious surroundings.

(i) The Factory and Offices

The site at Cheshunt and the modest factory and office premises built on it and mortgaged to the Eagle Star Insurance Company thanks to the intervention of Peter Kirwan-Taylor, certainly represented a substantial improvement over the facilities available at Hornsey. However, although the site provided room for further expansion by Lotus it was obvious that for a company with so diverse a manufacturing programme and with such underlying ambitions it was too cramped to be more than a makeshift arrangement. Nevertheless for the first three of the seven years that the Cheshunt factory was occupied by Lotus it was entirely acceptable. At that time, before further construction took place Elite bodies could be stored in the field at the rear without suffering too much deterioration.

Cheshunt is a characterless sprawl of buildings on the main A10 London-to-Cambridge road. The Delamare Road site of the Lotus factory was a piece of wasteland near the railway and was the nearest suitable location to Hornsey that could be found. Chapman was anxious that key personnel including Mike Costin, Fred Bushell, John Standen and Nobby Clark should be able to continue to work at the new site without the need to uproot themselves. Cheshunt was certainly acceptable from this standpoint. Some of us commuted from much farther afield but because we were young and foolish and perhaps a little wary of the long term prospects for secure employment with Lotus we were generally quite happy to journey from afar. It usually took me an hour to drive across country from Leagrave (Luton) and there were many others similarly

This frequently-seen (but not always correctly captioned) photograph was taken at my request in the autumn of 1959. It shows (from right) an ex-Team Lotus Sixteen fitted with early type front suspension (and for sale at any price); an ex-Team Lotus Fifteen with FIA spec. windscreen; one of the dreaded Works Seventeen cars also for sale, the original Seven Series One "A" demonstrator (703HNK) and a spare "borrowed" Elite. It was established practice to dispose of all Works cars at the end of the season; preferably to a distant market such as Australia or New Zealand where the ancient engines and fatigued suspension parts built into these cars would not cause unwelcome "comebacks" at Cheshunt.

placed although the majority of the new labour force recruited specifically to produce the Elite were locally resident.

At about the same time as the official opening of the Lotus plant in October 1959 our illustrious neighbours Tesco completed their Headquarters building in Delamare Road and whereas our opening was attended by a mixture of Ferraris and Ford Specials, theirs was mainly done courtesy of transportation by Rolls-Royce. Our interest in Tesco was that their building was an ideal vantage point from which to photograph the Lotus Works for publicity purposes.

The buildings on the Cheshunt site were in two blocks separated by a narrow roadway. The side walls opening on to this central roadway were provided with sliding doors to give good access. A great deal of thought had gone into the organisation of the companies within these walls so that the Northern unit was devoted to Elite production with the company's offices built on the front of it while the Southern building of roughly equal size housed manufacture of Lotus Components' sports and racing cars, Team Lotus, the Design Office, Development area, Service and Parts Departments. The whole thing was a miracle of compression and so too was the office block.

The lower floor of the main office block on the Northern side included a

Showroom with sufficient room for three cars and to the left of the entrance door the Sales Department including my office. There was a central staircase and at the top of this turning to the left were the Accounts Department and Production Manager Graham Lewis' office which had a window in the wall separating it from the Elite assembly area. Next to Accounts was Buyer John Standen and then Stan Chapman/Andrew Ferguson representing Team Lotus interests and beyond them Fred Bushell. Finally at the end of the corridor was Colin's office which had a real carpet and a low armchair for the intimidation of visitors. Lotus was one of the first British users of "Musak" – piped music – which was intended to keep us calm, motivated and productive. For the time it was quite luxurious and the whole thing bore the Chapman "neat and tidy" stamp although as we became busier it was progressively more difficult to maintain these high standards. Across the front of the building was an illuminated sign in Lotus Yellow and Racing Green with the characters of the company's name in contemporarily popular typeface. It was certainly a vast improvement on anything offered by Cooper, Elva, Lister and the like.

(ii) The Organisation

At that time only the ingenious survived in the kit car business. The definition of a *kit* was rigidly controlled by HM Customs and Excise and the corporate structure of Lotus was geared to these requirements. When one bought a Lotus

Photographed for publicity purposes at the entrance to the Parts Department in late 1959 is a Seven Series One "A"kit; the Morris Minor (or A35) power unit supplied in this case with standard single SU carburettor. The Series One cars had the benefit of a BMC rear axle with aluminium differential housing for which a wide range of final drive ratios was available. The Series One also featured 15″ wheels (in place of 13″) and was a 100% aluminium-bodied car finished to the usual high Williams & Pritchard standard. The Seven kit required only final assembly to complete; all trim, instruments etc., being in position. The exact degree of pre-assembly in which the car was supplied was agreed with Her Majesty's Customs and Excise in order to qualify for exemption from the British Purchase Tax of the time.

Kit the main chassis-body unit would be invoiced by Lotus Components Limited while the engine and sundry other parts would come from a mysterious concern at the same address entitled Racing Engines Ltd., which seemed to have no exclusive or visible employees.

Lotus Components and Racing Engines derived from the original Lotus Engineering Ltd., which flourished at Hornsey. Elites were manufactured by a new Company, Lotus Cars Ltd., which initially only produced complete vehicles on which purchase tax was payable on home market sales. Later when the Elite was also sold in kit form it became necessary to practice similar invoicing strategies.

There were two other Cheshunt bodies corporate in existence at this time; Lotus Developments., which provided design and development service to the car companies and which was the principal concern of Mike Costin; and Team Lotus Limited which then as always was a Chapman family operation.

(iii) Lotus Components

This company was a business name of the original Lotus Engineering Ltd., and was the medium for production and sale of all sports racing and single-seat racing cars. The daily running responsibility was Nobby Clark's and his lieutenant Roy Badcock. Nobby and Roy were two sterling individuals steeped in the Lotus tradition, endlessly calm and long-suffering.

The original Lotus Components building including the Parts Department shown here, Service Department, Team Lotus and the Design/Development area is now occupied by Omega Made to Measure Furniture doing a roaring trade. The sliding doors and gantry on the upper floor are a later Lotus feature not included in the original scheme of things.

As Group Lotus Sales Manager I provided a service across the board, but individuals within my team had special responsibilities. Racing car and other "factory retail" Lotus Components sales were handled by Peter Warr, who although never as calm as Nobby and Roy, was every bit as efficient. Peter was extremely adept at handling the complex paperwork surrounding the sale of cars for home assembly and his exceptional driving talent and familiarity with the racing world was invaluable. There were many occasions when Peter kept the peace between Chapman and unfortunate racing customers outraged to distraction by the delayed delivery of cars entered for races on the following day or which would not go round corners (the Seventeen) etc. Peter Warr had already been employed by Lotus for a year when I arrived on the scene. He was younger than I and had come straight from school, full of enthusiasm and considerable ability to serve a short apprenticeship under Colin Bennett, my predecessor. Bennett was one of the original Chapman circle and his departure and replacement by me was never satisfactorily explained. "Perhaps", says Mike Costin, "you were the flavour of the month, Robin". It always seemed that Bennett's relationship with Chapman remained cordial and yet it was generally considered that he had been pushed out. However, I am sure that Peter Warr's efficiency was founded on the training given by Colin Bennett.

Constant use of the local public roads by Lotus for testing the company's products resulted in a fairly high level of complaint to the Hertfordshire Constabulary who as was usual in such situations had to be calmed by Fred Bushell. We were able to keep the Elite test programme fairly well under control but it was the occasional exotic road testing operation which caused a major collapse of goodwill with neighbours and the forces of law and order. The night when the first Eighteen Grand Prix car was completed and then driven in the dark "up Delamare Road" by Chapman to ensure that all was connected correctly before being airfreighted to Buenos Aires is well chronicled. In fact having witnessed the occasion I know Delamare Road is too short to engage fifth gear on a Formula One car.

The worst testing incident in my time occurred when Lotus Components Works Manager Roy Badcock took out a Fifteen Series 2 fitted with a two-litre Climax engine. He was accompanied by a mechanic, and they reached the A10 dual carriageway at dusk. We could hear the Fifteen going up through the gears about a mile away as we stood outside the office and then there was a long silence. In due course a car was sent out to investigate and we were amazed by the outcome of what might have been an appalling accident.

Travelling at very high speed in the evening half-light and with his line of sight below the top of the moulded perspex windscreen, Roy had come upon a group of two or three schoolgirls on pedal cycles without seeing them in good time. The long, low front of the Fifteen had scooped up the luckless children who flew overhead, missing the mechanic who later graphically described the circumstances to us, but one of the bicycles struck Badcock on the head and stunned him. The airborne schoolgirls fell back to the road with scarcely more than a few bumps and bruises to show for their 100 mph collision. Badcock's foot was jammed hard on the accelerator and his travelling companion did not appreciate at first that he was unconscious. The car veered off the road and into a field at high speed. The mechanic desperately attempted to switch off the ignition, having considerable difficulty in reaching the switch on the driver's side door sill but eventually succeeding. The Fifteen had passed under a barbed wire fence, gashing the unfortunate Badcock's forehead and eventually came to rest several hundred yards away from the scene of the accident and well out of sight of the road. The search party was unable to locate the errant Fifteen until the mechanic struggled to the roadside and attracted their attention. The schoolgirls were

The appointment by the author in 1959 of Lotus Centres throughout Britain led to unprecedented demand for the Seven kit car. Until April 1960 the Seven Series One continued to be distributed through the trade but the very high cost of producing this finest of all Sevens forced the introduction of the much-cheaper-to-produce Series Two. This photograph taken without artificial lighting shows no fewer than seven Seven Series One in production and is typical of that hectic time in the last summer of that decade. The area immediately beyond the nose cone of the most distant car was used to store chassis frames but later became the area where Elan chassis development took place. The area in the far left corner eventually became Steve Sanville's engine shop with the dynamometer beyond that outside.

scooped up and taken away to hospital together with our damaged test driver and the crushed and battered remains of the Fifteen were dragged back to the Works where they now became even more overdue for shipment. This incident instantly made the headlines and did little to foster our reputation as socially conscious local employers.

(iv) The Parts Department

Before the Elite all Lotus supplied on the home market had been in "component" or "kit" form. The Parts Department was therefore efficient and well organised. The systems used to purchase components for both manufacture and replacement purposes were devised by John Standen who had occupied a loft (or mezzanine floor if you were John) at Hornsey but now at Cheshunt had relatively luxurious office accommodation. Buying components for very small scale car manufacture was extraordinarily difficult even at that time when the British Motor Industry was still afloat on a raft of successful component suppliers including Joseph

A general shot of the Works at Delamare Road, Cheshunt, early in 1960. Selsey Motors' Land-Rover in the foreground and behind it one of the returnable collapsible wooden crates in which the Seven kit was packed for delivery. The current Elite demonstrator stands outside the Parts Department and four completed Elites are lined up outside the Sales Office to trip up Colin on arrival and earn Brownie points for Graham Lewis.

Lucas (electrical equipment), Girling (brakes and suspension components), Automotive Products (Lockheed brakes and Borg and Beck clutches). In 1959 Lotus was very small beer to the component industry although there was a certain glamour and prestige to be had from association with the small company and its famous designer-owner. Nevertheless, we had constant difficulty in obtaining the tiny quantities of components required and John Standen was more than fully occupied in keeping a flow moving into Production. The whole system of after-sales service was built up for the Elite as we went along. It was more important to use parts for vehicle manufacture and sale than to keep a car on the road after it had been paid for. Jay Chamberlain – six thousand miles from Cheshunt – had to dismantle cars from his sales stock in order to keep others going and this caused endless justifiable friction with his distributors, dealers and the public.

At home we could generally keep vehicles running by the simple expedient of darting into Production and finding the necessary parts if they were not on the Stores shelves. Because of constant pressure imposed by the outside world, Stores personnel were generally extremely relaxed if not somnambulant. In charge of the Parts Department was "Jay" Hall with his Australian side-kick Mark Roberts; one of the legion of antipodeans who made the trip to Europe in pursuit of closer contact with motor racing. Jay and Mark good-naturedly kept the British Lotus owning public happy together with certain of our European agents (most notably François Staumont of Brussels) who after long experience found it advisable to arrive at Cheshunt bearing banknotes rather than attempt to operate through the so-called system. Just as Lotus itself had a well-earned reputation for sharp practice when it came to obtaining goods without due observance of payment terms, several of our customers intent on developing a racing career or new business used the same technique on the Parts Department. It would be unkind to mention names but one successful Lotuseer of the period (who has now achieved fame, distinction and financial stability) used to cause consternation when seen approaching up Delamare Road. The Parts Counter would be manned at full strength and all payment rules strictly enforced.

One day Keith Greene announced that he was coming up to see us with his latest Maserati and those of us who were Italophile in automotive matters turned out in force to witness his arrival; only to dissolve in hoots of laughter on seeing the son of the Gilby Engineering boss crouched low over the handlebars of a 50 cc moped of that illustrious make.

Another visit which I remember particularly was by Arthur Mallock whom I had long admired as an inspired Special Builder and whom I had encountered several times during my 750/1172 days before Lotus. Arthur was constructing his first U2 and ever-practical and pragmatic in approach decided to avoid wasting time in calculations by the simple expedient of buying a set of Seven suspension units for his new car. It was not long before Arthur and his U2 customers were harrying Lotus Sevens (and even Juniors) with members of this new family of simple competition cars.

(v) The Service Department

I was so occupied during my first weeks at Cheshunt with the Seven commercial development programme that some time elapsed before I was able to try the British Racing Green demonstrator Elite of that time. This car was in the care of Tony Caldersmith who was our expatriate Australian Service Manager; which exalted rank allowed him to wear a dark green overall coat. Tony was a most delightful fellow and an accomplished engineer whose monumental patience enabled him to come to terms with the huge workload that developed in pace with growing Elite sales. Eventually Tony took me out in the Elite so that I could form my less-than-favourable conclusions about this early Maximar-built Series One car.

A view down the central access road between the Elite factory on the right and Lotus Components, Service, Developments and Team Lotus on the left. Three new Elites and the Seven Series One "A" demonstrator in line at the rear.

The Service Department was situated immediately behind Parts on the left-hand side of the central drive way between the two blocks of the Cheshunt factory. There was barely space for work to be carried out on more than one or two cars at a time and Tony also had to grapple with the problem of being used as a convenient store for problem cars such as the Hill/Jolly Le Mans Fifteen which blocked one bay for several months in 1959 towards the end of the racing season. Very soon the tiny facilities at Cheshunt became wholly inadequate and the Service Department was moved bodily to accommodation at nearby Panshanger Aerodrome, used by the Company's flying enthusiasts as a base for the Messenger and Comanche. For the Service Department to be removed from Central Control was possibly dangerous in view of the inadequate systems in force to control stock and the allocation of labour. It was often suggested that Panshanger was the door through which a considerable amount of valuable material vanished but this was compensated by the fact that the majority of dissatisfied customers were kept at a distance from those of us who had sold them their cars. After the introduction of the Elite kit, owner-constructors were encouraged to drive to Panshanger to have their car inspected (and a certificate of roadworthiness issued).

After the transfer of the Service Department to Panshanger the area formerly dedicated to this purpose at Cheshunt became additional parts accommodation and was also used as a body panel shop serving Lotus Components.

(vi) Lotus Cars Ltd.

Manufacture of the Elite was under the control of two new recruits – Works Manager Graham Lewis and Len Street who in my time was operating as the link between Lewis and shop floor – the Works Foreman. Graham and Len made an odd pair but they certainly got the job done. Lewis was a Welsh bachelor, who treated Colin with exaggerated deference; usually calling him "Sir" while the rest of us he treated with contempt. Len Street maintained cordial relations with all including his difficult boss, and somehow or other managed to keep a steady trickle of Elites flowing. Graham Lewis saw his role as strictly competitive with the Sales Department. His motivation was to produce as many more Elites as possible than required by the Order Book.

We grimly took up the Lewis Challenge and Chapman very quickly learned to play one against the other. In the early days it was difficult for Production to keep up with demand – and we of Sales scored points. Later the boot would be on the other foot and Graham Lewis would line up Elites along the front of the building to ensure that Chapman could not reach his office without tripping over the fruits of his labour and our incompetence.

Elite sales were initially the responsibility of Ron Richardson who had attracted Colin's attention when he was acting as Racing Manager for Keith Hall. Ron was meticulous in all respects. His dress was immaculate and his dark-suited sobriety was matched by perfectly groomed hair, dazzling white teeth and trim fingernails. His car fascinated me. It was a converted Austin A30 van in which he had personally installed side windows and although it had covered a substantial mileage it always smelled and looked brand new. Despite constant interrogation Ron would never reveal how he achieved this remarkable situation. I could not have had two better men than Ron Richardson and Peter Warr to assist me.

In the Spring of 1960 a tall, young newly "bowler-hatted" ex-army officer arrived unannounced at Cheshunt, marched upstairs, knocked on Chapman's

In order to ensure that new cars reached the dealer without hitch, we transported them on simple flat bed trucks of the type shown here. The delivery operation was run on a full time basis by a small local contractor who could either mount a finished Elite or a crated Seven kit on his vehicle. At the height of the 1959-60 shipping programme to California there was a steady stream of vehicles from Delamare Road to the Docks.

door and offered his services to the company. Impressed, Chapman brought him down to me and we had the usual discussion. I explained that at the time we were well suited but that we would keep his name on file. This was not good enough for Capt. Ian McLeod who shortly afterwards turned up again – this time in an immaculate vintage Sunbeam Tourer complete with very attractive wife Dawn. We were beginning to find the system irresistible and I reasoned that if he could be as persistent as this on a permanent basis he could sell Elites to the less tolerant of our clientele. Eventually I took him on probation as an Elite retail salesman. With the minimum of training but using to the full his self-confidence and personal charm Ian McLeod then proceeded to astound us by selling Elites at an unprecedented rate. We preferred selling them directly to the public rather than through the dealer network for the simple reason that we enhanced profits by so doing. Most of such customers were initially from abroad and therefore did not present us with the complication of part exchanges. Later of course, Ian's talents were spread to include the sale of Elite kits when our marketing policy changed.

Ian McLeod saw himself as the Sales Department's champion and the main challenger of Graham Lewis' aggressive non-co-operation. Their rows became legendary and on one final occasion Fred Bushell was attempting to arbitrate in a heated argument between the two protagonists who had strayed into his office. Seated below with bated breath we could hear loud discussion overhead but then suddenly there was a crash of broken glass. At this point I realised that things had got out of hand and rushed upstairs to be passed by the vanquished Production Manager clasping hand to ear with blood everywhere. I dashed to Fred's office to find him standing white faced behind his desk with a radiant McLeod brandishing his fist gleefully. "Out you come, Ian" I muttered and closeted myself with Fred. Fred quickly explained the situation to me: how the argument had terminated when McLeod threw a right hook that jerked Lewis straight through Fred's glass office partition into the corridor and nearly severing his ear

The glass pane! (double skinned for sound insulation) in the rear wall of Graham Lewis' office allowed him to observe Elite production from his desk. This was a typical Chapman design feature and was the only window available to our Production Manager who otherwise relied on artificial light and the secondhand rays of the sun entering through the reeded glass panels of the partition behind the camera.

in the process. "He'll have to go" growled Fred. I returned heavy hearted to my office and made it plain to my best salesman that he had gone too far. We were very proud of him but of course there was no alternative response to such a serious breach of discipline.

Graham Lewis' ear was stitched back and he continued rather less obstructively than before. Ian McLeod's reputation was so well known among Lotus dealers that I had no difficulty in persuading Graham Warner of The Chequered Flag that McLeod was just the man he needed to keep Elite sales rolling. We were thus able to retain his services once removed and Ian did extremely well for his new employer.

Ian McLeod was a man of many parts (it was not until he hit Graham Lewis that we learned that he had been an amateur Army boxing champion). He was a good driver and because he was prepared to spend all the time necessary to pursue his Lotus duties frequently got involved in looking after visitors and journalists.

In June 1960 we were approached by the freelance Canadian Journalist Tom Davenport with an idea to prepare an article on the theme "Fastest Car; Fastest Driver". The idea was that Ian McLeod who had been personally vetted by Chapman and passed as suitable for all types of demonstration work would take Davenport as a passenger on a round trip involving some exciting mountain driving in North Wales. The journey began uneventfully and as the Elite began the climb out of Llanberis Davenport urged McLeod to "let her have her head" on the twisting ascent of the A4086 towards Capel Curig. As the Elite sped on Davenport marked on the palm of his hand with a ballpoint pen the swift passing of the milestones in order to calculate the car's speed over the difficult route. This was long before the time of compulsory (or even voluntary) seatbelts and both driver and passenger were braced firmly back into the seats of the rapidly ascending car.

The energy-absorbing properties of the Elite's fibreglass monocoque construction are clearly shown in this photograph of a substantially shattered Elite which crashed at Snetterton on 25 March 1962. The driver escaped with a broken leg. The identity of this car is uncertain but it is believed to be LOV1, the former Graham Warner/Chequered Flag car of hallowed memory. Note how the final drive unit has become completely detached from the remaining structure, and the characteristic ultra-short exhaust system of the highly developed short circuit racing Elite, ending under the driver's posterior. The remains of the car were stored behind the garage on the Norwich Straight and the engine stolen during the night.

The bus drivers of North Wales are thoroughly familiar with the difficulty of driving their bulky vehicles up and down the steep slopes of Snowdonia and the bus descending on that fateful day towards Llanberis was demonstrating the local knowledge of its driver by discreet corner cutting (as was indeed the ascending Elite). In evidence it was later claimed by McLeod's defence counsel that at a certain point the bus ran out of control and the driver, fearful of the nearside precipice, attempted to regain control by veering to the right where he struck the bank in the path of the oncoming Elite. It was suggested that the bus driver hoped that McLeod would pass the oncoming bus on the nearside as he fought to regain control but instead both vehicles, braking violently, collided head on at a combined speed of 30 mph. Poor Davenport died instantly; his neck broken by "whiplash" effect. Driver McLeod clutching the steering wheel was thrown against it and sustained numerous broken ribs, a fractured arm and jaw. The bodies were laid out on the verge and it was not until two days later than Ian McLeod rallied in Caernarvon hospital suffering from total amnesia. Ian claimed that he was extremely unpopular in hospital as a result of the local conviction that he was guilty and recalls only "blunt needles and horrible food" from this episode in his life.

Ian says that even today he finds it disturbing to drive on a "blind" left hand climbing bend and senses an involuntary lifting of the right foot. He duly recovered after an interval of three months and returned to his duties at Cheshunt. However, the police prosecuted him for allegedly causing "death by dangerous driving" – a charge for which if proved guilty, imprisonment was a possibility.

Back at Cheshunt we received the news of the accident in a short lived, stunned silence. This was a time when we were acutely sensitive to criticism arising from suspension failure on all cars including the Elite. The somewhat delicate mounting of the final drive unit which on the Series One car in particular absorbed most rear cornering loads was seriously suspect. Ian had carefully checked the security of the rear end on a vehicle hoist shortly before the accident after hearing an unusual (by Elite standards) noise. We were not surprised to see Graham Lewis set off at high speed towards the accident. We never got to the bottom of this episode but Ian McLeod maintains that the final drive unit of the

The entire Lotus sales team were generally enthusiastic (despite odd "bad moments" in 1961) but I am sure that both Peter Warr and Ron Richardson would agree that Ian McLeod was in a class of his own when it came to determination to succeed. As a "bowler hatted" regular army officer, Ian was anxious to establish himself in "Civvy Street" and threw himself into the difficult task of selling Elites with unbridled exuberance. This photograph is taken shortly after his appalling accident in Wales. A row of left-hand drive Bristol-built Elites (Maximar only manufactured rhd) are lined up to represent a good week's output, almost certainly intended for shipment to the US. The shadows indicate an early morning shot and we can assume that Graham Lewis has lined up these Elites for Colin's benefit as he drove onto the car park at the end of the building. You may be sure that McLeod knew all the answers and that on being questioned by the "Guvnor" would be able to assure him that we had already found a home for them all.

car was never found (an experienced mechanic could remove it in minutes). He claims that it is lost beneath the waters of Llyn Peris.

Despite the sterling efforts of Defence Counsel, the understanding support of poor Davenport's parents and wife and a generally favourable trial, the judge in his summing up was obliged to point out the facts of life. Today Ian McLeod feels that the Jury may have over-reacted to the summing up in reaching their "guilty" verdict. Ian was led down to the cells but on discovering this the Judge insisted that he be freed immediately and in passing sentence made it very clear that he had no intention of committing our man to prison or of depriving him of his driving licence and livelihood. A fine of £50 was imposed "with time to pay". Because of McLeod's total amnesia following the accident and certain aspects of the affair including the strangely missing final drive unit; differing interpretations of the causes persist. Ian himself is convinced that he was innocent of the charge of dangerous driving and based on a study of evidence on the spot claims that the bus must have been out of control. The incident cast a serious cloud over us all and the enforced absence of our number one salesman was particularly unwelcome at this crucial time. Fortunately Ian slowly recovered and came back to us almost as good as new, with a handsome beard to cover disfiguring scars.

Graham Lewis and Len Street were still in position when I left Lotus. Len Street subsequently left and gave his name to a company in Chelsea which still sells Lotus cars although Len himself has long since departed. Nobody to whom I have spoken knew what became of Graham Lewis but a few years ago I am certain that I spotted him crossing London's Regent Street although he vanished into the crowd before I could catch him.

One of the great joys of Lotus was the folklore which grew around the company and its founder and the amazing fund of stories that this generated. The very real difficulties of our daily work were constantly relieved by humour and Ian McLeod provided running commentary amusement on an hour-by-hour basis supplemented by tales of his pre-Lotus experience seeing the world with the British Army and doing his best to avoid contracting unsocial diseases. Another wonderful comedian was Andrew Ferguson who initially acted as Stan Chapman's understudy in Team Lotus and later took over the operation when Stan retired. Like Peter Warr he has been in and out of Lotus over the years and is currently back in harness with Team Lotus and its associated Club. Before he came to us Andrew had been employed by the Cooper Car Company and had organised their Racing Team with great success. I could listen endlessly to him recounting his experiences with Cooper; his best single turn being the re-enactment with all voices and sound effects of the famous occasion when Charles Cooper woke up to find the chest of banknotes normally kept under his bed, broken open and empty. Andrew was also a reliable source of information on the techniques used by Cooper's Chief Designer Owen Maddock and John Cooper which appeared to be mainly founded on the use of pieces of chalk, stick, string and clean-swept areas of the workshop floor in distinct contrast to the fully equipped drawing office and scientific approach at Cheshunt. All frame tubes at Lotus were straight and properly triangulated structures were *de rigueur*. The healthy contempt for Cooper's designs was tempered by their overwhelming success in Grand Prix racing contrasting with the consistent failure of Lotus' "technically perfect" designs before 1960. I think that the only really serious leading personalities at Lotus of this period were Graham Lewis and Fred Bushell and they both had very good reason for being that way. The only thing that would bring a smile to Graham's face was when he seriously embarrassed the Sales Department and Fred's good humour was mainly associated with the receipt of large, sound cheques or a period of absence from the office by Chapman.

(vii) Team Lotus

From the earliest Lotus days Chapman's motivation was increasingly that of making money (the simplest measure of worldly success), spurred on by the most competitive spirit I have encountered. Chapman behaved like a racing driver in all areas of activity. Faced with a logical argument that he didn't enjoy and sensing that he was losing the upper hand, he would devise a means of verbally "shutting the door" and enter the next corner ahead of the opposition with off the track excursions if necessary.

Chapman's love of money could well have been fostered at the parental knee. His father Stan, Landlord of the Railway Hotel at Hornsey, had a prudent and conservative nature but could become seriously agitated by low offers of start money to Team Lotus for which he was general administrator until Andrew Ferguson progressively took over this role after joining the racing team from Cooper. I am sure that Colin would have been carefully reared to understand the importance of having adequate funds in the hand and a little in the bank too. Chapman had a very personal feeling about the spending of "his" money by others. In fact when at our ultimate parting of the ways he needed a good justification for giving me the sack he was able to create a remarkably histrionic scene around the contractual continuation of an advertising programme in the US *Road and Track* magazine at a time when he was convinced that he had forbidden all expenditure of this nature. "You're spending my bloody money" was his anguished cry. This same impression was given to others and Ron Hickman tells the story of the day when due to poor internal communication the Elite aluminium dash panel was cut to the wrong profile and a substantial stock delivered to Cheshunt and the scrap bin. The group involved called a meeting on Saturday morning in order to decide who was to give Chapman the news that they had wasted "his" money . . .

Motor racing at that time had certain attractions for the man anxious to build up a fortune when taxation was high and controls on the illegal amassing of wealth strictly enforced. Despite the ministrations of the talented Fred Bushell, purchase tax eventually had to be paid on most of the complete cars produced for the home market and income tax at the correct rates on visibly paid salaries and benefits. Inevitably a certain amount of "hot" money came into the business to pay for new cars; particularly racing cars and a method could be developed over the years which allowed a proportion of this to bypass the system. Lotus would certainly not have been alone in this as the apocryphal story of the day that Charlie Cooper's money chest was stolen from under his bed suggests. At that time the financing of international motor racing was quite differently ordered from today. Although sponsorship was part of the picture it operated on a much more discreet basis and a commercial sponsor was prevented from emblazoning his logo on the side of the beneficiary's cars in the period before 1968. The principal sponsors, led by the fuel companies (in Lotus' case by Reg Tanner of Esso) would pay a retainer to "their" racing team – or teams; Esso supported both Lotus and Cooper for example. Additionally, bonuses were paid to manufacturers and drivers based on results. Payments of this type were clearly visible to the taxman and presented limited scope for creative accounting. However, the vital areas of start money and prize money particularly when racing abroad had special attractions.

The racing season and the weeks preceding it were marked by furious correspondence by telegram and letter between Team Lotus and the luckless organisers of National Grands Prix and major sports racing events such as Le Mans and the Spa 24 hour race. A process of bargaining determined the amount of start money that would be paid for each car and driver in an order of merit established by the race organiser; then immediately disputed and subject to counter proposals from Stan Chapman (urged on by his son) and Andrew Ferguson. This negotiation would continue until the last minute and it then became essential that as many cars as possible should at least appear on the start line and complete a lap or two to collect the precious funds. The start money technique had been refined by the Equipe Gordini during the early Fifties and had become something of a joke; immortalised in Ustinov's "Grand Prix of Gibraltar". The Gordini tradition was maintained during 1957, 58 and 59 by Team Lotus' efforts in Formula 2 and Formula 1 races with the front engined single seater cars; possibly the most fragile racing machinery in the history of the sport. Prize money was fixed by the organisers and generally not subject to negotiation. Therefore, if one's cars were unlikely to gain a place or even finish

Innes Ireland, a mainstay of Team Lotus in 1959, '60 and '61 was a hard driver and is here seen at Zandvoort, kicking up sand as he fights the understeering Sixteen in pursuit of always faster opposition. Observe the relatively narrow track front and rear in conjunction with narrow tread, large diameter (15") wheels of this car "in period use".

the race, start money became of paramount importance and Chapman raised the negotiation of this to a fine art.

Start money – and prize money too – was paid in the currency of the country in which earned. Such liquid funds could be used in a variety of ways and moved about the world relatively simply. Team Lotus was and remains very much a Chapman family property and although today it has become a multi-million dollar business that can only be run on impeccable lines, in its earlier years and under the strict financial controls of the time, the activities of Team Lotus became a cash cow (or calf, depending on results), of infinite value to Chapman. The rule was that money could flow freely from all Lotus companies into Team Lotus but never in the reverse direction. It could be argued that this was entirely logical since Team Lotus was the single major promotional activity behind the Lotus Group and it certainly pioneered technical changes (e.g. the Chapman Strut) later used on road cars.

A Chapman "first" was the juxtaposition of the words *Team* and *Lotus* in the continental style as in *Scuderia Ferrari* or *Equipe Gordini*. The English or the Scots with their cautious *Écurie Écosse* are usually self-conscious about this sort of thing but Colin being as British as roast beef ventured where others feared to tread and called his Scuderia or Écurie plain Team Lotus. Nowadays it seems completely natural although at the time some may have felt that *Lotus Team* would have been more acceptable; and in the tradition of *Monkey Stable*.

It was not until well into the Sixties that any form of advertising was permitted on racing cars. There was a great rumpus in 1950 when Tony Vandervell insisted on painting *Thin Wall Special* quite discreetly on his Ferraris, probably for very good tax deductible reasons. Vandervell had a considerable amount of clout with the authorities and ignored criticism but many of us thought it a little vulgar. If we had then known what would ultimately transpire I am sure the non-smokers in particular would have been utterly horrified.

The words *Team Lotus* were nicely and very discreetly painted on our cars together with the name of the driver again quietly done. Drivers' names on racing cars had been seen for many years; notably that of B. Bira and team names or badges such as Scuderia Ambrosiana (the Parnell-Lurani operation). But the eagle eye of the authorities was ever watchful to ensure that nobody stepped beyond the narrow confines of what was considered acceptable in this regard; and sponsors (such as Esso, Shell, BP, Lucas and Dunlop) were obliged to restrict the trumpeting of successes to stereotyped press advertisements of race results by cars strictly using their products. These severe restrictions ensured that sponsorship was limited to those manufacturers directly associated with the sport and we must ponder whether the decision to open the flood gates to all and sundry including tobacco companies, contraceptive manufacturers and woolly jumper knitters was really what the FIA intended.

Not only was the signwriting of Team Lotus very discreet but the premises of the organisation too were exceptionally modest in 1960. The Team Lotus workshops at Cheshunt were behind the Service Department and below Lotus Developments' drawing office. There was barely accommodation for three racing cars and the necessary paraphernalia to maintain them. Chapman pursued a policy fairly common at the time of "hiving off" certain racing activities to Works supported teams. David Buxton the Derby distributor ran Team Elite with considerable success, frequently driving with John Wagstaff. The team's administration was handled by Bill Allen, a good driver and solicitor to boot. By 1960 Chapman had more or less lost interest in systematic sports car racing and was concentrating Team Lotus efforts on Formula One. There were no Works supported sports racing car teams on the level of Team Elite although discreet support was given to Rob Walker and his driver Stirling Moss who used a

Nineteen with devastating success at home and abroad. Later, Ron Harris ran a supported team of Juniors with excellent results.

One of the problems at the time was the shortage of British-made power units for the large capacity classes. By diverting Coventry Climax FPF twin-cam engines to sports racing cars, supplies to the Lotus and Cooper Grand Prix Teams were jeopardised. In the smaller capacity classes the Coventry Climax single cam engines (FWA, B and M series) were rapidly overhauled after 1959 by Cosworth derivations of the Ford 105E series. It was not however until the advent of the Twentythree with Lotus Twincam Ford-based engine in 1962 that a viable British alternative with suitable performance for International competition in the medium capacity classes became available.

My early tasks with the company included disposal of the now very surplus front engined Team Lotus Sixteens as they were progressively replaced by the new Eighteen mid-engined Works cars during the 1960 season. They were ideally to be despatched to the most distant point possible to avoid after-sales service complications with the new owner; although they were all accompanied by the intended-but-never-fitted Rzeppa constant velocity propeller shaft universal joint which had not yet reached the starting line during Team Lotus operation of the cars. For £5 (yes) Mike Costin let me take away a brand new late type spare Sixteen chassis frame which I thought might make the basis of a quite good single seater hill climb car but I was so occupied by other matters that it went back later in exchange for my "fiver" and may well have eventually reached the circuit in HSCC events. The current success story of the Sixteen in historic racing suggests that it was potentially the most successful front engined car of its time although for well known reasons it never fulfilled that promise. In hard cash terms in 1960 the Works Sixteens were worth virtually nothing and went on their way for a few hundred pounds, usually fitted with the most clapped out FPF engine that we could find and a generally "dodgy" specimen of the always suspect transmission. They had caused so much chagrin to Chapman and Team Lotus that their departure was unlamented.

Team Lotus was administered by Chapman's father Stan and Andrew Ferguson but of course Colin was very much in charge of events. The chief mechanic was Jim Endruweit who had the characteristic air of resignation and putty-coloured complexion of a racing mechanic from a team with a particularly troublesome collection of machinery. Team Lotus mechanics were all capable of working round the clock regularly and were probably more experienced in this regard at the time than any other group in the racing world. Chapman treated his racing mechanics well by the standards of the company although he was probably more than aware that if he sacked any of the more experienced it would be difficult to find equally qualified replacements in view of the low standing of Team Lotus at the conclusion of the 1959 season.

At that time the whole business of motor racing even at Grand Prix level was totally different from today. If we disregard the relatively sophisticated operations such as BRM and Ferrari, most, including Team Lotus were gloriously amateurish by present day standards. In the first instance there were so few people involved. In those days track testing would involve loading the car on a trailer hitched behind a small van or car and motoring to Brands Hatch or Goodwood with a couple of mechanics to keep the thing operational for the benefit of the driver who would have arrived in Chapman's Zodiac or his own car. Of course, Grand Prix cars were ridiculously simple by the standards of today. Aerodynamics, for example, only existed in the sense of minimising drag and avoiding lift. Tyres until 1960 and the advent of high-hysteresis compounds required virtually no selection process at all. You used what was provided by the only (for British constructors) supplier – Dunlop – who changed the tread

pattern and compound every few years under pressure (from Chapman more than most).

No electronics or computer specialists were needed – or even available – at the time when the nearest thing to a pocket calculator was wheeled into the office on a trolley. The only computers that we knew were experimental devices occupying vast volumes of space at Manchester University and in the laboratories of one or two electrical manufacturers. If you wanted a rough idea of a dimension or calculation you used a sliderule, which was precise enough for the day. All suspension joints were by today's standards remarkably imprecise. The present universal use of rose joints and similarly exact metal-to-metal pivots was then

Happiness would have been complete if Chapman's first Grande Epreuve win had been accomplished by a Team Lotus car, but this was not to be. Astonished by the ease with which Innes Ireland beat him at the Easter 1960 races at Goodwood following the impressive debut of the Lotus Eighteen in the Argentine Grand Prix of February 7th, Stirling Moss persuaded Rob Walker to buy an Eighteen from the delighted Chapman. It was at the wheel of this car that Moss (shown here leading Jack Brabham) won the Monaco Grand Prix on the 29th May 1960 to set Lotus on what soon became the familiar road to victory.

virtually unkown*. Wheel alignment was achieved by methods used for the family car and the suspension geometry of Cooper and Ferrari was sufficiently vague as to be almost laughable by today's standards and certainly inferior to Lotus at that time. Chapman's main preoccupation was the design of a suspension system to allow the entire tread contact area of the tyre to remain fully in touch with terra firma under all conditions. Wheels under cornering load had to remain vertical to the surface of the track and photographs of Lotus and competitive cars cornering hard were frequently studied with laughter (Cooper) or satisfaction (Lotus Eighteen).

Apart from the ability to keep the wheels pointing in the designed direction, the 1960 racing mechanic needed to have a natural "ear" and "feel" for carburation and ignition, which were generally set empirically rather than to the dictates of a microchip. This was still the period of the contact breaker and magneto; devices dating back to the dawn of the internal combustion engine. Beyond these basic skills the Lotus racing mechanic had to be able to work all hours for a relatively small wage and very occasional bonus. Apart from caring for the team cars he would also have to be prepared to drive backwards and forwards across Europe in the transporter; replacing wheels and assorted bearings between traversing Alps and haggling with Customs Officers. In those days he was lucky to get a pair of dark green twill overalls and have them cleaned at his employer's expense once a fortnight. The modern practice of prancing about in multi-coloured 'designer' anoraks and shorts would have led to remarks about the uncertain sexual orientation of the wearer at the least. Today's racing mechanics never seem to get dirty and always seem be terribly fit and bronzed. Not for them the grimy hands, sallow cheeks and red-rimmed eyes of their forebears.

The Team Lotus workshop was theoretically out of bounds to all but those employed to work there. However, when routine activities such as new (as distinct from secret) car construction and between-race maintenance were in progress one would happily be admitted to enjoy examination of the excellent engineering and share the amusing banter surrounding the creation of the Lotus rear-engined Racing Revolution.

(viii)   Design and development

In the original Cheshunt plan it was intended that the majority of design and development activity would be concentrated on the mezzanine floor in the "Lotus Components Building". However, because this area had a wooden floor with limited load bearing capacity, an engine and gearbox assembly shop together with the Lotus Heenan & Froude dynamometer were located below at ground level behind the Lotus Components production area. Between the engine shop and Team Lotus was sandwiched a chassis development shop incorporating a surface table on which prototypes could be built and modifications carried out.

The staircase led up to a small landing from which doors opened out to Mike Costin's office, with a small office shared by Steve Sanville and Henry Lee separating Mike from the drawing office; all three constructed along the inner wall of the Lotus Components wing. Ron Hickman had a small office within the remaining large area which was devoted to the design and development of bodywork – in my time most conspicuously to that of the Elan.

* but tried by Lister on their first (unsuccessful) F2 car of 1956

In August 1986, Graham Arnold arranged a reunion of former Lotus employees at the original Cheshunt Works. On this happy day I was able to take a snap of colleagues (left to right) Steve Sanville (Engine and Gearbox Technician), Mike Costin (Development Director) and Ron Hickman (Design Engineer responsible for bringing the Elite to production form and for the design and development of the Elan and its immediate successors). The main office and Lotus Cars Limited building seen here is largely unchanged from 1959. My Sales Department was to the left of the entrance on the ground floor and above it were the offices of Colin Chapman, Fred Bushell, Stan Chapman, John Standen and the Accounts Department.

Mike Costin's office had a translucent wall dividing it from the fibreglass area and he was therefore able to get early warning of fires breaking out in the fibreglass shop where spontaneous combustion regularly reared its ugly head. We had to deal with such emergencies ourselves in order to avoid hostility from the Factories Inspectorate but nothing got completely out of hand in my experience. Steve Sanville and Ron Hickman were project engineers and had responsibility for specific development programmes. Ron for example was in charge of the Elan design and development programme whereas Steve Sanville was project engineer on the Seven Series Two and later the twin-cam engine. This formalisation of their roles had been preceded by a lengthy period during which Ron was heavily involved in Elite development and Steve built up a reputation as the expert on the notorious Lotus transmission used from the Twelve to the Nineteen.

Naturally the driving force behind all Lotus design and development was Chapman who maintained a drawing board at home at this time. Before moving to Cheshunt Ian Jones the Chief Draughtsman was also based at Gothic Cottage for security reasons and also to improve communication between him and the Chief Designer. Ian moved into the drawing office at Cheshunt as Chief Draughtsman (his previous experience at Lotus qualified him as a design draughtsman capable of working from the simplest brief). In the early days Ian was supported by Alan Styman – also a highly capable design draughtsman – Brian Luff as chassis project engineer and Bill Wells, remembered as the "bellhousing expert". One presented Bill with an engine and gearbox and he would design an elegant casting to link the two. The Eighteen and Twenty bellhousings are particularly good examples of his skill.

Chapman's heavy commitments with Team Lotus meant that he was not frequently to be seen in the drawing office during the greater part of the year. However, he enjoyed looking over the shoulder of the draughtsmen and in characteristic fashion commented on what he saw. On one occasion he noticed the engine bearers for the Elan being drawn in 16 gauge steel (thin enough). When Chapman's rage had subsided he instructed the luckless man to redraw in 20 gauge. Subsequently tests at this thickness resulted in breakage of the engine bearers which were then redrawn at "Halfway House" – 18 gauge – and again broke. Finally, the original 16 gauge dimension was used successfully. This is an example of the classical Chapman empirical design method which reached its apogee in the Sixteen Grand Prix cars although as Moss and others later learned to their cost the method and resultant breakages continued to plague the early rear engined racing cars.

(ix) The Cheshunt Routine

Over the period 1959-1962 the system of direct sales to the public was initially replaced by a fairly conventional distribution network and then finally as part of the continuing struggle for survival back to direct sales. The pattern of our working lives changed accordingly.

Continuity was provided by Ron Richardson and Peter Warr joined later by Ian McLeod. Customers arrived from all over the globe to buy cars; quite often with pocketfuls of currency some perhaps more than warm. We had no facilities to effect part-exchange deals (until after my departure) which made life simpler in several ways but in those days, before bank managers happily splashed out money for car financing to all and sundry, our clientele was rather restricted to the wealthy or distinctly suspect.

We always had a demonstrator Elite and Seven available and although I was occasionally involved in giving a trial run to the customer most demonstrations were performed by Ron, Ian and Peter; all of whom were accomplished fast drivers. The demonstration would involve a left turn into Delamare Road; left again at the top and then right to run north up the original A10 road. About a mile further on there was an island linking the by-pass to the road it replaced and this was the signal (when the engine was nicely warm) to expose the unexpecting potential customer to his (frequently) first experience of Lotus power-to-weight ratio. The best specimens we had for this were our brace of Super Sevens – initially 7TMT the FWA Climax engined Series One Car and later the first of the 1340 cc Cosworth Series Two versions, 8843 AR. Although many of our customers were naturally experienced fast motorists, at that time the raw and naked motoring offered by the Super Seven was relatively unknown and the initial drag up the by-pass in those days of no maximum speed limit could be relied upon to do the trick. Peter Warr in particular, about to embark on a very successful although short-lived racing career, rarely failed to clinch the sale. The customer would then return in varying degrees of good humour to the showroom on the right of the entrance door where we had built a counter for the purpose and where he could with our active assistance complete a set of order forms for his kit or complete car. In order to avoid the burden of British Purchase Tax this required him to buy certain components from one company – Lotus Components and the power unit from Racing Engines Ltd. In the case of pure

Parked in Delamare Road is the first Elite (pale green and probably No. 1045) that I drove – nominally a development car although used for sales demonstrations too. It has a Maximar body with the early exposed upper mounting points for the Chapman Strut rear suspension units. Later versions had these covered by the famous "Sabrina" domes which to a modest extent reduced the racket of the car crashing and banging over surface irregularities. The car points in the opposite direction to that taken for a demonstration run.

racing cars which were not subject to Purchase Tax in completed form this problem did not arise although we still used 'split' invoicing.

Building a Lotus kit involved no great hardship. In the case of the Elite which had never been intended for amateur assembly, the car was virtually built and then partially dismantled when we knew that everything fitted satisfactorily. In any case arrangements were made for the car to be thoroughly checked either by the Works (Panshanger) or one of our retail outlets on completion by the customer. Compared to the general standard of kit cars (then and now) Lotus cars in component form – a form of words that we felt more acceptable to our market – were a very straightforward proposition born of commercial expediency rather than engineering necessity.

Having obtained the signed order form and deposit the successful salesman would react according to temperament. The sober Ron Richardson would announce his success with a wry smile and a quip. Peter Warr would rub his hands with glee and engage in a little demonstrative arm waving while Ian McLeod could be relied upon to outdo all with a Scottish jig or a piece of outrageous mimicry. Ian was virtually unstoppable when in pursuit of an order and although an army career was hardly the ideal preparation for the harsh commercial world, his amazing self-confidence, personal charm and powers of 73 persuasion, which he used regularly on all of us from Chapman down and above all on the clientele kept him at the head of the field. "Man Management"! he told us, "you've got to have it to succeed". As recounted elsewhere it was a serious blow when we had to ask him to leave Cheshunt although we were delighted to keep him in the Lotus family at The Chequered Flag.

Chapman overawed most of us from time to time but he never seemed able to upset Ian who refused to be abashed by anyone. Ian McLeod's taste in cars was slightly bizarre and there was frequently disparity between the view of them held by Ian and the rest of us. I have already described his arrival in a magnificent Sunbeam Tourer of a kind which at that time was considered to be a rather dreadful "dog". He also appeared in an extraordinary vintage (just) Morris Minor saloon which had only done a couple of thousand miles in its lengthy lifetime. He spent a fortune having it refurbished and eventually it ended up with a Shorrocks supercharged MG PB engine which made demands (despite brakes converted to hydraulic actuation) on the driver's skill almost beyond those available from even the accomplished McLeod. He finally made a concession to modernity by buying a brand new NSU Sportprinz Bertone Coupé – a little rear engined air-cooled twin-cylinder car fitted with the type of swing axle independent rear suspension immortalised and outlawed by Ralph Nader's book "Unsafe at any Speed". 1961

Ian McLeod, Cheshunt's Number One salesman in 1960/61 was (and is) a great car fancier. This contemporary shot shows Ian with his Type 37A Bugatti and modern NSU Sportprinz – tested and commented upon by Chapman as recorded in the text. McLeod used the Type 37A to commute to Cheshunt from his home at Broxbourne during fair weather and negotiated a 5 minute delayed arrival time with Chapman to allow him to adequately warm up the huge sump of Castrol "R".
He bought the Bug from a French cypher clerk who had hidden it in Alsace Lorraine for the duration of the war and, because he subsequently had difficulty in driving it, sold it to the fortunate McLeod for £250.

was several years before Nader however and Ian felt that the Prinz (probably by comparison with the supercharged Minor) represented a pinnacle of roadholding achievement.

For weeks and weeks he worried Chapman to try the Sportprinz which he felt could give inspiration to Colin's creative drive. In the subsequent test run the car narrowly avoided violent inversion and a pale and chastened McLeod arose from the passenger seat to be told by Chapman that in his view it was "utterly f.....g horrible". Not long after that experience the little german coupé was up for sale and never seen or heard of again.

Most British Lotus distributors and some of the dealers collected their cars from Cheshunt. We devised an open sided crate for carrying component cars and these could be easily lifted on to a trailer for transportation. The arrival of dealers to collect vehicles in this way gave us an opportunity for contact to supplement the routine visits I made to their premises. We also contracted with a small local haulier to make deliveries; and for most of the time he had enough work to keep him fully occupied if not very regularly rewarded.

All export packing and transportation was carried out by the fledgling Howard Tennens company. We dealt with Ron Tennens who suffered mightily from our perennial inability to pay promptly for his services. However, like so many people he believed in the Lotus Dream and stuck with us through thick and thin. The peak shipment period to the States was throughout 1960 when we carried out massive deliveries to Jay Chamberlain with a total of 276 Elites sailing through the Panama Canal in that year. For Ron Tennens this represented important business in a world in which success is measured more by volume than weight.

The normal ebb and flow of retail customers, dealers and distributors was spiced by the more exotic visits of the racing fraternity and an astonishing variety of celebrities attracted by the Lotus legend and the irresistible personality of its creator . . .

There was a constant coming and going of the type of motor car that particularly appealed to me. I must admit to the belief that the finest things in automotive engineering originate South of the Alps and because these products of the great motor sporting tradition of Ferrari, Maserati, Alfa Romeo and Lancia were diametrically opposed to the ethos of Chapman's work I tended for political reasons to restrain my enthusiasm. Peter Warr's favourite car at the time was the Mercedes – he had a slightly Prussian approach to life which matched this – Ron Richardson was never terribly interested in cars as such and Ian McLeod's preferences changed with the moon and were generally beyond my comprehension. When something to my taste arrived at Cheshunt I would quietly saunter to the car park and enjoy it alone.

Chapter Four
Cheshunt – The Cars

Although the Elite was designed and finalised in Series One form during the Hornsey period, as a type it belongs in spirit to Cheshunt. Because Cheshunt was created for the Elite, this section begins with that car and traces the evolution of the series of types spawned during the first thirty months at Cheshunt; the most extraordinary period of creativity in Chapman's life. In this interval he brought the Elite to market, embraced and developed the mid-engined concept for his competition cars after a decade of commitment to traditional front-engined configuration and consolidated his position as the master of the space frame design technique.

This time also saw the pre-production evolution of the Elan, a car which for much of the three year period preceding launch in October 1962 was a three-dimensional "design doodle" passing through a massive process of evolution. The Elan project even underwent a title change in mid-stream as its character was transformed.

The climax of Chapman's first two years of design at Cheshunt was the birth of the Twentyfive Grand Prix car, often referred to as "the first of the monocoques" (even Chapman claimed this in later years although he never saw it that way when he first toyed with the idea of designing a racing car reduced to the smallest acceptable number of component parts). Chapman showed how to make a racing car without a spaceframe chassis and everybody else eventually either slavishly copied him or built on his example.

(i) Meeting the Elite

Behind the Cheshunt Parts area was the Service Department under the management of Tony Caldersmith, another Australian expatriate to whom I am grateful for my first opportunity to take a ride in an Elite. When I arrived at Cheshunt there was only one "spare" Elite – a road test car (6SME)* under Caldersmith's control. I felt that it would be highly desirable for me to try the car for which I would soon have commercial responsibility and prevailed upon Tony to take me out in "his" dark green, with tan interior, Series One Elite. As we drove out of the Works I appreciated immediately that here was a car unlike

For the exhibition "Eye for Industry" held at the Victoria and Albert Museum, London in November 1986 by the Royal Society of Arts, the designer Alan Irvine approached the author for assistance in obtaining an exhibit to record the achievement of Colin Chapman, a Fellow of the Society. Mrs Hazel Chapman kindly arranged the loan of a scale model of the Twentyfive. It is shown here in the company of a model Mini marking the contribution of the late Sir Alec Issigonis.

anything I had driven before (or since – including the only other fibreglass monocoque – the Rochdale Olympic). The all-fibreglass construction meant that it had a totally different "feel" and smell. All driving sensations were different. It was noisy and the structure magnified every road, transmission, engine and suspension noise. Vibration was an inherent feature of the car and was not helped by the fact that Coventry Climax seemed to spend very little time and money on balancing the FWE engine. On occasion this was so bad that we had to strip Climax engines on arrival, re-balance and re-assemble them before being able to mount them in the finished car. The roadholding and braking of this Elite was as astounding as one would expect from the Formula Two-derived suspension system. It was very light and of course so aerodynamically "clean" that the puny 75 bhp with which it was endowed, nevertheless provided good acceleration and very high top speed matched with outstanding fuel economy.

I must admit that my first impression of the car was an overall disappointment. Despite subsequently driving many thousands of miles at the wheel of Elites in the UK and North America, I never grew to enjoy it as a road car. As a racing car it was outstanding in its time but Chapman had intended it as a money-making vehicle primarily for high speed touring which could if required be converted for racing. On the track the car's limitations as a Grand Tourer could be forgiven. The buzzing, creaking and whirring and the general sensation of sitting inside an alarm clock about to ring were irrelevant in the context of its astonishingly agile handling and "urge". Even at that early stage it was obvious to me that the appeal of the Elite would be strictly limited even in its target market. Aesthetically it was irresistible and remains one of the most beautiful automotive shapes of all time. However, the Elite's beauty is perhaps only (outer) skin deep and when matched

*transferred from car to car . . .

with the roadgoing cars with which it was intended to compete – the Porsche 356 and Alfa Romeo Giulietta ranges – it suffered deeply by comparison although often beating them on the track.

But at the time that I tried the Elite for the first time in September 1959 I was like the rest of us at Lotus, confident that we had a winner and that with our youthful enthusiasm we would somehow find a way to convert the tremendous interest aroused by the car since its launch at Earls Court in 1957 into commercial success. How wrong we were!

(ii) The Elite – A General View

The Elite was an essential step in the development of Lotus and without it or something similar it is doubtful whether the company would still exist. Chapman knew that he would have to introduce a profitable road car if he were to attract large scale finance and provide a secure platform for the continuing development

An early and well known publicity photograph of the Elite (from 1958) showing the car in a typical English setting. It is almost certainly a show car, the specially made Firestone tyres being lacquered with the maker's name picked out in gold. The fit of the door is almost perfect, probably as a result of many hours of careful preparation. On this very early car the jacking point (below the front vertical join of the door) is faired in whereas on the later true production cars it is clearly exposed to view.

of the company. In this he was encouraged by his merchant banker friend Peter Kirwan-Taylor; an ardent admirer of the Chapman talent. The Elite broke new ground technically in one respect above all. Fibreglass reinforced plastic construction had been used for some time to produce compound curvature body panels for limited series car manufacture. Cars were often produced in numbers too great to allow the economical production by hand of metal body work but still too small to justify the heavy investment in body dies to allow panels to be pressed out. For the manufacturer on the horns of this dilemma fibreglass reinforced plastic (FRP or plain "fibreglass") was a godsend and already a well established technique in the specialist car world.

Fibreglass body panels can be produced with a good surface finish externally (on the surface in contact with the mould) and the resin panels have considerable additional strength conferred on them by strands of glass matting reinforcement. Fibreglass bodies are produced by making a prototype master (usually of plaster, clay, or aluminium) and from this taking a mould (itself of FRP). Into this is applied by hand firstly a "gel" release coat followed by resin and glass matting which then cures chemically to produce the characteristic panels which are smooth externally and rather like "Shredded Wheat" on the inside. The final colour of the panel is achieved by pigmenting the resin ("self-colour") or by subsequent painting. Apart from the need to take careful precautions to avoid spontaneous combustion during certain chemical reactions occurring in manufacture and of course the unpleasant effect on sensitive skin of working with fine filaments of glass and resin, FRP construction in its basic unsophisticated form is ideal for the small concern.

Chapman, familiar with fibreglass in non-structural applications, was intrigued by the possibility of using it in a more sophisticated manner. He would need to produce box section members to provide structural strength for a chassis body unit (CBU) and he would also have to avoid revealing much (or any) of the unsightly "Shredded Wheat" internal surface of the FRP panels. The task of producing a workable prototype was achieved relatively quickly but getting the car into production in a purpose-built factory took nearly three more years and it could be argued that sporadic development work then continued until the last example rolled off the line in 1963.

Chapman wished to demonstrate that his novel method of construction was capable of absorbing punishment, so during the development period the first examples of the Elite were produced for racing use in extremely thin section panels; resulting in a car substantially lighter than the later production versions. With hindsight it might have been better to have made prototypes suitable for crossing the Sahara rather than quickly accomplishing ten laps of Brands Hatch or even twenty four hours at Le Mans but the Lotus reputation was founded on racing successes. There was no lack of takers for the early pre-production prototypes which immediately achieved success wherever they appeared. The first Elites were not only light but were fitted with up to the minute running gear that ensured a very high standard of roadholding and braking. Power was by a version of the Coventry Climax engine (the FWE of 1216 cc) produced exclusively for the Elite.

The disc-brake wishbone front suspension was exactly as fitted to the Eleven Series Two and the Twelve single seater racing car. Rear suspension was by the first type of Chapman Strut with trailing radius arm and the cast aluminium final drive unit containing BMC crownwheel and pinion was mounted directly to the fibreglass structure of the car. The rear disc brakes were mounted on the final drive unit.

From inception the Elite was provided with rev counter, wood rimmed steering wheel, 15 in wire-spoked wheels and knock-off Rudge Whitworth

Cars externally resembling the later production Elites began to appear on the racing circuits during 1958. These were pre-production prototypes of lightweight construction built to test and promote the car ahead of regular production. By using extremely thin fibreglass laminate the weight of the car could be reduced dramatically and for racing purposes the resultant creaking and groaning from the flexible structure was bearable particularly since the engine was generally unsilenced. The two best known of these early racing Elites were LOV1 driven by Graham Warner of the Chequered Flag – ultimately the most successful Lotus dealer of my time and this car DAD10 owned and driven with success by Les Leston who had a motor accessory shop. DAD10 disappeared during the Sixties but more recently resurfaced and has now been lovingly reconstructed and brought back to life.

splined hubs which looked exactly right and were specified by Chapman to give his new car the proper Lotus racing image which (as he saw it) would be demanded by Elite owners. There was so much "tumble-home" on the door section that it was not practical to fit winding windows while at the same time providing sufficient clearance for the driver's arm. The clear Perspex side windows therefore detach completely and are stored in pockets on both seat backs on all but the very earliest examples. Although this sometimes alarmed potential customers, no rain would enter the car when on the move; so good were the basic aerodynamics. Small fittings were adapted from popular cars. For instance the ingenious little door handles came from the Hillman Husky; a stubby version of the Minx passenger car popular in the Fifties. One of the more fetching features of the Elite was the fingertip-operated headlamp flashing switch which was a new experience for British motorists and which did a roaring trade for the spares department for installation on cars of all types.

The very pretty wood rimmed steering wheel was unique to the Elite and the instruments although made by Lucas were not too noticeably "borrowed" from another maker's product. The hand-formed, welded front and rear bumpers of stainless steel were manufactured by the Miles Aircraft Company to aviation

The introduction of the Series Two Elite produced by Bristol allowed Ron Hickman and his team to design a new interior trim based on the use of Royalite plastic seen here in this late model car with ZF gearbox. Note the "push-pull" umbrella type handbrake under the steering column which replaced the conventional lever on the tunnel of the Series One car.

industry standards and were therefore excruciatingly expensive. The bumpers were typical of the "albatross" elements of the Elite's specification in which components were designed and subsequently manufactured in prototype fashion by expensive means without subsequently being "productionized". Still all these beautifully made bits and pieces gave great satisfaction to all but the luckless supplier, who soon tried either to wriggle out of the contract or secure (always unsuccessfully) massive price increases from his impoverished customer.

The spare wheel was laid horizontally behind the seats and covered by an FRP moulding that provided a reasonable surface area to support a briefcase and other small possessions. On either side of the spare wheel were the housings for the upper mounting points of the Chapman Struts. Viewed from the rear these resembled the physical attributes of the contemporary well-endowed starlet Sabrina and were the source of much ribald comment. The trunk or boot of the car provided a great deal of storage space as well as a home for the battery and fuel tank after the original intention of storing petrol in the hollow front wing structural sections (rubber sealed) had proved impractical.

The fact that certain elements of the car subject to wear were not designed in such a way as to allow maintenance or even adjustment did little to hinder the car's early success as a racing machine. Chapman averred that it was fatal to provide a means of altering suspension settings because this would automatically lead to uninformed adjustment away from factory set alignment. The RIV Italian

When Malcolm Ricketts and Robin Longdon found the remains of DAD10, enough Elite parts accompanied the famous racer to serve as a basis for the creation of two replicas of Team Elite Le Mans cars. The three beautiful restorations are seen here at Brands Hatch. The former Team Elite star driver John Wagstaff subsequently acquired the car on the left as a companion to his original Team Elite car which has been in his possession since 1961.

taper roller rear hub bearings were non-adjustable, expensive, and required weekly lubrication via an inaccessible grease nipple. Unless regularly checked they frequently wore away the outer ring locating bore in the soft aluminium strut casting. The front bushing of the Chapman Strut radius arm in both series cars was by means of a system adapted from the 1932 Y model Ford 8 hp family car (and lasted for about 100 miles of hard driving).

Although the Elite was born of Chapman's long felt desire to produce a true road car with the Lotus attributes of high performance, exemplary road holding and advanced technology, it shone best as a racing car where its failings as a Grand Tourer were unimportant. Despite all efforts the Elite was never other than a thinly disguised lightweight competition car. To those owners who had experienced Lotus ownership before, it was an acceptable package but to the new Lotuseers who viewed it as a competitor to Alfa Romeo and Porsche it was a disastrous and often traumatic experience. However, the Elite remains a classic motor car from aesthetic and engineering standpoints and provided the modern owner does not cover a high mileage, must surely be an eminently suitable subject for conservation and enjoyment. The FRP construction represents a peak of technical achievement in the pre-injection moulding era. Every element of the car is beautifully thought through and although individual components may be

inadequate for the purpose intended the design as a whole displays those intrinsic qualities that endear Chapman and his circle's creative work to the *cognoscenti*. Let us not forget that although Ron Hickman, John Frayling, Peter Kirwan-Taylor and Frank Costin (among others) had a hand in the evolution of the Elite, nothing (even those aspects to which he objected) passed into production without the full approval of Chapman as Designer-in-Chief.

Elite Series Two. The long commercial life of the Elite and its numerous inherent shortcomings meant that there were sporadic attempts to resolve them while production proceeded. There were occasional "campaigns" leading to alterations and improvements – albeit modest ones – in the basic structure, engineering, finish and specification of the car. The power unit too was upgraded to offer ultimately a choice of four stages of tune from the basic 75 to 105 bhp by the end of the production run.

The first changes occurred at the point where Maximar Mouldings refused to complete their contract to build the Elite CBU at any price: "Do you want to kill us slowly or quickly?" asked the disillusioned Max Johnson. Chapman forced them to produce 150 of the cars covered by the original agreement in desperation and with the prospect of having no visible follow-on source of chassis body units. By a very happy coincidence the Bristol Aircraft Company found itself in 1959 in a position where it would welcome work for the underemployed capacity in its Automotive and Plastics Division. Characteristically Chapman saw an opportunity to plug the gap left by Maximar's loss of interest and at the same time associate himself with a highly prestigious aircraft company which almost certainly would be able to manufacture a better quality product for him than the boat builder-turned-car manufacturer responsible for what were now to be known as the Series One cars.

The Series Two Elite (entirely manufactured by Bristol) was certainly a better quality-controlled structure than its predecessor. It also incorporated minor improvements to the structure itself together with an important alteration to the rear suspension which partially at least overcame one of the discerning driver's major sources of dissatisfaction. The original Elite rear suspension was based on that of the definitive version of the Twelve Formula car, using Chapman Struts

During the last months of 1959 the author was required to "prepare a survey and (the) necessary planning for marketing the Elite during 1960". One of the things the sales manager didn't like was the absence of proper sales literature so this was hurriedly put together and used well into 1960. The photographs and drawings were all inherited and the printing was carried out by the company's previous suppliers in this field in the pre-Birdsall/Balding and Mansell era. Even at this early stage of my short-lived Lotus career I tended to wax lyrical over the Elite although like most who had actually driven it I thought it a noisy little beast, albeit with remarkable performance in between the breakdowns. The incredibly long-winded period of development meant that most of the detail of the car (and of course Chapman never missed a point) was unusually well worked out for such a limited production machine. The cockpit view shows how perfectly suited to grand touring the car would have been had it not been closer to a racing car than open road transport.

Beneath the sleek slope of the bonnet lies the famous overhead camshaft Coventry Climax Power Unit—latent power at your instant call, yet so sweet tempered that the Elite will trickle through city traffic with utter docility. High efficiency yields twin virtues of flashing acceleration and remarkably low fuel consumption at three-figure cruising speeds. Enjoy Elite Economy!

The compact form of the Elite belies its spacious interior and boot. Suitcases, golf clubs and other luggage may easily be stowed. The Elite affords generous accommodation for two—truly luxurious travel

The brilliant 'brain child' of the highly successful Lotus design team, the Elite will carry you to higher realms of Grand Touring in superb comfort, speed and safety.

The unique lightweight monocoque fibre-reinforced plastic body unit draws unanimous praise for its strength, durability and refinement. It has been thoroughly tested and proved in thousands of miles of racing and high speed road use by the world's leading competition drivers.

The purity of line of this revolutionary thoroughbred excites admiration from any viewpoint. A superb combination of strictly functional aerodynamic form, first class driver vision and sheer elegance.

with fixed length articulated drive shafts and fore and aft location provided by a kinked (straight on the Twelve) trailing arm to a point forward and a little inboard of the hub casting. The system worked well until the rubber cup surrounding the ball joint on the forward end of the radius arm broke up, exacerbating the rear wheel steering effect inherent in the Chapman Strut by allowing the rear wheel to oscillate fore and aft in extreme cases with drastic effect on the handling coupled with an irritating rattle from the now metal-to-metal contact of the radius arm ball within the internally pulverised mounting block. Chapman's answer to the complaining customer was to suggest he carry a spanner, locking wire and supply of Ford 8 hp rubbers in the left-hand jacket pocket. Many Series One owners did (some – experienced Lotus owners – without requiring instruction) but these were from a besotted hard core. There were not too many such right thinking and reasonable (Chapman's definition) owners in the United States.

For the Series Two Elite Chapman adopted the new hub casting and wide based lower wishbone-cum-radius arm of the fully developed Sixteen Grand Prix car. In this installation the inboard pick-up point of the radius arm was near the

Enjoy an Elite—in Safety! *The suspension system of the Elite is directly derived from that used on the fabulous Lotus Grand Prix and Sports Racing cars, giving unparalled road adhesion and comfort. The unique self-compensating properties of the Chapman Strut independent rear suspension ensure consistent handling under extreme variations of load, and Lotus rack and pinion steering gear gives faultless steering control under the most hazardous conditions of surface and 'line'.*

Elite Emergency! . . *Feel the iron hand of the four wheel Girling Disc brakes safely sweep away all anxiety as they rush the car smoothly to rest . . .*

The Elite is tailored for travel in comfort. The thoughtfully designed seats establish new criteria for sheer luxury: cradling you restfully for all-day driving.

The wood-rimmed steering-wheel and short remote control gear-lever are arranged to reduce driver fatigue and give complete command.

Other features include matt non-reflecting dash-cowl, pile carpeting and read-at-a-glance instruments to satisfy the most critical judgment.

centreline of the car with a corresponding improvement in suspension geometry, straight line running and reduced wear and tear on the inboard mounting ball joint (still however based on the ancient Ford 8 hp system).

There was every incentive to avoid all but the most essential development work on the Elite. It was already far too costly and each change made could potentially magnify the loss on every car sold. Therefore our aim was to sell them as fast as we could and get on with the M2 (Elan) which hopefully would make money. Chapman was increasingly disenchanted by the Elite from late 1960 when the Bristol honeymoon period was over but it was more difficult to get rid of the now steady flow of cars themselves than the technical irritation they caused him.

Before the final drastic decision to sell the Elite as a kit car (a desperate measure decided by Chapman but given to me to implement) from October 1961 (at a saving of 30% largely represented by the now redundant British Purchase Tax, payable only on fully assembled vehicles) attention was focussed on the engine and transmission, unchanged since announcement of the Elite in 1957. The deteriorating personal relationship between Chapman and Leonard Lee of Coventry Climax had begun to affect the Elite by mid 1960. Chapman resented what he considered to be the better deal enjoyed by Cooper in the supply of engines for Formula One and Two cars. In turn, Climax disliked the failure of Lotus to pay promptly for FWE supplies and began to insist that engines must be collected from Coventry and paid for by a certified cheque carried by the driver. This was very restrictive on Fred Bushell's creative accountancy technique and added to the resentment. The final straw was the discovery that because of the now steady demand for the FWE from Cheshunt as a result of the uninterrupted flow of CBUs from Bristol, Climax were failing to meet the required quality standards. We suspected that the forklift truck department were assembling the complicated power unit to much lower standards than applied to the competition engines and FWEs to date. Climax simply refused to co-operate and in desperation we were forced to strip and rebalance a substantial proportion of the engine to ensure that the already strong tendency to roughness and vibration did not reach totally unacceptable levels.

In October 1960 the Elite SE (Special Equipment) was announced. This limited edition model incorporated an 85 bhp Stage 2 engine with twin SU carburettors and most importantly the specially developed ZF four-speed S4-12 all-synchromesh gearbox to at last replace the antiquated BMC transmission with "crash" bottom gear. Although offering better ratios and a slick, neat gearchange, the ZF is noisy and the lever itself has an infuriating tendency to buzz in sympathy with the Climax vibration periods.

During early 1962 the final development saw what was basically the "full race" Stage 3 version of the Climax prepared by Cosworth and offered in three stages of tune: Super 95, Super 100 and Super 105 (names inspired by Porsche). All SEs regardless of engine tune level were issued with silver painted roof section, Pirelli Cintura tyres and Lucas Le Mans PL700 headlights and heater/demisters fitted as standard. For the Series Two car there was a major redesign of the interior trim in Royalite thermoplastic, extending to new seat texture, transmission tunnel and door panels (now with ashtrays included). This attractive piece of Industrial Design by Ron Hickman and his small team won a major award in 1962. Ron was also responsible for the characteristic "see through numberplate" of the Elite, in

The Special Equipment Elite introduced in October 1960 was fitted with two SU carburettors and a fabricated steel 4-branch exhaust manifold. Power output was 85 bhp against 75 for the standard car. The MG gearbox was replaced by an all-synchro ZF S4-12. Here is an early specimen showing the Bristol body badge under the left-hand bonnet hinge. The Elite was never fitted with a bonnet or boot lid stay, Chapman having decided that his hinges were sufficient for the task without external assistance. The hardened Elite owner knew better and usually carried a suitable piece of timber for use under all conditions save absolute atmospheric calm.

which the (British) registration letters and numbers are mounted on black wire mesh in the air intake.

We may admire Chapman's characteristic persistence in the use of a fibreglass monocoque in the Elite concept but one can only wonder what might have happened had a simple sheet steel frame been developed earlier for that car before circumstances forced such a development on the floundering Elan development programme. The Elite would then have been perhaps no less successful as a racing car, just as beautiful to the beholder, infinitely more practical on the road and without doubt commercially successful. But the very failure of the Elite to achieve wide acceptance and therefore distribution in its day has made it desirable and admired today. It is a veritable triumph of development over design although Chapman – if still with us – might have argued that "if only Frayling had done as he (Chapman) had intended" the Elite would have succeeded commercially in chassisless form. His original decision to launch the Elan design/development programme as a self-supporting plastic monocoque concept bears this out.

(iii) Williams & Pritchard and why the Elite was made of fibreglass

It is natural that so creative a force as Colin Chapman should provide the impetus for the formation of satellite activities around the central Lotus endeavour. Progress Chassis arose from the original involvement of John Teychenne; Cosworth Engineering relied heavily on Lotus for business in its early months and a third enterprise – which like Progress never developed beyond a relatively modest level of activity – also owes much to Chapman.

Colin's highly critical standards resulted in an early decision that only the firm of Williams & Pritchard (virtually the two partners of that name) could produce aluminium panels of a standard acceptable to Lotus. Charlie Williams and Len Pritchard were a complementary pair; Charlie being the leading craftsman while Len made most of the business decisions. Len Pritchard weighed up Colin fairly early in the day and as was the case with so many Lotus suppliers laid down certain strict rules (such as "all goods must be paid for – promptly"). The partners decided on a certain pace for their business and this very rapidly became a major constraint on the rate of expansion possible at Hornsey. Because of the high standards expected by Chapman and delivered in full by Williams & Pritchard no other coachbuilder was able to replace W&P and Chapman became severely frustrated by the limited output and very high prices charged.

Interestingly it was not until the Seventeen that Colin introduced fibreglass panels on Lotus competition cars which continued to be fitted with W&P aluminium bodywork for the six years from 1953. Even after the introduction of fibreglass panelling at Lotus W&P always manufactured the aluminium prototype bodywork used to make moulds for the fibreglass panels.

Pre-1959 Lotus competition car bodywork is a combination of compound curvature panelling (beaten out by hand and wheeled) with a considerable amount of single curvature panelling riveted permanently into position on the chassis frame. The single curvature panelling was fitted in most cases by Lotus, requiring a relatively low level of skill. At Cheshunt there was a small panel shop situated between Team Lotus and the original Service Department dedicated to this process. The steel tubular chassis frames arrived from Progress lightly sprayed with pale grey paint before being stockpiled (indoors if lucky) often for a considerable period of time. The panels were then riveted over the rust.

Because Chapman had so high a regard for the workmanship of Williams &

Pritchard – high enough to prevent him from wishing to go elsewhere although he must have looked hard before reaching that conclusion – he knew that he must find an alternative method of manufacture for his new volume (by Lotus standards) car, the Elite. Fibreglass was beginning to gain acceptance in the highest circles as a material for bodywork manufacture (even the great General Motors had used it in their Corvette sports car). In the pursuit of profit, Chapman saw fibreglass as a means of escaping the tyranny of commitment to expensive small-scale body production in metal which implied reliance on hand-beaten panels produced in very limited quantities by W&P or Lotus itself.

As related elsewhere, the form in which he visualized the Elite at that early stage (1955) and the form in which it finally became a serious manufacturing possibility (1959) differed considerably, but in principle the production Elite remained true to Chapman's original concept of a fibreglass monocoque motor car.

In the meantime Williams & Pritchard continued gaily to manufacture aluminium coachwork for Lotus and others. Their work is clearly distinguishable by its wonderfully pure line and faultless curves. The quartet of Charlie Williams, Len Pritchard, Colin Chapman and Frank Costin between them developed a very characteristic form of competition car bodywork with widespread influence on others but harsh economic realities and Chapman's money-making ambition made it inevitable that the Elite should be constructed of fibreglass reinforced plastic.

(iv) The Elite – Body design and development

Peter Kirwan-Taylor spoke French fluently and it is believed that it was he who suggested the name Elite to Chapman with whom it became a favourite. We know that Chapman tried to apply it again to what eventually became the Elan but Ron Hickman was able to outwit him and secure the use of the name that he personally favoured for the successor to the original Elite. All Lotus employees were asked to vote for a name for the new car from a shortlist on which only "Elan" was acceptable. It won.

Like so many car names, "Elite" in this context is nonsensical and even misapplied but it is interesting how regular usage allows us eventually to accept names which might at first hearing sound incongruous. Chapman wished to brand his first real road car superior to and different from all others and in every sense a true Lotus. To him therefore the word Elite was perfectly acceptable as his cachet for a car at once efficient, exciting, beautiful, and exclusive.

The Elite was shown to the general public for the first time at the 1957 London Motor Show at Earls Court. It was without question one of the most aesthetically pleasing shapes ever mounted on four wheels and credit for the car's physical beauty in the first instance must go to Peter Kirwan-Taylor who sketched the original shape. Chapman and Kirwan-Taylor were fortunate in that they could call on the services of that most accomplished automotive artist and sculptor *manqué*, John Frayling. Frayling had been brought into the team together with Peter Cambridge (a specialist in car interior design) by their former Ford colleague Ron Hickman whose general talents are indelibly printed on the Elite and three other Lotus Types. The ubiquitous Frank Costin completed the group responsible for the design of the Elite.

The first of many meetings between the "Ford Three" took place one Saturday morning in October 1955 and Colin in his father's pub the Railway Hotel at

A photograph by Edward Sear of an Elite straight off the production line in 1960. From any angle the Elite has perfect lines and this shot shows the beautifully hand-made stainless steel bumpers and air intake surround, beaten out and welded by the Miles Aircraft Company and sold to us at a price substantially below cost. The fit of the door is somewhat suspect and there is probably more filing and "fudging" to be done before this car is ready for delivery.

Hornsey. They all presented their views eagerly and enthusiastically and discussed their individual abilities. Ron Hickman recalls that he and Peter Cambridge assured Chapman that John Frayling was far and away the best 3-D styling modeller at Dagenham, so it was John who became the official "modeller" assisted most closely by Ron Hickman as time permitted.

It is not generally appreciated that the gestation period of the Elite extended over four years between the original concept in 1955 and the manufacture of the first real production cars at Cheshunt.

Chapman and Peter Kirwan-Taylor would have begun with Chapman's own general concept or "package" of the car after which Kirwan-Taylor was able to produce his first outline and styling profiles for the design. Ron Hickman received ten dye-line prints of Kirwan-Taylor's outline drawings done within a week of the 1955 London Earls Court Show, which keys the Chapman general arrangement or packaging drawing for the Elite to summer of that year at the latest.

At the first formal design meeting for the Elite attended by Chapman, Kirwan-Taylor, Frayling and Hickman at Gothic Cottage, Kirwan-Taylor produced a $1/10$th scale bas-relief model of plasticine mounted on a Formica board and showing the proposed side elevation of the Elite body. Hickman and Frayling had never seen this technique used before and felt it to be of rather limited use, but nevertheless an improvement on a simple line drawing. Subsequently, John Frayling with occasional assistance from Hickman, worked flat out during his spare time to make a $1/5$th scale model of the car in his flat in Notting Hill Gate. This work continued every evening and weekend until just before Christmas when Hickman left for South Africa and remained there throughout 1956. The first model had partially enclosed wheels and because the original width planned for the body had by that time been considerably reduced by Frayling, it would have been impossible to steer the front wheels within the bodywork without a drastic track reduction. The first $1/5$th scale model already showed clear evidence of the Frank Costin influence – in particular the bubble-shaped roof with fixed side windows.

The first model had been made from American styling clay smuggled out of the Ford Motor Company, Dagenham (at the risk of instant dismissal if caught) by Ron Hickman. But because Hickman was now absent in South Africa, future supplies of clay were assured by the intervention of Kirwan-Taylor on one of his American business trips when he made the arrangement to buy and bring back further quantities.

It was now decided to make a second clay model with fully opened wheel arches and incorporating other Frank Costin recommendations. Costin was at that time working in the North of England but had received a set of photographs of the first model together with an analysis of the problem of front wheel steering clearance. Costin pronounced that in his view the benefits of a reduced frontal area for the car resulting from the slimmer cross-section would balance out the additional drag of exposed front wheels. The second Elite scale model incorporated these Costin-sanctioned alterations and the first model was kept as a record of the original concept.

John Frayling, apparently moved by study in a London Street of a Karmann-Ghia Volkswagen and having been particularly impressed by the design of the roof and window area, felt that there should be an alteration in this aspect of the Elite. He therefore proposed to Chapman and Kirwan-Taylor that the roof of the Elite should be moved bodily forward several inches. Chapman accepted this recommendation and at the same time an external boot lid was incorporated in the design.

The original design studies by Kirwan-Taylor showed the coupé top considerably further back than the definitive version of the Elite. John Frayling encountered a Karmann-Ghia Volkswagen in a London street for the first time shortly after the laying of plans for the new Lotus Grand Tourer. So impressed was he by the execution of the roof and glass area of the K-G VW and its relation to the rest of the structure of this elegant little car that he persuaded Chapman and Kirwan-Taylor that the roof of the Elite should be moved forward several inches. This change allowed the incorporation of an external boot lid in the design.

Early in the New Year 1957 Chapman invited John Frayling to join Lotus on a permanent basis to make a full-size pattern of the Elite, working in an industrial building in Edmonton (subsequently the first home of Cosworth Engineering); sufficiently far from Hornsey to ensure total secrecy. The objective now was to prepare a car for exhibition at the October 1957 London Earls Court Motor Show. Frayling obviously had to move like the wind. He was working in clay, largely by "eye" and the resulting full-scale model would have to be sufficiently accurate to allow the first production moulds to be constructed from it. We now see how fortunate it was that Ron Hickman had insisted to Chapman that John Frayling was really the one man to consider for this demanding task. Although Frayling is of the view that had Ron Hickman too joined the company on a full-time basis at that time, the Elite could have been "productionised" earlier and more satisfactorily, it is equally open to conjecture that this stage of the project could only have been a "one man" operation. Too much new ground had to be covered and Frayling was really the only member of the entire Lotus team of that time equipped to undertake it.

The very self-sufficiency of Frayling was at the same time both a strength and weakness. The strength was associated with Frayling's unerring eye which enabled him (plus or minus 25 mm) to model the car in space accurately from one side to the other, but the weakness of the situation was that Chapman was forced to rely on Frayling's superior knowledge to the extent that the original concept of the car as seen by Chapman became totally submerged by Frayling's reading of his brief. While operating at Edmonton Frayling could be easily supervised by Chapman from Hornsey but as soon as the project moved its centre to Maximar Mouldings at Pulborough where bodies were to be produced, Chapman lost control at a critical stage.

It was John Frayling (here seen as Ron Hickman's Best Man) who realised "in the round" the initial concept of the Elite created by Kirwan-Taylor, Frank Costin and Chapman. Frayling was ultimately responsible for the two outstanding attributes of the Elite – the beauty of its exterior in production form together with the aesthetically pleasing structural interior – completely at variance with Chapman's original concept of the car. Frayling is first and foremost an artist. His medium is modelling clay and with an unerring eye he realised the curving form of the Elite without precise drawings or other conventional design aids. He wanted "his" Elite to be as beautiful beneath the skin as on the surface and this led him to introduce an element of unplanned complication into the structure. Although Chapman responded angrily to this *fait accompli*, time was running out and he was forced to accept the costly Frayling alternative to his original scheme.

Frayling continued to work with Chapman from time to time (even to a few months before the latter's death in 1982) but the Elite must be regarded as his automotive masterpiece for Lotus.

One of the great beauties of the Elite (but beauty in the eye of the owner rather than the manufacturer) lies in its extensive use of double skinned construction techniques. The characteristic "shredded wheat" appearance of the inner surface of a fibreglass panel is neatly obscured by this technique in which all inner surfaces are enclosed within a second skin; of which the smooth surface faces outwards. This can be most easily seen in the case of the boot and bonnet lids; formed of two skins bonded together in production to form a strong, perfectly finished structure.

Colin Chapman is universally credited with the Elite double skin construction concept; but it is a fact that he originally intended the car to be a single skin monocoque with a small amount of local metal reinforcement (frames without interconnection) and the minimum number of essential box sections necessary for the achievement of adequate torsional and beam strength (the door sills, propeller shaft tunnel and roof perimeter). In the Chapman concept there were virtually *no* double skinned sections. Chapman knew that the single skin method would be the lightest and cheapest way to construct the Elite and he was quite prepared to conceal any of the inner "shredded wheat" rough areas with trim panels,

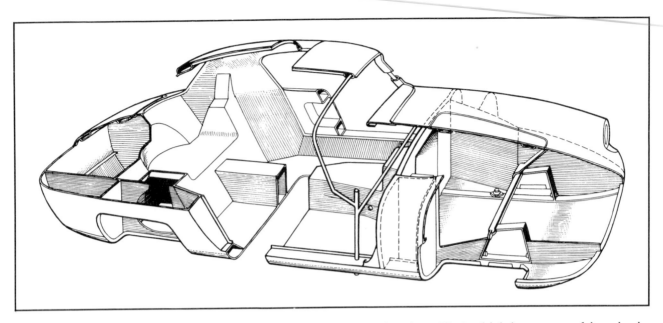

Comparison of this simplified sketch (by Ian Jones of the Lotus drawing office) which has appeared in print in one or two sources, with the final form of the Elite reveals innumerable discrepancies. In fact it is a fascinating insight into Chapman's thinking at a much earlier stage in the evolution of the Elite when the structure was quite obviously not intended to be double skinned in the way that John Frayling finally caused it to be. There is considerable ambiguity about intentions in the matter of rear suspension. A de Dion or even a "live" axle could be insinuated within this structure and there may have been one or more early prototypes built very closely resembling the form shown in this sketch. I was told on joining Lotus that Chapman had descended Tottenham Lane at speed in the first running Elite only to have the floor panel detach itself from the remainder of the structure under his weight. Such an eventuality would be quite possible in the case of the design shown here. Truly, Elite development was a perfect example of the blind leading the blind...

carpeting or even flow-coat filling if necessary. The first prototypes of the car were all built in this manner.

After the outstanding success of the 1957 Earls Court launch of the Elite (in single skin construction) Chapman appointed Maximar Mouldings to produce the chassis body units. Contact with Maximar introduced John Frayling to that company's 505 racing yacht designed by John Westall, Maximar's General Manager. John Frayling claims that he "fell in love" with the 505 constructional method and whereas up to that time he had only been interested in the external shape of the Elite, he now became seduced by the challenge of developing the internal structure of the car to be as much a thing of beauty as the exterior. When Chapman retained Frayling to work on the Elite, it was not clear to him (and probably not to Chapman, too!) that Frayling would ultimately end up, virtually single handed, creating the entire internal structure of the Elite.

John Frayling (and he alone) therefore found himself in the position of deciding to adopt double skinned construction for the Elite. At this stage nobody considered whether Maximar would be able to produce the car economically by this new technique. John Westall naturally accepted the position because he regarded Frayling as the official voice of Lotus.

Acting with his customary speed and dedication Frayling got to work with developing "his" internal structure for the Elite and had reached an advanced stage by the time that Chapman made his next official visit to Pulborough. Apparently Chapman's reaction was a furious outburst when he saw how his original plans for the car had been dramatically altered by the creative search for perfection of his stylist-turned-structural designer. Chapman realised instantly that the path taken by Frayling would add weight to the Elite structure; but that more seriously it would dramatically increase the cost of the body in terms of raw material and labour in construction. Chapman was the only member of the Lotus team at that stage who realised the size of the hole being dug for the Elite project by John Frayling but even he failed to appreciate the appalling production difficulties that would be presented throughout the car's life as a result of the double skinned technique.

In April 1959 Ron Hickman joined Frayling on a full-time basis at the latter's insistence in order to get to grips with the many practical and organisational problems presented by Elite manufacture. This return to the project by Hickman was sadly rather late in the day and later experience showed that had it been possible for Hickman to work with Frayling immediately after the initial full-size model had been constructed, the Elite production story may well have been entirely different.

During 1958 and into early 1959 Ron Hickman and John Frayling were based at Maximar Mouldings, Pulborough, where they were engaged in "productionising" the Elite. They regularly moved backwards and forwards from Sussex to Hornsey and later Cheshunt and this photograph was taken in London by John Frayling showing the youthful Hickman and the Sussex registration plate of Frayling's first Ford 100E (sidevalve) Anglia car.

This episode, so long imperfectly understood, to some extent exonerates Chapman from responsibility for the Elite's commercial failure. On the other hand it is not fair to blame Frayling for following his own path in the absence of direction from above. Frayling was never a structural engineer and Chapman obviously gave him no lead at all in this regard. There were certainly no working drawings available to Frayling to guide him in the design of the loadbearing internal sections of the car, and although Chapman clearly knew what he wanted and had some perspective sketches to show it, there was a total communication failure between him and his man on the spot at Pulborough. On the other hand the design characteristics of the car which ensured its commercial failure rendered it an object of beauty from any angle; internally and externally. Lotus' loss was the customer's gain.

In the latter part of 1958 and the early months of 1959 (by which time Hickman was beginning to make an invaluable contribution to the "productionising" of the Elite) the structural design of the car determined by Frayling created innumerable problems; some of which seemed almost incapable of solution. The one single element which caused the greatest difficulty was the installation of the steel body jacking hoop which ran continuously round the sides and upper edge of the windscreen and down to the floor of the car; providing a mounting point for the wheel change jack. However, the whole process of construction was complex beyond belief; the structure being formed of a series of separate, single skinned panels, taken from the mould and then dry assembled back-to-back and ultimately together to form the complete chassis body unit within a large steel tubular jig. In most situations it was impossible to observe the gluing process in action and great skill was needed to ensure that the correct quantities of adhesive were applied at the correct points so that on applied pressure to the two panels, an effective bond was achieved. There is no doubt that the experience of the Elite persuaded Chapman and Hickman that never again would they follow the double skinned route and from the beginning, the Elan was seen as a single skinned structure even in its original, chassisless, concept.

By the time that the Elite was finally dead and buried (after a brief and final reappearance to cover the initial "hiccup" in Elan production) most of those concerned with it were heartily sick of the car. It never made any money for Lotus. It was a constant drain on financial and human resources when frenzied attempts were made during 1961 and 1962 to keep production of the car "alive" as the Elan went through its extended process of development during which the original S2 concept was dramatically modified to the definitive M2 version. Nevertheless the Elite performed a vital role in Lotus history; teaching innumerable technical lessons; bringing home to Chapman that even his

Within the constraints of his busy schedule Chapman would motor down from Hornsey to Pulborough to see what his men were up to. Sometimes (as on the occasion when he discovered that Frayling had "double-skinned" the Elite) he would erupt in protest at the misdeeds before him. On the occasion when this photograph was taken he is obviously delighted by the finish of the car that he is about to test. No photograph survives of the Chapman expression on his return from a blast up the road.

remarkable genius had limitations but above all because it was a classic automotive design which despite failing to do that for which it was intended – make money – became a legend at Le Mans and on racing circuits throughout the world.

The Elite followed a general design concept which has rarely been copied. During the Fifties Porsche registered a patent for the manufacture of a car with a monocoque fibreglass reinforced plastic (FRP) structure but as far as we know did not manufacture a car according to this concept. Chapman was certainly unaware of the Porsche precedent when he dreamed up the Elite.

Chapman had never previously worked with FRP (at that period considered rather "down-market") but in considering the structures available to produce his money-making road car he had rejected the obvious alternatives. He had never used a "ladder" chassis – in which large (usually about 75 mm diameter) untapered steel tubes were welded to form a crude single plane frame to which the mechanical components and bodywork were attached. The type of steel tubular chassis construction favoured by Lotus for all types after the Mk. 3A (in which a similar superstructure had been added to the basic Austin Seven side members) was the so-called "space frame". This method of construction was ideal for a limited production competition car in that it could be assembled with minimal tooling and had all the advantages of good strength, light weight and ease of modification, maintenance and repair. It is however a relatively expensive way of producing a chassis for a road car and to be effective such a fully triangulated frame would intrude on vital touring car areas such as the door apertures and cockpit interior. So although Chapman was the most accomplished space-frame designer of his day he turned it down as a structural basis for the Elite.

Italian specialist Grand Touring car manufacturers frequently take the steel platform ("floor pan") of a popular saloon car and build on it a superstructure and body panels of appropriate elegance, aerodynamic form and light weight to transform the original workhorse into a thing of great beauty and efficiency. This however was impractical in the present situation for the lack of a car with basically adequate suspension system to satisfy the critical Chapman and the absence of an enthusiastic manufacturer-collaborator to supply a suitable platform. What was established practice in Italy was unknown in the British Motor Industry outside the luxury car sector. Having therefore rejected the conventional routes, Chapman was stimulated to evolve the remarkable technique used for the Elite.

Despite the grave misgivings of its designer and because of the intervention of his inadequately controlled "visualizer" Frayling, Chapman had in the Elite produced a dazzling *tour de force* – a massive albeit unwilling leap forward which did much to enhance Chapman's reputation as a designer if nothing else. With today's technology allowing extremely accurate control of moulded panel thickness there is no doubt that the Elite could have been made profitably but as it transpired, the many unforeseen technical conundrums presented by the double skinned Frayling structural system could only be solved by the dedication of much expensive attention.

Maximar Mouldings, the unfortunate company owned by Max Johnson and chosen by Chapman to manufacture the first group of production Elites, had won the contract because it had established technological leadership in the fibreglass boat manufacturing field. The company's general manager and designer John Westall was primarily responsible for this reputation but Max Johnson was

John Frayling in the foreground and the dimly discernible Elite chassis body unit on a trailer three vehicles down on the right gives a clue to the activity within the unprepossessing buildings shown here. This is Maximar Mouldings' factory at Pulborough where Frayling and Hickman initially toiled to "productionise" the Elite before the first Series One production bodies were manufactured within these walls. The Maximar reputation was founded on boatbuilding and the techniques developed in the marine field by John Westell of that company found their way in some degree to the Elite but later (the "Unimould" process) to the Elan. By late 1959 Maximar were so disenchanted by the Elite experience that Chapman had been forced to negotiate a new manufacturing contract hurriedly with the Bristol Aircraft Company which took over Elite production from early 1960 until the end of the car's life.

instantly recognised by Chapman (perhaps thus achieving an unwanted place in history as the first of a long line, ended by John DeLorean) as suitable for the "ego-trip routine" in which all the problems of working with Lotus would be concealed by the heady excitement of being Colin's friend and part of Team Lotus at race meetings and other prestigious occasions. The honeymoon period would last long enough to ensure that Maximar were well and truly hooked and unable to wriggle away from the contractual terms which in retrospect almost defy belief.

So obsessed was Chapman by weight and its effect on performance and manufacturing cost that he had conceived the original idea of a manufacturing contract with Maximar in which the price payable for chassis body units was related to an agreed design weight. Excessive use of materials therefore represented financial loss to the manufacturer. In the end the cleverness of his agreement boomeranged and caused the collapse of the arrangements with Max Johnson and the panic – almost as soon as production at Cheshunt had got under way – to find an alternative manufacturer for the body.

The Elite "dry assembly" method of production was immensely time consuming because it was impossible in a system of this kind to manufacture fibreglass panels with sufficient accuracy of thickness and dimensional tolerance to be sure that individual panel sections could be joined without excessive grinding of the mating surfaces and care and supervision of the application of resins and adhesives at all stages. A moment's relaxation of concentration could ruin a large expensively built-up structure. Failure to follow the strict instructions laid down by Hickman for the method of laying up chopped glass strand mat in the mould (requiring constant control) could result in structural failure on the road.

Among those concerned, John Westall was the first (and perhaps the only technician) to grasp the significance of the situation and the inevitability of ultimate failure to economically realise the design. But we must remember that even the experienced Bristol Aircraft Company was "conned" (his word) by Ron Hickman when the contract was transferred to them.

Two of the relatively few parts of the Elite committed to paper were the boot and bonnet hinges, designed by Chapman himself. On being told by Ron Hickman that neither "lid" would remain in the open position other than in conditions of total stability and controlled atmosphere and pressure, Chapman retorted that he knew that they would work and he didn't wish to be bothered by them any more. This was rather typical of the Chapman approach to the Elite throughout his life. Owners subsequently got used to carrying with them a suitable length of timber or plastic as in this case, to hold the boot lid safely open.

It is interesting to reflect that the empirical method of development applied to the Elite was such that very few drawings were produced and certainly none were made of the fibreglass reinforced plastic structure itself. It was largely due to John Frayling's remarkable eye and high level of artistic skill that the basic model and the early production moulds were completed and dimensional differences kept to an absolute minimum (one door is approximately 25 mm shorter than the other). Drawings were made of small components such as door and boot hinges although this was no guarantee that they would work in production. Elite door hinges are so dimensionally "marginal" that they have to be positioned to +/− 1 mm. for success. In the case of the boot hinge arrangements the development team gave up completely and the experienced Elite owner always carries a length of timber with which to prop open this vital aperture and instals a hinged prop for the bonnet, too.

There were no established formal design and development procedures; no clearly laid down criteria for costing; and when eventually it became necessary to transfer to the Bristol Aircraft Company the knowhow acquired at Maximar Mouldings the only method available was to produce a specimen of an "absolutely standard" Lotus Elite which took Ron Hickman and his assistant two months of hectic endeavour to manufacture. "Copy that!" said the Lotus lads and the Bristol Aircraft Company moved heaven and earth to do so without ever managing to repeat the fictitious standards of the hand-made Hickman original.

(v) The Elite – Frank Costin's contribution

Although Peter Kirwan-Taylor produced the initial concept which John Frayling later refined into the final form of the Elite it may be argued that the greatest single influence on the car's external form was wielded by Frank Costin.

This was the time of the collaboration between Chapman and Frank Costin on the design of the Vanwall Grand Prix car and the bodywork of the Lotus Mk. 8, 9, 10 and the Eleven were all Costin's work. His standing with Chapman was at its highest level, Colin considering Frank to be his best friend.

That most beautiful Lotus the Eleven had enclosed front wheels and during the evolutionary stages of the Elite's shape was achieving its greatest successes. Frank Costin as an aerodynamicist first and foremost (and in the racing application such things did not really matter) overlooked that the enclosure of the front wheels can only be tolerated where stiff springing and restricted turning circles are the order of the day. The Eleven had a considerable excess of body width over front track which made the enclosed front wheels less problematic, but unfortunately in the Elite case the desirable theoretical advantages of wheel enclosure brought with them many totally unacceptable side effects. Nevertheless Costin accepted the practical realities of the situation and was able to compromise by a reduction of frontal area and an acceptance of increased drag resulting from the use of "normal" wheel arches on the production Elite.

John Frayling has stated that although Frank Costin was not responsible for any single final detail of the Elite shape (and maintains that if that had been the case the Elite would have been very different if not positively ugly – as were some of Frank's other creations, by general consent!) the imposition of Frank Costin's aerodynamic principles was of the greatest importance.

The Costin influence may be summarised as dictating the Elite's smoothly flowing lines and above all the (at that time) unique bubble shaped roof structure. There was however yet another major compromise in the shaping of the tail. In

1955 Cooper had introduced their T39 "bobtailed" car in which the cut-off shape of the rear adhered to the aerodynamic principles of Professor Kamm. Although John Cooper subsequently claimed that the car was thus designed in order to fit into their transporter (!) it certainly had no adverse affect on the performance of this Lotus rival. Kamm tails were therefore "in the air" and apart from aerodynamic considerations it was certainly desirable if one could chop off the back end of a car and save a great deal of complication.

Frank Costin proposed that the rear of the Elite should be in the classical Kamm tailed configuration (rather like the Ferrari "Breadvan") and sent a drawing for consideration by the Elite design team early in 1956. The result would in the view of Chapman, Kirwan-Taylor and Frayling, have been hideous but in fact the final solution which is modestly in accordance with Kamm principles with the refinement of a finely turned-in periphery to the rear panel is undeniably elegant and effective. Poor Costin had to plead his case by post but had he been present at the meeting (and his usual forceful self) who knows what might have transpired?

(vi) The Kirwan-Taylor Frazer Nash

An interesting sideline to the Elite story cropped up early in 1957; before the prototype had been shown at Earls Court. Peter Kirwan-Taylor, who greatly

Peter Kirwan-Taylor was an amateur car body designer, happy to take on commissions for often unlikely subjects, including his "Bijou" design for the Citroen 2CV. In view of the cloak of secrecy surrounding the new Lotus at the time it was surprising that in April 1957 his rather ungainly body on a Frazer Nash "Continental" chassis intended for Le Mans appeared, bearing a striking resemblance to the Elite. The high chassis and BMW V8 engine of the Frazer Nash rather spoilt Kirwan-Taylor's attempt to make it appear sleek. No replicas were produced and the car did not start in the 24 hour race.

enjoyed his amateur body designing activities was approached by Paul Fletcher who had an entry at Le Mans in June 1957 for a new Frazer Nash car fitted with a 2¹/₂-litre V8 BMW engine which had originally been prepared by BMW for the Le Mans race in the previous year.

Although the configuration of the Frazer Nash chassis, which had a crude twin tube ladder frame (basically the Frazer Nash "Continental" type revealed at the 1956 Earls Court Show) was totally different from that of the little Elite Coupe, Kirwan-Taylor was so fired up with Elite spirit that he attempted to design a variant of that shape to fit this unlikely running gear. The height of the V8 engine with carburettors between cylinder banks demanded a totally different profile for the front end which now became tank-like in comparison with the elegant flowing curves of its model. The bubble top of the car however was distinctly reminiscent of the Elite despite having rear quarter lights and the treatment of the wheel arches in particular was almost 100% Elite. The tail, which had slightly protruding fins, again owed much to the proportions of the little Lotus Elite. However, the overall effect of the design executed in aluminium sheet by Peels of Kingston in a period of six weeks was crude in the extreme and one could feel sure that Williams & Pritchard would never have allowed such a poor interpretation to leave their works.

What is particularly interesting about this car is that although it in fact never took part in the 24 hour race of 1957 it was nevertheless clearly visible and a pointer to what was going on at Hornsey some months before the new Lotus was revealed in October. It is tempting, on examining this pure Kirwan-Taylor design, to consider the powerful influence on his basic concept for the Elite wrought most particularly by the excellent good taste of John Frayling whose talents were such that even Chapman was lost in admiration. Because Frayling was allowed so free a hand in his work on the Elite (and never again to this degree on any of the later designs with which he was associated), one appreciates just how gifted he is. The constraints of the Le Mans Frazer Nash chassis made it difficult to produce an elegant body but Frayling, I am sure, could have done wonders for that application of the Kirwan-Taylor concept as he did for the Elite.

(vii) The Elite – Suspension design and development

The fact that John Frayling was only available during 1956 on a part-time basis meant that the evolution of the Elite chassis body unit spanned a period when Chapman's thoughts on suspension were going through the first change of basic principle since the Mk. 3A. It was so important to perfect the external shape of the car that the final decision about the internal structure and running gear could be left until later but as 1956 progressed it was becoming increasingly important to firm up policy about the remaining aspects of the design. If Chapman had adopted his design practice current at the time (late 1955) when he first envisaged the Elite, it would have been fitted with swing axle independent front suspension and a rigid or de Dion rear axle similar to that used on the Eleven Series One. Much as he liked the swing axle however, there were serious problems on the road car if the desirable low pivot point of the half axles were to be achieved. Ground clearance would become seriously restricted. We may therefore safely assume that at a very early stage Chapman accepted the inevitability of providing the Elite with a form of wishbone suspension. His eventual design was devised to offer suspension geometry identical to that of a swing axle arrangement with a theoretical length of 40". So although the Elite system looked very different indeed, Chapman was moving relatively slowly and carefully in geometrical terms.

The new Lotus wishbone arrangement which was revealed to the public on the Twelve Formula Two car in October 1956 then became standard issue on the Elite, 1957 Eleven Series Two, the Fifteen Series One and the first models of the Seven Series One (October 1957). These early versions of wishbone IFS all used an upper wishbone member produced by modifying the lower link of the current Ford 100E family saloon car suspension and while the numbers of installations were low during the Hornsey period it was practical to proceed thus. Later however the upper member was replaced by a cross section Lotus forging which was generally used from mid-1958 onwards; being most clearly visible on the Sixteens and main production Sevens. The prototype Elite shown at Earls Court in October 1957 however retained the modified 100E Ford wishbone link.

Because the Elite was to make money, Chapman's earliest thinking about the rear suspension would have contemplated the use of a rigid axle. Study of the earliest Works drawing extant (Ian Jones' three dimensional sketch) shows

During the extended period of design and development of the Elite the only constant element was the external shape of the car. Within that envelope there grew a changing interpretation of what the structure of the Elite should be. No conventional drawing was ever produced although before John Frayling finally committed the car to double skin construction Ian Jones, the chief draughtsman, had produced a three-dimensional sketch which must be regarded as Chapman's own final view of how the car was to be internally constructed. Because Maximar Mouldings were in and around the prototypes as the design process continued they managed without any formality but the advent of the Bristol Aircraft Company at the end of 1959 as prime contractors for the Elite chassis body unit meant that standards had to be established and the design recorded. For this purpose, and with other motives such as the need for information to be included in the Elite workshop manual, James Allington was commissioned to produce this "ghost" drawing of the car – an extremely difficult feat in view of the masses of complex fibreglass panels surrounding the relatively simple mechanical elements of the car. The main obvious difference of the Series Two from its predecessor is the adoption of the more geometrically precise rear suspension locating system by means of a wishbone in place of the single tubular radius arm of the original design. The revised linkage system was adopted from Lotus Formula One practice where similar problems of directional instability had affected the Chapman Strut-equipped Sixteens of 1958-59.

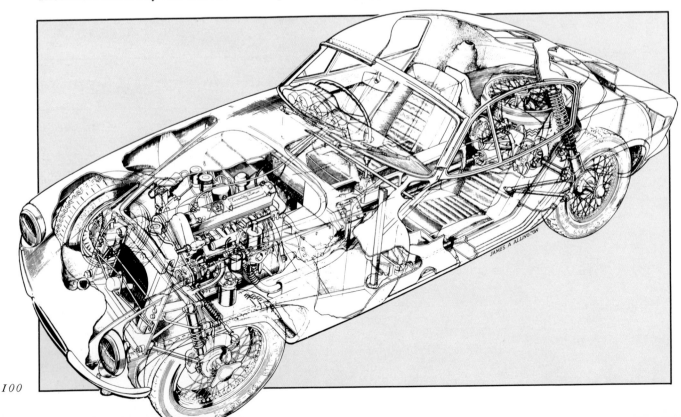

adequate clearance for an axle with the same radius arm and lateral location arrangements as the Eleven. Further weight is given to the theory that this was the original concept by the decision to mount the petrol tank within the offside wing of the car, thus providing more room behind the seats for installation of the rigid axle (or perhaps the de Dion tube which required even more installation space than the crude alternative). When it was found essential to abandon the installation of a fuel tank within the body structure – a leakproof arrangement could not be achieved – Chapman found himself on the horns of a dilemma.

It is conceivable that with sufficient dedication a way round the problem of the leaking front wing fuel tank might have been found. However, the methods tried to seal the tank area were sufficiently unreliable to persuade Chapman that alternative fuel tank arrangements would be necessary for the majority of cars produced although the wing arrangement was always available as a racing extra with expensive aluminium "liner". Quite separately from the Elite, other factors were intruding in the Lotus world in a way that would soon have significance for the Elite rear suspension.

For the 1957 racing season the FIA had announced the introduction of a new Formula Two for single seater racing cars of maximum $1\frac{1}{2}$-litres capacity unsupercharged. It was for this category that Coventry Climax developed their FPF engine and Cooper were the first to produce a car genuinely intended for this new Formula which raced experimentally during the latter part of 1956. By October of that year both Chapman and Brian Lister had produced new single seaters for Formula Two and although these two cars differed substantially in detail they were both front engined cigar shaped ultra light designs with wishbone IFS and de Dion rear suspension. Chapman more than Lister was familiar with the manufacture of low unsprung weight suspension systems and had really gone to town to reduce weight on his de Dion layout for the Twelve. A car was built for Team Lotus and taken out on test in March 1957; representing state of the art Lotus suspension design at that time. Lister also took out his prototype for Archie Scott-Brown to test and discovered to his horror that the modest output of the FPF could not be satisfactorily communicated to the track via his de Dion installation even with limited slip differential in position. The car was overall so tiny and relatively speaking the rear suspension so clumsy that the test was a disaster. The fact that the Formula Two Lister was the first racing car to incorporate Rose joint front suspension (Rose joints having been developed for use in sweet wrapping machinery) was obscured by the general air of disaster. Lister immediately withdrew and when he finally returned to the fray towards the end of 1957 it was with a completely different car with offset transmission but still with unsuitable de Dion rear suspension.

Chapman responded differently to the challenge. He decided to abandon the de Dion layout and adapt to his car an alternative independent rear suspension system that could be installed without major alteration to the existing spaceframe. This is where the plot thickens. There is no doubt that Chapman's "state of the art" design would be incorporated in the Team Lotus racing cars. This traditionally was where all new ideas were tested and we know without question that the first appearance on the Twelve of the Chapman Strut was in April 1957; six months before the Elite appeared for the first time in public at Earls Court. The Chapman Strut in the form used on the Lotus Twelve may be summarised as the simplest possible way in which to fulfil the functions of coupling the rear wheels to the main structure and applying drive. In this early form of the Strut there is no articulation between the outer extremity of the radius arm and the hub structure itself; the two are joined as one. In order to retain stiffness Chapman attached the inner end of the radius arm conveniently to a vertical chassis tube at the driver's hips and extended forward from this point a reinforcing strut to the original de Dion radius arm mounting in line with the front of the cockpit. The upper point of the suspension unit picked up on the original mountings behind the driver's shoulders and the fixed length driveshafts coupled the hubs quite simply to the final drive unit and provided lateral location. It looked as though the car had been designed that way and Chapman's thought processes in evolving this solution to the desperate and pressing problem of dramatically reducing the unsprung weight and increasing traction on his Formula Two car was accomplished by the same mental processes that he later applied to the evolution of the Twentyfive concept – a sort of restrained *reductio ad absurdum* which for the traditional designer "couldn't possibly work".

Here was Chapman, with a new rear suspension system designed under duress and against the clock, which although geometrically far from perfect (the radius arm was too far away from the centre line of the car – Chapman was always rather hasty about radius arm pick-up points) worked. Later developments of the Chapman Strut would show that he had faced up to the necessity of arranging a

By contrast with the previous photograph this modern picture of a Sixteen in historic racing guise shows the subtle modifications carried out by latter-day owners to improve the performance of this "ultimate" front-engined racing car. By extending the upper Strut mounting brackets outwards and fitting longer lower wishbones and drive shafts the rear track can be substantially widened. A similar process to match this can be executed at the front and the overall effect is finally enhanced by the use of modern compound wider section racing tyres fitted to appropriately cast "wobbly" wheels. I won't go into the other modifications that may be carried out to the transmission etc., to "improve safety and reliability", but Chapman would have admired the ingenuity and liberal interpretation of the rules thus manifested.

more central mounting for the extremity of the radius arm (Sixteen 1959 model and Elite Series Two) but for the time being he had found a solution to his immediate problem and the little Twelves showed much promise, but not a great deal more, with plenty of traction while they lasted and not bad handling by the standards of the day.

When the pace of Elite development quickened in 1957 as it became increasingly necessary to prepare one car at least for the 1957 Earls Court Show, Chapman was forced to make decisions about the rear suspension of the new car. How fortunate it was that with very little modification the Elite could be adapted to accept a "productionised" version of the Twelve Chapman Strut in which the coil spring damper unit was a press fit in the aluminium alloy hub casting to which a fully articulated radius arm would be attached. If the current concept of the car envisaged a de Dion rear axle then he need make no change to the mounting arrangements for the final drive unit – they would be the same. If he had contemplated the use of a rigid axle then he was immediately able to make a substantial reduction in the accommodation required for his rear suspension. The large clearances round the axle/de Dion tube were no longer necessary and the modest movements of the articulated drive shafts were all that had to be considered until making provision for the suspension units which would conveniently fit in more or less the same position as for a conventional axle/de Dion system. But most important in view of the need to make money from the Elite was that the Chapman Strut had to be the cheapest possible independent suspension system available. Leave off any more elements and there would be no suspension at all! What a splendid sales ploy too to be able to point to the use on the road car of the identical suspension system found adequate for the latest Team Lotus racing car! I think that we can safely assume that it was not until after April 1957 that the final specification of the running gear of the Elite was fixed by Chapman. By October 1957 the Show model was a long way from representing the final product. It was certainly not a "runner" – rather a highly developed mock-up. From early 1958 when John Frayling joined the company on a full-time basis and took up his position at Maximar he and Ron Hickman (later) with John Westall of Maximar had to go "like the wind" in order to produce something approaching a finalised product for Cheshunt.

(viii) The Elite – Body manufacture

A theoretical attraction of the use of fibreglass was that it could be made in varying thicknesses to accommodate different levels of stress. In practice however it proved extraordinarily difficult to communicate to the operators carrying out the lay-up process precise instructions to ensure a regular production of panels in varying thicknesses. Ron Hickman would work out the exact pattern for cutting cloth and stipulate how to lay it, but laminators, in the human way of things, would generally follow the easiest route. If they couldn't persuade the fibreglass to wrap nicely around a corner they might be tempted to cut the glass along the line of the corner and make a butt joint with no strength (this was ultimately found to be the cause of the Series Two differential mounting failure problem that caused so much trouble in the USA). The women operators thought that they had discovered an easier way of making the patterns but in the process had ruined the structure.

Chapman's cunning contract terms with Maximar Mouldings specified exact weights for Elite bodies in the knowledge that it would be so expensive for

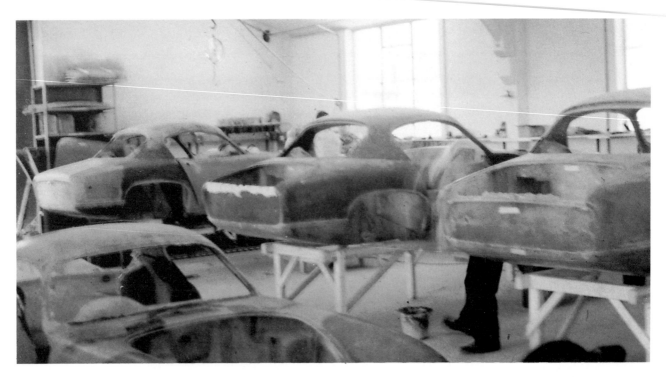

Here, inside the Maximar factory, Elite bodies are seen during the final assembly process. The Elite was composed of a number of sub-assemblies, dry bonded together and then progressively grouped and bonded to create the entire chassis body unit. This laborious process would have been even more so had not Hickman and Frayling concentrated on a process of simplification of the assembly procedure on realising the potential nightmare created by the elaborate structure evolved by the hitherto unsupervised perfectionist Frayling. The strange colouring of the semi-translucent fibreglass structures is caused by patches of polyester resin uniting the inner and outer skins. In the background can be seen a large spring balance suspended from the roof and used to check the weight of finished chassis body units. Payment was based on a guarantee by Maximar to restrict the weight of the finished car to tight limits imposed by Chapman himself. Excessive use of the costly raw materials involved would further erode the virtually nonexistent profitability available to Maximar and therefore for totally different reasons both Maximar and Lotus became acutely conscious of the finished weight of the chassis body unit. This neurotic use of the spring balance did not carry over to Bristol who subsequently found themselves using more than the specified material content (see Appendix 6).

Maximar to put more weight into each car without receiving payment for the surplus that they would maintain his target weights. In practice it was much more difficult to make the laminates down to the thickness that this required and infinitely more expensive in labour terms to use such reduced amounts of material because in order to make a satisfactory job the laminators had to work the resin into the glass with great thoroughness and to use ultra thin gel coats which raised serious production control problems. This was to some extent eased by using pigmented thin gel coats so that it was possible to detect where it had been sprayed into the mould. Conversely this had the disadvantage that when joining the mouldings it was impossible to see how the bond was proceeding.

The structure in the Frayling developed double skin form was so complicated and took so long to assemble that it was impossible to keep the resin adhesive flowing long enough. According to temperature it might begin to gel and set hard in as little as five minutes when it could take anything up to an hour to bond the structure. If there had been any inaccuracy in joining the panels the result was a car that was partially together and which would be destroyed if an attempt were made to get it apart.

The only solution to this was to carry out a "dry fit" of every moulding; grinding high spots and offering up panels to each other in the assembly jigs; dismantling where necessary, regrinding and assembling before carrying out the bonding process. John Westall (much to Chapman's annoyance) insisted that it was necessary to open up all clearances where the skins met so that instead of having an acceptable 3 mm clearance the gap could be as much as 10 mm. In order to achieve this it was necessary to make new moulds and patterns and in the assembly process it became essential to thicken the adhesive to bridge these new, unforeseen gaps. Chapman was furious and insisted that this change of plan would not only add weight but would also result in a brittle structure.

John Westall's cure for this complaint was to abandon the idea of pigmented laminates and gel coats so that it was possible to see through them and observe the adhesive which now became a darker colour. It was therefore possible to be certain where it had taken and where there was a breakdown at vital joints. As a remedy it was possible to "fluff up" the adhesive (by that time epoxy instead of the cheaper polyester) to give it greater strength using various lightening materials including chalk and micro balloons.

Away from the fabricated steel sub-frames used to mount the front suspension and provide the jacking hoop of the Elite it became necessary to devise a system to mount components to the fibreglass structure of this revolutionary car. The method chosen was that of the "bobbin" designed by Chapman and machined in three basic sizes from mild steel. The bobbin was "laid up" in the laminated structure as shown and great care had to be taken to ensure that it would not subsequently become detached. The bobbin was internally threaded to allow "blind" bolts to be used as the means of attachment.

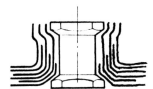

If all else failed and it was still possible to see through the skins that bonding had not taken place satisfactorily it was necessary actually to drill holes, sometimes even through the outer skin of the car, and with a giant syringe inject more resin, watch it spread, and hopefully achieve a satisfactory structural joint. In a nutshell, Frayling had created a monster and all concerned at Maximar (and later at Bristol too) became enmeshed in a manufacturing nightmare. Maximar quickly realised that they were losing large sums to Lotus and Chapman plainly refused to allow an increase, saying that Maximar should reduce their prices because they were making the cars too heavy. Rapidly the working relationship between Lotus and Maximar broke down and when Chapman talked in terms of legal action Maximar indicated that they were not really bothered – they were going out of business anyway so would Chapman like to kill them off quickly or slowly?

Despite these appalling difficulties about 150 bodies were manufactured by Maximar, painted, trimmed, fitted with bumpers, glazed and sent up to Cheshunt looking quite reasonable. Fitting the mechanical components was really child's play by comparison with making the body unit. When the Bristol contract was in the air Chapman was able to get Ron Hickman to incorporate the rear strut modification for the Series Two car into the moulds in order to produce the specimen cars for the instruction of the unfortunate new manufacturer. Ron was then able to write specifications, drawing on his knowledge of administration learnt in the South African Civil Service coupled with his legal knowledge to enable him to write a workable contract for Chapman, Kirwan-Taylor and Bushell to negotiate with Bristol.

(ix) The Elite becomes a Kit Car

Credit in full goes to Colin Chapman for the decision to sell the Elite on the home market as a kit car, bereft of the punitive British purchase tax applicable to fully assembled vehicles. All of us except Colin were reluctant to contemplate this irreversible step and we all felt that by so doing the Elite would become downgraded in the high performance car market. As usual, we were wrong. Chapman decided that we would announce the kit car Elite at the 1961 Earls

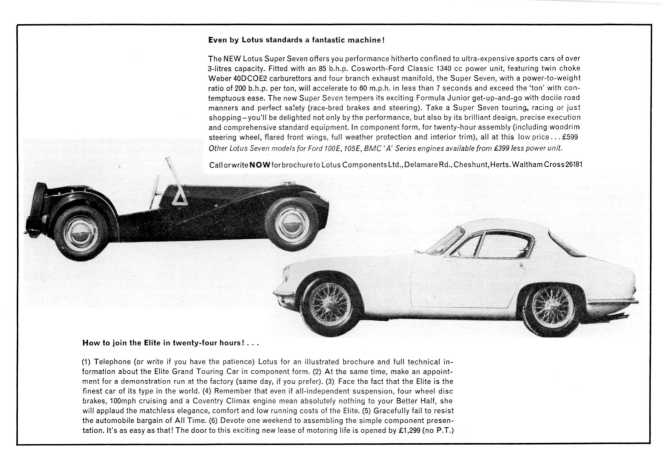

Even by Lotus standards a fantastic machine!

The NEW Lotus Super Seven offers you performance hitherto confined to ultra-expensive sports cars of over 3-litres capacity. Fitted with an 85 b.h.p. Cosworth-Ford Classic 1340 cc power unit, featuring twin choke Weber 40DCOE2 carburettors and four branch exhaust manifold, the Super Seven, with a power-to-weight ratio of 200 b.h.p. per ton, will accelerate to 60 m.p.h. in less than 7 seconds and exceed the 'ton' with contemptuous ease. The new Super Seven tempers its exciting Formula Junior get-up-and-go with docile road manners and perfect safety (race-bred brakes and steering). Take a Super Seven touring, racing or just shopping – you'll be delighted not only by the performance, but also by its brilliant design, precise execution and comprehensive standard equipment. In component form, for twenty-hour assembly (including woodrim steering wheel, flared front wings, full weather protection and interior trim), all at this low price . . . £599
Other Lotus Seven models for Ford 100E, 105E, BMC 'A' Series engines available from £399 less power unit.

Call or write **NOW** for brochure to Lotus Components Ltd., Delamare Rd., Cheshunt, Herts. Waltham Cross 26181

How to join the Elite in twenty-four hours! . . .

(1) Telephone (or write if you have the patience) Lotus for an illustrated brochure and full technical information about the Elite Grand Touring Car in component form. (2) At the same time, make an appointment for a demonstration run at the factory (same day, if you prefer). (3) Face the fact that the Elite is the finest car of its type in the world. (4) Remember that even if all-independent suspension, four wheel disc brakes, 100mph cruising and a Coventry Climax engine mean absolutely nothing to your Better Half, she will applaud the matchless elegance, comfort and low running costs of the Elite. (5) Gracefully fail to resist the automobile bargain of All Time. (6) Devote one weekend to assembling the simple component presentation. It's as easy as that! The door to this exciting new lease of motoring life is opened by £1,299 (no P.T.).

One of my favourite Birdsall advertisements was this, devised for the launch of the Elite kit and bringing in the Super Seven for company. Chapman always let me have a free hand in writing advertising copy and although he would frequently describe it as "bullshit" he never exercised a veto. In later years Lotus advertising and sales literature became far more conventional but by that time Birdsall was an extremely successful graphic designer and by Lotus standards costly to employ. In 1960-61 we appealed to a tiny and exclusive market that liked its advertising different whereas with the Elan a far wider audience had to be addressed, necessitating, I suppose, a "safer" line of patter.

Court Show and instead of hiding our heads in shame at our failure to establish the car as a factory built product, we would make as much fuss as possible about our new found ability to offer the Elite at a bargain basement price.

We would sell the car direct from the factory (although still retaining a foothold in the Trade) and we prepared a most impressive display for Earls Court in which the various components of the car were mounted in "exploded" form about the central body unit. The public reaction was favourable. We must be realistic and accept that we probably only gained a hundred or so additional sales by this technique; possibly appealing only to those people who hitherto could not afford a factory built Elite but had greater funds available than the average kit car buyer. This was yet another desperate step taken to stave off impending disaster and the Elite was marketed in this fashion in the United Kingdom for the rest of its commercial life; HM Customs and Excise being unwilling to allow an "authorised" kit car to be sold "either/ or". Once a kit car, always a kit car. The decision that Colin took was therefore a brave one and like his decision two years before to go into the Formula Junior field, he alone was willing to take the gamble – and win.

At this stage in our commercial fortunes with the prime market, the United States, in a state of disarray and the home market for the Elite in particular in a dangerously depressed state, it was only such inspired and intuitive acts by the super salesman Chapman that really kept us staggering forward until the advent of the Elan a year later would put the company once more back on to a reasonably secure commercial path.

In the face of declining sales at home and abroad, Chapman decided in October 1961 (with my grudging acceptance) that the Elite should be marketed in the UK as a kit, thus avoiding payment of the iniquitous British Purchase Tax amounting to nearly a third of the "assembled" price. As in the case of the Seven it was only necessary to fit the major mechanical components to the fully trimmed and finished body and there was every incentive to devote a weekend or two (or three despite what my advertisement said), to the task of assembly with such savings available. Note the final version of Chapman Strut used in the Series Two Bristol-bodied car in which the radius arm mounting is very close to the centre line of the car, ensuring more geometrically accurate suspension movement and reduced driveshaft loading. The standard car – although now fitted with twin SU carburettors – retained the crude cast iron exhaust manifold of earlier versions in conjunction with an exhaust system with twin tail pipes to give what Chapman would refer to as a "sexy" look. Although Firestone developed a unique tyre for the Elite, it was not found entirely satisfactory and the car in this shot is equipped with Michelin X alternatives.

(x) The fastest Elite

For Le Mans 1960 Michael Taylor of sports car specialists Taylor & Crawley, whose team was supported financially by Jonathan Sieff of the Marks & Spencer family commissioned something "rather special" from Chapman. This was to be the fastest of all time Elite and was perhaps (in moments of optimism) intended to go for outright victory on the Sarthe circuit. On paper the result of this commission might well have been capable of achieving that goal but in reality the result was a disaster and the "one off" special Elite only raced once – in a minor British event – before being converted back to standard specification.

A similar commission today would begin with consideration of the tyres to be used for the project. However, in 1960 tyre technology was still at a relatively early stage of development and even high hysteresis (known to the lads as "highly hysterical") rubber-mix tyres were just beginning to appear. The huge contact areas and "sticky" tyres commonly used today were unknown and to adapt an Elite chassis body unit for tyres of much greater section than standard was beyond contemplation. However, racing tyres of roughly Grand Prix standard (15 x 500 front; 15 x 600 rear) were accommodated in slightly modified wheel arches and the FWE Coventry Climax engine was replaced by a genuine FPF 2-litre twincam power unit half way between Formula 1 and Formula 2 in output (180 bhp) but certainly very much stronger than anything ever shoehorned into an Elite before. In the limited time available, and within the technical constraints

COLIN CHAPMAN'S LOTUS

of the Elite bodywork, appropriate supporting services were arranged including larger front brake discs and wishbones of Eighteen specification, strengthened spring settings and adjustable dampers. Despite these modifications, the FPF Elite had a distinct "nose-down" attitude and – nose-heavy weight bias notwithstanding – was found by Innes Ireland in practice to have an alarming tendency to "weave" at speed. The severe injuries sustained by Michael Taylor at Spa shortly before the French 24 Hour race resulted in the substitution as reserve driver of Jonathan Sieff, who although competent (he had already driven the 750 cc Elite at Le Mans in 1959) was hardly in the same class as Taylor and Ireland. Innes sent Sieff out in a standard Elite to practice night driving, with disastrous results – a monumental accident on the Mulsanne Straight from which Sieff was lucky to escape with his life (he achieved a certain notoriety as the first motor racing casualty to be rescued by helicopter). Ireland promptly refused to drive the 2-litre Beast and that was that.

Ian McLeod was one of the few to sample the machine before it left for France. McLeod is no daredevil but has certainly a great deal of experience of powerful motoring. He simply described the 2-litre Le Mans Elite as "a killer" and said that it made his heart beat as only a Ferrari otherwise can. He made it very clear to Chapman and anybody else who would listen that in his view the car should not be released.

(xi) The Seven Series Two

At the time at which I joined Lotus, sales of the Seven had fallen to a trickle. There is a lot of competition in the very small market for a hand-built rather expensive Clubman-level sports racing car and the Broadley brothers with their Lola and others had demonstrated that the gifted special builder using a combination of plagiarism and innovation could (as had Chapman earlier) build a simple car to take on the established Hornsey product with success. We desperately needed Seven sales to support Lotus Components Ltd., which at this time was struggling with the Seventeen albatross about its neck. I felt that it was going to be difficult to suddenly increase sales direct to the enthusiast and therefore recommended to Chapman that we should find a small group of enthusiastic established dealers to handle sales of the Seven kits on conventional motor trade terms to a range of buyers beyond the central core of club racing enthusiasts.

Up to this point the Seven was only available with two engine options; either the humble 100E Ford sidevalve or the costly Coventry Climax FWA. If we were to make the car acceptable to a broader clientele I felt that we should take advantage of the enthusiastic following for BMC products and the vast tuning industry built up round this rather old fashioned little engine by making a version of the Seven with a BMC A-series 948 cc power unit which in the A35 saloon was often driven by the stars (most notably Graham Hill who regularly took on and beat Jaguars in his Speedwell-prepared car). To set this in historical context it should be remembered that it was at this time (late 1959) that the Mini and Mk. II Sprite were launched; both fitted with variants of the A-series power unit. I felt that the intense interest aroused by these cars would rub off to the benefit of the new Seven A (for Austin). We marketed the other two versions of the car as the Seven F (Ford 100E) and Seven C (Climax 1100 cc).

During my schooldays in Wiltshire I had often visited the garage workshops at

Downton of Daniel and Bunty Richmond. This husband and wife team had set

108

Having decided in July 1959 to offer the BMC "A" series engine of 948 cc as an alternative power unit for the Seven Series One in addition to the Ford 100E and Coventry Climax FWA engines, we built this prototype car fitted with twin SU carburettors and four branch exhaust manifold as a prototype, demonstrator and general promotional car. I used it extensively in late 1959 as "my" company car for rapid trips in fine weather to visit the new Lotus Centres which were established during the latter half of that year as part of my distribution development programme.

up to provide a service for the very best cars with particular emphasis on Rolls-Royce and Bugatti. Daniel allowed me to wander around his Aladdin's Cave of engineering delight which included a remarkable Sprint car built up from a box of Lagonda Rapier parts that he claimed to have bought "for a fiver" and to which were fitted two Roots-type aircraft cabin blowers generating remarkable power output over very short periods of time; but usually long enough to reach the summit of Prescott or Shelsley. As the years passed Daniel's "cash customers" (as he called them) would frequently complain to him about the poor performance of the family shopping car and he was unable to resist the challenge of tuning certain of these mundane forms of transport. Soon remarkably quick Triumph Heralds, Renault Dauphines and Austin A35s could be seen in the neighbourhood. Fortunately Bunty Richmond was the business manager of this partnership and spotted an opportunity to develop an interesting and lucrative extension of the Downton Engineering Company's normal activity.

It was therefore natural that I should approach the Richmonds to invite them to become Lotus Seven agents. It was equally natural that they should build up a demonstrator based on the Seven A version with a 948 cc BMC engine to the highest level of contemporary Formula Junior tune. This car was road tested by David Phipps of Sports Car and Lotus Owner magazine and I myself had the opportunity to drive the car in the Brighton Speed Trials to experience at first hand its astonishing acceleration. Whilst in contact with the Richmonds during my Lotus period I designed for them their characteristic enamelled valve cover plate, to give the same professional finish to the power unit as Cosworth who fitted a named, finned cast aluminium rocker cover.

The Ford engined Seven had previously been sold in kit form at £499 and obviously we would have to study carefully the pricing of the car if we were to sell through the Trade. Depending on his position in the distribution network a British dealer at the time would expect a minimum discount of 17½% from the retail price before tax while the distributor would take a further 5% to allow him to make a return while supplying his sub-agent dealers.

I asked to see the cost sheets for the Seven and John Standen produced a set of figures which made it clear that even when sold at the full retail price direct to the public, Lotus made virtually no profit from the transaction. We therefore found ourselves with the following options available:

Abandon Seven production
Continue to sell only directly to the public at an increased price
Increase the price yet more in order to give a discount to the Trade *and* retain a profit
Redesign the car to reduce manufacturing cost and create a margin of profit

We decided to take the last course which led during 1960 to the introduction of the Seven Series Two car. The Seven Series One (as it then became known) had

to suffice as a means of getting the distribution network under way and although we knew that we were not going to make any money by selling the Series One car through the Trade its use as a launch vehicle dramatically increased activity for Lotus Components Ltd., and generated the necessary momentum to pave the way for the Series Two.

The design changes incorporated in the Seven Series Two, which in effect made it a substantially new car although it retained a superficial resemblance to the Series One, were with one exception (rear axle location – and that in part alone) intended purely and simply to reduce the cost of manufacture of the

Lotus sales brochures of the late 1950s were distinctive in shape if not content. The original Seven brochure of 1958 is illustrated in Dennis Ortenburger's "Legend of the Lotus Seven" as is my first Seven brochure printed in late 1959 to mark the availability of the Series One from the new Lotus centres. The illustrations in this brochure were of UOW 429 – the car used in the 1958 edition with a shot of 7TMT to update matters. We had no time in which to take new photographs. The 1959 brochure covered the Series One "F" and "A" models with passing reference to the availability of the Coventry Climax engine "C" model – not referred to at this stage as the Super Seven. To mark the introduction of the Series Two Seven Derek Birdsall designed a visually superb leaflet with text by the author. Play was made on the racing connection with a shot of Innes Ireland at the wheel of a Team Lotus Eighteen and there was a splendid shot of Ian McLeod accompanied by an elegant model in our first Series Two demonstrator Seven. Birdsall made skilful use of two colour printing to achieve maximum effect in this unusual brochure which like all subsequent sales literature in the Read/Birdsall period folded to almost square format.

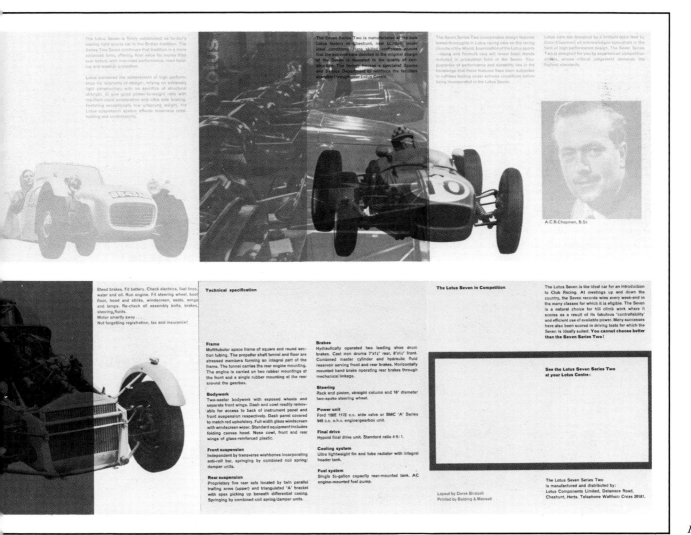

cheapest Lotus. It was my constant agitation that persuaded Chapman to take time to do a quick rethink of the design and specification and to instruct John Standen to re-source many essential components. This course of action led to the successful introduction of a car which in kit form at launch was sold at the incredibly low price of £399 less power unit – the cheapest Lotus kit-car ever.

The design changes began with the basic spaceframe. This was manufactured (as were all Lotus spaceframes up to that time) by John Teychenne's Progress Chassis Company of Edmonton. Teychenne had been a neighbour of the Lotus factory at Hornsey and had grown with them. Now he was located near Cheshunt and the burgeoning Cosworth Company; his fate closely tied still to Lotus. Broadly speaking the cost of a spaceframe produced in commercial series depends on the amount of material used and the number of welds made. Therefore to reduce the cost of the basic spaceframe Chapman had to delete as many tubes as possible from his original scheme. This policy did not create too much difficulty during the early life of a Seven Series Two but many present day owners of this model have experienced endless frame fatigue fractures as a result of the cheese-paring operation carried out in 1960. But at the time it provided an adequate level of torsional rigidity, was a good excuse to force Teychenne to reduce his price and was just a little lighter than the original.

Traditionally Lotus had used a BMC rear axle in the Seven. It was light, reasonably durable and had the advantage of suitability for a wide range of easily available ratios from 4.1:1 up to 5.55:1 – just what was required for motor racing. But it was rather expensive. John Standen had discovered that the Triumph Motor Company could offer an obsolete but similar axle (a little narrower and with a limited choice of ratios) at a much lower price and this was chosen for the Series Two car. The method used to locate the rear axle (whether "live" or de Dion type) in the Eleven and Seven had certain geometrical shortcomings. This therefore was a good opportunity to revise the system at the time of incorporating the new live axle into the design of the Series Two Seven. Location was effected by two single short tubular arms above the axle just inboard of the brakedrums in much the same position as on the Series One car. The outboard

That the model sitting with Ian McLeod in the Works demonstrator Seven Series Two "A" felt nervous even with the car at rest is revealed by the whiteness of her knuckles on the scuttle. Even at this late stage (February 1961) the Series Two engine line-up did not include officially the Ford 105E although during the summer of 1960 Caterham Car Services (most loyal and progressive of all Seven Centres) were inviting inspection of their 105E-powered demonstrator. The usual pressures on design staff at the end of the year meant that we had to wait some time before getting an official installation for the 105E which led shortly afterwards to the introduction of the Cosworth 109E Super Seven for which the same mountings applied.

Available with Ford 100E or BMC 'A' series power unit in component form (UK only) or fully assembled

Lotus Seven Series Two!

Manufactured and distributed by
Lotus Components Limited
Delamare Road Cheshunt Herts
Telephone Waltham Cross 26181

extremities of these radius arms picked up on brackets welded to the Triumph axle casing but Chapman's main cost-reducing technical improvement was reserved for the remaining element of the axle mounting system which would locate it fore and aft below the centre line and at the same time provide lateral location. In the installation of a "live" axle the radius arms not only bear cornering loads but also have to absorb driving and braking torque.

Having been obliged to weld brackets to the axle casing in order to attach the upper radius arms Chapman wished to avoid unnecessary expense elsewhere in the rear suspension system. He therefore hit upon the unconventional use of the rear axle oil drain plug as a means of attachment for the lower suspension member bracket. Not only was this a simpler solution but it also provided theoretically perfect location centrally of the triangulated lower radius arm which was extended to the lateral extremities of the space frame. At the time, words of caution were dismissed by the Designer-in-Chief. Repeated alternation of the right foot on throttle and brake pedal would fairly quickly loosen the axle drain plug with dramatic effects on crownwheel and pinion lubrication and the car's general handling qualities. This became particularly serious with some of the more advanced power units available as time went on and several beefing-up modifications were subsequently introduced. But when it was working it undoubtedly gave better suspension geometry than the Series One and improved roadholding under hard acceleration and braking on uneven surfaces.

The front suspension system was as before – it was cheap in any case. Smaller diameter brakes were fitted to the front wheels and a Triumph rack and pinion used in place of the modified Morris Minor system of the Series One. 13 in wheels in place of the Series One's 15 in were incorporated and this allowed cheaper tyres to be specified.

The appearance of the Seven Series Two was further changed by the adoption of a moulded fibreglass nose cone in place of the handmade aluminium nose used on the Series One car. This was designed by Peter Kirwan-Taylor and John Frayling and the opportunity taken to incorporate neat flares over the wishbone mounting brackets. The new nose was noticeably more elegant than its aluminium predecessor and infinitely cheaper to produce and repair.

Normally the car was supplied with cycle type mudguards but as an alternative the Kirwan-Taylor/Frayling-designed striking long flared wings from the Seven America were available. These resulted in a dramatic reduction in the amount of water flung through the holes where sidescreens are fitted to other cars and were either immediately hated or loved by the beholder. I rather liked them and they made the car a lot more practical as a roadster and instantly recognisable amid "Lotus look-alike" specials of the day.

In its basic form the Series One Seven was fitted with a horrid cheap steering wheel but a few pence more were saved here by John Standen who managed to find something even cheaper and nastier. The fastidious and well-heeled owner would fit a special wheel to his pride and joy. Much less obvious additional detailed cost cutting was carried out and at last we had a product that would enable us to spread Lotus Seven ownership further afield than was ever before possible.

The Seven Series Two kit was offered with a wider range of power units than its predecessor. Not only could it be built with the familiar 1172 cc 100E Ford, the 948 cc BMC A-Series (and the FWA Climax if you really wanted it) but there was now a new Ford engine available – the 997 cc 105E Anglia unit. To compete with the Mini, Ford had introduced their first overhead valve small car in late 1959 and its engine, known as the "Kent" type designed by Alan Worters and succeeding developments of it has played a greater part in the development of British motor sport than any other single power unit in history. At the time when

In April 1961 we introduced the Series Two Lotus Super Seven fitted with 1340 cc Cosworth-Ford engine and (by Seven standards) many refinements including wood-rim steering wheel, the famous Frayling/Kirwan-Taylor clam shell wings, electric radiator fan and twin windscreen wipers. The combination of 83 bhp and a dry weight of 436 kg gave performance adequate to keep ahead of anything off the Motorway system.

LOTUS SUPER SEVEN

Even by Lotus standards a fantastic machine! The Lotus Super Seven offers you performance hitherto confined to ultra-expensive sports cars of over 3 litres capacity. With a power-to-weight ratio of 200 b.h.p. per ton, acceleration to 60 m.p.h. occupies a mere seven seconds, and the magic hundred is at your beck and call . . . the Super leads the brilliant Lotus Seven family of light, low-cost sports cars.

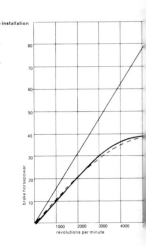

Alternative power units for installation in Lotus Seven

Engine	Ford 100E	Ford 105E	Morris Minor 1000
Type	4 cylinder side-valve water-cooled	4 cylinder o.h.v. water-cooled	4 cylinder o.h.v. water-cooled
Bore	2.5 in. (63.5 mm.)	3.1875 in. (80.963 mm.)	2.48 in. (63.0 mm.)
Stroke	3.64 in. (90.5 mm.)	1.906 in. (48.412 mm.)	3.00 in. (76 mm.)
Displacement	71.55 cu. in. (1,172 c.c.)	60.84 cu. in. (997 c.c.)	58 cu. in. (948 c.c.)
Carburettor	Twin S.U./Lotus manifold	Twin S.U./Lotus manifold	Single S.U.
Compression Ratio	7.1:1	8.9:1	8.3:1
Power Output	36 b.h.p. at 4,500 r.p.m.	39 b.h.p. at 5,000 r.p.m.	37 b.h.p. at 5,000 r.p.m.
Gearbox	Ford 100E 3-speed	Ford 105E 4-speed	Morris Minor 4-speed
Ratios	First: 3.894 :1 Second: 2.396 :1 Sync. Third: 1.00 :1 Sync.	First: 4.118 :1 Second: 2.396 :1 Sync. Third: 1.412 :1 Sync. Fourth: 1.00 :1 Sync.	First: 3.64 Second: 38 :1 Sync. Third: 1.41 :1 Sync. Fourth: 1.00 :1 Sync.
	Reverse: 4.793 :1 Remote control shift	Reverse: 5.464 :1 Remote control shift	Reverse: 4.67 :1 Remote control shift
Optional Equipment	Close ratio gears Ratios First: 2.294 :1 Second: 1.655 :1 Sync. Third: 1.00 :1 Sync. Reverse: 3.42 :1	Close ratio gears Ratios First: 2.917 :1 Second: 1.696 :1 Sync. Third: 1.280 :1 Sync. Fourth: 1.00 :1 Sync. Reverse: 3.83 :1	Close ratio gears Ratios First: 2.57 :1 Second: 1.68 :1 Sync. Third: 1.232 :1 Sync. Fourth: 1.00 :1 Sync. Reverse: 3.31 :1

Lotus Seven engine installation power curves

Ford 100E
Ford 105E
Minor 1000
Super Seven

(graph: brake horsepower vs revolutions per minute)

the Series Two Seven was launched in May 1960 the 105E in Cosworth Formula Junior modified form was producing more than 75 bhp and the basic unit from which this racing engine was developed was an obvious choice for the new Seven although it was not until later in the year that we listed the 105E option. It had a nice four-speed gearbox and in fact we sold more versions of the car fitted with this engine in the UK than any other form although initially it was the Sprite engined Series Two America which sold in the US before the potential of the little Ford engine was appreciated across the Atlantic.

To get real power from the "80-bore" 105E engine was expensive. It was necessary to fit two twin-choke Weber carburettors and to extensively modify the

Simultaneously with the Series Two Seven brochure a new Birdsall-designed brochure was produced for the Elite, now in Series Two form from Bristol. These two brochures continued into 1961 when a new brochure appeared in April to mark the introduction of the Super Seven with Cosworth 1340 cc Ford engine in kit form. The luxurious paper on which the first two Birdsall brochures were printed was now replaced by a rather less expensive "art" finished paper but the same style and originality was retained. The author wrote the text and supplied a selection of photographs which Birdsall then arranged with his "magic touch" to produce these little masterpieces of graphic design. The Super Seven was such a remarkable car that it didn't require a great deal of help from sales literature. However, we used an "atmospheric" shot of John Bolster at the wheel round Druids at Brands Hatch, impressive power curves and heavy linking to current Lotus racing successes (Arundell in the Formula Junior Twenty, Ireland driving the Twentyone and Moss at the wheel of his Walker car) to stress the pedigree of our new product (0-60 mph in "a mere seven seconds"...).

internals. In late 1960 however Ford introduced their Consul Classic car – a weird looking machine (Lotus components Works Director Nobby Clark had an early one as his company car), but the good news about this machine was that it was fitted with a 1340 cc version (109E) of the new Ford engine with longer stroke crankshaft and much better torque. We went to Cosworth and asked them to develop a low cost version of this new engine that would produce a lot of power. By choosing paired Weber 40DCOE carburettors – the "commercial" diecast version of the exotic Weber devices used by Ferrari and the rest – Keith Duckworth restrained the cost of his conversion which was mainly limited to increasing compression, opening the ports, increasing valve sizes, fitting a new camshaft and generally improving the breathing to give 85 bhp. Installed in what we announced as the Lotus Super Seven in January 1961 it made a devastating road car with sub-9 sec. acceleration to 60 mph which would leave behind almost anything available at the time. Apart from its tendency to aggravate the weaknesses of the rear axle location system the new Super was a very significant move forward in the saga of the Seven and the Cosworth 109E was the first of a series of large capacity gutsy Ford-based power units used to propel the tiny Lotus to instant driving fun.

(xii) "If you can't beat them" . . .

1959 was a year of mixed fortunes for Colin Chapman. There were moments of black despair, but his amazing drive and self-confidence enabled him to recover magnificently by engaging in a sudden and unexpected change of technical direction.

Although 1959 brought good news in the form of the opening of the new factory at Cheshunt, enabling the Elite at last to be produced in quantities sufficient to meet demand, in the area of traditional Lotus success – competitive motor sport – all was far from well. Three years of frenzied development had failed to turn the Team Lotus Twelve and Sixteen single seaters from "also rans" into race winners. The name Lotus which had earlier successfully appeared with monotonous regularity in the results of sports racing events had not yet featured among the first three in a Grande Épreuve. Chapman had an excellent string of drivers for the single seaters including Cliff Allison, Alan Stacey and Graham Hill but the frustration of Team Lotus membership had driven the first and last of these into the arms of Ferrari and BRM respectively while poor Stacey was killed in 1960 at the wheel of an Eighteen in an accident resulting from collision with a large bird which stunned the driver. The sorry tale of retirements, inadequate performance and hair-raising escapes from crashes caused by structural and mechanical failure had exhausted the patience even of Graham Hill, a highly experienced Lotus driver, race mechanic and erstwhile employee in charge of engine assembly and development. Chapman could ill afford to lose so talented a driver approaching his peak (he brought a string of victories to BRM and the World Championship in 1962), but with characteristic good fortune was able to pick up a new driver for the next stage of his Grand Prix endeavours – the gritty Innes Ireland – who although not in the same class as Graham Hill nevertheless was able to respond enthusiastically to the potential of the car that lay ahead.

Chapman had always looked down his nose at the relative crudities (as he saw them) of the Cooper racing car chassis and this may well have blinded him to the message conveyed by the disposition of mechanical components used by Cooper and none other in GP contention at that time. Whereas all successful Grand Prix racing cars before 1959 (with the only significant exception of the 1934–39 Auto Union cars) had incorporated the by now classical layout in which the engine was placed before the driver, usually with gearbox in unit with the final drive assembly behind him, the Cooper Grand Prix car was laid out like the pre-War Auto Union. The engine of the Cooper Formula One car was the same $2\frac{1}{2}$ litre Coventry Climax FPF used by Lotus, but mounted behind the driver. The engine was mated directly to a final drive unit (progressively developed by Cooper over the years from Citroen origins) in which the gearbox element lay behind the rear wheel centre line; the drive bypassing the crown wheel and pinion to the gearbox mainshaft and then back to the pinion via the layshaft. This arrangement allowed the engine to be installed nearly vertically as originally intended by Mundy and Hassan; the driver was able to sit as low as the seat cushion permitted and instead of allocating substantial sections of the interior of the car to power consuming angled propeller shafts connecting the rear wheels to the engine, the Cooper installation worked on the basis that the shortest distance between two points is a straight line.

It was fairly obvious from the way things were going in 1958 that it was possible to arrange heavy mechanical components in a rear engined car without creating the fearsome oversteering tendency demonstrated pre-war by the A-, B- and C-type Auto Unions (which had vastly inferior suspension and much greater power/weight ratio than the little Cooper). The GP car used by Cooper in 1959 moreover used far fewer of the inefficient curved frame tubes which were anathema to Chapman with his scientific approach to the triangulation of chassis structures. But most significant of all was the fact that Jack Brabham won the World Championship for Cooper. That was quite sufficient to break the mould of Chapman's design philosophy.

(xiii) A new Formula

Now we must transfer our thoughts to Italy. Several European countries had developed Racing Formulae to act as a nursery for rising racing drivers. In France for example there was a training Formula for racing cars based on the twin-cylinder Panhard front wheel drive power unit (the Monomill). In Italy the equivalent Formula was for unsupercharged 750 cc cars. These incorporated a four-cylinder engine developed from the Fiat 600 block to an exotic twin-ohc layout with dual Weber carburettors. The cars were reminiscent of current Ferrari/Maserati design in appearance with characteristically elegant offset single seater bodies. The little Stanguellini for example produced about 70 bhp on alcohol fuel and handled like a learner-driver miniature version of the contemporary Italian GP car.

The great Patriarch of Italian motor racing Count "Johnny" Lurani became increasingly concerned as the decade wore on by the dwindling store of Italian front line drivers (since 1950 Ascari, Musso, Farina, Fagioli, Taruffi, Bonetto and others had either retired or died) and there seemed to be no Italian potential World Champion emerging. In fact Ferrari and Maserati had been obliged to use a series of foreign drivers to achieve their Championship success during recent years. Lurani considered that the Italian 750 Formula Junior was inadequate as a nursery class because of the relatively high initial and running costs of the cars. He therefore in 1958 proposed a new Italian Formula Junior which would fulfil the important task of specifying a relatively simple and inexpensive car for a new generation of potential champions to learn the racing craft. This domestic

When the Italian-inspired Formula Junior was adopted internationally for 1959 the Italians understandably had a head start in fielding grids of cars, generally with Fiat engines and transmission. None of these usually very traditional cars was more beautiful than the OSCA, designed and built by the Maserati brothers in small numbers for the 1960 season. In that year, despite considerable opposition from the British contingent, an OSCA driven by Colin Davis won the World Trophy. But this was the last year of the front engined racing car and the Lotus, Cooper and Lola hordes overtook all these beautiful but hopelessly outdated relics of the past from 1961 onwards. Two OSCAs were shipped to the USA to the order of Luigi Chinetti the Ferrari importer. One was used by the Rodriguez brothers and this one by my old friend Sy Kaback, who much as he loved it rushed to buy a Lotus Eighteen replacement when he saw the writing on the wall. The OSCA was pushed to the back of the Kaback premises in New Jersey where I regularly and reverently paid homage to it as a wonderful example of everything that is good about classical Italian racing cars. Compared with the Eighteen the OSCA was crude in the extreme. It had a large diameter steel tube chassis with modified Fiat front suspension and rear axle. The 1100 cc Fiat engine was fitted with two twin-choke Weber carburettors and mounted at a considerable angle to the centre line of the car, the driver being offset beside the propeller shaft. The OSCA was fast in a straight line, easy to drive, quickly uncompetitive and utterly gorgeous.

Formula became adopted internationally by the FIA for 1959 and may be summarised as follows:

The basic mechanical elements including engine, gearbox, brakes (from the engine source) and axle (if used) had to be from a high volume production car. The power unit could be of either 1100 cc or 1000 cc capacity with an appropriately lower minimum weight unit for the smaller engine. In its definitive form the International Formula Junior imposed relatively few restrictions on chassis design which in effect meant that once they had got under way British constructors would dominate the Formula. However in Year One – 1959 – because they had been racing Formula Junior cars since 1958 the Italians had a head start and the European Championship winner in that year was a front engined Stanguellini using a modified Fiat 1100 engine and a crude chassis incorporating virtually unmodified Fiat 1100 front suspension and rear axle.

The subject of Formula Junior arose shortly after I joined Lotus in mid 1959. My self-imposed first task had been to bring life back into the Seven as a commercial venture. I therefore saw talk of Formula Junior as a potential diversion of Chapman's energies from the planned redesign of the Seven to reduce production cost. Chapman was initially persuaded against Formula Junior, but it was not long before the question began to prey on his mind. He possibly did not relish the task of spending time on cost-cutting revisions to the prosaic Seven which would render it less technically desirable. He may also have been anxious to demonstrate that the disastrous Seventeen project was a momentary aberration and furthermore he was conscious of the intense interest surrounding Formula Junior among fellow constructors. Elva and Cooper had Formula Junior cars on the stocks together with a host of smaller constructors; many entering the field for the first time. We followed one of our regular lunch meetings at the Waltham Cross cafe with a stroll along the River Lea towpath. Chapman had again raised the Formula Junior question with great persistence and asked me, Mike Costin, Fred Bushell and John Standen for our views. The others knew Chapman far better than I, so my objections were the only ones to be strongly expressed. However Colin announced that although we were already well into October he would launch a Formula Junior car in time for the 1959 Brands Hatch Boxing Day races. The die was cast and the Seven Series Two was temporarily shelved, leaving me to do my best with the Series One car which had to keep that product line moving until mid 1960 as the Formula Junior car and its F2 and F1 cousins occupied Chapman and the technical team.

(xiv) The Eighteen Formula cars – 1960

1959 represented the third consecutive year of intense struggle by Chapman to evolve a successful Lotus Grand Prix car. He had made valuable direct contributions to the success of Vanwall and BRM cars of this type as a consultant and his general influence on competition car design was everywhere apparent. But it was personal success as a designer in this most prestigious field that continued to elude him.

Several factors militated against Chapman's success in Grand Prix racing during that period. They began with his commitment to a front engined layout. Because of the influence over him of Frank Costin, a self-confident, highly qualified and older man with whom several earlier successes had been shared, a further complication developed from adherence to this basic layout. The only engine available to Chapman to power his Grand Prix cars was the Coventry Climax FPF. The twin-overhead camshafts of this extremely simple four-cylinder engine added considerably to its overall height despite the use of dry sump lubrication. When he first fitted the FPF in the Twelve single seater racing car of 1956, he used a body shape bearing none of the signs of Costin's influence and so narrow that it was essential for the propeller shaft to pass beneath the driver. Chapman was therefore content to mount the engine more or less vertically, the cam boxes nevertheless being below the height of the driver's chest.

The situation changed totally with the introduction of the Sixteen for the 1958 season. Chapman realised that the modest power output of the FPF engine would have to be offset as far as possible by every attention to the aerodynamics of the bodywork. Therefore the Frank Costin influence returned with the introduction of the Sixteen for the 1958 season. Although this car looked substantially the same throughout its two year life, by the time that Chapman had abandoned it at the end of the 1959 season a bewildering variety of developments had been tried including engine mounting positions in which the angle of inclination of the bores relative to the centreline of the frame had swung through an arc of nearly 90° while the propeller shaft had appeared both on left and right of the driver with a corresponding need to regularly redesign the gearbox/final drive unit. Similar variations in engine installation angles were tried on the Fifteen sports car

Chapman was acutely conscious (thanks to the tutelage of Frank Costin) of the importance of good aerodynamics in racing car design. It was therefore natural that in laying down the design of the Fifteen (1958) he should instal the rather tall Coventry Climax FPF engine at an extreme angle (60 degrees) to avoid interruption of the bonnet line. Although it was wonderful in theory, in practice the scheme was disastrous and very quickly it proved necessary to reduce the angle of inclination in order to avoid serious oil churning problems resulting in excessive internal friction. As originally conceived, the Fifteen was designed to use the Lotus final drive unit developed for the Twelve but like the canted engine this advanced feature was later discarded in the Fifteen Series Two car in which power transmission was via a modified BMC gearbox and chassis-mounted differential unit. Although not such a bad case as the Seventeen, the Fifteen suffered from the occasional Chapman failing of being too clever by half in its original version, the advanced features condemning the type among cash customers despite the many inherent virtues.

which was provided with a particularly low Frank Costin-influenced body making it impossible to mount the FPF vertically, although as that model developed the engine was tilted into an almost vertical position with accommodating bump in the body panelling.

This extraordinary determination to make the front engine installation work within a body of the lowest possible drag and frontal area satisfies me that until late 1959, at least, Chapman was convinced that the mid-engined layout had no real advantages to offer. The main examples of this layout in racing applications, with which one was familiar at the time, were the pre-war Auto Union cars which compared unfavourably in roadholding and handling with the front engined Mercedes-Benz competition. Latterly of course there were the various offerings of Cooper to consider. Chapman had a healthy contempt for the chassis designs of Cooper and this possibly blinded him to the fundamental truths understood by John Cooper and his father Charles from 1955 onwards by which time they had abandoned the construction of front engined racing cars. The Coopers appreciated perfectly that with restricted power (excellent though their engines were, Coventry Climax never achieved the power output regularly available to the Italians) it was of paramount importance to reduce loss in the transmission to the road of that power which *was* available.

We might not have seen a mid-engined Lotus racing car so soon as we did if Cooper alone had used this layout. It was quite possibly the realisation that others were very seriously considering placing the power unit behind the driver that riveted Chapman's attention. At Monza in September 1959 BRM actually turned up with a mid-engined prototype car. It was not raced but it existed. There were also rumours that Ferrari were studying a mid-engined development that added yet another nudge to the Chapman thought processes. The final incentive for change was Chapman's realisation that by simultaneously introducing a "universal" mid-engined racing car layout for Formula Junior, Formula Two and Grand Prix classes he could effect a dramatic reduction in the design and development time of a string of new models. By finally embracing the mid-engine doctrine he achieved in one fell swoop low frontal area, reduced drag, diminished transmission power loss, and avoided all the complication of severely angled engine installation. Incidentally too, he paved the way to a veritable transformation of Lotus' fortunes.

The great decision that Chapman made, which renewed his self-confidence and persuaded him that he could succeed in the new Formula, was the abandonment of the front mounted engine layout. Having overcome this massive psychological barrier and having braced himself for the inevitable taunt that he had finally copied the arch rival Cooper, Chapman set to work. A combination of the very limited time available, his lack of experience of rear (or mid-) engined design and the established success of certain elements of his single seater design methods dictated the general form of the new car, the Eighteen. Ever practical, Chapman saw the opportunity to establish the Eighteen as a basis not only for entry to Formula Junior but also as a means of reversal of Lotus fortunes in Formula One and Two. Not only did he now require a prototype Formula Junior car for the meeting at Brands Hatch on 26th December 1959 but he would also have to produce a Formula One car in time for the Argentinian Grand Prix on 7th February 1960. The switch to mid-engine installation was quite enough innovation under the circumstances with one significant exception – the rear suspension system of the new car.

The chassis frame of the Eighteen followed typical Lotus practice of the time with a combination of round and square section steel tubing and the characteristic single seater Lotus pierced steel oval bulkheads first seen on the Sixteen. These were placed so as to form the scuttle immediately ahead of the driver and the final bulkhead through which the tail of the Lotus five-speed transmission projected. Instead of following the very shapely "flattened cigar" profile of the Sixteen, the Eighteen body was by comparison rather shockingly crude and almost square in section; designed for low frontal area rather than drag-reduction. It seemed to be a throw-back to early Lotus Mk. 6 Chapman-only thinking. The prototype Formula Junior car – which came first – had a body entirely panelled in aluminium by Williams and Pritchard and this was used to make the moulds for the fibreglass panels of the production car.

Because his new design had to serve as the basis both of the commercial Formula Junior car and "Works" F1/F2 Grand Prix cars, the Formula Junior owner (and the few outsiders able to acquire the FPF engined version or make their own from a Junior) benefited from a specification of front line potential. The front suspension system was up-to-the-minute Lotus GP practice using two fabricated wishbones with separate anti-roll bar. At the rear Chapman again swallowed his pride and in addition to following the Cooper power unit location policy, now presented his version of the Elva/Lola rear suspension system

This historic photograph shows the original, prototype rear-engined Lotus racing car – the Eighteen in Formula Junior form prepared for the Brands Hatch Boxing Day (December 26th) meeting of 1959. Although the Cosworth 997 cc engine blew up in practice and with substitute engine fitted the car was only able to finish fourth, this new Chapman creation impressed all and marked the beginning of a new era for the company and for motor racing in general. Note the projecting gear rod mechanism for the inverted Renault transmission and the all-aluminium prototype body hurriedly prepared by Williams and Pritchard and from which the panels were used to make moulds for the fibreglass bodywork used in series production.

claiming that he had been forced to abandon the Strut concept "as a result of the low line" of his new chassis. Large cast aluminium hub carriers extended downwards to within a few inches of the ground and were located laterally by a long "reversed" wishbone picking up near the centre line of the car and a little longer than the articulated fixed length driveshafts providing the upper suspension link. Fore and aft location of the rear wheels was by parallel tubular steel radius arms which were also required to manage the torque of the outboard drum brakes; matching those drums fitted (in accordance with regulations) to the front wheels. By mounting the spring units to pick up the near ground-level hub spindles, the Lotus version of the Lola suspension looked superficially different enough to be "new".

The power unit of the Formula Junior Lotus was a combination of the brand new Cosworth-modified Ford 105E Anglia 997 cc engine and inverted Renault Dauphine four-speed gearbox with optional Pons-Redelé four- and five-speed clusters. The inversion was necessary to achieve the correct direction of rotation of the crown wheel and pinion as a result of turning the gearbox fore-and-aft through 180° in the Eighteen installation. Now transmission oil was poured through the former drain plug in this early example of the use "back to front" of a rear engined transmission in a mid-engined car. Later, of course, the same trick was applied to the superior VW gearbox and that led to the modern Hewland transaxle family. Chapman went to Keith Duckworth for a quick development of the 105E engine to power the new Junior. Apart from having a substantial weight advantage over the 1100 cc Formula Junior cars, Chapman's contender from the outset was to have a power advantage too because the engine with which Duckworth emerged from his test house produced a healthy 75 bhp and after initial lubrication problems, good reliability.

An end of season (1960) shot of a Team Lotus Eighteen Formula Junior car ready for disposal. From this low angle the Eighteen looks quite sleek. As Chapman's first rear engined racing car design, it occupies a special place in Lotus history. Of particular interest is that the haste with which the Eighteen Formula cars were evolved meant that no external influence was introduced at the design stage. This is very much a "Chapman-only" car.

The first Cosworth Ford engine (and so it was) was essentially standard below the cylinder head/block joint. The head was subjected to the usual increased compression and porting modifications; two 38DCOE Weber carburettors were fitted together with a freeflow tubular steel exhaust manifold and a special camshaft to enable the engine to take advantage of the better breathing capabilities. Other constructors – perhaps with a higher credit rating and more diplomatic manner had approached Cosworth for a special Ford engine and Lotus' planned back-up spare engine was not ready for the Boxing Day event. Fortunately for the venture, because Stacey blew up the only engine during practice, Graham Warner's Gemini crashed and its Cosworth engine was loaned to Stacey for the race in which the car ran reasonably well to finish fourth. The exercise had achieved its prime objective and Chapman knew that he was on the right track. He was now anxious to demonstrate that his new baby would be a World Beater with potential far in excess of the Boxing Day showing. In retrospect it is really astonishing – a mark of his great mental powers – that Chapman was able instantly to switch from the complex front engined Sixteen design to create a car which in a way was akin to the Twelve; a very simple expression of the desire to win, in which only the shortest, most direct solutions are followed.

The Formula Junior prototype having satisfied him that his inspiration was correct, Chapman pressed on with building for the 1960 Argentinian Grand Prix a full 2½-litre version of the F1/F2 variant of the Eighteen. The principal differences from the Junior (and you had to look pretty hard to see them with a body in place) were the use of the big FPF Coventry Climax engine with Lotus five-speed transmission, increased fuel capacity (a large scuttle tank and a smaller reservoir behind the seat), disc brakes on all four wheels (inboard at the rear) with appropriately larger tyres and rims. No sooner had the Formula Junior car returned from Brands Hatch on 26th December 1959 than attention was focussed

It is necessary to look hard at an Eighteen to be sure to which Formula it belongs. Here is Jim Clark at the Solitude Grand Prix (Formula Two) in 1960. Below the Lotus badge on the nose of the car is written "Lotus Coventry Climax" which is the first clue and the small diameter wide rimmed rear wheels with appropriate tyres together with offside exhaust system are the final give-away. Note too the prominent oil pipes from the dry sump engine to the forward oil tank mounted just behind the radiators. Although they cannot be seen in this photograph the brakes of the Formula One/Two Eighteen were disc (outboard at the rear) rather than the Formula Junior drum type.

on building the Argentine entry. This was a real day and night job and although the Team Lotus area of the works was generally closed to all, security became rather lax towards midnight, particularly when Chapman himself became increasingly and excitedly involved in the general rushing to and from the drawing office and component manufacturers. The prototype was completed at the last minute in running chassis form and driven off into the night by Chapman himself to make sure that everything was connected properly. We stood under the street light listening to the prototype thunder to the top of Delamare Road, then turn left and blast into the night. Fortunately it returned before long; the driver grinning widely. The car was then immediately partially stripped in order to fit into the crate in which it would cross the South Atlantic by air with wheels and body panels travelling alongside. The performance of the prototype F1 Eighteen driven by Innes Ireland at Buenos Aires measured against the two Sixteens sent along to raise a little start money and against some of the much more serious alternatives, made an indelible impression on us all. It was generally realised that something quite remarkable had occurred in Team Lotus and that the comic opera era of 1958/9 was at an end.

As the 1960 racing season wore on it became clear that the Eighteen was a car with which a good rather than brilliant driver could achieve success. At the Easter Goodwood Race Meeting Moss in the Rob Walker Cooper was unable to overtake Ireland in the 2½-litre Eighteen despite driving harder than he had

LOTUS JUNIOR

SPECIFICATION

FRAME
Multitubular space frame of 1 in. and ¼ in. mild steel round and square section tubes with fabricated scuttle hoop and roll bar.

FRONT SUSPENSION
By double wishbones of unequal length and separate anti-roll bar. Springing by combined coil spring/damper units.

REAR SUSPENSION
Fully independent with fixed length articulated drive shafts and single lower wishbone.

BRAKES
Hydraulically operated drum brakes. Internal drum diameter 9 in., x 1¼ in.

STEERING
Lightweight rack and pinion, 14 in., steering wheel.

POWER UNIT
Rear mounted Cosworth-Ford 105E 997 c.c. o.h.v. four cylinder engine fitted with twin choke Weber carburettors, alternatively tuned B.M.C. 948 c.c. or supplied less power unit.

TRANSMISSION
Single dry plate hydraulic clutch 7¼ in., diameter with special four speed close ratio gear box mounted behind differential in integral casing. Reverse gear, remote control gearchange.

FINAL DRIVE
Spiral bevel final drive unit mounted between engine and gearbox. Standard axle ratio 4.71: 1. Alternative ratios 4.44: 1, 5.03: 1.

COOLING SYSTEM
Crossflow radiator mounted in nose with remote header tank.

FUEL SYSTEM
Single light alloy tank, 10 gallons capacity. Electrical fuel pump.

BODYWORK
Removable panels with perspex aerodynamic windscreen. Twin lightweight rear view mirrors.

ELECTRICAL SYSTEM
Ignition by coil and distributor. Centrifugal advance and retard. Lightweight battery mounted in nose. Electric starter.

INSTRUMENTS
0-8000 r.p.m. tachometer, oil pressure gauge, water temperature gauge.

WHEELS AND TYRES
Lightweight bolt-on 15 in. magnesium wheels fitted with 450 front and 500 rear racing tyres.

DIMENSIONS
Wheel base 7 ft., 6 in. Track front 49 in. Rear 47 in. Overall length 11 ft. 3 in. Overall width 4 ft. 8¼ in. Height 2ft 10¼ in., (to headrest). Ground clearance 4 in.

PRICE (In component form)
Ex works, less engine £1050. With Cosworth Ford or tuned B.M.C. 'A' power unit £1276 5s. 6d.

SPORTS CAR & LOTUS OWNER

LOTUS JUNIOR
THE FINEST IN ITS CLASS

June successes include :—

B.A.R.C. Crystal Palace	First Heat	1st	LOTUS-FORD
	Second Heat	1st	LOTUS-FORD
	Final	1st	LOTUS-FORD
B.R.S.C.C Oulton Park		1st	LOTUS-FORD
Notts. Sports Car Club, Mallory Park		1st	LOTUS-FORD
Notts. Sports Car Club, Silverstone		1st	LOTUS-FORD

July successes include :—

Formula Junior Race, Reims (French G.P.)	1st	LOTUS-FORD
Formula Junior Race, Silverstone (British G.P.)	1st	LOTUS-FORD

MANUFACTURED AND DISTRIBUTED BY :—

LOTUS COMPONENTS LTD.

DELAMARE ROAD, CHESHUNT, HERTS.   Tel. Waltham Cross 26181

I told Peter Warr, responsible for racing car sales, that he had two pages of the August *SC&LO* to fill and this is his response. Although a total of 125 Eighteen Formula Junior cars were sold, sales made a rather slow start in 1960 and it was not until the early successes of the Team Lotus cars in April caused everybody to cancel their orders for Elva and Cooper Juniors that we were able to get going. August is late in the racing season to sell cars and therefore Peter made a special effort to "push" sales, in the knowledge that for the home market, the order bucket was virtually empty. The three photographs on the left feature at the wheel – yes – Peter Warr, with his crash helmet projecting well above the so-called roll-over bar required by Formula Junior regulations but so flimsy as to be virtually useless. On the facing page Jim Clark is at work to illustrate the list of successes at home and abroad.

been obliged to for some time. To Chapman, drivers were divided into two categories. Most were journeymen pilots with whom he would argue at the track and suffer frustration which might perhaps be eased a little by their off-duty entertainment value. I will not name names but instead turn to the other, infinitely more select group which earned his unstinted admiration, loyalty and friendship. This group included Alan Stacey, Jim Clark and Stirling Moss.

When it was known that feelers had been put out by the Moss/Walker Equipe indicating that they would be pleased to acquire an Eighteen, the mood at Cheshunt became electric. To Colin this was an honour indeed and an enduring source of intense pride and pleasure. Stirling of course got his car and proceeded to demonstrate that with equal equipment he was unquestionably The Master. He was also issued with an Elite for his personal use and is well known to have considered it an outstanding road car (while having the benefit of a group of racing mechanics to constantly care for it).

The stuffy Society of Motor Manufacturers and Traders (SMM&T) – organising body of the Earls Court Motor Shows in the Fifties and Sixties – generally resisted the inclusion of racing cars in their annual shop window until Colin Chapman put his type Twelve single seater on the Lotus Stand at the 1956 show. It was therefore natural in 1960 to exhibit an Eighteen Formula Junior car, fresh from an outstandingly successful debut year. This view shows the composite aluminium/fibreglass body panels of this type and the Cosworth-modified Ford 105E engine of 997 cc. The linkage to the inverted Renault gearbox may be seen above the exhaust pipe as can the "proper" fabricated tubular wishbone IFS used on this car. Between HRH Princess Margaret and Mr Anthony Armstrong-Jones may be seen the Hon. William Rootes, President of the SMM&T in that year. Answering questions is Ron Richardson, colleague of the Author and one of the three to whom this book is dedicated.

Most of Chapman's designs are of the greatest historical importance in the evolution of the competition car. The Eighteen is undoubtedly one of these; not so much because of its intrinsic virtues and merits but because it released Chapman from an extended period of disappointment and failure when for the first time he appeared to have lost his way. Once he had adopted the fundamental change of design philosophy represented by the switch to mid-engined configuration a whole vista opened up in which his influence on the course of automotive design could be renewed. The Eighteen is therefore one of the greatest and most significant classical Lotus designs, created almost intuitively and at breathtaking speed – the work of a human dynamo.

(xv) The Nineteen sports racing car – 1960

Automotive history is full of thinly disguised Grand Prix cars masquerading as sports racers to take advantage of opportunities in loosely constructed racing regulations. Ferrari did it all the time; Cooper and Gordini even produced sports cars with the driver centrally placed; Lago-Talbot did it for Le Mans. Most recently Cooper had introduced the Monaco, a mid-engined Climax powered machine closely resembling the single seater. The process of "GP-derivation" generally involves minimal drawing office work and because most of the technical elements of the design are well proven in competition, the result does not require much development and testing either.

Although the Fifteen in "Works" form and later Series Two revision with conventional transmission was a perfectly adequate sports racing car it had never made money for Lotus nor was it sufficiently distinctive to stand against the Eleven. Now Chapman considered the development possibilities of the Eighteen and saw a successful sports car within his grasp.

To generate a sports racing car from the Formula One machine involved opening up the frame design to the desired two-seater configuration and the evolution of a full width body to match. It is interesting that the Nineteen body is exactly in the spirit of the Eighteen; no bigger than necessary to fill the gaps and cover the subject; not self-consciously aerodynamic like the Costin-inspired cars but a thoroughly practical workaday machine. The only potential weakness was that it employed the same Lotus-designed transmission as the Grand Prix car with all the unreliability that that feature promised. The Nineteen was immediately nicknamed "Monte Carlo" to throw down the gauntlet to the old enemy Cooper.

A serious shortage of full $2\frac{1}{2}$-litre FPF Climax engines meant that only a few would be produced in this specification although the more available $1\frac{1}{2}$-litre FPF would also suit the Nineteen as it did the Eighteen Formula Two version. The total number of Nineteens to be produced was therefore fixed at 12 of which 6 would be fitted with the $2\frac{1}{2}$-litre Coventry Climax engine. Stirling Moss took delivery of the first and saw it as an excellent source of start and prize money in supporting events as well as the sports car Classics. The Nineteen allocation could have been sold several times over. Frank Arciero ordered one for his protégé Dan Gurney. He came to the Works to collect it in time for the big Riverside race in September 1960 only to discover that it was not yet ready (in fact Chapman had sold it to one of the more experienced Lotus customers who knew the ropes of jumping the Lotus queue). Peter Warr, Ron Richardson and I managed to assemble a collection of parts representing something like 75% of the complete motor car while the hapless Gurney (one of the World's most charming – and at that time trusting – individuals) stood by in damp-eyed misery. As usual we

JAMES.A.ALLINGTON

Traditionally, manufacturers of single seater racing cars had demonstrated the ease with which a 2-seater sports racing car could be derived from their pure racing car. Chapman's first essay in this direction was the Nineteen which was quickly evolved from the Eighteen Grand Prix car, using all the mechanical components mounted on a wider but very similar spaceframe. Because of the shortage of FPF 2½ litre power units production was deliberately limited, an initial batch of twelve being laid down. The Nineteen was instantly successful in the hands of Moss and others and continued to be raced for several years in the UK and United States, sometimes in the US with exotic non-original power units in place of the costly FPF.

eventually got him to the start line by robbing others on the factory floor and he like many others scored countless successes at the wheel of his "Monte Carlo".

(xvi) The Twenty Formula Junior racing car – 1961

Having made his first move in the new direction with the very simple Eighteen Chapman could immediately visualize improvements in the same way that he had been able to project forwards a whole range of technical developments from his earlier automotive concepts.

The outstanding commercial success of the Eighteen Formula Junior car (which had literally saved the company at a crucial stage by its high sales – over 125 during 1960) and profitability (about 30% of the selling price) coupled with excellent cash flow characteristics (you paid for it on collection and the luckless components suppliers waited up to a year for their share at rock bottom prices)

meant that Chapman, now pushed on by the rest of us, was anxious to maintain Formula Junior sales.

It was the Cooper 500 Formula Three car which established the basic commercial principles governing the sale of over-the-counter competition cars in the post-war period. Coopers would systematically introduce a new Mark (up to IX) each year until they effectively killed the Formula by the total success of their product and the annihilation of all opposition. Chapman had not made yearly changes in the systematic Cooper manner hitherto but the Junior class now provided an opportunity to produce for each season a car which was visually different to a degree sufficient to hold out the tantalizing prospect of superiority over the outdated preceding model. In the case of the successor to the Eighteen this illusion of novelty would not be difficult to achieve; the Eighteen being such an uncompromisingly distinctive shape.

The Twenty for the 1961 season broke little new technical ground but looked completely different from its predecessor. It was also a little heavier to allow use of the updated Cosworth Mk. IV 1098 cc Junior engine. The Twenty was no

The Twenty formula Junior Car (1961) was in effect a face-lifted Eighteen fitted with all-fibreglass streamlined bodywork. This model was fitted with the 1098 cc Mk. IV Cosworth-Ford 105E-derived engine producing up to 95 bhp. It is linked to an inverted Renault gearbox by an aluminium cast bell-housing. Note the "Y"-shaped detachable brace triangulating the engine compartment and the central fuel tank mounted behind and below the steeply reclining driver's seat which caused controversy at the time. The rollover bar met the spirit of the regulations without actually affording driver protection.

longer adaptable to F2/F1 racing like the Eighteen and the contemporary type Twentyone Works Grand Prix car had many similarities but was really beginning a new trend away from the commercial product. The form of the Twenty was now slim and handsome but with the exception of the "wobbly wheels" it looked just like every other rear engined Formula Junior car of the period whereas the rugged Eighteen is immediately identifiable as a Chapman Classic. The Twenty was equipped with the same suspension front and rear as the Eighteen but now had inboard rear drum brakes. It could be supplied with either the Renault inverted gearbox or a similarly treated VW transmission – again with close ratio four-/five-speed gear clusters. The introduction of disc brakes on the Anglia 105E Saloon from which the Twenty Cosworth bored-out 1098 cc engine derived, meant that under the Formula rules brakes of this type could be fitted as an expensive option instead of the aluminium finned drum brakes of the Eighteen Junior.

The Twenty continued on the winning Lotus way in the hands of the Works drivers and a multitude of private owners. The performance of these remarkable cars steadily advanced as Keith Duckworth continued his miraculous development of the Ford "80 bore" engine which after short-lived competition from modified Fiat 1100, BMC "A" and occasional exotics such as the DKW two-stroke became invincible in the class and despite its humble origins, capable of specific power outputs equal to the more complex Coventry Climax FWA in its most developed forms.

(xvii) The Twentyone Grand Prix car 1961

From 1954 until 1960 the capacity limit for Formula One Grand Prix racing cars was fixed at $2\frac{1}{2}$-litres unsupercharged or 750 cc with compressor. During this period two different fuel regulations applied; initially there was no restriction and the majority of cars raced on an alcohol-based source of energy, which allowed high compression ratios with freedom from detonation at the expense of lavish fuel consumption. For 1958 alcohol-based fuels were banned and Avgas (aviation spirit with an octane rating of approximately 120) was specified by the FIA, governing body of the sport. During the latter and major part of this second period the Formula Two category was restricted to engines of $1\frac{1}{2}$-litres displacement and generally speaking the same basic cars were used for both categories; the configuration of both categories of engine in the leading contenders being much the same. It was therefore logical that the FIA should have announced (and it did so in good time) that with effect from the 1961 season the premier class would be for cars with engines restricted to $1\frac{1}{2}$-litres capacity. This created a furore among the British entrants (in particular Lotus and Cooper with BRM caught up in the general fracas) who knew that there was no really competitive $1\frac{1}{2}$-litre engine available to them in the short term. It was feared by all that Ferrari would as usual generate newer and more powerful engines at the drop of a hat and to add to British misery the Commendatore too was switching to the mid-engined way of life.

The over-confidence of the British Constructors, who remained convinced that the $1\frac{1}{2}$-litre Formula would never materialise and had conceived their own Intercontinental Formula in the hope of prolonging the $2\frac{1}{2}$-litre era caught the principal British engine supplier Coventry Climax on the hop, forcing Lotus, Cooper and even BRM to fit the now hopelessly outdated and underpowered four-cylinder FPF engine of 1957 vintage. By dint of the driving ability of Moss,

Clark, Ireland and others using far superior British chassis an occasional victory or place was gained in 1961 with this simple engine in its strengthened Mk. 2 form. However, Coventry Climax were now under great pressure to develop an up-to-date power unit and it was decided that this should be a V8. Installation drawings were eventually produced and issued to Cooper, Lotus, Lola, (BRM were doing their own thing with another V8) and the Rob Walker team (for Moss). This group evolved suitable chassis designs (the Moss car was to be an updated version of the Walker Eighteen with Colotti six-speed transmission and Twentyone-style bodywork), installed the best FPF four-cylinder engines that they could find and pressed on in desperation while Ferrari's V6 engined cars demonstrated colossal straight line speed and won the World Championship.

Chapman's personal relationship with Leonard Lee of Coventry Climax was at an all time low. Lee used his power as purveyor of horsepower to the racing fraternity to indicate his displeasure where appropriate and Chapman anticipated trouble on this front of a serious deterioration in the relationship between Coventry Climax and Lotus Cars Ltd., as a result of the joint misery surrounding our use of the Elite FWE engine. There had been endless rows between Lotus and Coventry Climax concerning the quality of the FWE (which because of the quantities involved was produced in the general Coventry Climax forklift plant rather than the specialised racing engine shop) coupled with Lotus' precarious financial position and unreliable production scheduling.

Chapman correctly anticipated that he would be last in line to receive the new FWMV and had to wait until 1962, after a considerable amount of teething trouble had held back full-scale production during the latter part of 1961 when Brabham and Moss ran Climax V8s. Really it was only the strong backing given to Team Lotus by Reg Tanner of Esso that restored peace between them and Climax; a relationship which progressively improved from 1962 onwards after Elite production ceased and Lotus racing fortunes rose. When the first two V8 engines were delivered to Cooper and the Rob Walker team it was discovered much to the chagrin of the luckless recipients that the engine in reality differed substantially from the drawings supplied as guidance for the construction of the running gear to house it. The FWMVs were a little longer and a little deeper than planned and therefore much cutting and extending had to take place. Chapman had sensibly decided to ensure that his new F1 car for 1961 – the Twentyone – would be specifically designed to make the most of the limited output of the four-cylinder FPF on the basis that he could revise the chassis if necessary when the definitive V8 appeared.

The Twentyone which arrived for the Monaco Grand Prix in May 1961 certainly resembled the new Twenty Formula Junior car; a feature which would help sales of the latter by association. Although it had the same sleek profile as the Twenty it was in fact much less identifiable with its contemporary Formula Junior sister car than was the Eighteen Team Lotus machine for a number of highly significant reasons.

Because of lack of time Chapman had been obliged to install the troublesome Lotus gearbox in the Team Lotus Eighteens but had now had a lengthy period in which to consider alternatives. An agreement had been struck with the German transmission manufacturer ZF (Zahnradfabrik Friedrichshafen AG) to supply a standard four-speed automotive gearbox for use on the Elite which up to that time had relied on the rather agricultural MGA gearbox, lacking synchromesh on first gear. ZF manufactured a transmission which looked rather suitable for a lightweight tractor and a variation of this was developed by them in both four- and five-speed versions for use exclusively by Team Lotus in the mid-engined cars.

There were fundamental changes to the suspension system of the Twentyone   *131* too in comparison to that of the Eighteen. Although the spaceframe was strongly reminiscent of the Eighteen with characteristic pierced bulkheads at the scuttle and rear, the front suspension represented a departure in that the coilspring/ damper units were mounted inboard and operated by short extensions of the upper wishbones which were now beautifully fabricated in stainless steel sheet and pivoted on a lengthy spindle well supported at both ends in recognition of that fact at this spindle now carried all front suspension loads. In fact, so great was the concentration of force around this main spindle, that an additional cross brace had to be welded into the frame early in its life. By positioning the suspension units within the frame it was possible to use an attenuated anti-roll bar and to lose at one stroke the aerodynamic drag of the springs and dampers. Chapman lost no time in adopting successful devices used by his contemporaries but I doubt whether his sense of history was such that he was aware at the time that a similar technique was used by Maserati on the 4CLT/48 San Remo car thirteen years earlier. This particular feature may have been adopted at the last

There is very little that is really new in automotive design. When Chapman used an inboard-mounted spring compressed by an inward extension of the upper wishbone arm on the Twentyone Grand Prix car it was generally hailed as another example of his innovative approach. In fact, others had used the principle in several earlier cases – even I can claim precedence by quoting the example of a Dante 1172 Formula car of 1959 which had the same system. Here we see the 4CLT/48 San Remo Maserati of 1948 – a Grand Prix car used by Fangio, Farina, Villoresi and others and clearly fitted with a nice inboard mounted suspension unit actuated in precisely the same manner as on the Lotus Twentyone and its successors. The attraction of this system to Maserati was probably that they could dispense with the previous lengthy torsion bars which got in the way of everything forward of the bulkhead and which were tricky to adjust. This application even has a simple ride height adjuster built into the rocker arm!

minute by Chapman because I remember well a conversation late in 1960 with Mike Costin (as privy as any to Chapman's innermost technical thought) in which my suggestion that inboard suspension units would offer benefits (I had used the same system on a Dante design early in 1959) was rejected out of hand.

Apart from the reduction of suspension loading on the outboard element of the "wishbones" inherent in the new front suspension layout, the method of construction adopted for the upper arm (for the first time bringing a look of the aviation industry to a Lotus product) imparted far greater rigidity to this component than before. Additionally in the new $1\frac{1}{2}$-litre GP category of racing where the general lack of power output encouraged the avoidance of power-consuming drag, the outstanding aerodynamic feature of the Twentyone front suspension system was that the critical airflow between the wheels and the body of the car remained relatively undisturbed. Here again Chapman had consciously embarked on a new line of development pointing to universal future practice. At the rear there was another fundamental change in that the driveshafts were no longer required to do more than transmit power to the wheels. Instead of using the driveshafts as the main lateral locating element of the rear suspension system Chapman now controlled the wheel laterally by the same type of lower wishbone as hitherto but added a new upper link several inches above the wheel centreline and attached to a vertical extension of the cast aluminium hub carrier. Fore and aft location of the rear wheels together with the management of brake torque (the discs now being outboard) was again provided by two parallel radius arms. This was before the time of inboard rear suspension units and so by comparison with the front suspension system the rear was aerodynamically untidy. Chapman avoided the energy-consuming characteristics of a sliding driveshaft by ensuring that the geometry of the upper and lower rear suspension links followed very closely the path of the fixed length driveshaft and accommodated any slight conflict by using a rubber "doughnut" as the inboard universal joint. This peculiar design characteristic later cropped up regularly on Lotus road cars, not always with total success, but it derived from Chapman's deep dislike of splined driveshafts which under heavy power load can bind and inhibit suspension movement.

(xviii) The Twentytwo Formula Junior and Twentythree sports racing cars 1962

For 1962 we were to be given an inter-related pair of rear engined commercial racing cars; one – Twentytwo – for Formula Junior and a sports racing stablemate, the Twentythree, which resembled a baby Nineteen. The Formula Junior version arrived for the end-of-season Racing Car Show and although superficially resembling its predecessor the Twenty, differed in a number of significant respects to comply with the new Lotus commercial tradition of systematic annual design updating. The driver was in an evermore-reclining position to reduce frontal area and the spaceframe was substantially stiffer.

The front suspension of the Twentytwo was much as it had been before but with disc brakes fitted as standard. The rear suspension incorporated the subtle development first aired on the Twentyone Works Formula One cars. In this new layout the driveshaft reverted to its prime function of transmitting power from the final drive unit to the wheel hub and was relieved of all suspension locating loads. An inboard "doughnut" was provided as in the larger car. The Twentyone type cast aluminium hub carrier was extended above the wheel centreline to pick

The chaos that overtook our fortunes in the USA in 1961 held up deliveries of all Lotus types apart from the Elite, root cause of the trouble. Many of the Twenties did not appear on the track until the 1962 season, when the Twentytwo was officially the Lotus Formula Junior car. I managed to deliver a Twentytwo to Chamberlain in time for the late 1961 season events on the West Coast but unfortunately in its first and only race with Chamberlain at the wheel a wishbone fractured and I had to literally shield the car from photographers anxious to record that the plague of breakages affecting our fortunes in Europe was rearing its ugly head across the Atlantic. A batch of Twentytwos was brought in by Kaback for East Coast customers and within a week of unloading from the boat this car driven by Peter Ryan won the Formula Junior race in the Vanderbilt cup at Bridgehampton (here the car is seen at Marlboro, Maryland) by which time it had acquired a few individual touches such as the padded rollover hoop and distinctive colour scheme. Although structurally very similar to the "boxy" Eighteen Formula Junior car the Twenty had the advantage of low drag bodywork, disc brakes and an 1100 cc engine all of which enhanced its circuit speed.

up with a link mounted at virtually the same height as the upper mounting of the suspension unit. Separate roll bars were fitted front and rear. 1962 was the last year of the FIA Formula Junior before it was superseded as the "nursery class" by the new Formula 2/3 categories. The Twentytwo therefore may be considered the apogee of Chapman's small, low powered single seat racing car designs in the pre Formula Ford era.

The Twentythree was (as was the Nineteen to the Eighteen) an "opened-out" version of the Twentytwo. As described elsewhere, we were engaged in the evolution of a power unit for the Elan during early 1962 and this power unit (a twin overhead camshaft conversion of the Ford Kent engine) was being tried in various degrees of tune in a secret programme of road testing. What better test than to try the engine in the new Twentythree entered for the Nürburgring 1000 km race in June? The result was electrifying – Jim Clark at the wheel – and the Twentythree burst on the world as the 1500 that could take on anything regardless of capacity. For eleven laps before retiring it led the Works cars from Porsche, Ferrari and Aston Martin. A "pushrod" Twentythree driven by Ashdown/Johnstone finished eighth nonetheless.

Naturally enough, after such an arresting debut, the Twentythree became an excellent commercial proposition and we sold it strongly in all markets. It was so successful that it thoroughly eradicated the unhappy memories of Chapman's last unlamented small sports racing car, the 1959 Seventeen. The Twentythree occupies a special space in Lotus history in that it was the last small capacity pure sports racing car designed by Chapman; later vehicles used in this category being race-developed versions of road cars such as the Elan and Europa.

All Lotus designs in the series Eighteen to Twentythree were highly successful both in competition and commercially. They sold well across the globe and put us ahead even of Bugatti in the number of successes scored by Team Lotus and private owners. By this time Lotus had become the universal competition car and

Encouraged by the success of the Nineteen sports racing variant of the Eighteen Formula One car Chapman repeated the exercise for the 1962 season by producing the Twentythree sports racing car – a first cousin of the Twentytwo Formula Junior. Lotus re-entered the small sports racing car class by opening out the Twentytwo spaceframe but retaining the suspensions virtually unaltered. This tiny car was clothed in frame-hugging fibreglass panels with matching low drag windscreen etc., in accordance with FIA regulations. Although revealed at the Racing Car Show, the Twentythree really put itself on the map when in May 1962 driven by Jim Clark at the Nürburgring and fitted with an early example of the Lotus twincam 1500 cc engine the tiny Lotus led the field for several glorious laps before expiring.

every design contributing to this success bore the stamp of Chapman's genius. Because he was designer and owner of the company Chapman was able to indulge his remarkable talent almost without restraint and the variety of his personal output in the first decade since the appearance of the Mk. 6 – the first commercial Lotus – was prodigious and never subsequently equalled by him or any other creative automotive engineer.

(xix) The Twentyfour Grand Prix car – 1962

In due course a Coventry Climax V8 engine was provided to Team Lotus but too late for the Twentyone. For the 1962 season Chapman decided that he would produce a cleaned up version of the Twentyone (the Twentyfour) which turned out to have a dual role. Much prestige (and money) could be derived from the sale to selected top ranking drivers of Lotus Grand Prix cars as had been shown by the supply of an Eighteen to Moss. There were potential difficulties here and Chapman's very considerable charm was employed on occasions to soothe Reg Tanner who as the racing "baron" of Esso was not very happy to see "his" car supplied to Moss, (contracted to BP) winning all the races. Tanner had succeeded during 1961 in preventing the Rob Walker Team (or any other) from taking delivery of a Twentyone but for 1962 Chapman had cooked up a plan which met the Esso criteria for continuing support. The first role of the Twentyfour was to meet this pent-up demand for a Lotus GP "customer-car" and the second, as we shall see, was to act as a test bed for something quite different and top-secret.

Jack Brabham, who had been associated for many years with the Cooper marque, let it be known that he would be interested to purchase an up-to-date Lotus Grand Prix car and ordered a Twentyfour after a clandestine visit to Cheshunt which we all witnessed "Just up for lunch and a social chat with Colin . . ." UDT-Laystall ordered Twentyfours at the same time. The Twentyfour was substantially similar to its predecessor, being in effect a more compact, thought-through version of the 1961 Team cars. Its most important purpose was revealed within two months of the appearance of the Twentyfour at the Brussels GP on April 1st when Chapman unveiled the Twentyfive, for which the Twentyfour, representing no major technological step forward, represented the perfect decoy, at the Dutch Grand Prix. No previous Lotus racing car had ever been developed under conditions of such secrecy as the Twentyfive. The Team Lotus Twentyfours were raced alongside the new car but as soon as it became established, were sold off having fulfilled their prime purpose as a "belt and braces" machine to keep Team Lotus going had the Twentyfive failed to fulfil its promise.

(xx) The gamble that came off – the Lotus Twentyfive Grand Prix car – 1962

To the outside world it might have appeared that, Cooper-fashion, a process of steady development of the Eighteen/Twentyone mid-engined spaceframe cars would continue into the new 1½-litre formula. This view would have been confirmed by examination of the Twentyfour appearing at the Brussels Grand

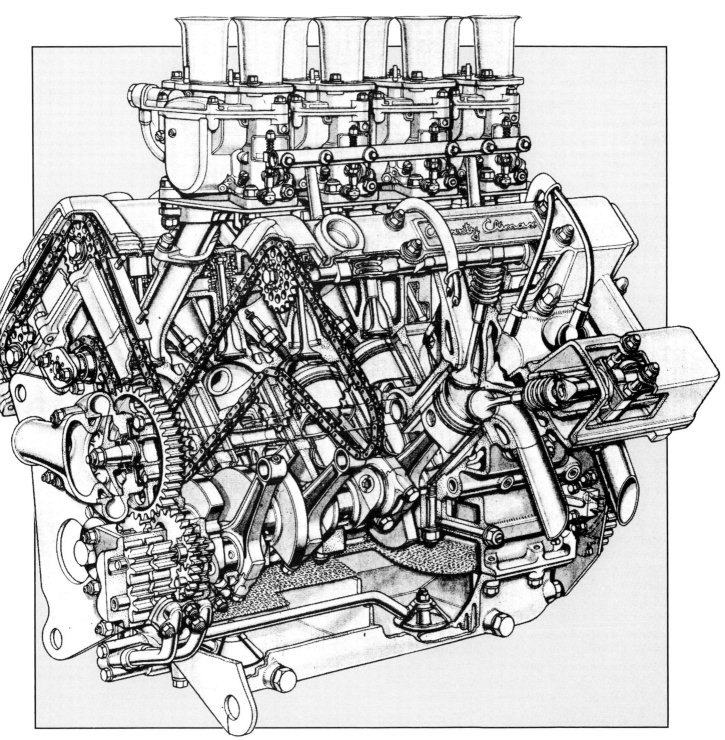

In 1953 Coventry Climax designed and built prototypes of a 2¹/₂ litre V8 racing engine (the FPE), encouraged by British manufacturers, most notably Connaught. The story goes that Coventry Climax were put off by the exaggerated horsepower claims of Mercedes Benz and Ferrari and felt that they would never be able to compete. In fact the FPE, had it been developed, could have brought earlier Grand Prix success to Britain, but that is another story. Lotus, Cooper and BRM had hoped against hope that they could persuade the authorities not to persist in the avowed intention of introducing a 1¹/₂ litre unsupercharged Formula One for 1961. That they failed in this is history and Ferrari who had developed an extremely powerful engine for the new Formula had a head start in the first year. The British manufacturers were obliged for most of 1961 to use an interim 1¹/₂ litre 4-cylinder Climax engine while Climax developed this new V8 FWMV power unit which in Lotus' case was not used until 1962. Surprisingly the FWMV drives its twin-overhead camshafts by single row chains instead of the more precise spur gears used on the FPF. The Lotus Twentyfour and Twentyfive were built around this power unit coupled to a ZF transaxle and we now began to hear some really high-revving little racing cars which, despite the lack of power, circulated at most impressive speeds, aided by the new technology introduced by Chapman and copied by others. The FWMV started life as shown here with carburettors and two valves per cylinder but by the end of the Formula was using fuel injection and a four valve set-up, very much the format chosen by Cosworth for the 1967 DFV 3 litre engine which followed on this formula.

Prix in April 1962, differing only in relatively minor respects from its Twentyone predecessor which had achieved reasonable success during 1961. Whereas the Twentyfour was obviously a competitive car and suitable for sale at a high price to prestigious independent drivers it was a curiously unadventurous design. The reason for this was soon to be revealed.

Those of us in the regular Chapman "core luncheon group" of Bushell, Mike Costin, Clark, Standen and me (when at home) had to a greater or lesser degree been aware that something was going on that caused Chapman's normally elevated level of personal excitement to rise to even greater heights. At a point early in 1962 he had subjected the design criteria of a Grand Prix car to the closest scrutiny. The very small power output available from unsupercharged $1\frac{1}{2}$-litre engines yielding about 100 bhp less than their $2\frac{1}{2}$-litre predecessors placed a valuable premium on other factors in the design equation. Only by attending to a ruthless reduction of frontal area and parasitic drag, coupled with the achievement of the highest levels of handling, road holding, traction and braking together with absolute adherence to the minimum permitted weight limit, could a designer secure the necessary advantage to win races. But Chapman's ultimate weapon in the search for superiority was his protégé, Jim Clark, a small Borderer offering very low frontal area, light weight and remarkable driving ability. Clark's greatest attribute in the environment in which he now found himself since joining Team Lotus for the 1960 season, was his ability to learn at Chapman's knee. This was to be the next collaboration of Chapman's career as a Racing Designer/Team Manager and the relationship stimulated him to conceive a car which would exploit to the full Clark's driving ability and extend his (Chapman's) technical skills to the limit.

The essence of this new car – the Twentyfive – was that it should consist only of the basic structural elements necessary for competitive operation. In effect this meant that it would abandon the conventional spaceframe chassis thus making space savings within the outer skin and the elements normally attached to the space frame could now be linked together and in several cases assume previously unconsidered stress-bearing responsibilities. As Chapman explained it to us at table: "All you need is four wheels, a fuel tank, power unit, suspension and brakes" . . . "Sounds wonderful, Colin" we all agreed. Mike Costin and John Standen in their capacity as Development Engineer and Buyer were "in the know" of course, but for me it was a fascinating experience listening to Chapman explaining his theories with knife and fork sketches on the starched tablecloth.

The Twentyfive project had to be conducted under conditions of the greatest secrecy. The Twentyfour was being produced as a back-up in case of development difficulties with the Twentyfive and as an effective decoy for those who were wondering what Chapman was up to that was causing the sparkle in his eye and the spring in his step. There was a very clear line of demarcation between our racing activities and the commercial side of the Group, which meant that one usually had to ask for information about Team Lotus. I was therefore pleasantly surprised when shortly after the lunch-time revelations, one Spring evening Chapman invited me to come over to the Racing Department to see for myself what was going on. That was unusual enough and an indication of his conviction that he was on to something of great potential importance.

It was dark when I arrived and in the strong lighting which enabled the Team Lotus mechanics to work round the clock, Chapman and Jim Clark stood talking and looking at the extraordinary new car taking shape. The prototype Twentyfive was supported on trestles at waist height. It was seen to consist of a large punt-shaped riveted aluminium monocoque structure in which Clark was to sit – or rather lie – with no room to spare. The punt provided enclosure for the lateral and transverse "rubber bag" fuel tanks and throttle-actuating cables and

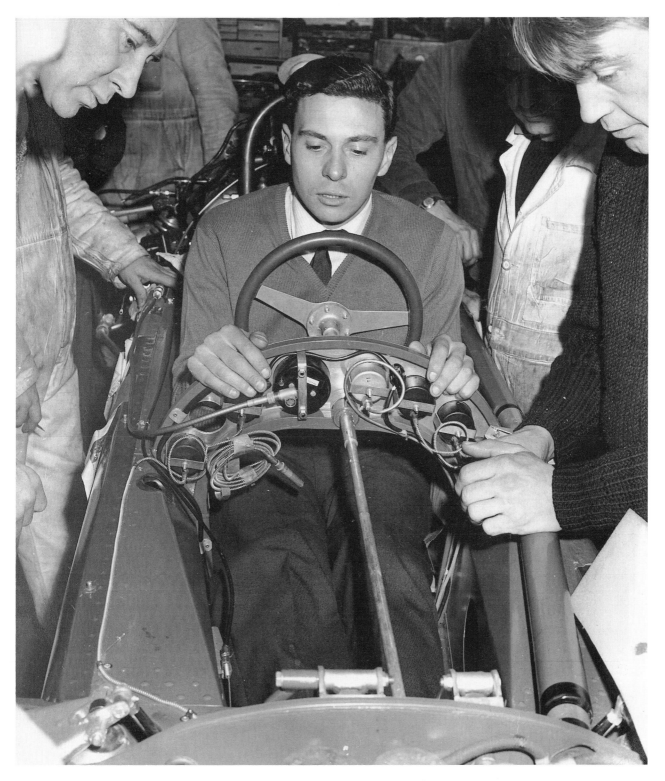

This shot of Jim Clark discussing pedal positions on a monocoque single seater (after my time – in 1963) reminds me of the occasion when I first saw the Twentyfive under construction in the Team Lotus workshops at Cheshunt. This car was in every sense designed for Clark – it fitted his physical proportions perfectly and was intended to give full rein to his remarkable driving talents which had been observed by Chapman with increasing interest from 1959. The car shown in this photograph is the first variant of the Twentyfive intended for the 1963 500 Mile Race at Indianapolis – the Twentynine. In its earliest form it closely resembled the Twentyfive as far as the main structure was concerned but carried an aluminium block push rod OHV Ford V8 engine giving approximately 350 bhp on gasoline. Various transmission and suspension components were beefed up for the American race to ensure reliability. On the right is the Team Lotus Chief Mechanic of my day, Jim Endruweit, and to the left of Clark the ubiquitous Len Terry (who departed just before I arrived on the scene in 1959 and returned almost immediately afterwards) considers the driver's point of view.

brake lines passed through a channel in the floor of the punt – "between Jimmy's cheeks", Chapman laughed. The Coventry Climax V8 engine was bolted rigidly to rearward extensions of the punt and the suspension system was arranged on a fabricated structure surrounding the ZF gearbox. At the front was the by now familiar inboard-sprung wishbone system first seen on the Twentyone but now with a number of detail modifications from the Twentyfour including repositioning of the steering arms in line with the upper wishbones – reducing yet further the minimal drag of the front suspension – and cast aluminium front suspension uprights at last replacing the ubiquitous Triumph Herald steel forgings. Although not yet to be seen, the car was completed by removable fibreglass panels forming the nose and covering the punt. Behind the driver the centrally positioned carburettors were enclosed within a snugly fitting cowl through the rear of which extended the long twin megaphones of the exhaust system. Even the beautifully moulded windscreen blended with Clark's personal aerodynamics.

From facial expressions and the manner in which they spoke I knew that designer and driver were already convinced that they had a winner and subsequent experience proved them right. As before, the individual elements of the Twentyfive were not in themselves new but what took our breath away was the manner in which Chapman had brought them together to create a single

Comparison of this drawing of the Twentyfive with the Twentyfour shows that all the mechanical elements of these two cars with minor exceptions are identical and interchangeable. The Twentyfive was a gamble for Chapman and the idea of completely abandoning the spaceframe chassis came to him after he had embarked on his new "play safe" car for the 1962 season. As Chapman strove to make his racing cars ever slimmer in order to reduce wind resistance and bulk, the awkward spaceframe was unwelcome. The constant problem of fitting fuel tanks into the conventional structure was overcome at a stroke by the use of self-sealing flexible fuel tanks within the riveted aluminium side members of the monocoque and the perennial problem of splitting and leaking tanks was overcome at one fell swoop. The Twentyfive had an enduring influence on motor racing design from its inception.

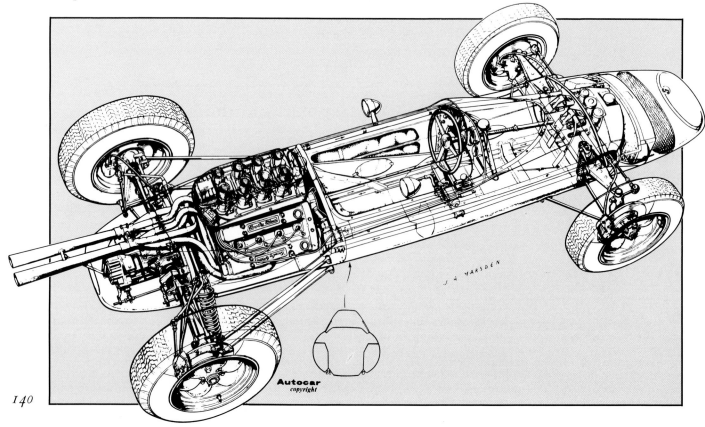

solution to the problem of winning the World Championship. Now that it was done we asked ourselves why so long to arrive at this departure? Not only had Chapman rejected at one fell swoop the *sine qua non* of current racing car design – the spaceframe – but in combining the elements remaining he had fashioned a structure of even greater torsional and beam strength. The impact on the racing world was electric and while Team Lotus continued to use the Twentyfive in virtually unmodified form for the remaining four years of the $1\frac{1}{2}$-litre Formula, the other contenders, with the odd quaint exception (not always unsuccessful) hurriedly adapted the new Lotus structural philosophy to their own cars. The influence of the Twentyfive on racing car design persists even though the latest manifestations of the original philosophy look so different and carry certain features present only as indicators in the Twentyfive – in particular aerodynamics – to levels undreamed of in the Spring of 1962.

(xxi) Note – Racing Transmissions

It is easy for us today, spoiled as we are by the range of Hewland racing transmissions available for almost every type of racing car from Formula Ford upwards, to appreciate that in the Fifties if you wanted an exotic transmission you made it yourself. Ferrari, Maserati, BRM, Vanwall and Aston Martin all designed and built unique transmissions for their single seater cars. Chapman had done the same with the Twelve and used this transmission in developed form in the Fifteen sports racing and Sixteen single seater cars with many variations to accommodate central, nearside and offside input shafts from the power unit. The final development, in which the gears were arranged behind the crownwheel and pinion was used on the Eighteen and Nineteen models. Brilliant in concept and when it worked, very efficient, the Lotus transmission was notoriously unreliable and yet another reason why the front engined single seater Lotuses failed to fulfil their promise.

(xxii) Note – Chapman and the ZF Relationship

Chapman had first contacted ZF (Zahnradfabrik Friedrichshafen AG) when he discovered that no British gear cutter would undertake the production of the internals for his new progressive change transmission designed for the Twelve. ZF carried out the work speedily and effectively; possibly recognising in this talented innovator a potential source of future business of a more commercial nature and on a broader front. In this they were right because the need to provide a sturdier transmission later for the Elite meant that the traditional MG gearbox would no longer fit the bill. In any case the MG box was in every way a crude thing with the gear change "feel" less pleasant even than the 105E Series Ford transmission which set new standards in this field. ZF had a gearbox available "off the shelf" and this became an expensive option on the Elite from the Bristol Series Two cars onwards. Although technically excellent the ZF gearbox had a rather harsh feel when changing gear and the shortened lever used on the Elite installation would buzz and vibrate (as did much of the rest of the car of course!) However, all-synchromesh gearboxes were not very common on British cars of the time and it was a helpful sales feature.

Chapman again used his own gearbox and final drive unit on the Eighteen Formula car and the Nineteen sports racer but it became increasingly obvious that this transmission was no longer acceptable as a result of its fundamental unreliability and high cost. He therefore turned again to ZF who selected a transmission system originally developed for military and off-road applications which was adapted within an aluminium housing for the Twentyone and later series Works cars. Although the relationship with ZF was therefore quite advanced by this stage the arrival on the scene of Formula Junior had fostered the search for suitable transmissions which complied with Formula rule that the basic gearbox should be from a FIA-recognised touring car. Initially the Eighteen Junior was fitted with an inverted Renault gearbox with Pons Redelé internals but within a short time the Volkswagen transmission with gears manufactured by a young man named Hewland began to take over from its French predecessor; having superior engineering and greater potential for development to offer. The advent of the Hewland company would do for racing transmissions what Cosworth was already doing for the power unit and the rest is history; ZF ultimately (with the odd exception) concentrating on purely commercial applications thereafter.

(xxiii)   Note – Chapman's Choice of Power Unit

Until the decision to design a twin overhead camshaft cylinder head for the 105 E Ford engine to be used in the Elan, Chapman had been content to take complete power units from external sources in what was becoming an increasingly strong British tradition. In the early days of the Mk. 3A, the Mk. 6 and the Mk. 8, Chapman had shown considerable ingenuity and skill in devising developments of humble power units such as the pre-war Austin Seven, Ford Consul and MG 'T' Type. But as soon as the FWA Climax engine became available, ready to slot in for immediate use, he transferred allegiance.

When Formula Junior replaced small capacity sports car racing as the main point of departure for aspiring professional drivers Chapman had the foresight to understand the implications for this formula of the newly announced Ford 105 E Anglia engine of 997 cc. The rule of Formula Junior racing which allowed a lower minimum weight for engines of less than 1 litre capacity than for 1100 cc, attracted Chapman's attention and the process whereby he, Mike Costin and Keith Duckworth together made it possible to produce from this ultra short stroke power unit a highly effective 75 bhp racing engine is shrouded in mystery. Did Chapman conceive the idea of using the Ford engine or was it Duckworth's brainwave? One thing is sure – only the presence between these two rugged individualists of the catalytic Mike Costin would make possible the collaboration that transformed this basic power unit and set in train a series of developments resulting in today's domination of motor sport at all levels by Ford-derived power. Although Duckworth had achieved success with his general engine tuning activities; particularly those associated with the Coventry Climax; it was the Formula Junior Ford engine which really established him as the high performance engine man *par excellence*. Only Duckworth was able quickly to master the development of this strange little power unit and even he had a great deal of difficulty in the early days in making the Ford engine both powerful and reliable. Serious problems were experienced in arranging suitable lubrication for the special camshaft required for high output and these early Cosworth power units are possibly the only examples of modern racing engine to have spent a period of development on castor (vegetable) based oils in the frantic pursuit of durability.

Inherent in the story of the development of the Lotus Ford Formula Junior car is the wide gulf separating the Italian and British traditions of competition engine design. The Italians were quite happy to evolve elaborate power units from scratch and quickly. Ferrari's ability to ring the changes on his stock of 4-, 6-, 8- and 12-cylinder engines in a variety of capacities and applications is legendary. Even very small manufacturers such as OSCA and Stanguellini could produce effective new power units sometimes perhaps based on a Fiat block but incorporating elaborate twin-overhead camshaft cylinder heads, special crankshafts and other engine internals. By contrast the Cosworth Ford Formula Junior engine and its subsequent larger capacity derivatives – before the advent of the Lotus twin-cam head – made use throughout of basic Ford castings and other components carefully selected to ensure correct tolerances and fits. By happy coincidence (it was not conceived for racing development as had been the FWP Climax engine) the little Ford 105E and its successors had all the basic attributes necessary for development of high output. The use of the same "80

The spaceframe of the Twentythree sports racing car was dominated by the characteristic "Terry-type" scuttle bulkhead of pierced sheet steel. If anything the wider Twentythree spaceframe was stiffer than the single seater Twentytwo from which it derived. The standard power unit was the 1089 cc Cosworth Ford with alternative 997 and 1470 cc versions. The standard transmission here is the familiar inverted Renault type with close ratio gears. This very early car is fitted with the hated (by Chapman) sliding spline Hook-jointed driveshafts. Later these were replaced by fixed length shafts with rubber "doughnut" inner joints. The fuel tank mounted centrally behind the seats (the filler projecting coyly between them) was also quickly replaced by side mounted tanks in production. This was an extremely successful car which rapidly put Lotus back at the top of the small sports racing car pile from which they had been tumbled by Lola in 1959.

bore" cylinder dimension throughout the range was purely for convenience and economy in ensuring that a whole family of different capacity power units could be generated about similar external engine dimensions and basic castings. That this wide bore and short stroke meant that the engine was able safely to achieve high rpm and accept large valves for appropriate breathing ability at racing engine speeds was a plus feature immediately recognised by Chapman, Costin and Duckworth. The era of the FWA/B-E and FPF Climax engines was ended by the advent of the Cosworth Ford Formula Junior package. Henceforth Chapman concentrated on urging Duckworth to develop larger capacity variants of the little pushrod engine (fitted to Series Two Super Seven and Lotus Twentythree) and the 1340 cc and even 1498 cc ohv engines were developed by Cosworth for sports racing and single seater power in appropriate classes before the Lotus twin cam head opened up new vistas for development of the basic Ford cylinder block. The breathing of the 105E engine modified by Cosworth was such that it was possible to fit two large Weber twin-choke carburettors to endow it with hitherto unthinkably high revving capability.

Cosworth – Ford four-cylinder, pushrod ohv, three main bearing engines used by Lotus 1959 – 1962

Type (year)	Dimensions (mm)	Capacity (cc)	bhp @ rpm	Principal applications	Note
Mk II (Dec 1959–60)	80.96x48.41	997	75 @ 7500	Eighteen Formula Junior	105E base. First 'customer' engine. 2 Weber 38 DCO E1 carburettors Wet sump. A2 camshaft
Mk III (1960 on)	80.96x48.41	997	85/90@7500	Eighteen (1960) & Twenty (1961) Formula Junior	Improved MkII. Steel main bearing caps. A3 camshaft. Optional dry sump
Mk IV (1961 on)	85.00x48.41	1098	90/95@7750	Twenty (1961)& Twentytwo (1962) Formula Junior/ Twentythree Sports Racing	Bored-out block. Developed from Mk III. Larger valves, etc. 2 Weber 40 DCOE carbs. Canted (30°) installation in Twentytwo with dry sump lubrication
Mk V (1961-63)	80.96x65.07	1340	85 @ 6000	Super Seven Series Two	109E base. A2 camshaft 2 Weber 40 DCOE carbs.
Mk VI (1962)	80.96x65.07	1340	105 @ 7000	Twentythree Sports Racing	Racing version of Mk V. Steel lower end/ A3 camshaft etc.
Mk VII (1962)	85.00x65.07	1475	120 @ 7000	Twentythree Sports Racing	Bored-out block. Developed from Mk VI

(xxiv)   Commercial Prudence – The Elan

The prototype Elite was conceived in 1955 and revealed to an admiring audience at the 1957 London Motor Show, but almost two more years elapsed before serious production began at Cheshunt in the summer of 1959. The long period of design and pre-production development was a completely new experience for Chapman who until that time was accustomed to seeing his concepts materialise and enter the market with minimal delay and (generally speaking) early commercial success. The Elite was in every sense a new dimension and one from which he was beginning to withdraw as early as late 1959. From 1957 when he introduced the Elite concept and his first generation front engined single seaters there followed three wearying years for Chapman and his entire team of collaborators, finding for the first time that the way ahead was not always easy.

The Elite was a Chapman/Kirwan-Taylor/Frank Costin *concept*. The task of realising it was principally delegated to John Frayling and (somewhat later) Ron Hickman whose complementary skills and temperament combined well as they struggled with the labyrinthine problems of developing this utterly novel production car. By the time that the Elite entered regular production in Summer 1959, John Westall, General Manager of Maximar Mouldings, (the first to appreciate the true situation) Frayling and Hickman had begun to suspect that the double skinned structural method of construction evolved by Frayling for the Elite was impractical. Chapman's initial rage at the discovery of Frayling's cavalier interpretation of his simple monocoque concept had been replaced by a gnawing suspicion that the main structure of the Elite was totally impractical for profitable manufacture.

The process of resolving the difficulties of manufacturing bodies at all – let alone profitably – was only possible with the total commitment displayed by Frayling and Hickman, exposed to the regular complaining and criticism of John Westall. Chapman's visits to Pulborough were infrequent and he was always able to motor smartly away from the problems. Nevertheless he had appreciated to the full that there could never be a repetition of the double skinned Elite structure in any future Lotus car.

Only desultory development work was done after production began (of which the main part was concentrated on the virtually inevitable updating of the Chapman Strut rear suspension layout for the Bristol-made Series Two cars plus interior trim improvements) all underlining the lack of interest from Chapman and Mike Costin. Any hope that the Elite might ultimately become a commercial success after the technical difficulties of design, manufacture and servicing were dashed by actual production and sales experience.

It is therefore not surprising that as early as the summer of 1959 when Chapman was deeply preoccupied with consideration of the next move in his racing car design series that a wave of new thinking washed over the jaded Elite development team. With characteristic bravura Hickman was writing (an almost unknown means of communication in Lotus at that time) his early thoughts on the Elite's successor. Some of us were convinced that we had to find a replacement as quickly as possible. Chapman himself toyed with the idea of producing a Ford engined 2 + 2 car to supplement the smaller Elite. There would hardly have been a single part in common between the 2 + 2 and the Elite and the larger vehicle could well have repeated all the shortcomings of its predecessor.

At this time however we were diverted by contemplation of the crude little Austin-Healey Sprite Sports Car. We reacted to it in different ways. Some saw it as a competitior for the Seven but in Hickman's mind it certainly revived memories of his Ford days when the idea of a small sports car based on freely

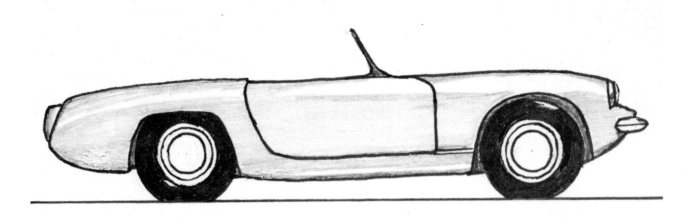

Although it eventually became the successor to the Elite, as originally conceived the Elan was to replace the Seven as a low cost, highly profitable sports car. Because of this Chapman insisted that it should incorporate certain key components from existing cars and John Frayling was directed to make up a model of a car which would ultimately use the mechanical components of the Ford Anglia 105E. Externally, the new car (code named S2) was to be fitted with a Mk.1 windscreen and miniature bumpers from the Sprite mounted horizontally at the front and vertically at the rear. Given that Chapman intended this Ford-based car to be distributed via the Ford dealer network in direct competition with the Sprite, it is clear that he would need all his legendary charm to persuade BMC to co-operate with the supply of suitable parts. Ron Hickman recalls that Chapman was determined to use the Weathershields-patented hood (matching the Sprite windscreen) and held that it would still be viable to arrange supplies from the BMC dealer network at prices much higher than OE levels. This drawing gives a rough indication of the original Frayling concept which should be compared with the ultimate Hickman M2 Elan unveiled in October 1962. Surely one of the most drastic development programmes of all time!

available road-car components was continually under consideration. The Austin-Morris combine BMC was well experienced in the art of producing simple but crude sporting cars from road going bits and pieces and the Sprite was in this "sheep in wolf's clothing" tradition. Several intimate members of the Chapman circle including John Standen and Ian Smith (founder of the Racing Car Show and author of the original history of Lotus) had tried the Sprite Mk. 2 at an official Press Day and were generally enthusiastic although critical of the road holding qualities resulting from the use of antiquated quarter-elliptic rear springs.

Chapman had a non-commital and "short-term" attitude to the Seven. Both the Series One and Series Two cars were "dashed off" designs to meet unfading demand from those who had originally bought the Mk. 6 and who like Porsche 911 owners later, refused to allow the suppression of their old love by "progressive" new models. Chapman (and Hickman) originally saw the Twentysix (coded S2) project as close to the AH Sprite concept and therefore a replacement for the Seven, but by early 1961 it had become *de facto* the successor to the Elite and therefore essential to the survival of Lotus.

Whereas the original S2 concept was a direct competitor for the Sprite (even using some of that car's body parts) but based on Ford mechanical components, Chapman's original intentions were modified by the advent of the Herald-based Triumph Spitfire in 1959. This car incorporated very simple independent rear suspension of much greater appeal to Chapman than the conventional rear axle originally chosen for the S2, although the Spitfire application of Swing-axle/IRS imparted road holding that appalled him on test.

Early in 1961 Chapman announced in my hearing that he would "never make another bloody car without a chassis". This heartfelt cry brought into the public domain his decision to abandon the original fibreglass reinforced plastics unitary construction planned for the S2. In the interim Ron Hickman had struggled with might and main to overcome the problems of creating a plastic monocoque without a structural top and incorporating large door openings.

The first clay model of the S2 – M2 Elan model made by Ron Hickman was this 3/8 scale hardtop version which tried to follow as closely as possible the beautiful lines of the Elite despite lacking the bubble-shaped roof inspired by Frank Costin and to which John Frayling attributes the Elite's aesthetic advantage over other cars. Hickman's first attempt incorporated regulation-height fixed headlamps which because they were positioned somewhat higher than those of the (illegal) Elite headlamps spoiled the wing line of the Elan model. Also to be seen are the characteristic Hickman fibreglass reinforced plastic bumper panels that he had conceived as early as 1956 together with a choice of sidelight/ flasher units; that on the nearside from an Anglia 105E matched by a Lucas unit upside down on the offside. Hickman made an attempt to flow the base line of the windscreen up the pillar and over the side window but this was not a great success in either hard top or open versions. The rear wing line was "hipped" which Hickman and Frayling always felt to be the best for an open car but which posed severe styling problems in conjunction with a fixed roof or hardtop. This first effort was in fact so good that Chapman expressed concern that if Hickman was too successful the new car could kill off Elite sales (Chapman not realising that the Elan was to be a long time coming to market).

Under the new system introduced by Hickman the S2 (Sports 2) project had been renamed M2 (M = Major Project 2) and was causing the greatest concern to Hickman as Project Manager. All the major components of the car were rapidly approaching design finalisation and yet there was no sign that the basic structure would soon be ready for test. The Elan was to be the first open car of chassisless fibreglass reinforced unitary (monocoque) construction. The Elite and the Rochdale Olympic which followed but which was manufactured much more closely to the original Chapman recipe for the Elite both had the huge structural benefit of an integral roof to "close the box" and provide sufficient rigidity.

Experience in manufacturing the Elite – even after the very earliest experiences at Maximar – was sufficient to persuade all concerned that never again should a Lotus chassis body unit be so constructed. The principle of a monocoque plastic structure was certainly acceptable; the objections surrounded the manner in which (largely as a result of John Frayling's development of the double skin technique) such a unit should be manufactured.

Taken a few weeks after the previous pictures, this photograph shows an improvement of windscreen and hardtop shapes and these elements are now in fibreglass and perspex form. The door and boot hinge details are being considered. Behind the head of the scaled human figure may be seen Ron Hickman's private office on the mezzanine floor next to the doors leading to the stair and Mike Costin's office.

By the time that this photograph was taken on 3 May 1961 Hickman had evolved what he calls his "Stage 2" design. This model shows the improved windscreen shape suggested by Peter Kirwan-Taylor (the only external influence incorporated by Hickman in what eventually became the Elan). Also seen is Hickman's first attempt at a retractable headlight intended to lower the wing profile and clean up the bumper panel design in the headlight area. The unacceptable element of this feature was that at a glance it resembled the current Porsche 356B and Chapman and Hickman were determined to avoid the Porsche path at all costs by following and developing what was an already established Lotus "family style". Therefore even though this initial solution to the headlamp "problem" would have been cheaper than that finally adopted it was simply unacceptable because of its affinity to the Porsche design.

With his extensive knowledge of fibre reinforced plastic construction, John Westall of Maximar stated clearly to Ron Hickman and John Frayling that the only effective way in which a car body could be made would be by developing one minor aspect only of the Elite production method. This arose from the need for a solution to overcome the very difficult access conditions where the mould returned on itself so that in laying up the laminate it was necessary to create a split mould to allow sufficient overlap of the two sections where they met. This procedure was followed without fuss for the production of small components such as the bonnet and boot lids of the Elite. It was certainly not an unknown technology as far as the team at Pulborough were concerned. Westall told Chapman that until he devised a system which would develop that principle of the split mould he would never be able to economically construct an entire car body unit. With a demountable mould it is possible to work with good access so that, as each section is laid up, it is progressively completed by adding new part moulds, laminating over the joins and as soon as the structure has set hard the entire mould is open to reveal a complete body shell with all returns, wheel arches, bulkheads and so on. It is necessary to design the car itself in such a way that it meets these criteria; the opposite of course of the Elite route where a beautiful shape was determined first and then all the remaining details designed afterwards without any real consideration for the demands of manufacturing technique.

Ron Hickman and John Frayling took on board Westall's advice and when it came to preparing the Elan the technique used for production of what was initially to be a monocoque open top chassis body unit but which ended as a straightforward unstressed body mounted on a backbone chassis, was in accordance with the method proposed by Westall.

Ron Hickman coined the name *Unimould* for this technique and Chapman's version was *Monolithic* because neither of them really liked the name chosen by the other. I prefer *Unimould* so we will adopt that. Chapman's idea was that before going further with the Elan they would produce a ¹/₅th size model in scaled down fibreglass construction using the thinnest possible cloth and resin layer so that by flexing the structure in the hand it would be possible to determine the location of weak points requiring the addition of a strengthening bulkhead or

This is the earliest interior mock-up of the Elan and is in very unfinished form (in the background can be seen the ³/₈ scale model of the car in fairly definitive shape) with the structural dash designed to eliminate scuttle shake. At this stage Ron Hickman intended the dash panel to be of aluminium or one of the proprietary steel products with bonded-on, simulated leather skin (BSC Stelvetite) which was also used in the Seven. Later Hickman told Chapman that he preferred a nice teak-faced plywood. To Ron's surprise Colin said that he would prefer this alternative for reasons of structural strength and lower weight in view of the fact that a metal dash might be subject to buckling unless flanged and swaged. Hickman attempted to incorporate a face-level fresh air vent for the driver at this stage which Chapman considered to be crazy and which was eventually dropped because of its complexity.

additional lay-up. Ron messed about for several months but failed totally to make a successful model of this size despite working with tweezers. The thicknesses that resulted were unrepresentative and eventually he and Chapman concluded that they could learn nothing from what had been done. Ron Hickman felt that he was struggling to prove that the Unimould system would work on an open car spurred on by the desperate sight of the Elite dying commercially on the one hand, while the Elan was developing mechanically at an alarming rate from the original down market concept to a high powered relatively expensive vehicle, with Chapman ultimately deciding to go to a twin-overhead cam conversion of the Ford Engine with high power output.

Hickman's continuing failure to devise a method of producing a unitary FRP open top body unit with door apertures was easy to understand. Nobody else has been able to achieve such a result and although Hickman and Chapman felt that ultimately they could achieve their goal they were both rapidly reaching the conclusion that it was still a long way ahead. Hickman was of the view that even if they did not resort to a conventional chassis of some kind they would need at least to provide substantial steel frames around the door openings, metal sub-frames front and rear for the rear suspension, engine mountings, radiator etc., together with a metal floor plate for the central tunnel.

Whilst Hickman was agonising over the difficulties of his task the mechanical specification of the car was racing ahead by leaps and bounds; all of which would

Here begins the final (3rd) stage of the Elan design saga. A very significant photograph indeed – this demonstrates how Ron Hickman worked at the headlamp scheme which would avoid the Porsche resemblance. He decided that if he moved the erected position of the headlamp back a few inches and folded it 90° or so forwards he could reach the profile drawn on this shot which in fact became his styling sketch. In production the headlamp "vanished" into the structure of the car and was surmounted by a perfectly matched fibreglass form completing the line of the wing.

have added greater demands on the structural strength of the body. With no central structure in sight, the engineers associated with the project were becoming desperate at their inability to test the suspension, brakes and power unit. Ron Hickman's M2 project engineer Brian Luff insisted that he *must* have some sort of run about "chassis" as a test bed and asked permission for funds to be made available for Ian Jones the chief draughtsman to lay down a simple one-off spaceframe for this purpose.

At a relatively early stage (June 1960), when faced with the possibility that the only way to achieve adequate rigidity for the Elan would be to mould in an assortment of complex and expensive metal local reinforcements, Chapman had suggested that it would be worthwhile to investigate the cost and suitability of fitting the car with a very simple folded metal backbone chassis which would fit within the central tunnel and extend outwards at front and rear to encompass the engine and mount the suspension systems. To have accepted this course of action then would have been tantamount to an admission of defeat – that the open top unitary construction car was too difficult to design and manufacture. However, the situation had now arisen where a chassis of some sort had become essential and remembering the earlier conversation Hickman took up the subject with Chapman so that it would become possible to build up a test vehicle to develop the power unit and suspension components without waiting for the final body unit.

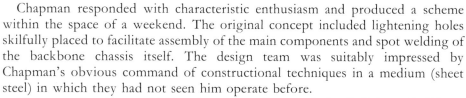

In this photograph the face-level vent has been dropped and the fascia trimmed. This seating buck still uses an Elite seat (manufactured by Cox of Watford) although John Standen made repeated attempts to persuade Ron to incorporate the much cheaper Triumph Herald seat which was subsequently re-engineered and used as the basis of the Elan production seat. Note the Triumph Herald steering wheel which, even with a Lotus badge in the centre, looks totally wrong for the Elan and which was dropped at an early stage.

Chapman responded with characteristic enthusiasm and produced a scheme within the space of a weekend. The original concept included lightening holes skilfully placed to facilitate assembly of the main components and spot welding of the backbone chassis itself. The design team was suitably impressed by Chapman's obvious command of constructional techniques in a medium (sheet steel) in which they had not seen him operate before.

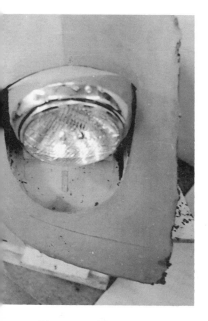

The test chassis was hidden beneath a "cut and shut" Falcon Caribbean fibreglass body of hideous shape. A floor was knocked up from plywood and with a couple of seats in position this car subsequently covered 50,000 miles of general testing. I remember well a run in it around Cheshunt and district with Ron Hickman at the wheel. He demonstrated to me the extraordinary "wind-up" (and "down") effect of the drive shaft doughnuts which Chapman had adapted from those to be fitted to the Hillman Imp saloon car. At a fairly early stage of development the rear disc brakes were moved outboard which cancelled this disconcerting effect under braking (but not during surges of acceleration) caused by the Rotoflex couplings which had been proved on the racing cars but which were one of the least loved characteristics of the production Elan.

Although the Falcon fibreglass body of the prototype car shook, rattled and vibrated like nothing on earth one had the impression that the strikingly simple backbone chassis of the M2 possessed remarkable rigidity despite its very simple construction. John Standen had costed the folded steel chassis frames in quantity at a price of £10 each and the fact that this nominal extra cost would at one stroke remove many of the difficulties of developing another Elite-type unreinforced plastic structure was more than welcome. Hickman therefore took the

To prove his theory before incorporating it in the 3/8 scale model of the M2, Hickman made the full size clay working model shown here. Much experimentation took place to determine the pivot axes for the headlight folding structure in both plan and front views in order to achieve an aesthetically acceptable result.

opportunity at the BRDC Annual Dinner in November 1960 to suggest to Chapman "Because the test car was so fantastic why should they not put a steel backbone into every car?" Chapman asked Hickman if he was serious. The reply was very strongly in the affirmative and when Hickman confirmed the cost Chapman immediately agreed with an alacrity which amazed Hickman particularly since Mick Costin (that expert Chapman-watcher) had forecast that Colin would "give the thumbs down." But this was an instant decision made possible for a variety of reasons not the least of which was that Hickman could now promise his boss a new car now desperately needed as the Elite became more and more difficult to sell and ever more costly to manufacture and service.

Hickman assured Chapman that with a separate chassis he could deliver the M2 at least a year earlier. That was finally the deciding factor and would avoid a hiatus in road car availability. Lotus would go out of business if M2 didn't have a backbone chassis. The final decision made it much easier to continue a programme of upgrading and design and execution of all mechanical components, the trim and general finish. Thus it was that the production Elan was announced with a chassis, establishing the precedent for all subsequent Lotus road cars.

Hickman was very much left to get on with the design of the M2 himself. Chapman was at this time so preoccupied with the immensely successful rear engined racing car programme that he was content to allow Hickman for whom he had a high regard and who survived the partnership a remarkably long time (1957–67) to evolve the new road car intended to ensure survival. Although Hickman was to some small extent diverted during this early period by the in-service problems of the Elite, most particularly those arising from bodywork discoloration and structural weakness of the final drive unit area, he had by the end of 1961 more or less established the final specification of the Elan. It had not been an easy task and Hickman was often provoked into threatening resignation.

Thrilled by this solution of the problem, Hickman installed his pop-up headlight and the new wing profile on one side of the 3/8 model in place of the "Porsche" one to give a truly "Lotus look": a beautiful wing profile and a clean bumper line. There was now a visually strong horizontal leading edge to the bumper (unlike the original version). The aerodynamic qualities of the design were now the best to date; headlamps could be kept clean and – perhaps the most important aspect – Lotus now had a unique feature on their new car, a "gimmick" which was 100% functional. On seeing it Chapman immediately liked and approved it much to Hickman's relief and amazement.

At this time Lotus had no formal costing techniques in force. There were never any final specifications issued or even drawings on a reliable and systematic basis. No professional estimators were employed and the majority of the costing activity was carried out by John Standen who had served his apprenticeship in the roof space parts department at Hornsey. When eventually a parts list for the Elan became imperative if production were ever to begin, it was found necessary to push a car into a corner of the development shop and strip it down, lay out all the individual components and list them in a process of "retrospective costing and design".

Unlike the Elite which had rapidly reached a relatively stable overall design specification the S2/M2 swung during the design period from the original concept of a cheap basic sports car to an Elite open car replacement and Lotus prime-product. By the time that it eventually appeared at the 1962 London Motor Show the Elan was openly announced as the Elite's replacement, but early supply difficulties necessitated an unwelcome final tranche of Elite production to keep the factory occupied. When one considers in retrospect the extraordinary process of evolution of the Elan and the total *volte-face* represented by the transition from original concept to finished product it is amazing that the result was so satisfyingly homogeneous and for this we must thank Hickman who throughout the extended evolution of the design was there in charge of development. We may never know the full extent of his frustration but we certainly know that Chapman steadfastly resisted Hickman's request to widen the car by 2 in and add a longer nose. That the result was not a really ugly duckling rather than a chubby, cheeky little shape, is a tribute to Hickman's aesthetic sense and patience.

By November 1961 in my "Proposed World Marketing Programme for 1962"

After the running Elan chassis fitted with a modified Falcon Caribbean body which provided road experience for the mechanical elements of the new car, Hickman prepared a virtually definitive version of the Elan seen here bearing a British tax disc with the expiry date May 1963 from which we may assume that it was ready to run in June 1962 – barely four months before the London Show launch. Naturally the car was made in left-hand drive for the prime US market and although unpainted the body shape was nearly resolved, although Hickman subsequently slimmed up the front "chin" of the car as his last modification before finalising the Elan body shape. Subsequently production moulds were prepared from which the "Press Release" car, shown at Ford's headquarters in Regent Street, London, was built.

circulated among the Lotus Board, the M2 was considered for introduction in mid 1962. By late 1961 the Ford Motor Company was taking an active interest in the new car and Chapman had persuaded Ford to allow access for distribution to the world-wide Ford dealer network; a significant and characteristic Chapman coup. Ultimately of course nothing came of this proposed Ford-Lotus association because of the developing nervousness of Ford about the potential reliability problems of the Elan. At this stage neither I nor any of my sales team had officially seen (nor had anyone else of course although we were not aware of that) a prototype of the new car despite frenzied activity by Hickman and his few helpers working on the upper floor of the Development Department. Ian McLeod had been drawn in at an early stage as a good example of an awkwardly shaped (tall, long limbed) customer and had been pushed into Hickman's plywood mock-up of the cockpit interior to measure up internal clearances. On this visit to the "inner sanctum" Ian had seen an early clay mock-up of the new car and (inevitably) volunteered criticism of the door/sidescreen depth relationship which he claimed was graciously accepted and incorporated. This criticism may have been engendered by the use at that stage of an original boxy Herald seat which was later modified and lowered.

While Hickman and his team were developing the body shape and structure others were designing a new power unit for the Elan. At an early stage in the development of the car the idea of using a gently modified version of the Ford pushrod ohv 105E–109E engine had been abandoned. Chapman retained Harry Mundy and Richard Ansdale (Mundy having been with Hassan the designer of the Climax FWA engine and Ansdale a Chapman collaborator on the Lotus progressive change transmission system) to design a twin overhead cam aluminium cylinder head to bolt on to a progressively larger Ford four-cylinder "80-bore" block assembly. The original designs were produced by Harry Mundy early in 1961. Richard Ansdale then took over responsibility for detailing the design during summer of that year and the first cylinder head castings were made locally. It was found that the first castings were unsuitable for machining and Birmid then produced a successful set which were machined by Laystall Engineering to enable the prototype power unit to be made at Cheshunt. As the process developed the proposed capacity of this engine rose from the original 1098 and 1340 cc engines (the prototype successfully ran "on the bench" in October 1961) to the 1496 cc five bearing 116E (later superseded after a short production run by the final 1588 cc version). Preliminary development work on this conversion was conducted from February 1962 with a 1340 cc engine installed in a left-hand drive Ford 105E Anglia family saloon of otherwise standard specification. The highly non-standard performance of this vehicle soon brought local notoriety but it needed a capable racing driver at the wheel to move safely about the countryside at the speeds of which it was capable with about three times the original power jammed under the bonnet.

Steve Sanville remembers discussions between Colin and Gibson Jarvie of United Dominions Trust (then a very active sponsor of racing with their own Team of Lotus GP cars) in which UDT were invited to fund development of the new Lotus engine. Apparently Colin was quite happy for the initials "UDT" to be cast on the cam covers if necessary but nought came of this . . .

The new twin-cam engine was to be manufactured for Lotus by J A Prestwich, the famous "JAP" engine-producing company that had been engaged primarily in the supply of proprietary power units to the motorcycle industry since the early part of the century. Although Cosworth later became involved in development of the M2 engine, they were not concerned with the original design. The twin-cam engine had immense potential for development and at an early stage of its life (before the launch of the Elan) the "Twincam" Twentythree of Jim Clark almost

In this view the 24″ (610mm) rule shows that the Elan headlights are definitely "legal" unlike those of its beautiful predecessor the Elite. The clean bumper line allowed by the Hickman-designed pop-up headlights and marked on this photograph by a black line was subsequently emphasised by the insertion of a strip of "Claylastic" bright trim (developed for the Mini) to "sparkle it up". Note also the edge of the wire mesh radiator grille evolved by Hickman for the Elite and its successor and on which the British registration numbers were mounted to allow the virtually uninterrupted flow of cooling air.

pulled off a win against cars of unlimited capacity at the Nürburgring in May 1962.

In keeping with Chapman's intention that the Elan should avoid repetition of the high production cost of the Elite, the suspension system was designed at the outset to be suitable for production at a much higher volume than hitherto. In this process much of the handmade appeal of the earlier car was lost but on the basis that the Elan was aimed at a less fastidious market than the Elite the relative crudity of execution of its suspension system can be overlooked: the design being no less admirable than before.

The welded tubular front wishbones of the Elite are costly in that much handwork is necessary in the preparation of the tubing itself; the welding of the wishbone requires a complicated jig coupled with the permanent risk that so vital a component may fail in extended service without 100% inspection during

These snapshots taken by Ron Hickman are all that remain of the Falcon Caribbean-bodied "lash-up" of the Elan in which the author rode early in 1962 with Hickman at the wheel. The Caribbean body was intended to provide minimal weather protection to the luckless test drivers who were out to develop the running gear of the Elan. At the same time it achieved a degree of concealment for the unusual contents of the bodywork which was normally fitted to a primitive Ford Popular chassis frame with teetering suspension and sidevalve engine. For my benefit Hickman performed a racing take-off to wind up the rubber doughnuts on the rear driveshafts but apart from that my memory of the experience is of a rattling, flapping and damp progress about the Hertfordshire countryside.

This must surely be the most interesting application of a Falcon body on the most exotic Ford Special of the period. The photograph right shows modifications to the dash area of the Caribbean body to allow the installation of Elan instruments. The photograph left shows alterations to the wheel arch area to permit clearance for the MacPherson Strut rear suspension system. It was also necessary to reduce the length of the Caribbean body to fit the Elan backbone chassis. Apart from adding a floorpan and bulkhead together with a windscreen, these photographs show just about all there was of the so-called bodywork. But lamps, screen and wipers made it "road legal" which was all that was required.

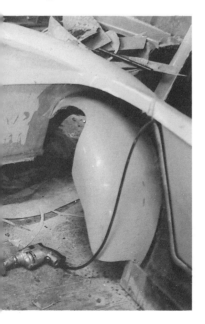

manufacture. So for the Elan, Chapman specified crude, pressed-up sheet steel wishbones for the front suspension, incorporating the same proprietary Alford and Alder uprights as the Elite. The system was partially at least of Lotus design but had none of the intriguing originality of the system first seen on the Twelve Formula Two car.

Chapman finally abandoned his "own" Strut in the Elan application and reverted to a purely MacPherson system in which the drive shaft was relieved of any lateral location duties. A wide-based welded tubular wishbone now performed this function but also largely absorbed the torque load from the outboard mounted disc brakes.

Because this was the first roadgoing application of the MacPherson Strut principle to the rear suspension of a car, there was no proprietary hub casting available for adaptation and the Elan is fitted with an Armstrong-made Strut spring/damper unit shrunk into a Lotus-designed aluminium casting carrying the ball races supporting the hub. We may assume that the rear suspension of the Elan is as it is for purely technical reasons. In the form used it is certainly no cheaper to manufacture than the Series Two Elite Chapman Strut. Whilst retaining the camber-control qualities of its famous predecessor it offers a lower roll centre as a result of the positive lateral location by a wishbone well below hub centre height. Lateral loads on the backbone chassis-mounted differential unit no longer exist and the drive shaft is purely that, now being equipped with doughnut joints to absorb any slight misalignment during suspension movement.

At the point at which I left the company in March 1962 I had not yet seen a complete M2 combining backbone chassis and the intended bodywork, nor could I have seen one unless I had been around in May of that year by which time Ron had put together a rough and ready "runner" embodying most of the final features of the Elan. The fully finished prototype of correct specification only just managed to "make it" to Earls Court in October. Despite the fact that the development team got their Falcon bodied runabout on the road early in 1961 it was not until November 1961 that Ron Hickman produced an air brush drawing of the complete car together with a chassis perspective drawing and a view of the interior. This was well after he had completed his scale model of the car but six months before the real thing finally took to the road. Ron produced his drawing principally to persuade Bristol to keep on with the Elite contract by holding up for them the prospect of a profitable follow-on product. Lacking a concrete sample Ron did his best with a very artistic rendering of the enticing prospect.

In retrospect Ron Hickman is amazed that it took so long to evolve the new car. However, the tiny development team was still engaged in keeping the Elite moving as it constantly generated new problems in production and use and first priority was always accorded to the source of cash flow. Nevertheless, it took well over a year to perfect the running gear of the new car including the development of the final form of the backbone chassis, the faired-in plastic bumpers (a story in itself – Chapman had resisted this feature – one of Hickman's most important automotive innovations) the evolution of the retractable headlamps, sliding windows and the 1001 other details requiring close attention.

The intense concentration on the original challenge of producing an open-top unitary construction body was not, he feels, wasted in the sense that even as a chassis-supported body it retained metal framed door openings, the specially developed bobbins and was still produced to the same overall dimensions by the same Unimould technique. Now the complete Unimoulded body would be lowered on to a free standing fully assembled chassis to which it was attached by means of the bobbins. Without Chapman's folded steel backbone chassis the Elan would never have come to market and Lotus would surely have crumbled away for lack of product in 1963.

Not only did the folded up sheet steel chassis of the Elan speed up the development of this car and thereby save Lotus from early extinction but it also provided a convenient means of displaying the mechanical components at exhibitions. The sheet steel chassis – at first simply a means of getting the mechanical elements on the road for testing but soon after adopted in the basic specification – was designed to fit within the structure of what was originally intended to be another monocoque fibreglass construction car. Chapman subsequently became rather fond of this low cost manner of construction and it features on the company's range to this day. Note the cheap, pressed steel wishbones of the IFS, the reversion at the rear to a MacPherson, rather than Chapman (in which the drive shaft is used for that purpose alone) Strut suspension system and the Lotus twin cam engine – one of the earliest conversions to this up-market layout of a humble production OHV engine. HRG pioneered such series conversions on the Singer SM Hunter engine of 1955 but after Chapman put the idea firmly on the map his example was followed by Fiat and Toyota, among others, to produce a cheap high efficiency engine offering transformed power and character.

Although the Elite had been conceived as a money maker for Lotus the Elan and the Seven Series Two were cars in which commercial considerations were even more strongly to the fore in Chapman's mind. A close study of both reveals that Chapman could happily allow his car design standards to be substantially compromised in the pursuit of economical survival. Nevertheless he always insisted that the commercial product range of the company should be exciting and highly saleable and truly Lotus in spirit (as the original S2 concept so manifestly was not). Nevertheless the £10 backbone chassis frame of the Elan has an "origami" look about it and the front suspension wishbones and other details give the impression of studied cost cutting. The infamous "doughnuts" of the rear suspension, like the easily rusting backbone chassis have spawned a thriving replacement industry manufacturing conventional driveshafts and galvanised backbones (which in 1962 would have cost perhaps £1 or so more than the rusting originals) to keep Elans and later models on the road. Elsewhere on the Elan the exquisite detail work and the almost total rejection of compromise of the Elite is absent. The very practicality of the Elan was a disappointment to me as an admirer of Chapman's perfectionist design skills. On the other hand one must accept the inevitability of this more robust, somewhat unglamorous design which led to the later Elan variants – the + 2 and Europa – and gave Lotus a commercial future after the almost fatal influence of the Elite. The Elite in terms of future development represented a beautiful blind alley whereas the Elan clearly established new Lotus design principles and revealed a practical way forward.

Chapter Five
Commercial Lotus

The launch of the Elite in 1957 at Earls Court stole the Show. The tremendous interest aroused was dissipated by the lengthy wait until the car entered production, its high price coupled with a quickly-gained reputation for unreliability. As a racing car it was supremely successful but to succeed in the sense intended it had to be attractive to a wider circle than the racing fraternity. In this the Elite was a signal failure and a commercial disaster for Lotus.

This section traces our desperate efforts to sell the Elite in what should have been the prime market – the United States of America – where Chapman had created an unholy mess by a combination of commercial ignorance and devil-may-care. At home, declining sales of the Elite forced us to present it as yet another Lotus kit car in October 1961. Every Elite sale was well and truly earned by the labours of the tiny Cheshunt sales team and marked with the sweat of their brow.

The narrative concludes with a summary of the advertising programmes current during my tenure as sales manager, notable for the participation of two outstanding talents – Derek Birdsall the now world famous graphic designer and Michael Boys, who was responsible for some of the very beautiful photographs gracing our advertisements and promotional material.

The first two years at Cheshunt saw the faltering introduction of conventional Motor Industry marketing methods for Lotus.

(i) The Home Market

In just the same way that the period 1959 – 62 was of outstanding interest from a technical standpoint at Lotus so these years saw a series of commercial experiments which broke new ground and enabled the company to survive a period of potential disaster while finding a way ahead.

Today nobody would embark upon a programme of expansion like that of the move from Hornsey to Cheshunt without extensive formal market research and detail planning. Commercial life in those days was very different and the whole Lotus expansion was typically based on hunch and "seat-of-the-pants" decision making. By moving to Cheshunt the potential volume output of Lotus was

That arch enthusiast and Lotus salesman Ian McLeod always carried a selection of snapshots (of which this is a good example) with which to entertain and cajole colleagues and the general public. Here Dawn, Ian's lovely actress wife, in suitable attire is "doing her stuff" by the Seven Series Two "A" demonstrator, bearing that ubiquitous number 8843 AR which popped up on a number of vehicles during and after my time. In 1960 we had not yet encountered the word macho, but this is a macho car by the standards of any age. The dedicated Seven owner hardly ever used the hood and even more rarely the virtually useless pieces of fabric intended to keep water from the elbows (not shown here). Side screens were a thing of the future and even the clamshell wings used on the demonstrator were faintly cissy. Note that when equipped with the sweeping Frayling/ Kirwan-Taylor wings, export type headlights were included in the specification so that even though the driver may not have been able to see through the screen at night, oncoming drivers could see him before he hit them.

increased by at least a factor of five. It was felt that distribution of the Elite could be handled in the UK and US markets by Michael Christie and Jay Chamberlain respectively. Neither of these two enthusiasts and their organisations had any prior experience of acting as a concessionnaire in this manner and both were led into their association with us by the admiration of all things Lotus that Colin knew so well how to exploit.

Because the main thrust of our sales effort with the Elite was towards the American market ("out of sight; out of mind") Michael Christie's UK operation continued to run while I occupied myself with the problems of finding a market for the increasing output of Sevens from Lotus Components. It suited me well to know that Michael Christie was steadily signing up dealers for the Elite and conducting an embarrassingly successful promotional campaign on our behalf. We had a photographic session at Michael's Aylesbury garage with a Seven and Elite and Michael and his entertaining Sales Manager Tony Kirkcaldy produced a series of photographs which were widely used in the Press. The Michael Christie concession ran to the ever increasing frustration of Michael Christie until December 1959 when the last deliveries to him were made. By this time we had established a network for the Lotus Seven and it was therefore relatively straightforward for us to add the Elite to the Lotus franchise of the Seven outlets.

As the new boy in Lotus and as the first member of the organisation who had ever previously been employed in the commercial department of another motor manufacturer, I could initially do no wrong in Chapman's eyes. I quickly realised that it would be impossible to increase Seven sales volume by continuing the established strategy of sales direct to the public. If we were to set up a conventional distribution network, which was the solution I proposed, we had to be certain there was sufficient profit in the Seven to allow a discount to cover the needs of distributor and dealer. Careful consultation with Buyer John Standen and Nobby Clark made it abundantly obvious to me that the Seven in its existing form produced no profit for Lotus even when sold direct to the public. To give a dealer discount would have been catastrophic and therefore it became necessary to conduct an exercise to simultaneously reduce the basic cost of the Seven kit and increase the general attractiveness of the product to a point where we could count on an increased sales volume without a reduction in price. The answer to this problem was the hasty redesign which emerged in April 1960 as the Seven Series Two with ultimately a choice of three power units; Ford 100E (and 105E later) and the BMC A-Series. Initially we planned to set the price at the same figure as for the Series One kit – £499 – but due to Chapman's commitment to the racing car design programme in late 1959, the catastrophic rebuild programme for Seventeens and all the follow-on complications of the move to Cheshunt it became necessary to take a calculated loss in setting up the distribution network by using the Series One to launch the campaign which could wait no longer.

When it came to selecting potential outlets ("Lotus Centres") for the Seven distribution network we turned in the first instance to companies with which there was an existing connection because the owner was a private Lotus competition car customer as in the case of Bill Frost of Shoreham or Tom Dickson of Perth. In the next rank were those whom I felt from a study of their advertisements and reputation might be favourably disposed to us. In this category came Woodyatt of Malvern (the most successful Seven kit sales outlet during 1960) and John Read's Holbay Engineering. It has amused me in recent years to read claims by sundry Lotus dealers to the effect that they are "the oldest continuous Lotus Agents" or that they have been a Lotus dealer "continuously since 1958". In fact the only surviving Lotus outlet in the United Kingdom dating from that early period is Rodney Bloor's Sports Motors (Manchester) Ltd. It takes an exceptional type of motor agent to survive a quarter century of direct exposure to "the Lotus Experience". These early Lotus Centre agents were intensely enthusiastic and threw themselves into the task of selling Seven kits with remarkable success. The production line was humming, Williams and Pritchard could hardly keep up with the pace, beating out compound curvature nose cones and we were delighted with our early success.

I like to feel that the appointment of my namesake John (Holbay) Read opened new vistas for an outstanding engineer and an opportunity to realise his full potential. Up to that point John had been running a relatively modest garage among the sand dunes of remote Hollesley Bay, Suffolk, caring for run-of-the-mill transportation with an occasional Bristol (his great love) to add interest. John Read initially signed an Agency Agreement with Downton in 1960 for Norfolk, Suffolk and Essex which gave him a wide range of conversions which nevertheless did not include Ford. As the trend became clear he later opted to tune the 105E for his own Holbay conversions working scientifically on a dynamometer, subsequently becoming one of the very few engine tuners able to equal or on occasion overtake the achievements of Cosworth.

At that time British engine tuners inclined temperamentally either to the Ford 105E or the BMC A-Series in the small capacity class. Both engines were

LOTUS DERBYSHIRE
David Buxton Ltd.,
Church Street, Spondon, Derby.
Tel.: Derby 55129.

LOTUS DEVONSHIRE
Bovey Motors Ltd.,
Bovey Tracey, Devon.
Tel.: Bovey Tracey 2124.

LOTUS GLAMORGANSHIRE
Maindy Stadium Motors Ltd.,
North Road, Cardiff.
Tel.: Cardiff 32747.

LOTUS GLOUCESTERSHIRE
G. P. Garage,
23 Grosvenor Place S., Cheltenham.
Tel.: Cheltenham 52219.

LOTUS LANCASHIRE
John Evans (Sports Cars) Ltd.,
782-818 Queens Drive, Liverpool 13.
Tel.: Stoneycroft 6424.

Sports Motors (M/C.) Ltd.,
126 Rusholm Road, Manchester 13.
Tel.: Ardwick 3015.

LOTUS LINCOLNSHIRE
P. S. Finney & Sons Ltd.,
Coningsby Service Garage,
Coningsby, Lincoln.
Tel.: Coningsby 374.

- UNRIVALLED ROAD-HOLDING
- PERFECT DRIVER CONTROL
- VIVID PERFORMANCE
- SUPREME SAFETY
- ECONOMICAL OPERATION
- EASE OF ASSEMBLY

LOTUS

LOTUS SUFFOLK
Holbay Sports Cars,
Hollesley, Woodbridge, Suffolk.
Tel.: Shottisham 687.

LOTUS SURREY
Caterham Car Services Ltd.,
36-38 Town End, Caterham-on-the-Hill,
Surrey.
Tel.: Caterham 4276.

Connaught Cars (1959) Ltd.,
Send, Surrey.
Tel.: Ripley 3122.

Crown Garages (Egham) Ltd.,
Egham, Surrey.
Tel.: Egham 54.

Paddy Gaston & Co. Ltd.,
43/51 Richmond Rd., Kingston, Surrey.
Tel.: Kingston 3288.

Pippbrook Garage,
London Road, Dorking, Surrey.
Tel.: Dorking 3891.

LOTUS SUSSEX
Frost's Cars Ltd.,
398 Lower Brighton Road,
Shoreham-by-Sea, Sussex.
Tel.: Shoreham-by-Sea 3584.

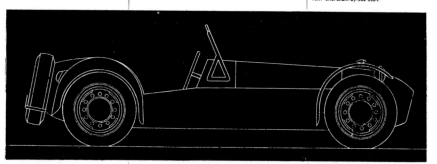

SEVEN

For use with the following power units :

FORD 100E

AUSTIN A35

MINOR 1000

CLIMAX 1100

Manufactured by :

LOTUS COMPONENTS, DELAMARE RD.,
CHESHUNT, HERTS. Waltham Cross 26181

Lincolnshire—continued
Kirk's Motors,
Longdales Road, Lincoln.
Tel.: Lincoln 25974.

LOTUS LONDON
Chequered Flag Ltd.,
492-496 Chiswick High Road,
London, W.4.
Tel.: Chiswick 7871.

Cornwall Garage (Finchley) Ltd.,
Cornwall Ave., Finchley, London, N.3.
Tel.: Finchley 4255.

LOTUS NORFOLK
Boshier of Norwich (Distributors) Ltd.,
Chapelfield Road Garages, Norwich.
Tel.: Norwich 24184.

LOTUS NORTHUMBERLAND
St. Andrews Motors, Ltd.,
Gallowgate, Newcastle-upon-Tyne, 1.
Tel.: Newcastle 2-8333/6.

LOTUS NOTTINGHAMSHIRE
The Chequered Flag (Midland) Ltd.,
5-11 Arkwright Street, Nottingham.
Tel.: Nottingham 89282.

LOTUS PERTHSHIRE
Dickson Motors (Perth) Ltd.,
Viewfield Place, Crieff Road, Perth.
Tel.: Perth 3892.

Sussex—continued
Selsey Motors,
Selsey, Sussex.
Tel.: Selsey 2528.

LOTUS WARWICKSHIRE
Ansty Garage,
Ansty, Warks.
Tel.: Walsgrave-on-Sowe 2569.

Monkspath Garage Ltd.,
Stratford Rd., Shirley, Solihull, Warks.
Tel.: Shirley 1645.

LOTUS WILTSHIRE
Downton Engineering Works Ltd.,
Downton, Wilts.
Tel.: Downton 351.

LOTUS WORCESTERSHIRE
Duford Motors Ltd.,
Headless Cross, Redditch, Worcs.
Tel.: Redditch 229.

Equipe Woodyatt,
Portland Road, Malvern, Worcs.
Tel.: Malvern 390.

LOTUS BELFAST
Easy Built Cars Ltd.,
Bankmore Street, Belfast.
Tel.: Dunmurry 3877.

four-cylinder ohv types, but there the similarity ended. The BMC engine dated back to the Austin A30 power unit of 1951 and was of the long stroke, relatively slow revving type with restrictive inlet and exhaust porting. On the other hand the bore/stroke ratio of the 105E was so over-square (80x48 mm) as to be almost incredible at the time. To Keith Duckworth of Cosworth it was immediately apparent that the generous piston area and low piston speed coupled with eight separate ports of the 105E engine promised unrivalled potential for development. Subsequent events proved him to be entirely correct although the achievement of high power output with reliability from the 105E gave Cosworth a hard task. In 1959–60 however, the A-Series engine – which responded more easily to conventional tuning practice – continued to enjoy a vogue in Club Racing circles and my promotion of the type as a power unit for the Seven was justified by its popularity before 1961, when the superiority of the rival Ford engine had been demonstrated beyond dispute.

The most successful independent tuner of A-Series engines at that time was the late, much lamented Daniel Richmond. A "hot" A-Series Downton engine has a particularly rich and powerful sonority which I found irresistible. The porting arrangements (siamesed inlets and three – one siamesed – exhausts) are inefficient and restricted the potential for exploitation in out-and-out Formula Junior form. However, for the Seven, a "fast road-tuned" Downton A-Series engine was probably the best choice for general use.

Equipe Woodyatt, the Seven distributor for the South Midlands and South Wales had appointed no less than five sub-agent "Centre Stockists" by mid-1960 including Monkspath Garage (a Mecca for the 1172 Special Builder), the GP Garage in Cheltenham, Chris Summers' Ansty Garage, near Coventry, Maindy Stadium Motors of Cardiff and Duford Motors of Redditch. The energetic Geoff Hopkinson of Woodyatt worked harder at the task of developing Seven sales than any other distributor and the results were appropriate.

Closely following the success of Woodyatt was the Chequered Flag with outlets at Chiswick (London) and Nottingham. Chequered Flag owner Graham Warner was one of the outstanding early Elite racers (LOV 1) and at that time was partnered by Alan Foster who subsequently ran the Gemini House Chequered Flag "upmarket" subsidiary at Edgware. Elites at Edgware; Sevens at Chiswick.

David Buxton was the natural choice for Derby. David's name crops up elsewhere in this narrative and characteristically, although like all Lotus Centres he had a clearly defined territory, his advertisements made it clear that he could offer "Free Delivery Anywhere". Buxton's major contribution to Lotus history of the period was his highly successful operation of Team Elite. Some of his later Chapman-related activities are best forgiven and forgotten.

I was nothing if not thorough in covering the ground and no corner of the Kingdom was left without official Lotus representation. In Belfast we had the imaginatively named "Easy Built Cars" as our Northern Ireland distributor. In the extreme North I appointed Dickson Motors of Perth, Scotland, where owner Tommy Dickson – a well established and successful Eleven driver – announced "This Enthusiast's Dream can be Purchased from £99 Deposit". In the deep South West was Bovey Motors of Bovey Tracey, Devon bidding "All Blithe bods welcome". Between these extremes were the Lotus Centres already mentioned together with Dan Margulies of Kensington, London, yet another successful Eleven driver and today a leading classic car dealer, who had first come to my notice in the early Fifties driving an indecently fast ex-Brooklands Talbot 105 with small wheels and fat racing tyres. Dan was so good a salesman that on one of my visits he nearly succeeded in selling me an extraordinarily dilapidated Lancia Augusta Saloon for £75. However, a test drive immediately fortified me to resist temptation.

Two Lotus Centres – Selsey Motors and Kirks Motors of Lincoln were a rather improbable choice but they achieved a modest local success. However, we were fortunate in the appointment of Paddy Gaston – at that time a leading rally driver and a very successful Lotus Seven agent although during 1960/61 he became heavily involved in distribution of the Frank Costin/Jem Marsh Marcos Mk. 2 which at that stage was rather like a slippery Lotus Seven with a lid. From the earliest days we had an agency agreement for the Seven with Caterham Car Services in which Ian Smith had an interest. The significance of this personal connection will not be lost on those who have read the first major attempt to chronicle Lotus achievements *Lotus – the Story of the Marque* of which we always threatened to write "the true version".

Ian Smith ran a successful electrical component business and had competed with a Mk. 6 on the hills and circuits since 1955. He was a close friend of

Chapman and apart from establishing the enduring Lotus Seven Caterham connection, Ian performed a great service to the component car industry by his creation and organisation in the early years of the Racing Car Show – at that time held in the Royal Horticultural Halls, London. The later acquisition by Caterham of the right to continue manufacturing the Seven (without "Lotus") was a happy chance of fate. The Caterham Seven of today is as enjoyable in every way as the early Lotus models although its astronomical price is far removed from that of our humble engine-less offering at £399.

I put the Lotus Centre dealer network into place at high speed and all of them did a remarkable job under very difficult circumstances throughout 1959 and 1960, a year of frenetic activity at Cheshunt as we churned out Elites for the American market and those who had waited two or three years to take delivery at home and on the Continent. It was the time of the astounding success of the Formula Junior Eighteen which without question saved Lotus during its first major financial crisis at Cheshunt. However, we began to run out of commercial steam at the end of 1960 and the underlying reason for this situation lay in the disastrous developments in the United States market where for the small European high performance car manufacturer success was essential. The crisis extending into 1961 arose from the improved ability of the Cheshunt production facilities to supply at a time when sales were falling. The impending disaster had its origins in California but the ultimate responsibility for it lay at our door.

(ii) Trying hard abroad

Having gained much of my previous Motor Industry experience in export I was anxious that we should not neglect the opportunities available in Continental Europe as well as the established North American market. Shortly after joining Lotus I was approached by an organisation staging a "Do-It-Yourself" Exhibition in Rotterdam. In 1959 DIY was a very new thing and newer still in Holland than in the UK. This seemed to be a good opportunity to link up with our new man in the Netherlands, Tony Hildebrand and accordingly I took over a car for exhibition on the Harwich–Hook of Holland Ferry during the night of 3–4 October. The little Lotus aroused immense interest, despite the fact that the Benelux taxation arrangements did not encourage legal evasion via the kit-car loophole as in Britain at that time. Nevertheless, we got good PR coverage and Hildebrand was able to sell a number of cars in the next year or so. Tony Hildebrand was also able to forge a business connection with Downton as a result of his Lotus Agency and my introduction, and subsequently acted as our Netherlands distributor for the Elite, too. My visit to Rotterdam was memorable for a drive on the Dutch Autobahn in an open Mercedes Benz 300SL driven by Hildebrand when we cruised for mile after mile at an indicated 200 plus kph; the fastest on four wheels for me at the time. Hildebrand also taught me the gentle Dutch art of drinking Bols without using the hands.

I decided that we should establish an exclusive distributor in each of the principal European territories. This was done before Britain was a member of the EEC and therefore different rates of import duty and other conditions applied in each of the individual European markets.

Without a doubt our two most enthusiastic continental importers were Hildebrand in Holland and François Staumont of Brussels. I have always considered the Belgians to be difficult as business partners. They strike the hardest bargains and in the case of motor cars even at that time the Belgian market (which has no indigenous manufacturer) was a highly competitive arena where fought a multiplicity of importers seeking a niche for their wares in the face of intense competition. Furthermore from the Lotus point of view there was the agonising Belgian pavé – a traditional cobbled surface which was sufficient to rattle to pieces the most carefully constructed all-metal motor car. Driving on pavé in an Elite – even at 20 mph – gave the impression of imminent collapse of the suspension system and the creaking structure housing it. In dealing with Staumont I had not only to overcome the conventional objections (and there is no one like a Belgian motor dealer to imagine inherent shortcomings in any product for which money is demanded) but I had also to reassure him that in the event of collapse of our cars he would in some way be indemnified against warranty claims. In the end we had to treat him as we subsequently treated others by building into the price structure a cost factor of $2^{1}/_{2}\%$ to allow for the virtually inevitable reconstruction of a major part of the vehicle within the first few months. Staumont was an undoubted Lotus enthusiast and without that enthusiasm the relationship would have died. He had imported the Eleven before my time and therefore knew something of the problems.

It was not necessary to educate him in the strange ways of Lotus parts supply. François would arrive at Cheshunt with a pocketful of banknotes to exchange for parts immediately stowed away in the trunk of his waiting car. He knew that this was the way to get sparkling service from us. Throughout my period at Cheshunt Staumont continued to do his level best with Elite and Formula Junior cars and although we often cursed his nitpicking approach to a company which was frankly not equipped to get involved in any sort of detailed correspondence about anything – particularly disintegrating motor cars – he did better for us than most.

In Germany our agent was Autosport Wolfgang Seidel. On arriving by air to visit him for the first time he met me in an exotic Boano-bodied 250GT Ferrari which was quite a handful on cobble stones in particular. Wolfgang's wife Margot was somewhat younger than he but gave us the impression of being rather neglected. To compensate we always devoted ourselves to her entertainment and under the right circumstances she would demonstrate to us an unforgettable rendering of the Twist with scant regard for the surroundings – on one occasion the concourse of Heathrow airport. Seidel, unlike Staumont, had other strings to his bow and therefore tended to sell Elites on demand. The self-confident Germans, spoiled by the wonderful range of Porsche cars available at the time found difficulty in accepting the all-plastic Elite as a worthy

My Lotus business card with (on the reverse) selected delivery figures to end October 1961. This is an old trick to give the impression to Chapman and any other enquirer that Lotus' Sales Manager is "on the ball" with all information at his fingertips.

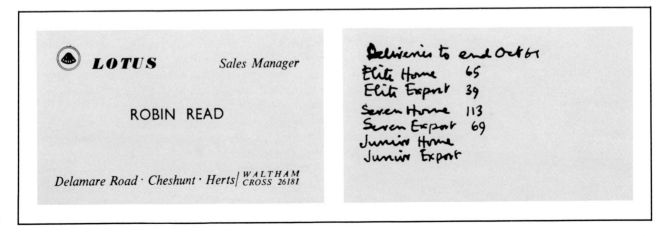

competitor but Seidel sold one to his friend Peter Lindner, successful driver of a Lightweight E-Type Jaguar.

In Switzerland I appointed Hauri Motor Service of Biel (Bienne). Hauri had an excellent but small operation in the German speaking part of Switzerland a few kilometres from Berne. Lotus had traditionally exhibited at the Geneva Motor Show and this was one of "Jabby" Crombac's spheres of influence. The Elite was greatly admired in Switzerland and in France too where British automotive products often acquired a chic corresponding to the response frequently accorded to products marketed in the reverse direction. At this time the Mini had been accorded an instant vogue in France and the popularity of this little car rubbed off on other British motoring products including ours. Regular success at Le Mans also did no harm to our French reputation.

In Portugal, Auto Boavista; Canada, Autosport Equipment; Sweden, Yngve Nystrom; and in Japan, Fuyo Trading Company Limited, struggled against all odds to work with us to sell Elites, Sevens and the racing car range.

Worldwide we had twenty (official and unofficial) Lotus Importers by the end of 1961, none of whom (apart from poor Chamberlain very briefly) ever over-extended our manufacturing resources. We experienced a traditional heavy demand for racing cars at the beginning of each season but what we were desperately striving to achieve was consistent and regular demand for the road going production range. The majority of agents were like so many of our customers: wealthy, successful enthusiasts who made money elsewhere and enjoyed the association with the glamorous Lotus product and reputation. It was not until the Elan went seriously to market in 1963 that Lotus had a suitable product for overseas exploitation.

(iii) The United States of America

The Chapman – Chamberlain Friendship

In 1956 during his first visit to Sebring Chapman met Jay Chamberlain, a gifted race car mechanic and driver who had during 1955 campaigned a Mk. 9 on the West Coast with considerable success. Jay's business life was centred on an imported car dealership in North Hollywood and he had a good knowledge of and appreciation for European cars. This was a crazy time for the imported car. It was possible over a short period to sell almost anything small and European whether it was a genuine sporting car such as an MG or Triumph or even a vehicle as totally unsuited to that market as the Renault Dauphine. The really improbable car that sold "like it was going out of style" as Chamberlain would say, was the ubiquitous Beetle – so diametrically opposed in every way to standard Detroit Iron and advertised everywhere by the simple medium of billboards showing the Beetle in full colour with a price tag as the only written message.

The whole of Europe's sports car industry had been churning out its best products for shipment to the other side of the "Big Pond". On my arrival in 1960 the odd early Testa Rossa Ferrari was still able to win minor events and California and the Mid West in particular teamed with racing OSCAs, Maseratis, Abarths, Porsches and other exotica rarely seen in the UK. Into this established heavy metal charged the featherlight Lotuses which while they held together were capable of winning races against more expensive Italian and German opposition. When Chamberlain and Chapman met, the Lotus star was in the ascendant and Chapman was flattered by the attentions and fulsome praise of the charming and

A reminder of the happier days before I met Jay Chamberlain is this well known photograph of Jay (left) and Herbert Mackay Frazer on a ceremonial lap of Brands Hatch on the bonnet of the Héchard-Masson Le Mans Team Lotus Eleven here driven by Chapman to commemorate the class win of 1957. Shortly after this photograph was taken Mackay Frazer was killed but the business relationship between Chapman and Chamberlain flourished happily for two more years.

assured Chamberlain who was so successfully racing and promoting the Hornsey product. Having spent so much time with both of them I can understand how easily their friendship would have developed in those halcyon days. Chapman in the right mood (or when it suited him) could present an unusual combination of Britishness with his moustache and sober haircut while displaying a sense of humour and fun with accompanying flashing smile and a total absence of stuffiness and the air of superiority that can so infuriate our transatlantic brethren. Equally, Chamberlain could exude charm and enthusiasm in abundance, but by the time that we met in April 1960 this had largely evaporated thanks to the Elite Saga and its effect on his morale and material wellbeing. The two Cs were made for each other and formed a mutual admiration society that endured until mid 1959 although by that time the heady joy of the early years was fading rapidly .

Chapman persuaded Chamberlain to come to England in 1956 and shortly thereafter Jay was advertising his new position as "Exclusive West Coast Distributor for Lotus Sports Racing Cars". In the following year Chamberlain returned to Europe and in this most memorable period of his association with Chapman was invited to drive an Eleven (with his close friend Mackay Frazer) at Le Mans. Lotus had an outstandingly successful race with victories in 750 (Allison/Hall) and 1100 (Chamberlain/Frazer) classes with the coveted Index of Performance award (Allison/Hall – with Chamberlain/Frazer runners-up),

UNITED STATES DISTRIBUTOR
JAY CHAMBERLAIN AUTOMOTIVE, INC.

Jay Chamberlain commissioned artwork for an early promotional campaign for the Elite of which this is a typical example showing one of the very early Series One cars sent over for the 1959 Sebring Twelve Hour Race. In the form shown here the illustration has been reproduced by the German Lotus Seven Club as a postcard and is available through Club Lotus.

hitherto the exclusive preserve of the French, finally snatched for Britain. In the following year 1958, Chamberlain driving his favourite Fifteen with Pete Lovely, retired from the 24 hour race. The injuries that he sustained at Reims in the previous year had taken a long time to heal and may well have sapped his competitive spirit. One can be sure that the car was paid for by the driver but to be selected for Le Mans was a great honour and the fact that Chamberlain won the vital 1100 cc class in 1957 set the seal on the Chapman-Chamberlain association. At the time that Chamberlain was injured at Reims poor Mackay Frazer was killed and this was the first of the great personal losses from motor racing accidents experienced by Chapman which included the one-legged Alan Stacey (1960) and worst of all (because of the long perfection of their collaboration) Jim Clark in 1968. These bereavements were deeply affecting to Chapman and there is no doubt that when he made his few great friendships based on reciprocal admiration between designer-mentor and brilliant driver willing to accept him in this role, they were of enduring strength. Such friends were friends indeed.

When Chamberlain saw the Elite he realised that here was a perfect car for the Californian market. It had style, uncompromising European looks and that unique Lotus speed and handling combination that endeared him to Chapman's sports racing cars. As an established and successful trader – albeit on a modest scale – Chamberlain knew the ropes of the imported car business and the two agreed that Chamberlain should hold the sole US concession for the Elite. In this act lay the first potential flaw in the jewel of their association. Chapman understood perfectly well what "sole" and "concession" meant. However, he was intensely forgetful when overwhelmed by dollars, and exclusive agents had to learn to turn a blind eye to sundry "black" imports arriving in their territory as the personal baggage of enthusiasts back from the European tour.

First find the finance . . .

Before Chamberlain could operate effectively as the sole importer for what Chapman intended to be by Lotus standards a high volume product, he had to find finance on a far greater scale than hitherto. Let us not forget that before 1957 Chamberlain's experience of the imported car business was as a gifted mechanic and driver at that stage just beginning with imports of the Eleven to gain experience of handling relatively large transactions. None of us knew the true extent of the promises made, but one could guess that Chapman would have promised Chamberlain all that was required to enable the latter to arrange a large line of credit to underwrite the establishment of the Cheshunt factory and Elite production within it.

Chamberlain decided to separate the Elite import concession from his other activities under the umbrella of a new corporation: Lotus Cars of America Inc. By 1959 when cars began to arrive, this "paper" operation was based with Jay Chamberlain Automotive Inc. (from whom you could buy an Elite at retail) at 4110 Lankershim Boulevard, North Hollywood. California abounded with wealthy amateur enthusiasts and it was not long before Jay wooed and won as the guarantor of his letters of credit Dr. John Briggs, scion of the founding family controlling the Briggs and Stratton industrial power unit corporation. John ("Jack") Briggs was a modest, shy, charming man with a liking for fast cars and planes and the glamour surrounding them. Chamberlain had learned the ropes quickly from Chapman. Despite his inherited personal wealth, Dr. Briggs was recognised as an outstandingly successful chest surgeon and was dedicated to his career in the medical world. He had two junior partners, one a specialist in vasectomy who had reputedly snipped his way to a fortune from what was at that time a novelty in California and unheard of in Europe. We discussed it in hushed tones.

Dr. Briggs must have wondered what all the fuss was about because months passed before examples of the product for which funding had been arranged arrived on the scene in March 1959. For the 1959 Sebring Endurance Race – vital as a shop window for sports cars aimed at the US market – Chapman sent over two cars, neither of which was in full racing trim. Chamberlain and he drove them to a rather unimpressive 21st overall (Chapman) and DNF (Chamberlain). The two cars were then shipped to the West Coast for exhibition and to canvass sales. Chamberlain spent large sums on advertising, appointing dealers and in creating unfulfilled demand. Four more cars arrived in July but 1959 dragged on and by the end of that year the ether between North Hollywood and Cheshunt was carrying regular waves of invective between the two former friends; one of whom had passed more than a year geared up to sell cars which even now were only beginning to appear in a trickle. In March 1960 Chapman made his annual pilgrimage to Sebring but Chamberlain stayed put in North Hollywood utterly disillusioned by the turn of events. Chamberlain and Chapman had astonishingly similar temperaments characterised by extremes of emotion extending to screaming rage and wailing and gnashing of teeth as the need arose. Chapman now became worried by the threats of refusal to extend letters of credit arriving from nearly bankrupt Chamberlain and his impatient backers and decided that the time had come to dust off the olive branch. By this point in my career at Cheshunt I had demonstrated that deep cracks in Lotus' reputation could be papered over by a new and positive approach. I suspect that Chapman felt that I would represent new hope to Chamberlain which might just calm him down and ensure the continuing availability of funds. The crunch came at the end of March 1960 after Chapman's return from Florida when a letter arrived from Chamberlain (certainly prompted by Jack Briggs and his partners) insisting that there must now be an immediate improvement in both number and quality of Elites supplied if we were to have any chance of entering a market grown accustomed to the Teutonic efficiency of Porsche and the sophisticated engineering of Alfa Romeo. Chapman grabbed the telephone and told Chamberlain to stand by for the arrival of his new Sales Manager who would sort out everything. Fortunately Peter Warr's sister worked at the US Embassy in Grosvenor Square and was able to speed up the issue to me of a visa on 24th March. On 2nd April 1960 I entered the United States for the first time at San Francisco having followed the Polar route with a refuelling stop at Gander in a Boeing 707 – a real marvel at that time. From San Francisco I immediately flew on by propjet Lockheed Electra – then enjoying a macabre reputation for suffering mainspar failure and accordingly obliged to "fly low, slow and dangerous" to Los Angeles and thence (because my booking was nothing if not thorough) by helicopter to North Hollywood. I was the only passenger on board the helicopter for this leg of the journey and shared the freight compartment with the local mails, deafened by the screaming rotor gearbox. That was my first helicopter flight and I have never liked them since.

In at the deep end

Imagine a jet-lagged, lonely, but determined figure clad in British sports jacket and grey flannels stepping into the Californian warmth of a deserted heliport clutching a suitcase – at the tender age of 26 the innocent and unsuspecting envoy of the apprehensive Chapman. The outcome of the task that must now be undertaken would govern the future course of Lotus in that the company's survival depended absolutely on a swift resolution of the conflict with Chamberlain. The tone of the tragicomedy that followed was set by the henchman sent by Chamberlain to bring me back to headquarters.

My driver turned out to be a sort of elderly minder. He introduced himself to me as "Tiger" explaining that he was commercial advisor to Chamberlain and the father of the new Lotus Cars of America Wholesale Sales Manager to whom he referred as "Tiger Cub". For this narrative we will adopt those names. Tiger led me to a huge Chrysler Sedan with the inevitable air-conditioning system and wafted me in luxury to Lankershim Boulevard – still today very much a centre of imported car activity. Chamberlain's premises incorporated a modest showroom with adjacent servicing booths and a secure parking area. His windowless fully air-conditioned office was behind (or "in back of" as he would say) the showroom. I was led into his presence and he remained seated, regarding me with a sullen air as we shook hands and I was grudgingly invited to sit down.

"Why has that ba-a-astard (enunciated lingeringly) sent you over? Is he scared to come himself?"

I felt uneasy and muttered a few platitudes.

"Chicken shit!" shouted Chamberlain "That man's screwing me."

He slowly got the frustration out of his system and I began to understand why Chapman had sent me as the sacrificial lamb with no more than a sketchy and very one-sided view of events leading up to the crisis. I had been so engaged by the task of setting up UK and European distribution for the Seven and had hardly had time to get to grips with the problems now flooding in upon us as the Elite began to go to market.

Since the arrival of the 1959 Sebring cars barely 50 more Elites had been shipped from England, but few had completed the long sea journey via the Panama Canal to Los Angeles by April 1960. Chamberlain had set up a string of agents between San Diego and San Francisco along the Camino Real and these few cars were inadequate to feed the hungry market. There were many niggling problems with the first consignments of Elites and no spares available to resolve them. From the beginning Chamberlain had been obliged to cannibalise complete cars for parts and with such sophisticated opposition in the market place this was the route to disaster. By now interest in the Elite was rising strongly. Chamberlain had campaigned his ex-Sebring car in local events and *Road and Track* (January 1960) printed a somewhat hesitant joint road test of this car (which they disliked – "our first ride in an Elite was disappointing") and one of the first Cheshunt cars which arrived just in the nick of time. The pressure to supply the market was intolerable.

Chamberlain decided that Tiger Cub should drive me Northwards to San Francisco to placate all the Californian Elite dealers. Fortunately we found them considerably more relaxed than their Importer. Our furthest point North was to visit Rod Carveth, the man responsible for San Francisco sales. Rod came from a wealthy East Coast wine-producing family and had raced a Testa Rossa Ferrari and other exotica before becoming involved with Lotus. He was a typical enthusiastic dilettante-turned-car salesman – an old Chamberlain friend, perhaps chosen for all the wrong reasons. Carveth and his wife lived in a typically Californian wooden mansion with two Dobermann pinscher dogs who regarded me with baleful glares as they lay on the thick woollen rugs strewn on the floor of the huge living area.

Tiger Cub promised me an evening to remember in San Francisco; taking me to Finocchio's nightclub which on close examination was seen to be peopled with extraordinary folk whom I eventually calculated must be lesbian, transvestite or worse. This was long before Lord Arran's liberalising Sexual Offences Bill, and I was a little shocked. The cabaret was astonishing for the time. There were several staggeringly beautiful young ladies in the chorus who on removing their clothes turned out to be members of the opposite sex. The star turn was a very youthful Danny la Rue making his North American debut. I was expected to know all about my famous compatriot, but in fact had never heard of him until that day. I must say he revealed a very high standard of talent to our American cousins. I enjoyed the evening but left behind the bearded ladies and balding queens without regret.

On our return to North Hollywood after a week's absence Tiger again took charge of me. On one occasion he led me to a barber shop for a haircut while he at the same time had a shave, facial massage and accompanying removal of surface imperfections while bombarding me with his usual paeons of praise for Chamberlain: "Jay's a charger" and Tiger Cub: "Finest Salesman in the West". He asked me what I would most like to see in the way of entertainment as his guest before I returned to England and I suggested a Burlesque show thinking naively and in ignorance that this might have something to do with cowboys. I am happy to say that in contrast to my experience in San Francisco the ladies of the Burlesque show were entirely female and gave me my introduction to the famous American bump and grind routine which is never done quite so well elsewhere.

Chamberlain was as opinionated and dismissive as Chapman, but at a lower level of intensity, as in all things. He developed a negative attitude towards the Elite as a competition car, possibly as a combination of his developing antipathy towards racing following the nasty accident to his arm at Reims in 1958 and the disappointing performance of the two Sebring Elites in 1959. On the few occasions that I watched him race in California his once obviously superior talent was on the wane, and after his abortive attempt to make a racing comeback in Europe during 1961 he completely abandoned that pursuit on his return to the States. Chamberlain's European racing venture (with Formula Junior and Formula One Lotus Eighteens) was a saddening gesture of defiance by the jilted former Chapman friend, incapable of believing that the man in whom he had vested so much trust, could (as he saw it) reject and nearly destroy him. To those of us who knew the circumstances and the men concerned, it was upsetting to see the bewildered, once carefree Lotus-eater vainly attempt to recapture the former joys of his association with the glamorous Chapman circle and to re-enter a world of which he was once a vitally important element.

However lukewarm Chamberlain may have been towards the Elite as a track car (and the tormented saga of the SCCA classification and re-classification of the Elite so that it ended up lumped with 300SL Mercedes, Porsche Carreras and Jaguars in C Production did nothing to encourage owners to compete against massive odds) he wholeheartedly believed in it as a Grand Tourer, while it continued to tour grandly. The Lotus association for Chamberlain was very much the ultimate ego-trip (as it was for so many others from the earliest days of Chapman's activities) and he relished particularly involvement with the more exotic models beginning with his first Mk. 9 in 1955 and including the Fifteen he owned when I met him. It was no surprise that there was not a Seven to be seen anywhere in the Chamberlain organisation on display or even listed for sale. Perhaps he remembered the funny old Mk. 6 – rather obviously home built and reminiscent of Californian hotrods – and so regarded the bottom of the range cycle-winged Lotuses as peculiarly suitable for the peasantry of Europe. However, my activities since joining Lotus had been largely concentrated on getting the Seven moving as a commercial venture, and I therefore arrived in North Hollywood fired with proselytising zeal for "my baby".

The Lotus Seven America

The occasional Seven had reached the US prior to 1960 – some privately imported, others brought in by sporting dealers including Chamberlain on

Early Americas were fitted with virtually standard Sprite engines of 48 bhp. We chromium-plated the valve cover but retained the standard inlet and exhaust manifolds. Later Downton in particular produced highly successful conversions for the Seven "A" series engine installation which gave the car up to Formula Junior power output to propel 450 kilos of motor car. Downton themselves had a Seven to this specification which I was invited to drive in the Brighton Speed Trials (standing start kilometre). The getaway (in pouring rain) with limited slip differential was more than impressive and the rate of climb such that the water in the flooded undertray was driven violently up my flapping trouser legs.

occasion, but there was no concerted effort to promote the type. Early in 1960 we had received a visit from Gei Zantzinger and his sales manager of Suburban Foreign Car Service Inc, Philadelphia. Although this visit was prompted by the troubles created by Chapman's forgetful but characteristic appointment of two "exclusive" East Coast Importers (of which more anon), I took advantage of the contact to open discussions about the Seven. Zantzinger was enthusiastic – apart from being a member of a wealthy Pennsylvanian colliery owning family he was a passionate motorcyclist for whom the Seven was a relatively civilised mode of transport and one he understood well. We promised to give the Seven a new lease of life for the US market by revising the specification and Zantzinger placed his orders – independently of Chamberlain of course – who although he automatically objected to the arrival on the scene of rival Lotus importers was only in fact considered by Chapman to be "exclusive" thoughout the US for the Elite at this time despite having had the complete franchise granted to him in 1958 during the honeymoon period.

"You'll never sell that here" said Chamberlain when I broached the subject on my April 1960 visit. "Too goddam expensive, crude and crappy". I told him that Sevens were on the way to Suburban and that he could not ignore the interest. The odd Seven that Chamberlain had encountered earlier was to the British kit-car specification; either with Climax FWA or Ford 100E sidevalve ("L-head" in the US) power. The former (the Super Seven) was very expensive indeed, and awkwardly comparable with that "mainline" Lotus 1100 cc competition car the Eleven, which won all the races, made money and was loved by Chamberlain and his dealers. The Seven F with old fashioned iron engine was frankly way off beam for the US, where Ford L-head engines whether with four or eight cylinders were hopelessly old-hat.

But the good news that I brought was that we had developed a Seven exclusively for the US market; taking into account previous criticism and at last exactly what was needed. Chamberlain mustered a modicum of enthusiasm as I told him the specification. One of my first acts on taking over responsibility for sales was to extend the appeal of the Seven beyond the 1172 Formula racer (F-Type) and very occasional oddball driver (C-Type FWA Climax). Sales had dwindled to virtually nothing and the Seven needed a shot in the arm for the British market. This was initially accomplished by adapting the Series One car as it would soon be known to accept the 948 cc "A" series engine and gearbox from the Morris Minor, A35 and other BMC models and "majoring" on this as the top of the line. The "F" was demoted and the superb "C" Super Seven hardly got a mention in my new brochure, but could be had "if desired". The new Seven "A" would provide a basic car to accept tuning equipment from Downton, Speedwell and others up to Formula Junior (70 bhp) standard and would result in a relatively low cost, high performance sportster. Of course while all this was going ahead, Chapman, the Development department and John Standen the Lotus Buyer were frantically redesigning the Seven into what would be known as the Series Two, and hopefully its lower cost would allow us to make a little profit from the loss-leader Seven range.

The Seven "A" Series One, rarity that it is, is one of the nicest versions of this classic Lotus, but we had to make more changes to the basic car before it could be considered suitable for the US market. Morris Minors were commonplace in the UK but rare indeed across the Atlantic. We therefore chose the Austin-Healey Sprite power unit for it, knowing that parts and service facilities were available throughout the US. A full set of "options" was standardised including wire wheels, FIA specification canvas "doors", tonneau cover, carpet, spare wheel and "proper" windscreen wipers. Even the side-mounted silencer was chromium plated and suitable mountings were provided for US license plates. But the most striking feature of all was the appearance of new long "clam shell" front fenders replacing the cycle-type wings fitted hitherto. These were designed and moulded by Kirwan-Taylor and Frayling and were so skilfully conceived, executed and elegant that they eventually became standard wear on subsequent models although initially being reserved to Americas and Super Sevens.

This little car started something and from that point the Seven became accepted in the US and a particularly successful car in SCCA racing events where with the correct tuning and skilful driving it was competitive with almost anything on a twisted circuit. With the co-operation of David Phipps in the UK and Suburban working with *Sports Car Illustrated* in the US we managed to get the Seven America on to the front cover of the June 1960 issue of this most prestigious journal. The road test within was largely the work of Phipps who had tried the car in the UK with photographs taken in Pennsylvania just in time to catch the SCI closing date for copy in March. Even Chamberlain ordered a batch of Seven Americas when I sweetened the bitter pill with a promise of early delivery of Formula Junior Eighteens.

I cultivated Karl Ludvigsen, Editor of *Sports Cars Illustrated,* and my pressure, aided by Jay Chamberlain, resulted in the excellent publicity of the June 1960 issue of *SCI* which featured the new Seven (Series I) America with Sprite engine on its cover and also included tests of the racing Elite and Eighteen Formula Junior cars. David Phipps provided a great deal of help from the UK by conducting the Eighteen test by remote control at Goodwood and he was also responsible by a similar sleight of hand for the Elite write-up. The Seven test was an Anglo-American cooperation by Phipps in England and Mike Davis on the other side of the Atlantic. The Lotus message certainly dominated that issue and sales of the Seven and Formula Junior cars benefited accordingly. Nobody doubted that the Elite in racing form was a good proposition and they didn't really need to be told so again. What we would have preferred would have been a favourable touring test but even at that stage the reputation of the Elite for use off the track was already tarnished.

THE MERCEDES-BENZ 300SL STORY— WITH CUTAWAY

SPORTS CARS ILLUSTRATED

50¢ JUNE 1960

design·economy·competition

HOW TO DRIVE THE JAGUAR XK150 IN COMPETITION·BY WALT HANSGEN

3 LOTUSES TESTED

SPARKLING NEW SEVEN
RACING ELITE
FORMULA JUNIOR

ROAD RESEARCH REPORT— AUSTIN 850 and ITS RELUCTANT REVOLUTIONARY DESIGNER

During my ten day diplomatic mission to Chamberlain he relaxed sufficiently to invite me to join him in meeting that famous early Elite owner and Chapman friend Chris Barber at Los Angeles Airport as he arrived for his first US appearance at the Hollywood Bowl Jazz Festival. Thoughtfully, Chamberlain provided his famous guest with an Elite for use while in LA. On the following day we had tickets for the Festival and sat under the stars in the balmy night air listening to the Greats – including Count Basie, Louis Armstrong, The Fire House Five, and of course Chris himself. It was a highlight of my visit "out West" and with my head ringing with Jay's stern admonishments and personal messages polite and otherwise for Colin and with my mind full of impressions and memories I flew across to New York to get to grips with a gnawing problem that had reached dangerous proportions and which was another reason for my visit to the United States.

Life among the lawyers

American commercial law is full of pitfalls for the unwary. At this time there existed a whole raft of so called Anti-Trust legislation designed originally to prevent the creation of monopolistic cartels intended to tie up a market and exclude competition. Regrettably the laws concerned tended to be born out of over-reaction and now that the danger had largely passed, were frequently counter-productive in that they fostered petty litigation and often impeded the creation of efficient marketing arrangements. One suspected that the prime purpose of the Anti-Trust legislation was now to protect domestic industry from imported goods and keep the rapacious US legal system well rewarded. Chamberlain and Chapman had walked head first into the Anti-Trust trap probably out of pure ignorance and a mighty row was now brewing up. Lotus Cars of America Inc was on shaky ground in its attempts to reserve the overall US Lotus franchise for itself. Chamberlain had grudgingly compromised to some extent by allowing European Motors Inc. of Detroit and Suburban Foreign Car Service of Philadelphia to import Lotus sports racing cars but he was determined that the Elite – which he saw as the big money spinner – should be his alone.

In addition to the reluctantly accepted Surburban Foreign Car Service, there was another "exclusive" East Coast Importer who had "just happened to do a deal with Colin". This was Sy Kaback's Grand Prix Imported Cars of Rutherford, New Jersey. Now Gei Zantzinger had unhelpfully decided that Suburban, a few hundred miles south of Grand Prix was the legal East Coast distributor. Furthermore he was going to sue and slap an injunction on Kaback,

I understand that it is nowadays difficult to obtain permission to use the Lotus logo or badge without running the risk of legal action. However, in the good old days, everybody borrowed Lotus graphics if they felt that it would help the commercial cause. Here is a nice little sticker made by Sy Kaback a long way from Cheshunt to promote his East Coast distributorship. Hopefully Hethel will not object to its reproduction in these pages.

Chamberlain, Lotus and anyone else who disagreed. Delightful person though he is, Zantzinger was mad at Chapman and Lotus in general and, what was worse, he had the resources and determination to do something about it. Were he to succeed in this action, all exports of Lotus to the States would have halted forthwith.

This was serious and so on arrival at New York I reported to another Chapman friend, John Dugdale, the US representative of the British Automobile Manufacturers Association which maintained a very smart office suite in Fifth Avenue. John Dugdale is a pillar of the British Motoring Establishment and by the time of our meeting already had a distinguished career behind him which he has chronicled in his enthralling book *Great Motor Sport of the Thirties* (1977). John began his working life on the staff of *Autocar* magazine and since that time has done many fascinating things – always in the world of motoring. At the time of writing he plays a vital part in the Jaguar and MG world of North America.

In 1960 John was very much "Our Man in New York" and although I was small fry in the order of things, nothing was too much trouble for him as far as I was concerned. Apart from entertainment extended to me in his home by John and his beautiful Guatemalan wife Carmen, he was constantly available to me for advice and guidance. To help me resolve the legal wrangle looming ahead he directed me to a New York Law practice where the Lotus case was assigned to a Senior Partner – Mr. Honey. The firm was principally concerned with Customs legislation which was inextricably linked to Anti-Trust law and the perennial US concern to avoid the "dumping" of goods from low labour cost sources to the detriment of local industry. If a complaint was made that imported goods were too cheaply supplied US Customs and Excise would levy a countervailing duty based on a notional cost of production calculated to restore the balance. So any serious importer needed a good lawyer who could operate with equal facility in the fields of Anti Trust and Customs legislation. In one celebrated case Mr. Honey and his Partners had saved several million dollars for Lodge Plugs and this had established their reputation in motor industry circles. Fortunately they had a close association with the law firm of Glad & Tuttle of Los Angeles which later was to prove very useful to us as the nightmare of Chapman's US legacy became clear.

The fourth Lotus importer in addition to Chamberlain, Zantzinger and Kaback was John Posselius of European Motors Inc. The EMI responsibility was the Mid-Western region centred on Detroit and Chicago; after the West Coast the most important market for imported cars. Thankfully Chapman had only appointed one exclusive importer/distributor in this area – and that with Chamberlain's grudging acceptance – and our relationship with Posselius was always as friendly and successful as one could hope under the generally difficult circumstances. By comparison with the rest of the distribution network European Motors never gave us the slightest legal hassle and this had a great deal to do with the temperament and personal circumstances of John Posselius the controlling shareholder. John had spent much of his life in the bosom of the US Auto Industry, was married to a member of the Chrysler family and lived in splendour in Grosse Pointe Farms, residential nerve centre of the Auto Industry Establishment. Posselius and his associates had made a great success of their Mid-West distributorship of the Triumph sports car range and by comparison any business that they might do with Lotus would be seen as a minor interest although very much in tune with their personal enthusiasm. Posselius had seen manufacturer/importer aggravation before and was therefore well able to tolerate the occasional transgression.

The opposite was the case on the East Coast where both Suburban and Grand Prix were newcomers to the relatively "big time" represented by Lotus. Jay

Chamberlain was determined to hold unto himself the Elite for as long as he possibly could in order to recoup his massive investment in launching the car on the US market. He was determined that no other company should import Elites from us and throughout 1960 we maintained this exclusivity, influenced no doubt by the huge letter of credit which with buoyant Formula Junior Sales at home and abroad represented our main prospect of survival. However, Chamberlain had to accept as *fait accompli* that we were supplying cars other than the Elite to his own sub-distributors as direct importers and acceptance of this situation was formalised by the data panel for the Lotus Seven America road test appearing in Sports Cars Illustrated of June 1960. Although Chamberlain was prepared to allow Lotus Cars of America to appear on an equal footing with Suburban and European Motors (but not Grand Prix Imported Cars) in the case of the Seven he resisted it completely for the Elite and the SCI road test in the same issue included only the name of Lotus Cars of America Inc. as importer.

The Elite fades fast

By April 1960 Chamberlain's feelings about Lotus were coloured by the fear that he had embarked on a disaster course. Because he was exposed and alone in the fiercely competitive Californian market place – capital of the high performance car world – he saw this more clearly than any of us at the time. Chamberlain and I got on well despite the fact that I was never able to restore his relationship with Chapman, irretrievably damaged by what Jay regarded as incessant and unforgivable abuse of his personal friendship. I therefore concentrated on reassuring him of our long term intention to work wholeheartedly with him and his financial backer Dr. John Briggs. Nevertheless the resultant easing of his fears and the effect of that on his commercial judgement, leading to a willingness to become more deeply involved with us in 1960 contributed to his eventual personal and commercial undoing.

On returning to Cheshunt from North Hollywood I made every effort to ensure that no effort was spared to support Chamberlain by fostering increased Elite production and shipment to California. By the time that I returned to Los Angeles five months later on 21 September, we had shipped a further 100 cars which under normal circumstances would have provided an adequate flow to support the small Californian network of dealers and to enable Chamberlain to begin at last to exploit the East Coast and Mid Western markets.

Sadly the improved rate of supply failed to ease his problems. With the benefit of hindsight it is easy to see that both Chamberlain and Chapman were then ill-equipped to understand what was involved in the successful acquisition and retention of a position in the US performance car market. At that time Chamberlain represented to Chapman the Golden Goose which would fund Lotus during the build up of production before and after the move to Cheshunt. Any visitor to the USA at that time saw how Volkswagen (and in the high performance market its first cousin Porsche), had achieved success by massive investment in parts and service training before beginning to ship cars for sale. VW and Porsche too were obsessed with manufacturing quality and this combination gave them such high levels of success with a virtually obsolescent product. Porsche were buoyed up by the close association with Volkswagen although Max Hoffman the Porsche importer of the time was not averse to insisting that each highly desirable and instantly saleable Porsche 356 car had to be accompanied by a couple of the relatively unpopular Lancias or Alfas for which he also held the concession. Nevertheless, the profitability of the Porsche line was such that dealers could afford to knock out the Lancias at least at cost and with a lot of grumbling.

The US market for sports and competition cars at this time was dominated in

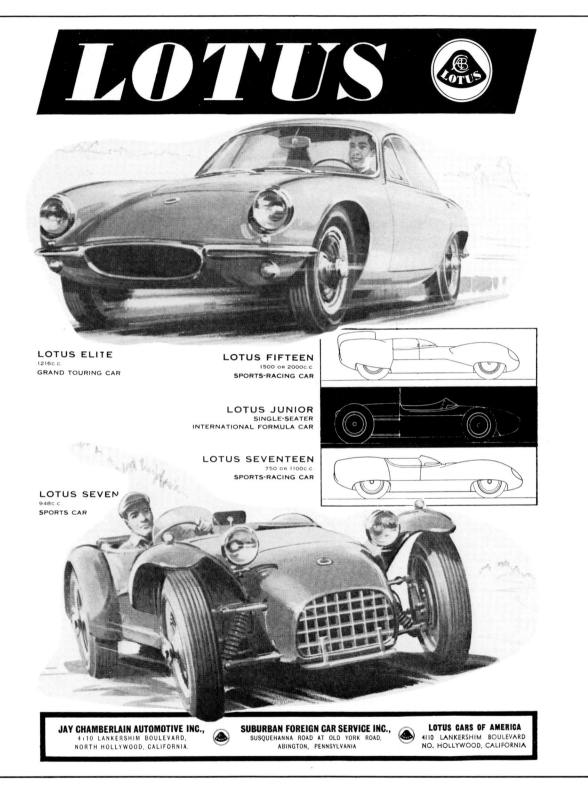

LOTUS

LOTUS ELITE
1216 c.c.
GRAND TOURING CAR

LOTUS FIFTEEN
1500 OR 2000 c.c.
SPORTS-RACING CAR

LOTUS JUNIOR
SINGLE-SEATER
INTERNATIONAL FORMULA CAR

LOTUS SEVENTEEN
750 OR 1100 c.c.
SPORTS-RACING CAR

LOTUS SEVEN
948 c.c.
SPORTS CAR

JAY CHAMBERLAIN AUTOMOTIVE INC.,
4110 LANKERSHIM BOULEVARD,
NORTH HOLLYWOOD, CALIFORNIA.

SUBURBAN FOREIGN CAR SERVICE INC.,
SUSQUEHANNA ROAD AT OLD YORK ROAD,
ABINGTON, PENNSYLVANIA

LOTUS CARS OF AMERICA
4110 LANKERSHIM BOULEVARD
NO. HOLLYWOOD, CALIFORNIA

Chamberlain was fed up with the lack of general promotional support (come to think of it – any support at all) from England, and because Chamberlain's advertisements were rather anaemic the author prepared this "busy" advertisement for use in the US Press during early 1960. The version shown here was printed virtually unaltered for the British market *(Motor Sport)* despite the Elite having left-hand drive and the Seven clearly a Series One America at a time when the Series Two car was available on the home market. Both the Fifteen and Seventeen, although still listed and supplied, were very much *passé* but Chamberlain still had some to sell so we stuck them in for good measure. Note that at this stage politics ruled that Chamberlain appeared both as importer (Lotus Cars of America) and retail outlet from the same address while only Gei Zantzinger's Suburban Foreign Car Service was admitted as an alternative source in view of the litigation pending between Suburban, Lotus and Sy Kaback's Grand Prix Imported Cars of Rutherford, NJ.

the lower price sectors by British manufacturers while the upper strata were the preserve of Ferrari, Maserati and Mercedes-Benz. However, the vital sports car middle market was dominated by Porsche with Jaguar and Alfa Romeo in hot pursuit while innumerable other minor marques – including "exotics" such as Abarth, OSCA, Elva (and Lotus of course) controlled the competition car market and now increasingly were looking to enter the commercial sports car sector, too.

Chamberlain and Chapman were absorbed by the need to overcome complete car supply shortages. There were never sufficient parts available from Cheshunt to provide a proper back-up service and the situation got seriously out of hand in mid 1960 with constant hysterical transatlantic telephone messages from the distraught Chamberlain. Jay wrestled with a multitude of warranty problems all of which threatened to incur massive expense for which inadequate provision had been made by him or the factory. Furthermore, there was no formal back-up at Cheshunt to handle warranty and other service claims beyond the tiny Service Department of Tony Caldersmith.

Some of the reported claims met with incredulity. For example Elite doors, bonnets and bootlids were changing colour after the cars were delivered. We were not aware that some of the earlier cars had been sitting in the sun for months while later specimens went straight from the ship to dealers. Little snags like accelerated wear of the rear radius arm ball joint bushings of these Series One cars were difficult to explain to customers brought up on Porsche and Triumph who had moved to the Elite in search of a different kind of excitement from that which now regularly impeded daily motoring. It seemed that all the problems that had afflicted us at home were now repeated, but more drastically, in California. Solutions were well beyond Chamberlain's financial resources and technical ability. Jay became so concerned by the situation that he was reluctant to press ahead with a determined follow-on sales campaign; and this only shortly after cars had begun to arrive to meet demand created in 1958 and 59. He threatened to withhold further letters of credit until the situation was resolved. A cold shiver ran through Cheshunt.

Since returning from my first visit to the West Coast I had been occupied by the launch of the Series Two Seven kit-car. I was nevertheless closely following developments across the Atlantic and by September 1960 it had become obvious that I would have to return immediately to sort out the nightmare situation now paralysing our most important market. On my next arrival at Los Angeles Airport there was no sign of Jay's old Minder "Tiger". He was replaced by a young man to whom I took an instant dislike. The Elite that he had chosen for the journey to North Hollywood seemed to have been selected deliberately to make the point that the pride of the Lotus range was totally unsuited to the market. The radius arm ball joints rattled as of old; the final drive unit growled to indicate that at least once it had dumped its oil and the engine was even by FWE standards exceptionally noisy and harsh. A bouquet of Elite faults, in fact.

Whereas Tiger was a genial old rogue who had seen an opportunity to use Jay for the benefit of himself and his son, the new Minder was without question a minor member of the Underworld. At various moments during the day he would dart off on activities connected with a call girl enterprise. I suspect that he may have had a "hold" over Jay and used it to exploit the situation. He was undoubtedly a car enthusiast but his allegiance was to Porsche. He had a superb 356 Super 90 which he used to demoralise me. Unfortunately for him I rather enjoyed this punishment and the experience of the many other delightful (often unseen in Britain) types of car which I took the chance to test whenever possible. In short my task was simple to describe but virtually incapable of fulfilment – to clear up the appalling mess that had been generated in California by the joint efforts of exporter and importer and to restore confidence in the Elite.

When we realised during the late Summer of 1960 that something was going horribly wrong in California, Colin decided that I should go back to reconnoitre and to do whatever was necessary to maintain the flow of orders. We had no idea what we might find and therefore I was issued with this letter reminiscent of 19th Century diplomacy which, it was hoped, would open all doors. In actual fact it was not required, but I have kept it as an interesting souvenir of the time.

LOTUS CARS LIMITED

CHESHUNT · ENGLAND

Telephone: Waltham Cross 26181

20th September, 1960.

To Whom It May Concern

This letter is to introduce Mr. R.F. Read, Group Sales Manager, who is responsible for all marketing arrangements for Lotus Cars.

Mr. Read is authorised to enter into arrangements and conduct negotiations on the broadest basis to ensure proper distribution of the Group's products.

A.C.B. Chapman

A.C.B. CHAPMAN
Managing Director

As we buzzed and rattled along the freeway in the Elite I began to feel a growing mixture of anger and concern aggravated by the tiredness of jet flight – then a relatively new experience. By the time that we arrived at Chamberlain's office on Lankershim Boulevard I realised that this was going to be an extremely difficult meeting; requiring all the reserves of youthful optimism and professional tact that I could muster. Failure on a mission of this kind could result in a situation which might well close down Lotus or permanently damage the company.

Following the initial meeting with Chamberlain at North Hollywood during which I parried insults with pleasantries, it became obvious that the first priority was to examine Elites forming the subject of the repeated complaints that we had received at Cheshunt and to get to grips with the problem. You must imagine the impact on me of seeing not one, but most Elites (particularly those in white or pale colours) of which the doors at least had turned a darker shade than the rest of the bodywork. White doors went brown; red went yellow and blue changed to green. Chamberlain and I had no idea what caused this and he had been unable to obtain satisfactory advice locally even though there was considerable fibreglass expertise available. I got back to Chapman for help only to find that he too was dumbfounded for we had never experienced this problem in Europe. His response was to immediately fly Ron Hickman to California to investigate. Hickman is a perfect example of Chapman's "Pied Piper" ability to attract people of remarkable talent and provide them with an environment in which their abilities can flourish – to Chapman's advantage. Seduced from Ford, Hickman had been intimately involved with the design and development process (such as it was) of the Elite and had acquired at Lotus encyclopaedic knowledge of plastic construction techniques. He later became known for his invention of the Black and Decker Workmate, but before that with minimal intervention from Chapman he designed the Lotus Elan and later the Elan +2. It didn't take Ron long to come up with the answer after he had consulted an industrial chemist called in from New York to confirm what at that time were just his suspicions about the discoloration and severe glassfibre cloth "patterning".

As described earlier the external surface of the Elite was of resin backed by matting formed from a multitude of fine glass strands skilfully laid with the "grain" running such that maximum strength was imparted to the structure. In order to achieve a smooth finish a layer of pure resin called gel-coat is concentrated at the surface during lamination and later rubbed down by hand and painted with cellulose. What Chamberlain and I had not fully appreciated was that whereas polyester resin was used for the main structure of the car, the doors, boot and bonnet lids were moulded with epoxy resin to reduce surface distortions where inner panels met the outer ones, due to shrinkage. The Elite was formed of clear resin without filler or pigment. This had been found to be essential to enable the bonding (by a dark-coloured epoxy resin) of the ultra-lightweight panels of the car during manufacture to be carefully studied through the translucent material.

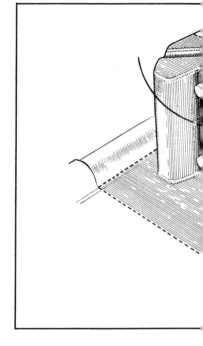

In the relatively cool, dull climate of Northern Europe the paintwork of Elites had given little trouble. Furthermore, most of the early often wafer-thin skinned "lightweight" cars had covered relatively small mileages and were primarily used for racing (often involving respraying after accident damage). In California a completely new situation applied. Hollywood was chosen as the birthplace of the

You can just discern the windscreen of this Elite resting btween the seats. The unfortunate Ron Hickman, during his trouble-shooting visit to California at my request during 1960, was presented with a bewildering array of problems to solve in double quick time as we strove to rescue our fast-vanishing reputation. Whether this car suffered from excessive leaks, contraction of the Claylastic surround (developed for the Mini) or whether the screen just popped out we don't know. The epoxy resin doors of this worst-case-of-all white car do not yet seem too noticeably discoloured by the California sunshine, but they soon will be. In the background you can see "Jay's Lube-Lab", where ministrations to Fiats, Borgward, MG and so on helped to provide a little cash to stave off the inevitable disaster building up as a result of the Elite débâcle.

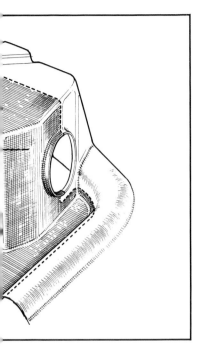

Much sleep was lost by all during the early weeks of Bristol production when failure to adhere to the stipulated lay-up procedures resulted in local weakness of the structure in the area of the "differential box" shown here. The final drive unit was secured by four bolts and failure by Bristol Laminators to allow the strands of glass matting to follow the prescribed route caused early fatigue cracking under load, requiring the cutting out of the diff. box and surrounding area and replacement by a new, correctly made unit. We lost a lot of time and money with that little problem before Bristol brought it under control.

American film industry because of its outstanding record of continuous sunshine. For much of the year the sun rises each morning in a cloudless azure sky and remains unshielded for the entire day. One can rely on two or three weeks on end of perfect climatic conditions for filming and there is little incentive to keep a car in a garage in such glorious weather. So, decided Hickman, our Elites were receiving a daily dose of ultra violet light on unprecedented scale. As a result of this, the epoxy resin responded vigorously and continued to cure and thereby darken under the paint. Even three or four coats of cellulose (particularly white or light coloured) were inadequate to prevent the passage of UV rays and in the opposite direction the inexorable migration to the surface of surplus hardener. On passing through the "soft" cellulose paint the hardener in combination with UV rays had a photo-chemical effect on the pigments in the paint, concluded Ron. This was a potential nightmare and Ron and I put our heads together with Chamberlain to seek a solution which would hopefully avoid bankruptcy for all.

Fortunately, Los Angeles abounds with small specialist paint shops engaged in the custom finishing of hotrod and imported cars. There was therefore a choice of locations available to us where we could set up a systematic programme of rectification. It is virtually impossible to repaint on a piecemeal basis odd doors, bonnets and boot lids of cars of which the overall paintwork had been exposed to the elements for several months without achieving some form of mismatch. We therfore had to carry out a total repaint. The task was further complicated by the need to introduce some means of sealing the doors and then priming them. By a process of extended bargaining we were able to agree an overall unit price of $150 for repainting which naturally was added to the cost of every sale made and had to be borne by Lotus in England. This arrangement unfortunately was overshadowed by the discovery that the ever more desperate Chamberlain had earlier fraudulently altered invoices for rectification by the crude expedient of adding digits to invoice totals and, acting on instructions from Fred Bushell, Hickman gathered evidence to prove fraud.

Our difficulties had at the same time been compounded by the discovery by Chamberlain that the method of attachment of the final drive unit to the main structure of the car was another problem area on Bristol-built cars. The final drive unit of the Elite is an aluminium casting housing an MG nosepiece on which are mounted crownwheel, pinion and differential. The Lotus housing has four lugs which are bolted to the fibreglass. Because the disc brakes were mounted inboard against the final drive unit in order to reduce unsprung weight the entire rear braking and driving torque was transmitted to the structure of the car via the four lugs. In many cases the fibreglass structure of the car at this point began to show signs of collapse and, more seriously, detachment from the surrounding area.

Owners of fast cars naturally enjoyed hard acceleration and braking and it was just these forces that aggravated the on-off loadings applied to the structure of the car. The situation was further complicated by the difficulty of carrying away heat generated by the rear brake discs which had a further weakening effect. Chamberlain had attempted to effect a jury rig repair by fitting steel strips to brace the mounting bolts and by shielding the brake calipers as fully as possible to reduce heat transfer. In fact the bracing modification, although apparently logical, was totally ineffective because the weakness was further afield. It was not until after a blazing row about "wasting his time" that Chapman agreed something might be wrong and took an Elite from the production line which he (with Mike Costin in the passenger seat) then drove up and down Delamare Road alternately braking and accelerating for twenty minutes until the final drive unit and the fibreglass to which it was bolted detached itself in a fairly major fashion from the structure. The damaged car was hurriedly dismantled and investigated only to reveal that the lay-up of fibreglass matting in manufacture had been applied so that, instead of correctly reinforcing the final drive mounting area in the manner intended, there were now areas of fundamental weakness surrounding the final drive. All chassis-body units at Cheshunt were modified by cutting out the offending areas and bonding-in new, correctly laid up sections. Some were also fitted with "psychological" steel braces while in the longer term the problem was ultimately resolved by reverting to the correct method of lay-up and by Hickman's improved pictorial display instructions for the laminators, better training for them by Bristol, and tightening inspection procedures during manufacture.

Whereas these were the two principal areas of agonising embarrassment at the time, there were in addition a multitude of minor complaints coming from all directions each of which had to be rectified and funded from the virtually non-existent profit margin of the Elite. Later we had to increase the warranty allowance margin and this was always used up. The major casualty of this episode however was Chamberlain himself who was totally demoralised by the bad reputation gained by the Elite almost before it had entered the market. Despite all subsequent changes in distribution the Elite never at that time gained acceptance in the United States except as a lightweight GT racing car. Its claim to excellence in that sphere was undisputed.

Chamberlain goes under

By the end of 1960 our success in shipping nearly 300 cars to Chamberlain – all of which had been paid for by drawing against his Letter of Credit – coupled with our failure to resolve fully the inherent technical problems of the car which were causing difficulties for Chamberlain in the market, sounded the death knell for Lotus Cars of America Inc. The ultimate downfall of Chamberlain was engineered by the financial backers of Lotus Cars of America led by Jack Briggs as the principal stockholder but guided by his Attorney. We do not know exactly what precipitated the unhorsing of Chamberlain; it was probably a combination of events and I suspect that we were viewed as fellow conspirators; to some extent equally culpable.

We were advised that Chamberlain was no more "in the picture" and that the new head of Lotus Import Operations in the USA was to be one Peter Hessler. Apparently he enjoyed the full confidence of Jack Briggs and had a background in the motor business. He was even of British origin (this probably in the hope that he would be able to understand us better and keep one step ahead). My preliminary investigations at home had been unable to discover information about Hessler but it seemed to me imperative to return to the West Coast as soon as possible in order to ensure that the break in continuity of orders was kept as short as possible.

We were unable to terminate the contract with Jack Briggs and his group even if we had wished to do so because his legal advice was certainly now of a far higher standard than the commercial expertise that had previously been available to him. Furthermore, with over a hundred unsold Elites in California or on the high seas we ran a grave risk of destroying the American market for the Elite for all time if we took any precipitate action that might flood what was in effect severely distressed merchandise on to a market already surfeited with unwanted Lancias, Alfa Romeos, Daimler SP250s and even from time to time Jaguars. We had to live with Jack Briggs and the unholy mess to which we had made our unique contribution.

The combination of serious technical problems and the loss of the key man Jay

Chamberlain augured badly for our immediate prospects in the US. I therefore decided with the full support of Chapman and Bushell that I should return to the States and remain there until our affairs were on a reliable commercial footing.

I flew from Heathrow on 26 October 1960 to New York and later on to Los Angeles where I was met at the Airport by Peter Hessler. He seemed to me a little unrelaxed or even apprehensive but bright, positive in his views about the situation and compared with my two previous sorties to California, this was a relatively calm welcome. Jack Briggs and Hessler had decided to abandon the old Chamberlain site and had set up a new wholesale and retail operation, Western Distributors Inc. at 317 North Victory Boulevard, Burbank. They had moved a number of Elites, Sevens and Juniors into position and it was heartening to see the new Lotus import operation based on a solus site without the usual Chamberlain clutter (the clutter being the only merchandise which he could comfortably sell and profit from). My preoccupation was simple – I needed to know Western Distributors' plans for new orders for the Elite; stocks of which were now building up at Cheshunt at an alarming rate. Hessler was evasive, promising that things would "soon be better", but there was nothing definite for me . . . I returned to New York to face Sy Kaback and to satisfy myself about Peter Hessler. I called on Colin's old friend at the British Automobile Manufacturers Association in Fifth Avenue, John Dugdale, told him about Hessler and my misgivings about the situation in general. At the mention of Hessler's name a frown appeared on John Dugdale's normally relaxed features. He made a telephone call and asked a few questions. "You'd better go round to the Rover people," he said. "I think that they can tell you something more".

Wanted by the Mounties

On arrival at the Rover offices I was shown a group photograph and asked if I recognised any of the faces. Only one aroused my interest and recognition. It was Hessler. I pointed him out.

"Well, well, well" came the reply. "Wanted by the Mounties for fraud . . . They can't extradite him but I should steer clear if I were you. I think we're talking about half a million dollars – Canadian of course" (in mitigation).

My heart sank. I went back to the Hotel Taft and called Fred Bushell to tell him the story. Ever-practical Fred reminded me that we had no alternatives at the moment and that the future of our company currently rested in the palm of Peter Hessler. I told Fred that I would discreetly raise the question of Hessler's provenance with Jack Briggs on the basis that although he had not consulted us about his new man, he should at least in view of his earlier experiences in ventures associated with us, know exactly the risk (if any) to which he might be exposed. When I eventually got through to Dr. Briggs he affected some surprise at the news that I gave him but did not seem to be too concerned. He reminded me of the close involvement of his Attorney who had "vetted" Hessler before the appointment was made. "Under the circumstances, Robin, I am prepared to give him a try", said the ever benign guardian angel of our fortunes.

I knew that my duties in the States would keep me there for some considerable time. It was expensive staying at the Hotel Taft and therefore it seemed practical to locate an apartment in Manhattan, particularly since Colin and Fred had agreed that my wife should join me (she eventually arrived by air early in January 1961). Sy Kaback introduced me to an exotic and artistic couple who had branched out into the purchase, renovation and letting of traditional brownstone apartment buildings in the upper reaches of Manhattan. I found a pleasant and commodious apartment in East 76th Street.

The Wildest

Trained and tamed 'til your foot says, "Sic 'em !"

For the person who appreciates the *pure* sports car, it's Lotus 'Elite'. This $6,000* British Grand Touring champion was designed for those who hunger for an original and have a taste for the genuine.

When you go Lotus 'Elite', you go avant garde (translation — front bunch). The blood line is racing, the breed is speed. Lotus 'Elite' is a thoroughbred.

LOTUS ELITE

Lotus 'Elite' has four cylinder engine, disc brakes and independent suspension all around. Built to get there quicker, ride surer, with tremendous fuel economy. Lotus cars are on immediate delivery everywhere by Western Distributors, Inc., 317 North Victory Boulevard, Burbank, California. Write for illustrated brochure.

*Equipped ready to roll — slight freight variances

Dealer inquiries welcome

After the demise of Chamberlain at the end of 1960 his eventual successor Peter Hessler, employed by financier Jack Briggs to run Western Distributors Inc which had taken over the US stock of the Elite, was determined to show how it should be done. The author was horrified to discover that Hessler had devised his own advertising programme of which this abomination is a manifestation. The Hessler advertising campaign is completely out of touch with the Elite and signally failed to achieve its objective. Eventually the message got home and Hessler abandoned his ghastly campaign. There was then a modest amount of advertising in US periodicals directed from Cheshunt but it was not until late 1962, and Bob Challman's Ecurie Shirlee, that a half-way reasonable US advertising campaign for the Elite resumed.

East coast episode

Accepting that it was unlikely that we were going to receive serious orders from Western Distributors other than for the strictly seasonal Twenty Formula Junior Cars I turned my attention to encouraging the other importers/distributors from the Chamberlain days. Nearest at hand was Sy Kaback's Grand Prix Imported cars of Rutherford, New Jersey. Sy's main business was the Weathermatic Corporation (a highly successful air conditioning contractor) based in Queens and therefore contact for me was a simple matter. Sy and I got on extremely well and his wonderful sense of humour coupled with sound business sense (he went into the Lotus venture with his eyes wide open), made working with him a welcome change from my experiences elsewhere in North America.

For Sy, motor racing was a serious passion taken up a few years before I met him. Characteristically he went in at the deep end and devoted himself to midget racing which in the United States involved driving extremely powerful four-cylinder Offenhauser powered cars running on methanol round quarter – mile oval indoor tracks. Although Sy subsequently graduated from this rather down market American type of racing to the sport as conceived by the SCCA, he would periodically revert and on one occasion took me and my wife to an indoor event in which he was going to make a modest comeback. On the way he regaled us with a story so entertaining that I almost ruptured myself with laughter.

There was always a certain amount of political conflict between the various organisational bodies of US motor sport and at one time the "indoor" track organisers decided that they would hold a Le Mans type race on a quarter mile oval for European cars. At this time Kaback owned a potent Aston Martin DB4 which he considered ideally suited to this event.

The organisers felt that since many of the drivers were familiar with the track in their midget racing mode, it would be only fair to avoid giving the regulars an advantage over the SCCA drivers with whom they were to join battle. What better course to take than to alter the direction of travel from anti-clockwise to clockwise? And then because the race was intended to simulate Le Mans and in fact taking place at night, indoors, why not switch off the Stadium lighting? One should imagine a Le Mans start with drivers crouched opposite their unlit, motionless cars. A maroon explodes and the drivers sprint across the narrow track. Engines roar, headlights are switched on and almost immediately the carnage begins. One or two cars stall at the start; headlight beams trace a crazy zigzag course around the circuit (lap time about 15 seconds) to an amazing background cacophony of rending metal, screeching tyres and roaring 4-, 6- and 12-cylinder engines of immaculate breeding operating in an entirely alien environment. Within a minute or two the organisers began to realise the error of their ways. The noise subsided with a remarkable rapidity as the number of snaking headlight beams was dramatically reduced by events. Soon the organisers felt it their duty to order that the Stadium lights be switched on again. With unexceptional prescience, they covered their eyes and gradually forced themselves to view the scene. As Sy explained "most of the goddam cars were upside down on the straw bales by this time. I won that race but it cost me 15,000 bucks to straighten out the Aston afterwards". I understand that this was the first and last indoor blacked out Le Mans start sports car race ever held in North America.

But to more serious things: Kaback bought a Lotus Fifteen and very quickly blew up the 1½-litre Climax FPF engine with which it was issued. To obtain spares for this sophisticated European power plant was a difficult and expensive operation by remote control and the standards of maintenance required were somewhat ahead of the resources of Grand Prix Imported Cars, Inc. Accordingly, Kaback decided to replace the FPF engine with a modified version of one of the recently introduced General Motors compact V8s; the all-aluminium Buick/ Pontiac engine. This beautiful little (3.5-litres was small by American standards) power unit had been designed to help GM, whose behemoths were rapidly falling out of favour, combat the imported car invasion; then reaching its peak. Knowing that lightweight = low cost, GM had decided that the cylinder heads and very complicated block casting should be manufactured in diecast aluminium. The technical difficulties of this process were such that GM were never able to reduce the scrap rate in production to an acceptable level and early in their life the Pontiac Tempest and its Buick running mate were dumped and the rights for manufacture of the engine acquired by the British Rover Motor Company who (because their volumes were so much lower), successfully produced it by simple sandcasting methods. This engine has only recently been abandoned as a power unit for the products of Austin Rover who inherited it.

Kaback was the first to take the route of fitting a lightweight V8 in a European chassis (his example shortly followed in the famous Lotus Fifteen-Buick of "Dizzy" Addicott). Because the V8 was no heavier than the four-cylinder Climax which it replaced and because its power output in lightly modified form was

During 1959 Sy Kaback became increasingly frustrated by the performance of his 2 litre Coventry Climax FPF engined Fifteen. There was no formal servicing set-up for the twin cam Climax engines in the US at that time and as an enlarged version of the original 1½ litre engine, the 1960 cc Climax was not one of the most reliable sources of power. Kaback had the bright idea of dropping one of the new General Motors (nominally Buick in this case) 3½ litre all aluminium V8 pushrod engines into the space normally occupied by the British thoroughbred engine. The Buick not only weighed less than the engine it replaced but with a little encouragement delivered an extra 100 bhp. The installation was cramped if not crude but it certainly worked. The idea was copied elsewhere most notably by "Dizzy" Addicott in the UK, giving the Fifteen a new lease of life in the early Sixties. The Buick flywheel housing intruded to such an extent in the footwell that Kaback (no giant) was forced to drive without shoes. He adopted heavy wool socks taped to his feet but even this protection was inadequate to avoid third degree burns which he never noticed until after the chequered flag.

Kaback was not too fussed about the niceties of aerodynamics and accommodated the huge radiator judged suitable for the Buick engine by bashing out the existing svelte Williams & Pritchard bodywork. A big radiator requires a big air intake, he reasoned, and out came the tinsnips. The conversion was an instant success. On its first outing at Vineland, New Jersey in 1960 Kaback came first overall - "a massive high that compensated for all the disappointments, frustrations and money spent," he recalls. Sy then went on to achieve six consecutive overall wins at Lime Rock and Vineland. In this photograph he is shown on August 5 1961 being passed by Walt Hansgen – the latter on his way to overall victory in Briggs Cunningham's Tipo 63 V12 Maserati "Birdcage"; the Maser too much for the Fifteen, even in revitalised form.

noticeably in excess of the original four-cylinder engine, the results were highly satisfactory. Kaback found the American engine much harder to destroy and of course its technology was easily understood by his mechanic who could now obtain parts over the counter at any GM dealership. Kaback still had this car when I met him but had moved on to Formula Junior. He owned what I consider to be the most beautiful car of this class – the OSCA – of which very few were made. The Rodriguez brothers had one, Kaback another and Colin Davis successfully campaigned the Works car in the early Junior races in Europe. Beautiful though the OSCA was it could not hold a candle to the much lighter, nimbler, all independently sprung British cars, most particularly the Elva which in the US swept all before it in 1960. Kaback bought a Twenty but his interest in single seater racing of this type never rose to the levels of his passion for larger, hairier racing offered by the Lotus Fifteen Buick and shortly afterwards he concentrated his sporting attentions on ocean racing, forming his own waterborne Team Lotus for this purpose. This must be one of the few abuses of the racing team's registered name that has so far passed unnoticed by the Hethel lawyers.

Enthusiastic though Sy was and good as our business relationship became we could never expect his modest operation to provide us with sufficient demand to meet more than a fraction of the ever increasing output at Cheshunt. Sy entered into the SCCA Show activities with all his remarkable energies but rumours of the Elite's disaster on the West Coast were already abounding and beyond selling a few Sevens and racing cars there was little that Grand Prix could contribute. After all, Kaback's main commercial activities were in the lucrative air-conditioning field and he was not about to jeopardise that by dabbling dangerously in the imported car business.

Early in February 1961 my wife and I drove West to Detroit to spend a week with the Posselius family. Like all Americans with whom I came in contact they treated us exceptionally generously and we entered a delightful social world as relief from the regular business discussions that proceeded during the day. Because John Posselius' European Motors Inc. relied heavily on its high volume Triumph sales he was reluctant to prejudice the success of that part of the operation by over commitment to Lotus. He had had one or two Elites from Jay Chamberlain and I now suggested to him that he should continue to concentrate attention on the Seven and Formula Junior market. John Posselius was possibly the most enthusiastic of the American importers of the Seven at that time. He and his associates had the vision to see its immense potential for SCCA racing and when I returned to the Middle West in September of that year I was able to see for myself in local SCCA events how the Seven was carving out its remarkable reputation in American sporting circles.

The utter frustration of our situation in the United States during these early months of 1961 is difficult to imagine. I was completely hamstrung by the fact that I had inherited such distribution as there was in the United States from the joint efforts of Chamberlain and Chapman. If Lotus was to have any hope for the future at all – and not just in the United States – I had to ensure that none of the cars already in the American pipeline would find their way on to the market as distressed merchandise. Additionally I had to find a way to avoid entering into actual litigation (as distinct from running the gauntlet of its continual threat). If news of our perilous situation ever got out we would find Lotus totally discredited in North America; our cars dumped on the market and with the exception of racing car sales, no future whatsoever. In the meantime, because of the impact such a disaster would have had on Cheshunt, there would have been no future even for racing cars. One false step and the whole pack of cards would have collapsed and the story of Lotus ended.

We were locked in the vice of the monstrous predicament that had been created largely by the inexperience and folly of Colin Chapman above all followed closely by Jay Chamberlain; a wonderful illustration of the old adage that one should try to avoid mixing friendship and business. Colin and Fred understood that they really had no alternative available to them than to let me try to cut the Gordian knot by preserving the peace between East Coast, West Coast, and Middle West; at the same time trying to help Western Distributors to move Elites and restore the confidence of Jack Briggs and his advisers to the point where they would be willing to place new orders and appropriate letters of credit to keep the supply line from Cheshunt open. The supply line was certainly flowing but at that time it was mainly leading into speculative shipment to the US and the field behind the factory, while Bank Manager, Bristol and other component suppliers went screaming up the wall.

I was fortunate in that I had developed good friendships and working relationships with all parties in the drama. Litigation may have been in the air but we all got on very well together. The most awkward potential disaster on the East Coast was that surrounding the dismay of Gei Zantzinger when he discovered that his Suburban Foreign Car Service Inc was joint exclusive East Coast distributor for Lotus with Sy Kaback's Grand Prix Imported Cars Inc. We had several cordial meetings on the subject but there was no doubt in my mind that unless some reasonable accommodation could be found we would end up in court. After protracted negotiation we agreed that the East Coast territory should be divided so that the Zantzinger influence extended Southwards from Philadelphia while Sy Kaback looked after New York and its environs. Gei Zantzinger felt sufficiently relaxed to announce his forthcoming marriage and to invite my wife and me to attend the ceremony. I was introduced to all as the representative of the defendant in the forthcoming legal battle, although I had a sneaking suspicion that disaster had been averted. Zantzinger lived at his parents' huge mansion (their wealth founded on coal) set in a magnificent park. Gei's interests were somewhat at variance with the superb style of his family's way of life and consisted of firing off representative examples of his collection of World

War II machine guns, pride of place going to a USAAF Browning which projected from his bedroom window rather like the side armament of the Flying Fortress. Having shouted a warning Gei would open up with gleeful abandon. When tired of this pursuit he turned to his collection of motorcycles in which pride of place was held by a beautifully restored Ariel Square Four. I suspect that he preferred his two wheelers to the Lotus Eleven garaged with them. I had temporarily abandoned direct involvement with motorcycling in 1955, encouraged by my wife and the onset of family responsibility. I finally saw the light and returned to motorcycling ten years later.

The ever-puckish Zantzinger, observing my Eurasian wife's distinctly Japanese features, took us to the local Honda agent. Now in 1961 Hondas were only just beginning to appear in the United Kingdom and they had been seen in the United States for very little longer than that. However the pride and joy of the local Honda agent was a race kitted CB92 Honda of 124 cc. When suitably excited he was known to start up this fascinating twin cylinder 4-stroke machine and Zantzinger did the trick by introducing my enigmatically smiling wife as "Miss Honda 1960". The result was electrifying. Immediately the button was pressed and from the two open megaphones came that sound heard by very few Europeans who had not attended the 1959 and 1960 Motorcycle Grandes Epreuves. I had not and therefore 12,500 revs from a 4-stroke twin beggared belief. Later of course we grew accustomed to the "impossible" exploits of the Japanese motorcycle industry as they swiftly destroyed all European competition on and off the race track. Gei Zantzinger was by nature a charming fellow and fortunately did not depend on Suburban in any way for his livelihood. Our personal friendship saved the day for Lotus.

I had last seen Jay Chamberlain in the Fall of 1960 when we lunched at René Dreyfus' Le Chanteclair Restaurant, the accepted New York meeting place for all motor racing enthusiasts and where Jay – one of that select band with Le Patron Dreyfus himself who had raced at Le Mans – would be particularly well received and fussed over in the ego-boosting manner known only to the French restaurateur. I never saw him again in the United States (and only at all in the distance during his sad European swan-song racing season) and never spoke to him again. He was bundled away by the lawyers surrounding Jack Briggs as the official scapegoat for the California débâcle.

My attempts to persuade Peter Hessler that he should issue new orders for the Elite had been totally unsuccessful in real terms although soothing promises were made by all and sundry. I informed Colin and Fred that I would now return to Cheshunt for a Council of War on the basis that they should become directly involved in the situation in order to emphasise how seriously we regarded our predicament. Colin was now deeply engaged in the rear engined racing programme; totally fired-up by the first Grand Prix successes achieved by Lotus during the previous year and confident that the tide had finally turned on the highly diverting racing front. To have to return to the misery of the American market was an unbearable prospect, particularly since although my own energies and initiatives had to some extent been exhausted there was still dear old Fred Bushell to throw into battle. Accordingly, Colin decided that we should volunteer to return to California with the objective of securing a major order for the Elite.

The thirty day party

Fred and I very nearly failed to leave the ground at Heathrow when the undercarriage of our Boeing 707 struck a large object on the runway with a resounding crash that shook the entire airframe "Don't worry Fred," I said "It's far worse where we're going". I warned Fred that we were faced with an appallingly difficult task and we agreed that we might as well accept the need to stay locked in negotiations with Hessler and Briggs and their legal advisers until we had secured an order. Without an order there was no future for Lotus. Little did we know at that stage what it was we were about to experience . . .

On arriving at Los Angeles we took a cab to "my" customary resting place, The Bel Air Palms Motel at Burbank which although it had been originally chosen for its proximity to the Chamberlain Lankershim Boulevard operation was also well placed for access to Western Distributors. After recovering from the lengthy flight we called on our Attorney Ned Glad at his down-town Los Angeles office and laid our cards on the table. We made it plain that we were desperate and that we were here to fight to save Lotus in the only way possible – by securing a large, properly financed order for the Elite which would enable us to placate the Bank and Bristol. We had no money to pay the law firm of Glad & Tuttle, but we would find some way to reward Ned for his support and advice. In actual fact I had spent a considerable amount of time drinking with Ned Glad and we had become good friends. Although Ned Glad's driving experience was restricted to commuting from Santa Ana to his office, bumper to bumper with thousands of others on the seven lane freeways of LA, his regular exposure to the heady world of Lotus was beginning to make him yearn for a slick shifting "four on the floor" European sportster. This was very convenient because in the end we were able to settle our account by giving him an Elite – an experience which took at least ten years off his demeanour and resulted in an invitation to me (in the absence of his wife and family on vacation) to join him for a splendid evening at the Burlesque shows.

In early 1961, following the collapse of Jay Chamberlain Automotive, Dr Jack Briggs the financier of Lotus Cars of America Inc. backed a new distribution company to be managed by Peter Hessler at Burbank, California. Worried by the absence of new orders for the Elite, Fred Bushell (then Company Secretary) and the author travelled to California with the intention of staying put until an order materialised. This led to the "Thirty Day Party" episode. Posing for the Press with a Seven Series Two America and Elite after agreeing terms are (left to right) Robin Read, Fred Bushell, Peter Hessler and Dr Jack Briggs.

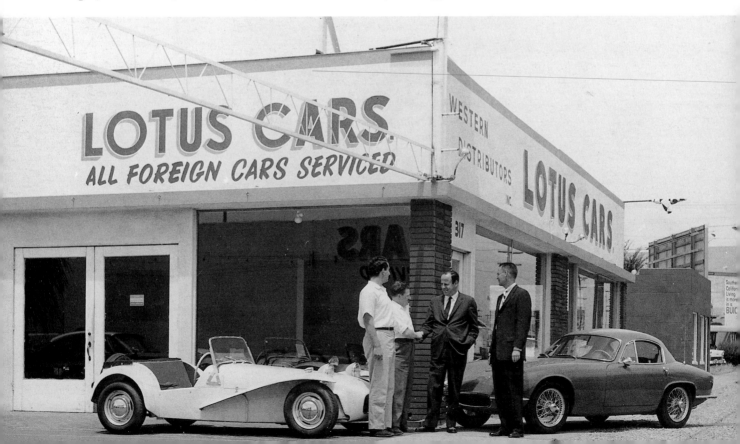

Fred and I were therefore fully fired-up when we met Peter Hessler and Jack Briggs on the following day. We made it clear that we were not able to return to England without an order and that although we appreciated the difficulties of Western Distributors and were most grateful to them for protecting our United States market by transferring the original inventory of unsold Elites to the new company, new orders were essential and the only means of survival for us.

There then followed the remarkable episode of the "thirty day party". Fred and I were so determined to get our order and Letter of Credit that we refused to let Hessler have any peace. This meant that we had to be with him constantly during working hours and his very extensive periods of play.

Peter Hessler shared a delightful house, perched above the Sunset Strip and close to the Warner Bros. Studios where Peter's wife ("girlfriend" said Fred with a knowing wink) entertained a galaxy of friends and relatives from the film world. Peter's companion was the daughter of a doyen of the British acting contingent based permanently in Hollywood. Exile had if anything strengthened their Britishness and cricket was regularly played and tea drunk despite their presence in the heart of the American Dreamworld.

It was extremely interesting for Fred and me to find ourselves in such a congenial milieu. As visitors from the Old Country we were treated royally and it suited Peter to keep us as occupied as possible and away from entanglement in his thinning hair. He almost certainly knew that I knew who he was and the presence of Fred at my side made it doubly clear that we were determined to get our way. So on the one hand we were taken to the Warner Brothers Studios where we met Paul Henried, Hazel Court (a well known British star of the time); went on the lot with Marlene Dietrich, watched soundtracks being dubbed, visited sets and

Eventually we got round to making the Seven Series Two with left-hand drive and much larger US-legal headlamps. The characteristic American license plate holder can be seen on this Cosworth-Ford Super Seven America, together with the electric (Elite) cooling fan for traffic jams and the cheap and nasty "toast rack" grille replacing the "egg box" original of the Series One.

found it all very fascinating. At weekends we would be taken into the hinterland to relax (Fred as an accountant managed to get to Las Vegas, but I generally preferred the Pacific beaches). In the intervening periods the great thirty day party continued. Each evening Fred and I would shower and travel up the winding track to the Hessler residence where we would remain entirely and intensely sober while everybody else had a wonderful time. We resisted the blandishments of charming young ladies (and they were prolific in Hollywood) and at the end of each night's jollifications Fred and I would take home some of the more enfeebled of our fellow revellers before finally returning to do the washing-up and making our own way back to Burbank. Hessler became very nervous. We obviously meant what we said. We were there for the duration; we had our own lawyer at hand; we seemed to know a great deal about him and he may even have imagined that it was our machinations that had deposed his predecessor Jay Chamberlain. We ourselves were becoming desperate and we made it clear to Hessler that we wished to have a serious round table discussion with him and Jack Briggs who, like Chapman, was a shadowy off-stage "presence" at all our deliberations. The meeting took place and our by now grubby draft contract came out once more for inspection and discussion. We made clear to Dr. Briggs the seriousness of our predicament and the impact that the collapse of Lotus in England would undoubtedly have on his own heavily committed private fortune backing the Elite stock in California. The pace of negotiations quickened and we concluded an agreement for another 100 cars to be supplied in a slightly imprecise pattern during the rest of 1961. With Jack Briggs we went to his Bank and watched the necessary Letter of Credit being raised. A huge sigh of relief from Fred marked the end of this period of stress and anxiety. We telephoned Colin instantly and gave him the good news. Colin announced to the Press that he had won substantial orders in the US. Fred returned to England while I flew across to New York to explain the situation to Sy Kaback before finally crossing the Atlantic.

I knew that although we had gained a respite by the outcome of the thirty day party negotiations, we had only really bought a little time and that if we were to enjoy any long term success in the United States we must strengthen our distribution. The fatally flawed character of Peter Hessler was too obvious. The Lotus attitude to him, coupled with the ever present threat of his Canadian past

The advertising material used by Jay Chamberlain was hardly very imaginative and the advertisements issued by his successor at Western Distributors were downright bad. However, there were one or two nice little touches like this visiting card which attempted to imbue the Elite with personality.

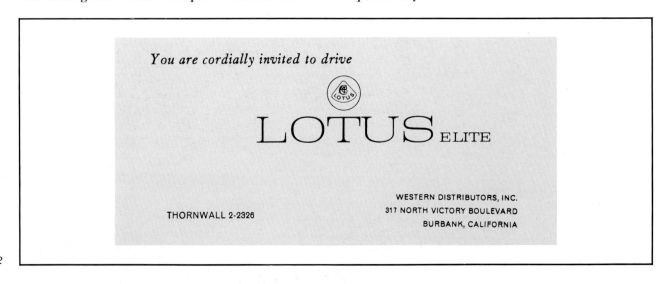

created a sense of paranoia. Matters later came to an appalling head when Hessler was killed driving a Lotus Twenty Formula Junior car at Riverside at a Press Day and champagne reception. Inevitably Jack Briggs had had enough at this point and so it was therefore fortunate that we had begun to examine alternatives in secrecy throughout the early part of 1961.

Where else to turn?

My planning and negotiations to find an alternative Lotus importer for the United States followed two distinct paths and the pressure to achieve a result increased after Fred Bushell and I returned from California having averted total disaster by the skin of our teeth. We knew that time was not on our side. I was particularly keen to persuade John Posselius of European Motors Inc, to become more involved than previously. For John, Lotus was a tiny sideline which amused him while he proceeded to run his main business as a major distributor of Triumph sports cars. I attempted to persuade John and his associates that with years of experience in the imported car business coupled with their well established network of sub-dealers, they would be able to achieve success at what after all were the relatively modest volumes of sales we needed.

John Posselius professed himself interested and I have no doubt that he very seriously considered the possibility. However even Triumph sports cars at that time were going through a difficult patch and I suspect that the financial resources of EMI were fully committed in the established direction. As a good friend of Chapman and in his usual more than helpful way to me, he had examined alternatives on his own initiative. John's suggestion was that we should talk to an old business associate Ray White, a long established Buick dealer in Detroit who had also developed a successful import sales operation for Fiat. I had not met Ray myself at that stage but planned to enter discussions directly during my next visit.

At the SCCA Show in New York I had been approached by one Walter Schapiro who introduced himself to me as an entrepreneur working between the US and the UK. His business was to introduce people to each other and set up deals – what the Americans would call "an operator" which covers a multitude of sins. Walter had a distinct appeal although I found it perennially difficult to be absolutely sure about his background. What was clear was that he had at one time trained as a rabbi and although he had not proceeded further with that potential career, had remained deeply and actively religious. He was more willing to discuss his religion than the commercial elements of his background. He was at that time particularly involved with the promotion of a book written by that most extraordinary of rarities a Roman Catholic priest turned rabbi. I was so intrigued by this tale that Walter arranged to introduce me to the convert who was currently on a fund raising visit round the faithful of New York – so at least I know that that part of the story was clear.

Walter knew nothing about cars in general or Lotus in particular but this was not to prevent him from offering any assistance that we might need. Chapman and I scheduled a visit to the US in late September 1961. This was intended to enable us to meet Ray White and John Posselius in Detroit and was timed to allow Colin to proceed thereafter to join Team Lotus at the Third United States Grand Prix at Watkins Glen on 8th October. I was somewhat put off by the fact that Colin's main interest at the time was to pursue the acquisition of a replacement for his faithful Comanche aircraft and he spent much of his time scouring the classified ads in flying magazines rather than preparing for the important discussions ahead.

In fact nothing came of the discussions with Ray White who probably knew too much by that time about our disastrous experience in his market. Colin and I

In 1961, while desperate for orders, Colin accompanied me to a meeting in Detroit with John Posselius (left), friend of Chamberlain and Chapman and a major Triumph distributor, who had proposed Ray White (centre), a Buick and Fiat distributor, as a possible major importer of Lotus. Nothing came of this despite the smiles evident in my snapshot.

spent a pleasant day with John Posselius, staying at his home in Grosse Pointe Farms. This was the only occasion when I shared a room with Colin and saw for myself the medication needed by my unfortunate boss to deal with his allergy-related hay fever. By this time I was getting desperate to find a substitute for Western Distributors or even a prop for them and Walter Schapiro was my only hope. I met him in New York and told him how desperate was our situation.

Shortly after my return to Cheshunt Walter Schapiro visited me and I gave him a full briefing on the situation telling him that we needed a reputable, well established household name American importer to handle the whole Lotus range and to establish a successful distribution network. At that time I had focussed my attention on the Roosevelt operation which imported Fiat cars together with some of the more exotic derivatives such as Abarth. The company was owned and run on a day to day basis by the son of the former President of the United States, Franklin Delano Roosevelt. FDR Junior, it seemed to me, would be exactly the man for us. He had a successful reputation in the business, was involved in the sporting import field, was well financed and offered a dazzingly unforgettable name . . .

"What can I do for you?" asked Walter Schapiro. Much as I liked Walter personally and much as I appreciated his determination to help us against all odds, I was at a loss to see how he could accomplish anything practical. So it was perhaps a little unkind of me to suggest the impossible: "I want you Walter, to just do one small thing for me. I want you to get FDR Junior over here to Cheshunt as quickly as possible"

"But I've never met him", said Walter . . .

Within a week Walter called from New York to tell me that he had pulled it off. He had in his usual remarkable way found a way to meet FDR, had probably told him some amazing story about his personal friend Colin in order to achieve

```
        R.F. READ - COMMISSION STATEMENT.              RACING ENGINES LIMITED - TO BE CONFIRMED.

        FEBRUARY AND MARCH, 1961.

 LOTUS CARS LIMITED.                                     Sales              £20,715.


                    Home Sales      9,479.
                    Export Sales   26,069.
                    Spares          6,687.
                    Servicing       2,316.
                                  £44,551.    GROUP TURNOVER              £116,114.


 LOTUS COMPONENTS LIMITED - TO BE CONFIRMED.
                                              Commission at .1%             £116.
                    Home Sales     29,735.
                    Export Sales   21,113.
                                  £50,848.    Paid on account until confirmed £111.   May Salaries.
```

Each month I was to be issued with a formal commission statement, the total amount being payable two months in arrears. In the first months of 1961 I was permanently stationed in New York wrestling with the problems of that market and did not discover that Fred Bushell and the accounts department had "forgotten" to calculate my commission entitlement. This was done in a combined February/March statement after I had protested but even then Fred held back £5 until he could be absolutely sure that the sum was truly mine. At this period the cost of maintaining me on the other side of the Atlantic was considerable and there may have been a psychological element in the lapse in routine.

the miracle. FDR was to be with us in a few days. I went upstairs to Fred and Colin and told them the news. Even Colin was impressed.

FDR Junior *did* arrive; we *did* have a lengthy business meeting with him – even took him out to lunch – but sadly nothing came of that interesting and very promising episode. It was left to my successors to find a way out of the US dilemma and I suspect that it was many years before (thanks to our friend the Elite) the situation reached anything approaching normality.

(iv) The SCCA and the 1961 New York Show

The importance to European car importers of the SCCA was that it dominated the genteel section of US motor sporting activity and had evolved a series of "production" and "modified" racing classifications which enabled imported cars of widely differing levels of performance to compete on a reasonably equitable basis. It was crucially important that eligible cars should be accepted for an SCCA racing classification in which they had a good chance of success and we were particularly fortunate in that the Seven and Elite were ultimately well placed. Variants of each type were allowed to run in many of the available classes – usually finding a niche in which to develop a winning streak. The SCCA was controlled by the wealthy amateurs who had begun to race after the War at East Coast and later Californian road circuits using the very best of European competition cars for the purpose. Many of the finest Ferraris, Maseratis, OSCAs and other Italian exotica were shipped to the States in this period and the great established European sporting car manufacturers such as Jaguar, Triumph, MG, Porsche, and Alfa-Romeo built their US business and reputation on the exposure and glamour of success in SCCA-organised competition. So powerful an influence was the SCCA in the market that it had created and fostered for European cars, that some manufacturers almost unknown at home developed successful business operations in the United States with the assistance of an

For the 1961 SCCA New York Region Motor Show we put on a demonstration of building the Seven America in public. I organised our participation with the full co-operation of Sy Kaback, the local Lotus distributor. We organised a free competition in which members of the public had to guess the actual time taken to assemble the Seven which we described as the "Twenty Hour Sports Car Kit". The grand door prize to the winner was in fact the car itself which was assembled by staff from Grand Prix Imported Cars in substantially less than the allotted time. This is a general view of the Stand showing an assembled Seven America in the foreground, left-hand drive Elite just visible to the left and the assembly demonstration proceeding in the background.

Middle: **A close-up of proceedings at the SCCA Show with the author (bending, left) checking progress with the partially hidden Grand Prix Imported Cars Service Manager in suitable white coat.**

enterprising local concessionaire. A particularly good example of this is the Elva case. The Elva importer was Carl Haas, known today of course for his association with the Lola-Cosworth-Ford Grand Prix and USAC cars. Haas, based in Chicago, was an outstandingly energetic businessman who encouraged Frank Nichols of Elva to produce a range of Sports Racing and eventually (with consummate timing, for delivery in time for the opening races of 1960) Formula Junior cars for the US market where by dint of early arrival on the scene they enjoyed success out of proportion to anything they later achieved in Europe. The Elva was a particularly ungainly, somewhat agricultural device fitted mainly with the BMC A-Series engine in its first year of competition during which, supported by Haas and driven by Walt Hansgen, Briggs Cunningham's No. 1, it was virtually invincible throughout the US. Similarly obscure European sporting cars such as Siata, Stanguellini and Arnolt-Bristol provided variety in other semi-amateur events, ranged against an increasingly successful domestically produced selection of cars with Detroit V8 power. A stock (Chamberlain once joked: "Stock? Of course it's stock; it cost 30,000 bucks to get it that way") or modified V8, driven well, and in a European inspired chassis such as Cunningham and Scarab could give the best imported cars a good run for their money.

Lotus had never previously participated in the SCCA New York Show, but encouraged by Kaback, for whose local operation it would have been of direct benefit, I decided that it was essential for us to use the Show as a means of increasing public awareness of the Seven in particular, which was now arriving in the US market in Series 2 form as a kit in order to qualify for lower import duty (categorised as "parts" rather than as an "unassembled car"). We faced a certain amount of competition for attention in that the same venue was being used by Jaguar to give the eager North Americans their first glimpse of the fabulous E-Type which had been launched at the 1961 Geneva Show. Like so many Jaguars the first version was the most beautiful of the series and the E-Type — seen for the first time and not much more expensive than the Elite — took our breath away. Although we had an Elite and Junior on display it was on the simple

A view in the opposite direction at the SCCA Show, revealing more of the Elite and an unsold 1960 Eighteen awaiting a buyer before being superseded by the new Twenty Formula Junior. Standing in the centre is (left) Sy Kaback talking to the bespectacled Luigi Chinetti, Ferrari Importer for North America whom I persuaded to draw the winning ticket from the boot of the Elite.

Seven in basic specification suitable for SCCA Class 'A' racing that I wished to focus attention. Remembering the success of the Seven in the Do-It-Yourself exhibition in Rotterdam in October 1959 where we had assembled a car publicly for the first time, I decided to repeat the process. The Service Manager of Grand Prix Imported Cars was provided (unusually) with clean coveralls for the purpose and with an assistant was set to assemble a Series 2 Seven Kit against the clock with a target of completion in less than twenty hours. At the same time we ran a competition to guess the actual time taken to complete assembly; the first prize for which was to be a Seven Kit. The attention aroused by this stunt was enormous and we were besieged by interested would-be winners. The competition entries were eventually loaded into the boot (propped open by the jack handle of course) of the largely ignored Elite and the winner drawn out by Dorothy Brown, Kaback's Personal (and personable) Assistant and Manager of Grand Prix Imported Cars.

I was unable to resist the opportunity to ask the admired Luigi Chinetti, North American Ferrari importer and winner at Le Mans in 1949, to present the prize. The whole operation was a great success for us and really helped to put the Seven range on the map in America. During 1961 Sevens achieved overwhelming success in SCCA races; winning both Class A and Class C (Super Seven). The SCCA Show was in fact the only automotive exhibition in which we participated during my period with Lotus in North America and was a most welcome diversion from the high level of stress and difficulty characterising my working life at the time. We were able to capitalise on our achievements in New York by booking substantial orders from Sy Kaback and John Posselius which gave us cheer and comfort at this particularly gloomy point in Lotus fortunes.

(v) My Company Cars

Because I continued to live twenty five miles across country from Cheshunt at Leagrave, Luton, it was agreed that contrary to established practice for non-directors, I would be provided by the company with transportation to enable me to commute. In the first instance transportation was provided by a Lotus Developments Ford 300E Van or Team Lotus' rather tall Thames 15 cwt van powered by a Ford Consul 1703 cc engine. Whereas the 300E was a fairly manageable vehicle, the big Thames – which was much narrower than the later Transit – had to be driven with caution. In the wet it had an alarming tendency to continue straight ahead when one wished to round a corner and even on dry surfaces it would demonstrate similar understeering characteristics at higher speeds.

My travels in the late summer of 1959 when I was engaged in setting up the United Kingdom distributor and dealer network for the Seven were courtesy of Nobby Clark's Ford Consul Saloon car. This was a series 2 model and had originally been Colin's company car before he bought the Zodiac. The Consul is rather like a foreshortened Zephyr/Zodiac but fitted with a 4-cylinder engine. Modified Consul engines were used from time to time in the Lotus Mk. 6 (beginning with the prototype of 1952) and we even had an unsuccessful experimental version of the Elite at Cheshunt with a Ford Consul engine in a desperate attempt to work out a means of avoiding the aggression of the commercial relationship with Coventry Climax. Unfortunately, the Consul, like the FPF engine intended for Le Mans, is so much heavier than the FWE Climax, that the project was abandoned. For my 1959 promotional trip the Consul covered 1500 miles in a week of hard driving and did very well. The noble Nobby used one of "my" vans for the period, having in his long-suffering and good-natured way made my task easier. It was back to the vans on my return. However, one learns not to look a gift horse in the mouth and soon I was rescued by the introduction of the Ford 105E Anglia Saloon in October 1959. The arrival of this vehicle meant that Mike Costin's A35 Saloon became surplus to requirements and was allocated to me as Mike took over his new baby; the first small Ford with overhead valve engine and a very different kettle of fish from the sidevalvers that preceded it. The A35 differed superficially very little from the earlier A30 but in fact it was a drastically different animal. The only visual changes were a larger rear window and chrome plated radiator grille, but the greatest advance was the installation of the 948 cc A-Series BMC engine and gearbox which although directly derived from the 803 cc unit of the A30 was a much tougher, perfect power source for saloon car racing. The 948 cc engine would respond well to tuning and with modest suspension modifications A35s in the hands of John Sprinzel and Graham Hill regularly took on and often beat Works Mk. 2 Jaguars.

On my first visit to Downton after acquiring the A35 I discussed with Daniel Richmond the possibility of fitting a pair of Amal motorcycle carburettors which I had retained from my Dante Engineering days. Daniel was interested to try the experiment and designed a tubular steel inlet and exhaust manifold which was fabricated by his star welder Janosz Odor (later to found Janspeed a little further up the road from his point of departure). I would not normally recommend Amal carburettors for road use; they are not as forgiving as SUs and must be opened progressively by a sensitive right foot to ensure smooth pick-up. However, my Downton A35 which also featured a gasflowed high compression cylinder head made a wonderful noise from the unrestricted inlet venturis and relaxed silencing arrangements. Unfortunately the suspension and brakes remained absolutely standard so that the heightened acceleration and general speed capabilities caused frequent moments of acute anxiety. Later, while absent on one of my trips abroad the Amal carburettors and Downton inlet/exhaust manifold disappeared while the car was in the care of the Service Department and nobody, strangely enough had any ideas as to why or how this could have happened or could even

remember that the car had been thus equipped. Nevertheless, I am quite sure that

another little A35 or A40 not a million miles from Cheshunt was going rather faster than hitherto.

Later in my career I was handed the Costin 105E Anglia 744 HNK when Mike moved on to a Consul Classic 315. "My" Anglia was very well loosened up by this time and certainly motored impressively. I asked Mike whether he felt it would be a good idea to have a little Cosworth handiwork incorporated in the engine which brought forth the immortal admonition "never bugger about with the bread and butter car, Robin". My totally standard Anglia served me well until the end of my time with Lotus.

Although I had made my first UK sales tour in Nobby Clark's Series Two Ford Consul, I needed a more appropriate car for promotional purposes. Lotus Components built up a prototype of the Seven Series One "A" which was the interim model intended to revitalise Seven sales and hold the fort until the Series Two cars could be ready in the following year. This delightful Sprite engined Seven Series One finished in bright red with silver wheels and registered 703 HNK became my "company car" for fairly long journeys visiting British distributors and dealers when the weather was reasonable. It was also used as our regular demonstrator during late 1959 and early 1960. The two Series One Sevens 7 TMT, the "Super" with Climax engine and my little Sprite engined roadster gave me the most enjoyable motoring in my time at Lotus. Although the later Series Two Super Seven with Cosworth 1340 cc engine was at least as fast as 7 TMT there was never any doubt that the original Series One version of the Seven current from October 1957 to early 1960 was a better car in every way. We made

John Bolster of *Autosport* could always be relied on to give Lotus a good press. He had been an enthusiastic advocate of the Chapman philosophy since the days of the Mk.6. As an ex-hillclimb and sprint expert and former ERA driver, he took to the Super Seven like a duck to water and conducted a marvellous road test in April 1961 which featured this photograph rounding Druids at Brands Hatch. It was the allegedly unauthorised expenditure of funds on an advertisement incorporating this photograph in the United States which finally gave Chapman the excuse to sack the author so it occupies a special place in his memory. At a price of £599 in kit form the Super Seven Series Two with Cosworth Ford 1340 cc power unit was the Bargain of the Century and had performance which is astounding even by the standards of nearly thirty years later. The high power of the Cosworth engine overtaxed certain elements of Series Two Seven design – most notably the rear axle location arrangements – but apart from that it was a perfectly practical all-round road car that gave a glimpse of real motor racing performance for a song.

Even by Lotus standards a fantastic machine!

The NEW Lotus Super Seven offers you performance hitherto confined to ultra-expensive sports cars of over 3-litres capacity. Fitted with an 85 b.h.p. Cosworth-Ford Classic 1340 cc power unit, featuring twin choke Weber 40DCOE2 carburettors and four branch exhaust manifold, the Super Seven, with a power-to-weight ratio of 200 b.h.p. per ton, will accelerate to 60 m.p.h. in less than 7 seconds and exceed the 'ton' with contemptuous ease. The new Super Seven tempers its exciting Formula Junior get-up-and-go with docile road manners and perfect safety (race-bred brakes and steering). Take a Super-Seven touring, racing or just shopping—you'll be delighted not only by the performance, but also by its brilliant design, precise execution and comprehensive standard equipment. In component form, for twenty-hour assembly (including woodrim steering wheel, flared front wings, full weather protection and interior trim), all at this low, low price . . .

LOTUS SUPER SEVEN

£599

more Series Ones in the last six months of its life than were sold during the first two years and with a well tuned BMC A-series engine it made a wonderful all round clubmans sports car; very much a four-wheeled motorcycle.

The Works Demonstrator/Road Test fleet disposed of its Series One Sevens (7 TMT going to Peter Warr) as soon as the new Series Two cars came on stream. We had a Downton-modified Seven Series Two "A" and eventually the first of the Series Two Super Sevens powered by a 1340 cc Ford 109E engine with Cosworth-modified cylinder head, camshaft, and two Weber 40DCOE carburettors to gobble the atmosphere. The Super Seven was of course a wonderfully exciting road car easy to drive relatively rapidly and up to 80 mph capable of holding off virtually anything encountered in its day.

During my first year in New York (1960) while I was very much under the wing of John Dugdale and through him the Rover Company of North America I was provided with a 3-litre automatic Rover Saloon which was used to accomplish relatively long journeys in and out of Canada and on the East Coast. This car represented the most extreme case of unfulfilled wishful thinking on the part of a British motor manufacturer trying to develop the North American market (Land Rovers sold well in Canada and parts of the US as an expensive alternative to the Jeep). Although I was extremely grateful to Rover for their generosity in providing the car, it was an experience forgotten instantly after the arrival of my Elite.

I drove demonstrator Elites in the UK and eventually while on my longest stint in the States an Elite Series Two was sent over for me in January 1961 (Chassis No. 1712). This car was garaged in New York and used for out-of-town journeys to the Middle West, up and down the East Coast and an unforgettable trip to Sebring in February 1961 which involved leaving New York in mid-Winter and gradually during a period of 48 hours travelling through the seasons from Spring to Summer in Florida. Miraculously the Elite reached Sebring intact, but on the return the clutch slave cylinder expired and although being a commonly available type from the MGA, and despite MG being extremely popular in the States, I was unsuccessful in my attempts to locate a replacement. I therefore achieved the minor distinction of driving from South Carolina to New York without the facility of a clutch. This was done by setting the tickover at 2000 rpm and using the light weight of the Elite to permit moving away from rest on the starter motor and sticking to major highways requiring a minimum of clutchless gearchanges.

I cannot disguise my lack of enthusiasm for the Elite. When everything was functioning properly it had many excellent qualities even though these were best suited to the race track. Apart from the episode of the defective clutch slave cylinder the only misfortune experienced with my US car was when I was forced off the road by a belligerent truck driver while attempting to overtake on an icy surface in Upstate New York. There was no other vehicle in sight and the truck driver must have welcomed the opportunity for a little light amusement. Inevitably I eventually left the road after attempting to hold a series of monumental slides but fortunately the snow covering the central reservation was so deep that the Elite was instantly buried and brought to rest before reaching the other carriageway. Removing my window in the approved fashion I was able to scoop away enough snow to allow the door to open and emerge to the amazement of a passing group of college students returning from a skiing holiday. They easily managed to heave car and occupants clear of the snow and return us to the roadway without a single scratch to show for the mishap. My wife in the passenger seat was somewhat shaken by events and we therefore halted at the next motel to recover her composure before proceeding the following day, although I was so relieved that I was ready to continue forthwith.

The Elite faced competition in continental racing from two principal rivals. During 1962-63 the Abarth Simca although possessed of evil handling characteristics derived so much power from its twin-cam 1300 cc engine that it was virtually uncatchable on any circuit with reasonable straights. Shortly after the Elite began to race internationally the Alfa Romeo SZ appeared on the scene and under the right circumstances (races requiring powers of endurance rather than sheer speed) gave a good account of itself against the Elite. The SZ is constructed on the contemporary Giulietta floorpan and mechanicals on which a superstructure of steel tube and aluminium panels was designed and erected by Zagato. The result was much heavier than the Elite but developed a little more power in compensation. It certainly did not handle as well as its British competitor but adequately enough and of course it had remarkable durability to keep it going when others fell by the wayside. This photograph shows Biscaldi driving to a class win in the May 27 1962 Bologna Raticosa.

My real motoring joys were reserved for the opportunities – mainly in California – to drive some of the marvellous European cars imported at that time and to be found on car lots throughout the States. On my first visit Jay Chamberlain handed me an almost new white Jaguar XK 150 Fixed Head Coupé taken in part-exchange from Jack Lemmon. The heavy Moss gearbox of this car and its handling reminded me of an extremely potent truck, but the Special Equipment 3.8 litre Jaguar engine is unquestionably a thing of joy and I felt absolutely at home on the Sunset Strip in this genuine Hollywood speedster.

More to my taste were the small Italian sporting cars which abounded. The Porsche Importer Hoffman of New York had a simple technique to move unwanted Lancias which he also distributed. The Porsche sold like hot cakes and therefore for a dealer to earn the opportunity of selling one Porsche 356 he was obliged to take a couple of unwanted Lancia Sedans. Jay Chamberlain had a pillarless Appia which he could not give away, but which was in my eyes a thing of modest beauty and marvellous engineering. I also drove my first Alfa there; the 1300 cc Giulietta Spyder (sic) which despite a small capacity engine and substantial structure performed in undramatic well-bred style and with the indefinable Alfa "feel" which keeps a Milan-built car of this make in my garage today.

Fred Bushell and I had fun with a Fiat Abarth 750 Zagato Coupé; another car very much to my taste. The Abarth was about the right size for Fred and we used it to go to and from our motel during the famous thirty day negotiating party. The Italians are uniquely able to take something as mundane as the 600 Fiat

Towards the end of the competition life of the Elite its pre-eminent position (and that of the contemporary Alfa Romeo SZ) was usurped by the fiendishly rapid Abarth Simca 1300 (this is the Davis/Cuomo entry at Sebring 1963). Carlo Abarth was responsible for a dazzling array of high performance cars, some of which – particularly in later years – were entirely of his manufacture. However, the Abarth reputation was built on the conversion of humble roadgoing cars and components into machinery suitable for international competition. For the first decade of its existence Abarth & C. of Turin produced performance conversions for Fiat cars and a wide range of complete vehicles based on the Fiat 500 and 600 floorpan in the main, to which were fitted aluminium bodies (some by Zagato and Allemano) and engines generally of 1 litre or less. In 1961 Abarth began the construction of a car based on the Simca 1000 Saloon chassis and this new Abarth Simca 1300GT raced for the first time in the following year. Although the floorpan was fairly standard (but with wheelbase shortened by 100 mm) Simca 1000 beneath the very beautiful aluminium body built by Carrozzeria Beccaris, the 1300 cc DOHC engine was the first 100% Abarth power unit, even the cast iron block at last being specially made. The general layout of this three bearing engine closely resembled the earlier Fiat Abarth Bialbero type which in itself was a design (little known) of the great Gioachino Colombo. The standard version had four-speed transmission but options were later available (within the Simca transaxle casing) to give five or six forward gears. Once early handling problems had been overcome the outstanding power-to-weight ratio of the Abarth Simca gave it total superiority over the Alfa SZ and the Lotus Elite.

floorpan, graft on to it a thing of beauty like the Zagato "double bubble" body and a collection of Abarth "go faster" bits to produce a gem of a motor car so beautifully made and equipped (with large Jaeger instruments, Nardi steering wheel and all the trimmings) as to link it directly in style and engineering quality with the great Italian sporting mainstream crowned by the products of the Prancing Horse. Fred preferred his Ford Consul Classic so I was happy to act as chauffeur.

(vi) Lotus Advertising and Sales Literature

The move of Lotus from Hornsey to Cheshunt had psychological undertones. Cheshunt represented a fresh start; a new leaf would be turned and the misdeeds and inadequacies of the recent past would henceforth not be repeated. I had been brought into the company to manage the process of improving our image in the public eye as well as to strengthen commercial methods and performance. I understood the problem well because my own perception of Lotus before joining had been poor – a company that had lost its way; that might even fade away – and I and a thousand others had reached that conclusion without knowing a tenth of the whole story.

However, having familiarised myself with the company during the first weeks of my tenure, I was filled with enthusiasm to present Lotus as it could be if the innate talent and promise were revealed. It was essential to present Lotus in a completely new light if the Elite were to succeed commercially. The Elite was the key to change and the way to greater things, therefore it must not be confused with Lotus kit cars and the rough and tumble of motor racing represented by its predecessors. At that time the Seven was seen in a completely different light from its present day, expensive Caterham successor. In those days the Seven was a very basic kit car (eventually the cheapest version was priced at £399). It was way below the Morgan class and certainly not to be considered by the potential Elite buyer. Fortunately the Elite raced among Grand Touring cars and was beginning to establish a Le Mans reputation which was quite sufficiently up-market for our purposes.

The Elite had to be seen against the background of competition from Alfa Romeo and Porsche. These too were expensive but had established a reputation for superb engineering, durability and finish. They also bore household names from the world of high performance motoring. For a dealer it was not necessary to persuade an enthusiast of the virtue of Porsche or Alfa, only to enable him to find some way of finding the large sum of money to acquire one. With very few exceptions the Elite customer would be a sophisticated buyer who had probably already experienced ownership of the direct competition or at least something expensive and well established such as Jaguar, Lancia or Austin-Healey. After the first few madmen, seduced by the racing connection (or even wanting a car purely for racing purposes), it was going to be a hard uphill struggle to move the relatively large numbers (up to 750 cars in a year) that we had in mind.

There was only provisional sales literature for the Elite. Because the car had been a long time in finalisation and because too there were no cars available to satisfy demand that might thus be aroused, my predecessor had no incentive to rush seriously into print. Chapman had studiously avoided encouraging the Press to conduct road tests in the United Kingdom and most particularly, in the US. There had never been discussion of a co-ordinated advertising or promotional programme or consideration of how literature might be jointly produced and financed. My first duty therefore was to rush out a simple brochure for the car and this was done much in the style established before my time, using antiquated photographs with my wording representing the new thinking.

We had to present the Elite in a way that would appeal on the broadest possible front to people with both taste and money (and there were even fewer of them then than now). We had also to be sure that the car would appeal beyond the male enthusiast to his wife and family; perhaps even to his parents. Therefore it was necessary to play down the racing element and project the Elite as an elegant and sophisticated product in impeccable taste that would add to the stature of the owner. In order to convey this image and message I felt it essential to use the very highest standards of photography and graphic design.

Several years previously I had met Michael Boys, who after photographing my wedding in 1954, went on to take some excellent shots of the products of the Dante Engineering Company. I knew Michael well and admired his work for the fashion world. It was therefore appropriate to invite him to come up with a series

Lotus Elite

Lotus Elite

Beneath the sleek slope of the bonnet lies the famous overhead camshaft Coventry Climax Power Unit – latent power at your instant call, yet so sweet tempered that the Elite will trickle through city traffic with utter docility. High efficiency yields twin virtues of flashing acceleration and remarkably low fuel consumption at three-figure cruising speeds.

The compact form of the Elite belies its spacious interior and boot. Suitcases, golf-clubs and other luggage may easily be stowed. The Elite affords generous accommodation for two – truly luxurious travel.

The suspension system of the Elite is directly derived from that used on the Lotus Grand Prix and Sports Racing cars, giving unparalleled road adhesion and comfort. The unique self-compensating properties of the Chapman Strut independent rear suspension ensure consistent handling under extreme variations of load, and Lotus rack and pinion steering gear gives faultless steering control under the most hazardous conditions of surface and 'line'.

Emergency ? . . . Feel the iron hand of the four wheel Girling disc brakes safely sweep away all anxiety as they rush the car smoothly to rest . . .

The Elite is tailored for travel in comfort. The thoughtfully designed seats establish new criteria for sheer luxury: cradling you restfully for all-day driving.

The wood-rimmed steering-wheel and short remote control gear-lever are arranged to reduce driver fatigue and give complete command. Other features include matt non-reflecting dash-cowl, pile carpeting and read-at-a-glance instruments to satisfy the most critical judgment.

I commissioned Michael Boys (today an internationally renowned fashion photographer but then known to me as the man who photographed my wedding in 1954) to take a series of photographs to be used in advertising and sales literature during 1960. Graphic designer Derek Birdsall evolved this six-panel double sided leaflet for the Series Two Elite using an "atmospheric" Boys side view of the car with attractive model coupled with a revealing, doors, trunk and bonnet lid open shot from above and a discreet reference to the Elite on the track. The copy in this and all other Lotus sales literature until early 1962 was written by me and the unusual 150 mm square folded format then became the norm during my period as Sales Manager.

Those interested in competition work will find the Lotus "Elite" well up to any demands made. The prices and specifications of competition modifications can be obtained on application to the Factory Sales Department.

OPTIONAL EQUIPMENT APPROVED FOR

THE LOTUS ELITE Series Two

The Lotus Elite is the finest compact Grand Touring Car in the world. Brilliant 'brain child' of the highly successful Lotus design team led by Colin Chapman, the Elite will carry you to the highest realms of modern motoring in superb comfort, speed and safety.

The unique lightweight monocoque glass fibre-reinforced plastic body unit draws unanimous praise for its strength, durability and refinement. It has been thoroughly tested and proved in thousands of miles of racing and high speed road use by the world's leading competition drivers.

The purity of line of this revolutionary thoroughbred excites admiration from any viewpoint. A superb combination of strictly functional aerodynamic form, first class driver vision and sheer elegance.

Subtle detail improvements have led to the introduction of the standard Series Two car. The basic conception of the Elite has been retained and modifications introduced to further refine the suspension and interior appointments.

Peak of perfection is represented by the Lotus Elite Series Two Special Equipment model, fitted with supertuned engine, all synchromesh close ratio gearbox, exclusive interior appointments and range of colour schemes.

The Lotus Factory at Cheshunt was specifically created for the production of the Lotus Elite. In the most modern high-performance car factory in the world, specialist craftsmen produce the Elite under conditions of the utmost precision and cleanliness, reinforced by a strict multiple-inspection system – the finest guarantee.

With monotonous regularity, the Lotus Elite has consistently gained success in motoring competition throughout the world. Class and Index of Thermal Efficiency Wins at Le Mans; success at the Nürburgring, the T.T. – at home and abroad the Elite emphasizes again and again its unchallenged superiority as the world's finest compact Grand Touring Car.

Technical specification Standard model

Frame
Integral chassis/body construction. Unique, extremely strong chassisless structure of glass reinforced polyester resin, conferring the important advantages of exceptional strength, impact resistance, sound damping and thermal insulation. Two seater, two door coachwork offering spacious accommodation for two persons with provision for luggage in separate compartment. A wrap-around glass windscreeen and side windows with hinged quarter lights for ventilation. Large wrap-around rear window. Attractive colour schemes.

Front suspension
Independent by transverse wishbones incorporating anti-roll bar. Springing by combined coil spring-damper units reacting through a single attachment point at each end.

Rear suspension
Independent rear suspension by latest Chapman Strut system, incorporating combined coil spring-damper units and including double articulated drive shaft giving lateral location. This system has been expressly designed to offer a certain amount of camber change with increase in load, to maintain good handling characteristics under all conditions.

Brakes
Hydraulically operated 9½in. disc brakes, outboard at the front, inboard at the rear. Horizontally mounted umbrella type hand brake operating rear calipers through cables.

Steering
Lightweight rack and pinion steering gear.

Power unit
Coventry Climax 1216 c.c. engine. Single o.h.c., 4 cylinders bore and stroke 3in. · 2·62in. 74·25cu.in. (76·2 m.m. · 66·6 m.m. 1216 c.c.) Max. 75 b.h.p. at 6100 r.p.m. Compression ratio 10·0:1. The engine is water cooled and has a steel crankshaft of fully counter-weighted design with a large overlap between crank-pins and main journals, carried in three 2⅛in. diameter and 1in. wide main bearings of lead-bronze steel backed thin strip type. The aluminium pistons are fitted with plated top rings Connecting rods are split diagonally. Big end bearings are renewable lead-bronze strip type. High mechanical efficiency is provided by a piston speed of 2500ft. min. at 5750 r.p.m. Cylinder head of heat treated aluminium. Valve of XB steel rest on shrunk-in Austenitic cast iron seatings. Chain driven camshaft directly operating the valves through piston type cast iron tappets. Spur gear type oil pump with built-in relief valve. Renewable element type full-flow filter. Horizontal 1½in. S.U. carburettor.

Transmission
Single 8in. diameter, dry plate clutch hydraulically operated. 4-speed gearbox with the following ratios: 1st, 3·67:1; 2nd, 2·20:1; 3rd, 1·32:1; top 1:1; reverse 3·67:1.

Final drive
Hypoid final drive unit, standard ratio 4·22 to 1, the following axle ratios available at option: 3·7, 4·55 and 4·875. Typical speeds per 1000 r.p.m. (with standard 4·80 15 rear tyres) 3·7 19·33 m.p.h. (31·2 km.p.h.) 4·22 16·95 m.p.h. (27·3 km.p.h.) 4·55 15·73 m.p.h. (25·3 km.p.h.) 4·875 14·66 m.p.h. (23·6 km.p.h.).

Cooling system
Tube and Gill radiator with integral header tank. Thermostatically controlled electric cooling fan.

Fuel system
Rear mounted fuel tank, total capacity 6½ gallons. A.C. fuel pump.

Electrical system
Special heavy duty 12 volt amp.hr. battery. Coil and distributor; centrifugal advance and retard. Belt driven dynamo; automatic voltage control. Fuse box mounted under bonnet. Recessed Lucas P700 7in. head lamps. Separate side lamps. Flasher units. Twin stop-tail lights, twin rear number plate illumination lights, twin high frequency horns. Instrument lighting with brightness control. Two speed electric screen wiper.

Instruments
4in. tachometer, 0–8000 r.p.m. 4in. 0–140 m.p.h. speedometer. Oil-pressure gauge. Petrol gauge. Water temperature gauge and ammeter.

Wheels and tyres
Knock-on 15 in. wire wheels with identical rims front and rear are fitted with 4·80 × 15 4-ply rating high performance tyres. Spare wheel mounted at rear of body.

Dimensions
Wheel base 7ft. 4in. Front and rear track 3ft. 11in. Overall length 12ft. 6in. Height to roof 3ft. 10in. Overall width 4ft. 10in. Minimum ground clearance 6½in.

Weight
Standard Elite, less fuel 11½ cwt.

Optional extra equipment
Heater/demister unit; radio; seat belts; full range of special competition equipment (details available on request).

Lotus Elite, Series Two Special Equipment model incorporates twin carburettor 84 b.h.p. engine; 4-speed all-synchromesh gearbox; heater/demister unit; exclusive range of dual and single colour schemas.

The Lotus Elite is protected by a six month Warranty. Specialised service facilities for the Elite are available throughout the United Kingdom at established Lotus Centres, and internationally in the workshops of overseas Lotus Distributors.

See and try the Lotus Elite Series Two now, at your Lotus Centre:

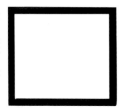

The Lotus Elite
is manufactured and distributed by:
Lotus Cars Limited, Delamare Road,
Cheshunt, Herts. Telephone Waltham Cross 26181

Layout by Derek Birdsall/printed by Balding + Mansell

Opposite page bottom and below: **To accompany the new Birdsall Lotus Elite brochure we later produced the supplementary optional equipment leaflet shown here, bearing a Michael Boys photograph of an elegantly-clad model by the side of our promotional car. On the reverse Team Elite's John Wagstaff is seen accelerating away from a wide-running TVR at the Mallory Park hairpin.**

SPECIAL EQUIPMENT SERIES

A complete set of Special Equipment Components can be supplied with a new car which when built will bring the car to the Series II "Special Equipment" model specification. This extra equipment comprises: ZF close ratio, all synchromesh four-speed gearbox, 4.2/1 final drive ratio, heater/de-mister unit, Lucas PL head-lights, Special Equipment engine, ash trays, dual tone finish, "Monza" quick release filler cap. **£152 0 0**

Fresh air heater/de-mister unit (on basic model) **£18 15 0**

Special coachwork finish to customer's own colour
(i) Complete finish in one colour **£45 0 0**
(ii) Complete finish in dual tone colours **£55 0 0**
(iii) Dual tone finish with any one of the three standard colours as the main finish **£12 10 0**

Tyre options
(i) Pirelli "Cintura" (set of five) **£6 10 0**
(ii) Michelin "X" tyres **£4 10 0**

Alternative final drive ratios
Comprising 4.9/1, 4.2/1, 3.7/1 **£7 10 0**

Filler cap
"Monza" type standard diameter quick release type in alloy **£4 10 0**

Long range fuel tank
Constructed in light alloy 10½ imperial gallon capacity **£23 10 0**

Brake vacuum servo
Giving feather light, but progressive pedal pressure, with immense stopping power, fitted complete **£27 16 1**

Stage II 90 b.h.p. engine
This unit can be supplied with the Standard or Special Equipment Model. The specification comprises high lift camshaft, extractor 4-branch exhaust system, carburation and ignition modifications. This unit raises the maximum speed of the "Elite" to 120 m.p.h. and reflects a considerable improvement in acceleration times.
(i) With Standard Model **£87 0 0**
(ii) With Special Equipment Model **£76 0 0**

Red spot. Heavy duty road wheels
Set of five **£10 10 0**

Air duct to carburettors
Moulded into the bonnet, this duct directs fresh cold air to the carburettor intakes **£14 12 6**

Weber carburettors
Pair of twin choke 40/DCOE/2 type carburettors to suit Standard, Special Equipment or Stage II engines complete with inlet manifolds, fuel piping, etc. **£79 10 0**

Z.F. gearbox
All synchromesh close ratio as supplied on Special Equipment Model, but supplied on Standard Model to replace the M.G. unit. **£98 17 6**

Oil cooler assembly
Complete with special filter mountings, radiator, high pressure piping, duct, unions, etc. **£31 0 0**

Seat belts per seat from **£8 10 0**

All prices are stated net ex works and are subject to change and/or alteration without notice. The factory sales department will be pleased to advise on the supply and availability of any of the above items of extra equipment. All prices quoted are extra to the basic price.

LOTUS ELITE

QUEEN OF GRAND TOURING

Glassfibre reinforced plastic unitary construction, all-independent
suspension, four wheel disc brakes, Coventry Climax 1216 c.c.
power unit.

MANUFACTURED AND DISTRIBUTED BY :—

LOTUS CARS LTD.

DELAMARE ROAD, CHESHUNT, HERTS.   Tel. Waltham Cross 26181

In 1960 the author commissioned Michael Boys – a friend of several years – to take a series of promotional photographs of the Elite. Here is one of the most beautiful, taken in the rain, in an English country lane and used with characteristic Lotus typography for "Lotus Elite" in a crudely assembled advertisement for *Sports Car and Lotus Owner* of August 1960. *SC & LO* depended heavily on subsidies from Lotus in the form of paid advertising and the August issue threatened to become a disaster financially without special effort on our part. Pat Stephens came up to Cheshunt with a big stick and we responded in magnificent style by creating instant advertisements to fill any blank spaces remaining after the enthusiastic support of the Lotus Centres had been spread among the text.

of photographs of the Elite to create a style for the car which would appeal to the target audience. Boys responded by selecting a top model, dressing her elegantly and then photographing car and driver in a series of striking settings. While not "atmospheric" in the style that we know today they are certainly photographs with a message and were "different" from general run-of-the-mill automotive illustrations of the time.

Michael Boys was purely a photographer and I therefore needed to track down a graphic designer who could take the photographs and listen to the message that I wished to convey before putting the whole thing together. Michael Boys led me to Derek Birdsall and I recognised in him the remarkable talent that has led him to the top of the tree in the international design world. Derek began by creating advertisements in which Boys' photographs stated the message virtually unaided. Our first advertisement for the Elite showed the Boys photographs with a simple message within the border of the photograph itself. People began to see Lotus in a completely new light and the visual impact of our advertising was immediate and effective.

Subsequently Derek Jolly, Lotus importer for Australia and extremely accomplished photographer took similar photographs of the Seven Series Two in which driver and passenger were carefully chosen and dressed to position the cars above the oily mechanic/racing driver owner image associated with Lotus

pre-1960.

Lotus Seven Series Two

............Latest expression of the Lotus theme

..................the Lotus Seven is firmly established as today's leading light sports car in the British tradition

....and the Series Two continues that tradition in a more advanced form, offering

............even finer value for money than ever before, with improved performance, roadholding and weather protection

........................Available in easy-to-assemble component form, suitable for Ford or BMC 'A' power-unit

....Write today for the address of your nearest Lotus Centre to

...............................Lotus Components Ltd, Delamare Road, Cheshunt Herts. Telephone WALtham Cross 26181

Derek Jolly, the Lotus importer for Australia was an excellent photographer and, arriving in the UK with the attractive lady shown here, offered to take a set of photographs for us in the original Seven Series Two "A" demonstrator. This is an early (August 1960) Birdsall advertisement using the inclined text written by the author and later developed for the 1961 advertising campaign.

The new presentation carried through to the sales literature that followed my original hastily produced Elite leaflet and the competent but not particularly imaginative sales literature used for cars in the Hornsey days. The first 100% Birdsall leaflet was for the Elite and he produced his famous (now a collector's item) Elite leaflet which folded to form a 150 mm square pack. Opened out the Elite appeared atmospherically through a selection of orange and blue tones linking it to the Grand Prix successes of 1960 but in all other respects positioning the car well above the old Lotus. Subsequent sales literature for the Seven and later (1961) the Super Seven followed this established pattern; all the Birdsall leaflets folding to the same square and opening out with six panels of information front and rear. I wrote the "copy" and attempted to match my wording to the avant-garde presentation of visual images. Not everybody liked our sales literature but they certainly noticed it and it was used too in overseas markets with translated text where appropriate.

We employed Michael Boys alone to photograph the Elite and having run the initial campaign and established the Elite as an up-market product, the emphasis switched more to the written message. This became particularly important in the case of the Elite in October 1961 when the car was presented in kit form. Now we had yet again to face the problem of putting over the car as an up-market product justifying what by kit car standards was an immense price tag, despite being much less than that of the factory-assembled Elite. We strenuously avoided use of the word "kit" and from October 1961 in the British market the Elite was supplied in "component presentation". I coined the phrase "How to join the Elite in 24 hours! . . ." and with as much abandon as could be summoned wrote copy making light of this sudden change of emphasis. In fact the Elite had a new lease of life as a kit car although it still sold at a relatively modest level. I played no part in the launch of the Elan but felt that I (had I been there) or my successors would have been forced to start again with this new model to present a credible image after the débâcle of the Elite. To switch to kit presentation after selling the car as an up-market international-quality Grand Tourer was just "not-on". At the time I felt strongly that we should have persisted with marketing it as intended but Chapman overruled me and I suspect that he had even less confidence in the staying power of the product. Nevertheless the Elan sold ten times the volume of the Elite so my nervousness was unjustified.

LOTUS ELITE

The unique lightweight glass fibre-reinforced plastic body unit draws unanimous praise for its strength, durability and refinement. It has been thoroughly tested and proved in thousands of miles of racing and high speed road use by the world's leading competition drivers. Beneath the sleek slope of the bonnet lies the famous overhead camshaft Coventry Climax Power Unit, latent power at your instant call, yet so sweet tempered that the Elite will trickle through city traffic with utter docility. High efficiency yields twin virtues of flashing acceleration and remarkably low fuel consumption at three-figure cruising speeds.

The suspension system of the Elite is directly derived from that used on the Lotus Grand Prix and Sports Racing cars, giving unparalleled road adhesion and comfort. The unique self-compensating properties of the Chapman Strut independent rear suspension ensure consistent handling under extreme variations of load, and Lotus rack and pinion steering gear gives faultless steering control under the most hazardous conditions of surface and 'line'.

Emergency ? ... feel the iron hand of the four-wheel Girling disc brakes safely sweep away all anxiety as they rush the car smoothly to rest. With monotonous regularity, the Lotus Elite has contrived to win the index of Thermal Efficiency award throughout the world. Outstanding index of Thermal Efficiency Wins at Le Mans, success at the Nurburgring, the T.T. – at home and abroad the Elite emphasizes again and again its unchallenged superiority as the world's finest compact Grand Touring Car.

The Lotus Elite is the finest compact Grand Touring Car in the world. Brilliant 'brain child' of the highly successful Lotus design team led by Colin Chapman, the Elite will carry you to the highest realms of modern motoring in superb comfort, speed and safety. The Elite is tailored for travel in comfort. The thoughtfully designed seats establish new criteria for sheer luxury; cradling you restfully for all-day driving. A compact form belies the spacious interior and boot. Suitcases, golf-clubs and other luggage may easily be stowed. The Elite affords generous accommodation for two – truly luxurious travel.

Wood-rimmed steering-wheel and short remote control gear-lever are arranged to reduce driver fatigue and give complete command. Other features include matt non-reflecting dash-cowl, pile carpeting and read-at-a-glance instruments to satisfy the most critical judgment. The Lotus Factory at Cheshunt was specifically created for the production of the Lotus Elite. In the most modern high-performance car factory in the world, specialist craftsmen produce the Elite under conditions of the utmost precision and cleanliness, reinforced by a strict multiple-inspection system – the finest guarantee of consistent quality.

General specification: Lotus Elite

Chassis/body unit: integral chassis/body construction. Unique, extremely strong chassis-less structure of fibreglass – reinforced polyester resin, combining the important advantages of exceptional strength, impact resistance, sound damping and thermal insulation. Two-seater, two-door coachwork offering spacious accommodation for two persons with provision for luggage in separate compartment. Wrap-round front and rear screens. Removable side windows with hinged quarter lights for ventilation. Stainless-steel front and rear bumpers. Luxurious adjustable seats, washable non-reflecting interior door panels and full trim. Matt non-reflecting instrument binnacle. High-quality floor carpeting. Rear parcel shelf beneath facia. Spacious door pockets. Front parcel shelf beneath facia. Foot-operated windscreen washers. **Front suspension:** independent by transverse wishbones incorporating anti-roll bar. Springing by combined coil spring-damper units reacting through rubber bushings at each point at each end. **Rear suspension:** independent by Chapman-strut system, incorporating combined coil spring-damper units and double articulated drive shafts giving lateral location. This system has been expressly designed to offer a regulated amount of camber change with variations in load, to maintain constant handling characteristics under all conditions. **Brakes:** hydraulically operated 9¹/₂" (24.13 cm.) discs on inboard rear. Handbrake mounted at front. Inboard rear brakes. outboard front. **Steering:** rack and pinion. **Power unit:** Coventry Climax FWE, light alloy water-cooled, wet-liner, single o.h.c. 4 cylinders, bore and stroke 3" × 2.62" = 74.25 cu. in. (76.2 mm. × 66.6 mm.). Capacity 1,216 c.c. Three-bearing crankshaft. Twin S.U. variable choke carburettors on light alloy manifold. Cast-iron exhaust manifold with twin silencer/tail pipes. Compression ratio 10:1. 80 b.h.p. @ 6,100 r.p.m. **Cooling system:** tube and gill radiator with integral header tank. Circulation by engine-driven water pump. Thermostatically controlled electric cooling fan. **Fuel system:** rear-mounted fuel tank, total capacity 6¹/₂ gallons (29.5 litres). Chromium-plated screw fitting fuel filler cap. **Transmission:** hydraulically operated 8" (20.32 cm.) diameter single dry plate clutch. Four-speed and reverse gearbox with remote-control shift. Ratios: First, 3.67:1. Second, 2.20:1. Third, 1.32:1. Fourth, 1.00:1. Reverse, 3.67:1. Synchromesh on upper 3 ratios. **Final drive:** Hypoid bevel final drive unit in light alloy casing; rubber mounted to chassis/body structure. **Electrical system:** Lucas 12-volt heavy-duty 12-volt battery. Coil and distributor ignition with centrifugal advance and retard. Belt-driven generator; automatic voltage control. Fuse box mounted under hood. Recessed Lucas 7" (17.78 cm.) headlamps. Separate sidelamps. Flashing direction indicators. Twin stop-tail lights; twin rear registration plate lights; twin high-frequency horns. Instrument lighting with brightness control. Two-speed electric screen wipers. Dipping mechanism controlled from steering column. **Instruments:** Tachometer 0–8,000 r.p.m. 4" (10.16 cm.) diameter; Speedometer 0–140 m.p.h. (0–225 k.p.h.) 4" (10.16 cm.) diameter; oil-pressure gauge; fuel contents gauge; water-temperature gauge; ammeter. **Wheels and tyres:** five knock-on, wire-spoked, steel rim wheels fitted with 480 × 15, 4-ply rating, high-performance tyres. **Dimensions and weight:** wheelbase 7' 4" (223.5 cm.); front and rear track 3' 11" (119.38 cm.). Overall length 12' 6" (381 cm.). Height to roof 3' 10¹/₂" (118 cm.). Overall width 4' 10" (147.32 cm.). Minimum ground clearance 6¹/₂" (16.5 cm.). Weight: 1260 lb. (572 kg. **Colours:** Tartan Red, Conway Yellow, Light Blue and Cirrus White paintwork. Black, Red or Tan interior trim, and seats. **Principal performance figures:** maximum speed: 115 m.p.h. (185 k.p.h.). Acceleration: 0–60 m.p.h. (0–96 k.p.h.) in 11.4 sec.; 0–100 m.p.h. (0–160 k.p.h.) in 33.8 sec. Fuel consumption: 35 m.p.g. (8 litres/100 km.). **Optional extra equipment:** heater/demister unit. Alternative final drive ratio 4.2:1. Seat belts. Special paintwork in single- or dual-colour schemes to own specification. Quick release fuel filler cap. Full Race specification to F.I.A. regulations, details available on request)

To succeed the first brochure for the Elite from my time at Cheshunt (pages 84–85) Derek Birdsall designed a companion high quality six panel version matching the style and quality of the Seven Series Two brochure (pages 110–111). This was so designed to allow translation into foreign languages as required although to my knowledge it only appeared in English and French. Later when *force majeure* obliged us to relaunch the Elite as a kit car at the 1961 London Motor Show (October) a new brochure was necessary. The quality of the paper was downgraded to the same chosen for the Super Seven but my copywriting exuberance was undamped as will be observed from the text which I wrote for this edition. At that stage DAD10 was a legend and with its non-standard Frank Costin aerodynamic improvements reminded the prospective owner of the direct racing pedigree of this "...passport to a completely new world of motoring".

My working methods with Birdsall were simple but successful. The process of producing an advertisement began with my "copy" and a sketch showing how I thought the thing should be presented. This was then discussed exhaustively with Derek and between us we would come up with a final solution. Such touches as the slight angle from the horizontal of presentation of the combined Seven/Elite advertisement were entirely Birdsall's. It was a fruitful collaboration and the brochure printers concerned – Balding & Mansell of Wisbech – have remained close collaborators of Derek Birdsall since those Lotus years.

Chapter Six
Colin Chapman
The man and his circle

The only element of Lotus more fascinating than the cars of that name is the man who created the company and all that it represents.

In many ways Chapman was self-taught. He began as a civil engineer and based his technical achievement on knowledge acquired while training for that career. He had an unrivalled ability to absorb information and knowhow from others and having exhausted their usefulness would move on, having mastered yet another skill.

Colin Chapman was surrounded by a throng of disciples, sycophants, servants (my category!), collaborators and occasionally friends. I have selected a few of those whom I knew personally to give an idea of the variety of his acquaintance and the appeal of the man across a wide range of social standing, intellectual achievement and personality.

(i) Colin Chapman

On the occasions when I have watched Chapman during a television interview since the period when I knew him personally (and I had never met him or spoken to him since 1962) I have remarked upon the veneer of sophistication on the man I knew before he became a millionaire and international celebrity. Nevertheless I was conscious when observing the mature Chapman at work that the fundamental characteristics remained. I have never met a man like him before or since and to encounter and observe at first hand such an extraordinary amalgam of qualities within one human frame was an exceptional experience indeed.

Chapman was driven by an ultra-competitive approach to everything that he undertook whether it be his life work – Lotus – or what was nominally regarded as "relaxation". It was well known that when he was employed by the British Aluminium Company in the early Fifties he would work all night on Lotus matters and some of the day on British Aluminium's behalf. If things became too wearing he would – it is said – cat nap on his office drawing board set in the horizontal position. If necessary, he could work on and on to achieve his objective, regardless of the effect on others. Some of his friends and associates were able to obtain relief by walking away but others (most notably the

This previously unpublished photograph was taken at Monaco in 1981 just before Essex sponsorship of Team Lotus evaporated and only a little more than a year before Colin Chapman's untimely death. It shows the man as many prefer to remember him: totally dedicated to motor racing, enjoying life to the full and relishing the explanation just given of the cause of his black eye – a direct hit from a bread roll the night before. The flying bread roll was another Chapman hallmark.

unfortunate Mike Costin, brother of Frank the Aerodynamicist) suffered greatly. The strain on those involved in design and development during a period of high creativity (for example in 1960 as a result of the switch to mid-engined layouts) was prodigious.

From time to time Chapman would divert his attention from the technical people and lash the rest of us. His father Stan was often verbally abused for difficulties real or imagined affecting the administration of Team Lotus which was his responsibility prior to the arrival from Cooper of Andrew Ferguson. Stan after all had provided the space behind his pub The Railway Hotel, on which the first commercial Lotus operations had taken place. The Lotus factory at Hornsey grew to overshadow the pub and at the time of the move to Cheshunt Stan retired from the licensed trade and concentrated on getting Team Lotus to and from races around the world. For this service he received an honorarium, plus a 2.4 Jaguar which was as immaculate as the man himself – and regular abuse from his brilliant son. Colin could be notoriously rude to his closest employees and colleagues (the closer, the ruder). For example, if he was having a discussion with me in his office and Stan put his head round the door at the wrong moment, the conversation would quickly assume an Anglo-Saxon dimension followed by the hasty retirement to his office of the luckless parent. Fred Bushell, for whose services Chapman had so much to be grateful, was regularly subject to insults. Fred would flush bright pink with anger when treated thus, but like the rest of us would bite his tongue knowing that the wrath of ACBC was short-lived.

Not all of us perhaps were as tolerant as Costin, Bushell and Chapman Père. Colin didn't particularly mind if answered back and in fact enjoyed a good "ding-dong" when the occasion arose. During this period Peter Warr, then a junior member of the organisation but with an extremely important role, was able to control his fiery temperament but I can imagine that in later years, as his responsibilities and proximity to the Master grew, the sparks would fly.

Chapman treated me better than most for a variety of reasons. One of these was that I was carrying out duties which were new in the Lotus experience and although it never took Chapman long to pick up new ideas, while things were going in the right direction, it was possible for me to keep that little bit ahead in the world of distributor and dealer networks, importers, sales and marketing. He had a real need – and knew it – that Lotus should cast off its "cowboy" commercial image in the search for and expansion of stable markets. He may too have been intrigued by the suspicion that I was probably the least under his personal spell of all in the working circle and probably best able at that time to survive in the outside world should he tire of me.

Extended patience was not one of Chapman's characteristic virtues. Whereas he could be very charming and easy to get on with much of the time, there were moments when his violent temper touched us all. There was one occasion while I explored the furthest reaches of his unusual patience and tolerance with me personally as, in the middle of an argument, he suddenly coloured up when I asked why he was taking a particular line and answered "Because I'm the bloody Managing Director, that's why". The decision resulting from that confrontation was in fact prejudicial to our cause but Chapman presumably felt that I was encroaching too far on his prerogative.

My nature allowed me to be highly diplomatic with him and to withdraw whenever I felt the temperature rising, but this was often not possible for many of his colleagues and associates. From among a number of such occasions I recall Sir John Whitmore standing at the bottom of the office block stairs for a conversation with Chapman at his office desk some fifty feet away. We felt that Chapman won that particular challenge about some trivial Parts Department matter affecting the ability of Whitmore's car to race that weekend. Then there was the day when Keith Duckworth conducted a conversation with Chapman from the same (disad)vantage point but in which he was the decisive victor. Duckworth knew Chapman well from the period when he had briefly been an employee. He also knew that his personal future was to some considerable extent at that time linked to the fortunes of Lotus. Nevertheless being Duckworth and a bluff northerner, he liked to be paid for his services and on this particular occasion had arrived, oily-handed with shirtsleeves rolled up straight from the test house, to sort out the overdue account. From the bottom of the stairs he informed Chapman in no uncertain terms "No money – no more bloody engines". I am sure Chapman enjoyed these goings on, but I am equally sure that

COLIN CHAPMAN'S LOTUS

In November 1986, Graham Arnold of Club Lotus arranged for former Lotus employees to visit the Delamare Road factory. Few tears were shed by Mike Costin, Steve Sanville, Ron Hickman, Len Street and me but although the original Lotus Works no longer have their pristine appearance they remain largely unaltered as my snapshots show. Here is the fully triangulated, stressed skin monocoque Chapman-designed staircase leading from Reception to (ultimately) Colin's office. It was at the bottom of these stairs that disgruntled individuals including Keith Duckworth and John Whitmore would stand to inform Chapman remotely and loudly of their displeasure.

he understood the strengths and weaknesses of given situations extremely well and that Duckworth would have been paid promptly thereafter. But it was probably "Fred's fault"; Fred Bushell had many uses. After these tense moments Colin would be found sitting at his desk with a huge grin, savouring the cut and thrust of it all.

Chapman treated his working colleagues with considerable harshness on occasions but in his domestic life – from what I observed – the reverse was the case. His courtship of and successful marriage to Hazel Williams has been described elsewhere. Hazel was the ideal partner, having a relaxed and tolerant nature and a considerable understanding of the demands of her husband's chosen métier. We all liked Hazel and Colin was unquestionably devoted to her. I am sure that he discussed all his personal and business problems with his wife before making decisions. It was very much a marriage of true minds. By the time I joined Lotus Hazel was occupied by a young family and was not often seen at Cheshunt, but I remember on one occasion visiting the Chapman household at Gothic Cottage with my wife for dinner to discover Colin working at his drawing board, watching television and conversing simultaneously (one of his legendary attributes) and then sitting down to a meal and light-hearted banter. He certainly enjoyed provocation and on that occasion we had an amusing and convivial evening. When in the right frame of mind he could be an entertaining companion with an infectious laugh and inexhaustible charm. There is a good story to illustrate the Chapman sense of humour and the legends in which it is enshrined:

With Colin at the wheel of the tuned automatic Ford Zodiac, Mike Costin and one or two others were travelling at the usual breakneck speed to a Channel port for a continental race when they spied a frail old lady teetering towards a pedestrian crossing ahead. Chapman slowed; but perhaps rather too rapidly for the little old lady who immediately retreated to the kerb. On satisfying herself that the squealing, lurching hulk was really going to stop in time she again ventured forth only to change her mind once more. By this time Chapman had brought his large motor car to a halt, lowered the window and enquired firmly of the lady "Madam, how the hell am I going to hit you if you keep moving about like that?".

Colin divided his friends, associates and acquaintances into clear categories. To certain of them he gave enduring loyalty. This group included a wide range of personalities and talent. He was specially attached to the small group of helpers and employees who were undoubtedly essential to the company's early success. I never knew such early influences as the Allen brothers and Frank Costin, but his original full-time paid employee "Nobby" Clark and other early Lotus personnel including John Standen and Fred Bushell, had all been promoted to senior posts by the time that I joined the Company.

Chapman's circle included a very select band of motor racing people of whom without question the most important was Jim Clark. Colin had unlimited admiration for Clark's driving ability and the two of them formed the remarkable partnership which brought Lotus its first World Championship in 1963 using the Twentyfive – a car built expressly for Clark and in which he was able to exploit his talent to the full. The untimely death of Clark in 1968 at the wheel of a Lotus Formula Two car at Hockenheim was deeply upsetting to Chapman and I suspect that he may never have been able to develop quite the same rapport with any

other team driver. Before Jimmy Clark there was Alan Stacey, tragically killed at the wheel of an Eighteen in the 1960 Belgian Grand Prix. Stacey, who may indeed have had some of Clark's potential, was highly regarded by Chapman. His death was profoundly shocking to the emotional Colin and there hung in Gothic Cottage a framed photograph of Stacey, a tribute unique at the time.

Chapman had the highest regard for Stirling Moss whose stature at the time was such that he operated within the elevated and independent environment of the Rob Walker Racing Team; very much a law unto himself and now the respected "elder statesman" of motor racing. Chapman also had great admiration for Graham Hill. Hill's remarkable racing career is well documented, but it is appropriate to recall that his first period as a professional driver was with Team Lotus. Hill held the job of Engine Shop Foreman at Hornsey in the belief that if any chance of a drive cropped up he would be in the the right place at the right time. However, the story goes that his very relaxed attitude to duties as Foreman resulted in being fired by Chapman on an occasion when he was caught with his feet up on the stove reading while the engine shop's other employee got on with the work. Two weeks after his departure he was back again because it had resulted in total collapse of output. I do not think that Chapman ever quite understood how Hill exerted influence on events in the engine shop, but by 1958 he was promoted to Works Driver and that particular problem was thereby solved.

Graham Hill was an extremely patient member of Team Lotus and even for a brief period tolerated such indignities as the partially enclosed exhaust system of the Sixteen which while aerodynamically efficient tended to toast the driver's legs. I believe that he eventually went on strike and had the offending system moved outboard. The frustrating performance of the Sixteens in 1958 and 1959 finally wore down even Hill's patience and he accepted an invitation to move to BRM. I accompanied Chapman to a meeting with Graham Hill at the Steering Wheel Club when Chapman leaned gently on his former driver to whom he could now offer a car which had won the Monaco and French Grands Prix. But there may have been other reasons why Hill preferred to stick with BRM and in the long run he probably made the right decision. The BRM team was very receptive to his ability to help them as one of the best development engineer/drivers and he undoubtedly played a great part in the renaissance of that marque and its World Championship successes. Among his contemporary constructors Chapman only considered Enzo Ferrari with respect. Ferrari had been actively involved in motor racing since 1919 and although his cars were somewhat conservative in chassis design, the engine was the most powerful available throughout the period and frequently compensated for the road holding deficiencies of the Ferrari racing chassis which remained front engined throughout 1960.

Outside the intimate commercial and racing circle of Lotus, two of the strongest of Chapman's personal relationships were with Peter Kirwan-Taylor and "Jabby" Crombac. These two were early customers for the Mk. 6 and both interestingly had fitted their cars with modified bodywork. Whereas Crombac was principally a racing journalist he was extremely helpful to Lotus as general representative in France and elsewhere on the Continent and was a constant help in dealing with the Le Mans authorities and others with whom Team Lotus traditionally had a turbulent relationship. It was generally understood that Jabby would arrange anything that was necessary both on and off the track in French-speaking areas.

Peter Kirwan-Taylor is a merchant banker and over the years fulfilled this professional role for Chapman and Lotus. Without his commercial and banking skills and interest in all things Lotus, the company would not exist today and his support during its rise and "rocky" years forms Kirwan-Taylor's main contribution to the Lotus story. In the period covered by this book however, he performed an additional role of great significance. His early bodywork designs to convert his Mk. 6 from ugly duckling to a quasi-elegant road car had not gone unnoticed by Chapman who at the time was nevertheless not particularly concerned by aesthetics. Kirwan-Taylor also designed a very pretty little body for the Citroen 2CV and this car – the Bijou – with fibreglass panels on standard 2CV platform was assembled at the Citroen works at Slough. Quite a few were to be seen at the time, one of which was regularly used by Kirwan-Taylor's wife for shopping. With the 425 cc 2CV engine of the period the Bijou looked much faster than it actually was.

When he began work on the Elite, Chapman as his first move asked Kirwan-Taylor to sketch the bodywork. The result, very much Kirwan-Taylor's original concept despite later input from John Frayling and Frank Costin, is certainly one of the most beautiful small cars of all time and a permanent tribute to Kirwan-Taylor's abilities in this field. Later Kirwan-Taylor's involvement was principally limited to acting in a consultative capacity after Frayling and Hickman joined Lotus. He was however involved with Frayling in the design of the (still going strong) flared wings of the Seven and his influence at least can be traced in later models. I have nothing but admiration for Kirwan-Taylor's contribution to the Lotus story and he was the main restraint on the mercurial Chapman at a time when he needed the best possible financial counsel and general business advice. Whereas Fred Bushell's views were regularly overridden, Peter Kirwan-Taylor's professional voice was that of the City and Chapman fully appreciated the need to follow the rules of the game if he was to become a "real" motor manufacturer and thereby wealthy and successful.

Over the years there were legions of "friends" (real and imagined) and acquaintances who came and went in the glamorous world in which Colin Chapman moved. Many were sorely wounded by the experience because they failed to understand Chapman's nature and the tenets that governed him. In my time I think of Jay Chamberlain, the original US Importer of the Elite, and Derek Jolly who represented Lotus interests in Australia; men who gave their all to Chapman and who ultimately were either ruined or wounded by the experience, having failed to appreciate Chapman's *caveat emptor* approach to business and life in general. Equally many of his lesser drivers were used and passed over peremptorily. In this category in my time was Innes Ireland and a little later, Trevor Taylor and Peter Arundell. Several Lotus personalities have over the years left and rejoined the company after a "breather". Early cases were Peter Warr and Andrew Ferguson, the latter pair still associated with Lotus having been "abroad" for varying periods since I knew them.

The period 1959–1962 was long before today's universal passion for keeping fit. We spent none of our time running unless to reach a destination, nor did we skip or do press-ups, but Chapman was like most of us, faintly obsessed by his health. He suffered two curses, hayfever and a perennial tendency to overweight. In this latter regard he was totally unlike his automotive creations which tended to go the other way with resultant fragility in use. Chapman was known to some of his intimate circle as "Chunky" and depending on the year and time of year at which photographs of him were taken the waxing and waning of his figure was there to be seen. He had immensely strong willpower when it came to matters concerned with making money, work and the designing of motor cars and his tendency to over-indulge the pleasures of the table was also subjected to the famous willpower from time to time with remarkable results. Hayfever was another thing and caused him much misery, particularly since the racing life meant that he spent a lot of time at the height of the pollen count season in the open air. Chapman had a battery of pills for the purpose of reducing the adverse effects of hayfever and these would be taken openly at regular intervals during the day. Whether fat or thin, suffering from hayfever or not, Chapman generally exhibited an aura of good health and wellbeing to the outside world. Apart from stocky build his physical characteristics included a high colour to the cheeks, gently greying hair (long and curly) and a moustache which characterised him throughout his life. It was the archetypal British moustache adopted too by Graham Hill and quite unlike the drooping dago versions inspired by the film "Viva Zapata". Chapman's blue-grey eyes sparkled and he had extremely white teeth. My dentist at the time Dr. J. L. Karp of Upper Wimpole Street practiced discreet hypnosis on patients nervous of the chair. He had managed to cure one of my daughters of thumb sucking by his process and also claimed to be able to help hayfever sufferers. At my suggestion Chapman went along and obtained considerable temporary relief.

In matters of dress at that time Chapman did not show the interest in sharp outfits and natty headgear of his later years. He dressed just about as badly as the rest of us, but spent rather more money on doing it. At this stage a good old English flat cap was adequate to keep the unruly locks under control. Jackie Stewart was not yet a force to be reckoned with and the characteristic corduroy cap, affected in later years by Chapman, had not been seen. Chapman had a chameleon quality which enabled him to blend easily with a wide range of people and environment. On returning from Sebring 1960 he appeared dressed in American seersucker tartan slacks, T-shirt and tan, with a decided Stateside cockney accent. He was equally at home with the Captains of Industry with whom he frequently came in contact including Tony Vandervell, Sir Alfred Owen, Leonard Lee and their peers. His self-confidence, even in extreme adversity, was such that although he might address his more imposing acquaintances as "Sir" (particularly if they were about to pay him large sums of money) his philosophy was firmly based on reserving high regard for those first past the post in their chosen field. The rest of us were in the "also ran" category.

Although it would be true to say that we generally appreciated what was happening to us at the time or shortly thereafter and although most of us eventually grew to accept the situation with reasonable grace, a large body of people sharing Chapman's world were fairly systematically used and abused on his way to the top of the pile. Chapman's charm was so legendary that he could talk and wile his way out of almost any "impossible" situation. If he couldn't get out of it himself, he would summon one of us to sort out matters for him. For example he would occasionally sell a Team car when abroad racing and forget both to tell us and/or to hand over the cheque. Problems of that order were relatively straightforward, the difficult ones being those with heavy emotional overtones. Among these, one of the worst was the case of Dan Gurney's order for a Nineteen.

One of my old distributors summed up Chapman's cavalier attitude beautifully when he wrote to me (referring to a conversation he had had with a fellow importer from another quarter of the globe) "He realigned my thinking by explaining that Colin Chapman would rather sell one Lotus Seven to a naked French w...e swinging from a chandelier than sell a hundred Lotus to a Distributor". That is an accurate paraphrase of the situation I found on arrival at Cheshunt and I am grateful to my old friend for his apt form of words.

The sad story of Jay Chamberlain is told elsewhere in some detail in these pages. Of all Lotus Distributors in my time he suffered the most in both personal and financial terms from his links with Lotus. Most of the distributors who became "walking wounded" in their relationship with Chapman and the rest of us, were better equipped to handle the situation than Chamberlain. They either had substantial uncommitted personal fortunes on which to fall back or a more sophisticated approach to life and business which enabled them to understand better what was going on and take the necessary steps to survive it.

(ii) Fred Bushell

Fred began his career with accountants Peat Marwick and did the Lotus books in his spare time. As things progressed Chapman invited him to join Lotus on a full time basis and Fred saw the opportunity to speed up his career development. Chapman showed remarkable acumen in these early appointments and Fred was the outstanding member of the group. He was intensely loyal to Chapman and shrewd enough to appreciate as a non-Establishment "type" that he would probably never have an equal opportunity with the potential for making money that this represented. Chapman's tendency was to sail close to the wind in financial matters and Fred was able to exert just enough restraint to avoid disaster although it took a constant toll on him. It was Fred's job to calm down the Bank Manager, to entertain the Purchase Tax Inspector to lunch and to explain why Colin was out although the visitor was sure that he was in. Fred knew everything about the financial aspect of Chapman's business and racing activities. This gave him a degree of security unique at Cheshunt and although he was regularly cursed and insulted by Chapman, he was never sacked like the rest of us. Fred would maintain a fatherly influence over the Lotus personnel and was able to keep the peace during the most difficult times by careful advice *sotto voce* as the temperature rose. Occasionally things got out of hand as on the day when Ian McLeod punched Elite Production Manager Graham Lewis through the glass partition of Fred's office, but generally he kept all of us including even sometimes Chapman reasonably calm. Fred was officially in charge of administration although I could never at the time understand his technique. Large piles of paper accumulated on his desk and when tackled he would explain by expounding the Bushell philosophy that most matters would resolve themselves if left long enough. In fact my subsequent experience proved this to be very largely true and it was advice that I never forgot. Fred was the only "internal" member of the organisation on whom Colin leaned heavily; the other early associates all played an important role but were never listened to in the manner that Colin heeded Fred.

(iii) "Nobby" Clark

Poor Nobby died shortly after I left the company in 1962. He was the original Lotus full-time employee and the story goes that one day he walked into the Hornsey premises out of curiosity and eventually, on announcing that he was a welder, was roped in forthwith. Nobby was one of the most charming people I have ever had the pleasure to meet and had the perfect technique for dealing with Chapman. Nowadays Nobby would be described as "laid-back" but in those days he was simply calm and allowed criticism to flow over his head while he twirled a propelling pencil and made his own decisions. In 1959 Nobby was in charge of Lotus Components, manufacturing all cars other than the Elite and this complex operation was always beautifully organised and well capable of maintaining planned levels of output even under the heavy pressure of the pre-racing season panic.

(iv) Mike Costin

Another delightful, ever-patient and tolerant character, Mike took an immense pounding from Colin as head of Development in my time. This position inevitably meant that he had to work extremely closely with Chapman as Chief Designer and the strain on Costin was immense.

When Keith Duckworth left Lotus in 1958 to start his own business after a spell of ten months grappling with the so-called "queerbox" transmission, Mike joined forces with him on a part-time basis. Chapman's response to this "alienation of affection" was to insist that Mike concentrate on his Lotus responsibilities (day and night). A deal was struck by which a favourable contract of employment with – not so usual for those days – fringe benefits including a company car (at one stage the 105E Anglia saloon "handed down" to me) was offered by Chapman. Since Mike and Colin had been together "full time" since 1955, and because Mike (unlike Keith at that time) had wife and young family to support, he accepted.

Shortly after I left, Mike moved into Cosworth Engineering where for many years he was Technical Director. Today he is Chairman of the Cosworth Board, hopefully at lower levels of stress than at Lotus. There is no doubt that Mike's influence on Colin was as important as that of his older brother Frank the aerodynamicist in the early years of Lotus. Although in no sense a "formal" engineer, Mike has unequalled practical understanding of high-performance automotive design and development and has experienced at first hand many times most of the things that can go wrong with the engines, suspension systems, and the general structure of fast motor cars. He was never too busy to pause to explain to me the technical intricacies of his work at Cheshunt and I had many fascinating discussions with him.

Mike Costin's principal role was to act as a sounding board and to make the Chapman concept function as originally intended. He ran the drawing office and supervised the general engineering development operations that supported the whole production and racing endeavour, including regularly acting as Test (and occasional racing) driver. After 1958 too, he performed the essential function of maintaining the peace between Chapman and Duckworth; thereby allowing them both to progress at greater speed.

(v) Ron Hickman

A measure of the esteem in which Chapman held Ron Hickman was the duration of his employment with Lotus (1957–67), during which time he enjoyed remarkable freedom of action. Although he regularly and prudently referred his design thinking to Chapman for approval and agreement the latter's preoccupation with other matters frequently meant that Ron had to work on his own initiative and the Elan and the Elan + 2 (Type 50) are very much Hickman's cars. There is no doubt too that had Hickman been able to play a truly substantive design role earlier in the original Elite project rather than just being around when it was conceived and later involved only with the "productionising" of a finalised design concept, the first new road car from Cheshunt might well have been more practically designed and executed.

Hickman, a South African, originally studied law and intended to enter the Judicial system of that country. However, he was diverted from this course by the overwhelming ambition to become a car designer and although he never had any formal training in engineering, art or design, he had a natural talent for all three and was fired by an irrepressible creative urge. In 1955 at the age of 22 he arrived in London and nine months later joined Ford as a styling modeller. He lost no opportunity to use this opening to gain experience and learn as much as possible about the techniques of his chosen field. He enrolled at the Central School of Art and began his innovative career with a series of concepts including even at this early stage that characteristic Hickman design feature – a body colour co-ordinated bumper panel. Chapman initially resisted this for the Elite as strongly as had Ford, but Ron eventually won acceptance of the idea for the Elan but with the panel painted silver and (on the front) a strip of chromed plastic as a compromise.

Ron Hickman's first encounter with Chapman was at the 1955 London Motor Show at which the Mk. 9 was displayed after a remarkably successful racing season. He had organised an overseas press pass and was accosted by Alfred Woolf who was acting as a freelance PR man for Chapman. Woolf introduced Hickman and his friends the New Zealander John Frayling and Peter Cambridge to Chapman, and there followed a further meeting with Chapman, Peter Kirwan-Taylor and Frank Costin. On that occasion the original drawings for the Elite were on the table and the young Ford stylists were deeply impressed. Hickman and Frayling were enthralled by the Chapman magic as others before and after them. Frayling then became deeply involved with the evolution of the Elite from this point but Ron went back to South Africa for four months (but not before persuading Chapman to accept his "breathing numberplate") before returning and working with Frayling every evening at the latter's basement flat until the end of 1956. Finally, Ron returned again to England and the Ford Motor Company in May 1957, and a year later became totally involved with Lotus and the "productionising" of the Elite at the Maximar Mouldings factory at Pulborough.

Ron Hickman photographed while a contemporary of the author at Lotus during the early days of his development work on the Lotus Elan S2 – M2 project.

The Hickman-Chapman association was the quintessential Chapman-led creative partnership. It was equal to those with the Costins, Jim Clark and Fred Bushell. Chapman's personal charm, virtuoso design engineering abilities and man-manipulative powers brought out Hickman's own extensive talent in a way which could not have occurred elsewhere so soon. Chapman recognised in Hickman the inventive qualities which later evolved the Elan and Elan + 2. Hickman's talent led ultimately to the registration of more than 200 patents including those protecting the ubiquitous Workmate portable workbench, the success of which ultimately made his fortune.

During the period when our paths crossed at Lotus my personal contacts with Ron were restricted by frequent absences abroad and the fact that his work was largely behind locked doors at Cheshunt. However, we had an excellent opportunity to get to know each other in the "Great Door Discoloration Affair" that caused so much havoc in California. Despite the veil of secrecy drawn over the Elan project Ron made it his business to keep me informed about aspects of commercial interest as well as giving me one of the very first drives in the original Falcon-bodied prototype.

Although he had a quiet self confidence, Ron was always the modest "backroom boy", mixing well with the Lotus Developments team under the nominal control of Mike Costin but in reality dominated by Chapman himself.

Hickman understood Chapman's personality and moods well, and although they "rowed" from time to time Ron discreetly avoided the limelight and never precipitated the sort of crisis that might have resulted from demanding a title recognising his true position in the scheme of things. He also produced results as fast as anybody else in the organisation (but of course never fast enough for

Chapman) and his solutions were always reasonable and rational. Chapman was not able to out-argue Hickman and (as I knew from my own experience) respected him for not giving way to the appalling pressures that Chapman would sometimes bring to bear on his employees.

Ron Hickman had a unique combination of talents not present anywhere else in the organisation. To this was added personal qualities of endless patience and persistence, on a scale necessary to handle a 2–3 year project. The respect was mutual but Ron Hickman was never a crawler as were some members of the team. He didn't form part of the Chapman social circle but it can be seen with hindsight that Hickman was ideally suited to the needs of Lotus in that period in that he would get on with his work without demanding priceless Chapman time for decision making or discussion and only varied this method of working if Chapman or others came on the attack.

The Chapman-Hickman collaboration was one of the most perfectly balanced of Colin's partnerships. Chapman undoubtedly inspired Hickman to develop his talents at an earlier age than would otherwise have been possible. Hickman's ability to extend plastic body moulding technology well beyond current practice was appreciated, absorbed and built upon by Chapman and eventually led to the sophisticated moulding techniques in use at Lotus today.

(vi) Michael Christie

Michael Christie who in 1957 had the foresight to arrange with Chapman to be the supremo of Elite sales in the United Kingdom later had cause to regret that initiative, but because he was experienced in the motor business was able to handle the situation well and avoid excessive personal damage. Michael had achieved considerable personal success as a hillclimb and sprint specialist in the early Fifties. He was extremely handsome (Bunty Richmond of Downton Engineering would swoon in recollection of his Greek profile) and had achieved remarkable commercial success with his Alexander Engineering Company, one of the earliest "bolt-on-goodie" speed equipment and accessory manufacturers. Stirling Moss had an "Alexanderised" Standard Ten saloon fitted with wire wheels and k/o hubs which Christie was able to exploit for its considerable publicity value. Michael Christie performed the useful function of soaking up the early Elites for the British market, but as soon as we got under way he was left behind a sadder and wiser, but thankfully not so much poorer man.

(vii) Peter Warr

I have referred earlier to Peter Warr who with occasional lapses maintained the closest links with Chapman until his death. Peter (who during his period with me in the Sales Department always referred to the boss as "Mr. Chapman") had all the qualities necessary to survive prolonged exposure to Chapman and the motor racing temperament: a burden which became stronger over the years. Peter Warr's career in the seventies and eighties is well known, but when he set out along the path to fame and fortune he began as a burning enthusiast of the characteristic type found at Lotus in the early days. In addition he offered a high level of educated intelligence, steely determination and innate business acumen.

Peter bought one of the very first Mini Vans at the time when you could have any colour you liked as long as it was a sort of bright orange and then very conveniently bought the Works demonstrator red Super Seven Series One car TMT 1 immortalised by Graham Hill at the Brands Hatch Boxing Day 1959 meeting. Peter subsequently bought an Eighteen and later a Twenty Formula Junior car which he campaigned with considerable success and a little Works support. Peter Warr's personal connection and experience of the racing world made him ideal to handle Lotus Components retail business in my time and he concentrated on pure racing and sports racing car sales with great efficiency and overall success.

(viii) Derek Jolly

The original Australian Lotus Importer Derek Jolly was another devoted and regularly damaged Chapman admirer. Jolly was a good driver but above all had plenty of money, as the heir to the Penfold Wine fortune. In the mid Fifties it was difficult to import motor cars into Australia and Derek had built for his personal use a virtually unbeatable close replica of the Eleven which bore the name Decca – a personal nickname which he applied to several of his activities, business and otherwise – which frequently centred on a passion for music.

In time Jolly was successful in persuading Chapman to appoint him as the Australian Lotus importer and one or two cars found their way in by devious means. Derek could be relied upon to finance certain operations such as the entry of a Fifteen Series Three (Lotus transmission) car for Le Mans in 1959 which he co-drove for a short time with Graham Hill. This car was stuck in the Cheshunt Service Department on my arrival and was eventually shipped to Australia whence it has now finally returned to the UK. Jolly conducted his importership mainly from Europe which he seemed to prefer to the Antipodes. He had a sophisticated taste in music and the opposite sex and managed to cater for the requirements of both by cruising around Europe in a large Citroen DS19 Estate car. This was ideally suited to the provision of nocturnal accommodation whilst en route from one French cathedral to the next and to transport the recording equipment that he needed to capture the sound of French organs playing baroque and earlier music. This was an area of common ground that I shared with him although I found his interest in photographing stained glass somewhat esoteric for my tastes. I have always preferred the real thing to photographs.

Life is full of coincidence and when I discovered that his family wine business was Penfolds it occurred to me that there might be a link with two of my godchildren of that name. Indeed we discovered that Derek's family originated in Sussex and later the oldest child of the English Penfold family in question travelled to Australia and spent a couple of years working with the Penfold businesses in that country.

I admired Derek Jolly's ability to temper strong personal admiration for Chapman with the making of vast allowances for Chapman's treatment of his

We did not ask too many questions about where Derek Jolly went on his photographic tours with our demonstrators but here the faithful Series Two has been fitted with the clamshell wings originally introduced for the American market more than a year earlier. Eventually of course these flared wings would become a standard feature of the car and very much part of its character. Derek has hesitated at low tide on a lonely shore with his beautiful girlfriend and we now admit to the 105E engine as an alternative to the faithful old sidevalve 100E. Now too we emphasise the lowest ever price of a Lotus kit car (admittedly without engine and gearbox) and we had a good year.

Latest expression of the Lotus line, the race-bred Lotus Seven Series Two. Available now with a choice of three engines and gearboxes: Ford 100E, BMC Series 'A', and Ford 105E – the engine that powers the championship-winning Lotus Formula Junior. The Chapman-designed frame and suspension permit complete realisation of full tuning potential.

The specification of this most-easily assembled, most successful sports/racing car includes as standard full weather equipment, and the new flared wings in fibre-glass are obtainable to choice.

And, incredibly, this 1172 Formula Championship winner can be obtained, less engine and gearbox, in component form for £399!

NOW £399!

friends. Eventually Derek was replaced by other, hungrier outlets in his native country but I have no doubt that he now harbours no lasting malice as a result of this and other events.

(ix) Friends in the Media

Chapman was very accomplished in his relations with the motoring and popular Press with whom in the early days he enjoyed a somewhat exaggerated prestige. For a short time (1958) he even had his own column in the *Sunday Dispatch* newspaper ("ghosted" by a professional hack). The personal relationship was extremely important when a press car broke under test and had to be rebuilt or replaced. We could usually count on the absolute discretion of testers, who greatly enjoyed the opportunity to drive such fabulous products while they lasted. Apart from the devoted "Jabby" Crombac, Colin's roving pressman on the Continent, two other lifelong friendships in the literary world were established in my time. David Phipps was a schoolmaster with a passion for motor racing, an erudite style and outstanding talent as a photographer. Although coming belatedly to the journalistic profession, he had every quality to ensure success. Additionally he was well and truly under the Chapman spell and in exchange for "scoops" on all new models David could be relied upon to give us an excellent press, particularly in the "tame" Journal, *Sportscar and Lotus Owner* of which Phipps became the Lotus Editor and Patrick Stephens was the Advertising Manager.

Sportscar and Lotus Owner depended absolutely on a covert subsidy from Cheshunt to survive. We flooded it with advertising and it was unquestionably required reading for all Lotus owners although it was impossible to imagine anything more sycophantic than this remarkable publication which is today sought after as a collector's item. We forced our luckless distributors to cough-up for advertisements in its pages and generally kept it afloat under difficult circumstances. Patrick Stephens is remembered in the first instance for his early books on building Austin Seven and Ford Sidevalve Specials. Subsequently Pat set up his own publishing company which prospered mightily and has since become a cornerstone of the automotive publishing world. Pat would take me out for a beer and sandwich and persuade me to increase the company's advertising with *SC & LO* and of course we always obliged with the favourable Phipps editorial material in mind. The energetic Phipps and his equally accomplished wife Priscilla disseminated favourable information about Lotus throughout the world in these and successive years and probably have done more than anybody (Crombac and Ian Smith – author of the original Lotus History – included) to promote Lotus internationally by the written word.

(x) Chapman at the Wheel

Chapman embodied the personal attributes necessary for success at the wheel of a racing car. Where both he and his Development Engineer Mike Costin differed from the conventional successful motor racing driver was that their high level of intelligence told them that they had limitations and that these might sooner or later bring their career to a premature end. After the débâcle at the wheel of the

COLIN CHAPMAN

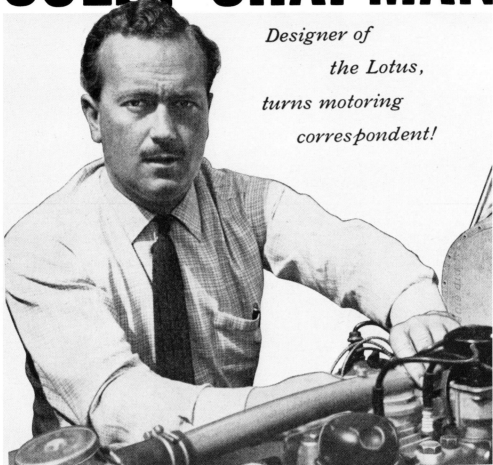

Designer of the Lotus, turns motoring correspondent!

How do you get a new slant on the motor car business? Where do you find a man who speaks with personal authority on every topic that crops up in the motoring world? You read the new motoring correspondent of the Sunday Dispatch, Colin Chapman. He is one of the most successful car designers of the decade, and will bring you the news, and the news behind the news.

He's entertaining, discerning, a mine of information. His column will be of vital interest to you.

READ **COLIN CHAPMAN** IN THE **NEW**

Sunday Dispatch
MOTOR RACING

The Great British Public were well aware of Colin Chapman by 1958 when he launched Team Lotus into serious Formula One racing. The *Sunday Dispatch* signed up Colin as "Motoring Correspondent" and for a short period this advertisement appeared in motoring journals. The most important outcome of the episode was the friendship that developed between Colin and the then editor of the *Sunday Dispatch*, Walter Hayes. Hayes left the Dispatch and joined the Ford Motor Company as head of PR. This fortuitous chain of circumstances led to a gradual cementing of the relationship between Cheshunt and Dagenham including the Lotus Cortina contract; the supply of major engine and gearbox components for the Elan and ultimately, in collaboration with Cosworth, the development of the DFV Formula One engine designed by Duckworth. In this photograph Colin holds tightly to an Aquaplane cylinder head mounted on the Ford 100E engine of a Seven Series One. The look of concentration has less to do with leg cramp than consideration of his likely fee for the promotion.

COLIN CHAPMAN'S LOTUS

Vanwall at Reims in 1956 and missing a drive at Le Mans in 1957, Chapman gradually retired from motor racing proper although he indulged in occasional forays in minor events thereafter. He was persuaded to join the Lotus Seven Team in the 1961 Eight Clubs race meeting at Silverstone, but perhaps the most unforgettable of these latter-day Chapman racing occasions was the Production Race at the 1960 British Grand Prix when Colin undertook a unique test drive in a Jaguar Mk. 2 3.8 litre saloon. His Primrose Yellow Ford Zodiac Automatic was reaching a point where it needed replacement and "Lofty" England suggested to him that the ideal car would be a Mk. 2 Jaguar for which he just happened to have an entry in one of the supporting races at the British Grand Prix. Those of us who were fortunate enough to witness this hilarious occasion will never forget the duel for the lead between Jack Sears and Chapman. The two leading contenders drove with headlights ablaze and door handles enmeshed for ten laps before Chapman pipped Sears to the post and placed an order.

Chapman's brilliance as a driver greatly assisted him in the development of his early cars although it may also have allowed him to tolerate and compensate for certain design shortcomings. Here he is seen at the wheel of the Works Mk.9 leading its main rival of the era, a "bobtailed" Cooper Type 39. The Cooper (with "Ivor the Driver" Bueb at the wheel) appears to be much closer to the limit of adhesion than the Lotus which probably explains Chapman's relaxed smile as he speeds to certain victory at Brands Hatch in October 1955.

It was only some such device which took his fancy that provoked Chapman to race and certainly those were the only occasions that I can recall when he went beyond routine testing. He was a brilliant driver and although extremely fast on the track drove carefully and with consideration on public roads. I count myself fortunate to be one of the few people to have been driven by Chapman on a racing circuit. It was an experience which effectively cured me of any youthful desire whatsoever to engage in motor racing and since that event I have often felt that the majority of would-be racing drivers could save themselves a great deal of money, anguish and possibly injury if they were able to sit by the side of a master, enjoy a few high-speed laps of a racing circuit and learn what it really takes to succeed. Judging by my own experience at Goodwood with Chapman during the 1961 Motor Show Press Day where the proceedings were enlivened by the presence on the track simultaneously of several relatively slow-moving, inexpertly driven cars and a number of brimming puddles, only the determined should continue to aspire to this level of achievement.

The occasion was one of a series of events at Motor Show time when British manufacturers and importers would take examples of their wares to Goodwood to be test driven by the motoring press. Occasionally a car would spin off but generally speaking the proceedings were fairly steady. We had laid on an Elite and Super Seven Series Two (Cosworth Ford 1340 cc.). Chapman decided that we would travel to Goodwood from Panshanger in his Comanche single-engined aircraft and because I was brought up in the shadow of Goodwood I was to do the navigation. We landed at Denham to pick up veteran journalist Gordon Wilkins and flew down towards the South Downs, which on arrival were hidden by dense cloud. The Comanche began to descend and to my horror we narrowly missed the radar aerials on the Trundle. At least we knew where we were and almost immediately thereafter landed on the grass surface in the centre of the circuit.

Chapman intended to test both cars to be sure that they were functioning correctly (at this point with production rising, there were many instances of build quality shortcomings and even failures and we were all somewhat neurotic about them). We went out in the Super Seven first, Chapman with cap well pulled down. By the time we had completed Madgwick Corner from a standing start with no slackening of pace, I realised that I was in for a new experience; one to be endured. By the time that we had completed the first lap Colin shouted across to me "Bloody thing's going to boil". He must be one of the few people who could drive a Seven so hard under those conditions (it was a rather cool, damp day) but we then proceeded to execute two more laps at even faster pace with the little Seven skirting all the puddles in a series of skips and swerves, passing the sedate saloons on the track to left and right at will. Fairly soon the occupants of other cars realised who it was at the wheel of the Seven and I shall never forget the looks of sheer amazement on the faces of passengers way above us as we left them for dead in a car with a top speed of barely 90 mph.

No sooner had we climbed out of the Seven (which failed to boil for anyone else during the day) than we were into the very standard Series Two Elite and out once more on the track. In this case my enduring memory is of the extraordinary noises of protest made by the Elite at speed. With standard suspension, the demonstrator Elite assumed amazing angles of roll under fast cornering, so much so that I found myself looking down at Chapman while at the same time being barely able to see out of the window on my side of the car. Meanwhile the fibreglass structure creaked and groaned incessantly as it was subjected to these extraordinary cornering and braking forces, Chapman again darting around the puddles and past cars to left and right. His mastery of the Elite was absolute and as he drove he shouted comments about tyre pressures, wheel alignment and

The British Society of Motor Manufacturers and Traders (SMM&T) held an annual Test Day at the Goodwood racing circuit to enable the Press to take the wheel of cars exhibited at the London Motor Show. In 1961 we took down an Elite and this Super Seven. Chapman is here "checking out" the Super Seven with me as passenger. It was an unforgettable experience and when Peter Warr found this photograph of the occasion, he hung it in the Cheshunt sales office with the caption: "An absorbing pictorial representation of cold, all-consuming FEAR..."

brakes, never relaxing for a second. One of my treasured possessions from that day is a photograph of Chapman and me in the Seven on which Peter Warr wrote the inscription "An absorbing pictorial representation of cold, all-consuming fear." My facial expression tells all, and this photograph adorned the sales office until I took it with me on departure.

By comparison with this track-driving experience travelling with Chapman on the public road was very relaxing. He would rarely drive so unreasonably fast as to cause one the slightest nervousness – and in fact the only time that this happened to me was the occasion when Graham Warner of The Chequered Flag drove up in a Maserati 3500GT for lunch. Chapman took the wheel on the return to the office from the Broxbourne restaurant and Graham invited him to "give it a whirl' which he certainly did. As we swept on to the dual carriageway section of the A10 the big Maserati broke away and went sideways on to the grass. With a lightning reaction Chapman instantly "gathered it up" and returned to the hard surface with a laugh and a "whoops!" while I mopped the perspiration from my brow.

226   Colin's personal car at the time that I arrived at Lotus was a pale yellow Ford

Zodiac, 467 FKL. It was an automatic transmission car fitted with a two-carburettor Raymond Mays cylinder head conversion which gave it a characteristic exhaust beat rather like a powerful boat. As a motor enthusiast I was rather intrigued that Chapman preferred such an unglamorous road car. He had no doubt that automatic transmission was the thing for practical motoring and as far as he was concerned at that time the main attribute of a road car should be its ability to pull a trailer with a racing car in total reliability at high speed. I must say that I was glad when he finally exchanged the Zodiac for the 3.8 Jaguar and it was on a journey with him in this on our way to Heathrow on one occasion that he explained to me the Chapman philosophy of "look for the gap". This involved continuous anticipation of the inevitable accident and presumably stemmed from the experience of his racing years. Since then I have always followed this advice and tried to avoid placing myself in a position from which there is no escape in emergency.

Through the medium of Alan Stacey and Jim Clark, Chapman was able to maintain a very close personal link with racing driving and I am certain that both these Team Lotus members were so successful because their modest personality allowed them to absorb information and technique from Chapman. Others such as Innes Ireland, never, it appeared to me, had the humility or ambition to listen to the Master.

(xi) The Flying Craze

The modern Grand Prix circus is invariably accompanied by an incredible collection of hardware. Motor homes crowd the paddock and drivers arrive in sleek twin-engined aircraft or helicopters. The racing cars themselves are overwhelmed by this impressive show. One thing is certain; a real racing driver never arrives by road.

It was not ever thus of course. In the Fifties the most lavishly furnished international teams would appear in a large ostentatious transporter-cum-mobile workshop while others would continue to rely on an old converted bus or van for the car, tools, spares and mechanics. The drivers and team owners would arrive by car, the drivers usually having exotica of Italian or German origin, perhaps from the factory of the company for whom they raced. Chapman would arrive in the lemon Zodiac until he led the great airborne revolution in 1960. Team Lotus had at their disposal a Ford Thames based "one" off low-loader with tuned 6-cylinder Zephyr engine, modelled on the famous Mercedes racing transporters or a cheerful old panel van carrying two cars and the workshop equipment.

There has always been an affinity between high speed on terra firma and in the air and there have always been racing drivers in flight at and above ground level. Chapman learned to fly while a member of the University Air Squadron and completed a fourth year in the Royal Air Force as part of his National Service.

It was Chapman who laid the foundations for the now universal motor racing fraternity practice of flying by private aircraft to the circuit; an area of activity in which the competitive spirit is manifested by the need to be seen in the latest and most expensive aircraft that sponsorship can provide.

Shortly after the move to Cheshunt, Chapman introduced the question of a company aircraft into our lunchtime conversations. Mike Costin warmed to the idea because of his own earlier connections with heavier than air transportation (he remains a skilful and dedicated sailplane pilot). John Standen liked the idea because he generally thought that Colin could do no wrong, while Fred Bushell went slightly pale as he considered the financial implications. From my commercial point of view I wondered aloud whether Colin was interested in designing and manufacturing aircraft as a sideline but he denied this and with one exception (the Moonraker boatbuilding joint venture with David Buxton) has never ventured outside the automotive field.

Colin and Mike went into a huddle and the result was a rather tired and inexpensive Miles Messenger aircraft, a single engined military four-seater type of all-wood construction. I am told that Miles glue tends to deteriorate over the years, but the Lotus specimen seemed to be acceptable as a stopgap. I think it cost little more than would have bought an Elite with sufficient change for spare parts to keep it going during the first year.

Fairly soon the Messenger began to pall on Chapman whom I suspect found it rather pedestrian and unglamorous – certainly out of character with the increasingly successful Lotus image. The Messenger was abandoned by Colin and passed on to Mike Costin and John Standen. Even Fred Bushell had a lesson or two although I never quite saw that sort of activity as being Fred's scene, he being even squarer than I. The Messenger was replaced by a secondhand but relatively young Piper Comanche. This miracle of modernity had retractable tricycle undercarriage, variable pitch propeller for its "flat-six" engine and all-metal construction with very comfortable accommodation for four with luggage.

I never experienced the Messenger but when flying in the Comanche was impressed by Chapman's prowess as a pilot, despite his slightly swashbuckling air. I am glad that I was not on board when the merry Lotus band of aviation enthusiasts made an ill-advised crossing of the Alps in the Comanche on the return from the 1961 Italian Grand Prix at Monza. The experience was subsequently laughed over but I suspect by the way the tale was told by John Standen that he at least had been utterly terrified when the little single engined aircraft iced up so that nothing could be seen from the cockpit. The propeller was also affected by ice and large chunks were flung back against the canopy as the air speed and rate of climb progressively fell, the Comanche apparently "hanging on its prop" a few hundred feet above the invisible Alpine peaks. Colin and his greatly subdued crew were heartily glad to finish that journey and never attempted such a foolhardy route again in the Comanche.

It was fortuitous that Team Lotus cars at this time ran on 120 octane Avgas supplied free of charge by Esso.

Lotus was ever more inclined towards the aviation world than the conventional motor industry possibly because the greatest single external influence on early Lotus design was Frank Costin. Frank's younger brother Mike too was ex-de Havilland. The modern racing car draws heavily on aviation practice but it was really Chapman who first began to make car parts in the manner of the aviation industry. The upper front suspension rocker arms of the Twentyone Grand Prix car are the first major examples of this type of technology in use at Lotus and increasingly the more precise standards of the aviation industry overtook the "rubber-bushed" sports and racing car design philosophy of the Fifties.

Chapman's enduring interest in the world of aviation later formed the inspiration for the rapid transition in racing car design philosophy which saw the pursuit of aerodynamics away from the goal of drag and lift reduction ("streamlining") to the positive application of aerodynamic science to improve road adhesion (starting with the crude suspension-mounted wings of 1969). All this had its roots in Chapman's return to the air in 1960 and his lifelong love affair with and awareness of the importance of aerodynamics is an essential part of his make-up as an automotive designer.

Chapter Seven

Colin Chapman
Automotive Designer

Motoring enthusiasts discuss Chapman's achievement ad nauseam. Was he a brilliant designer – or an ingenious plagiarist? What was it about the man and his work which assured the immortality of his name in the annals of automotive history?

I offer an entirely subjective view of the result of his activities at the drawing board and his influence on others.

(i) Colin Chapman – Automotive Designer

"It is only the unimaginative who ever invents. The true artist is known by the use he makes of what he annexes, and he annexes everything."

Oscar Wilde

The task of assessing Chapman's importance as an automotive designer in the overall historical context presents difficulties.

There are designers such as Ernest Henry whose influence (inspired perhaps by Goux, Boillot and Zuccarelli) has been all-pervasive since 1912 in that it established the classical form of the high performance four-stroke engine. The Henry influence may even today be glimpsed in the products of Cosworth and Honda among others.

On the other hand there have been gifted designers such as Ferdinand Porsche *Père* whose work although brilliant and enduring, was exploited within a narrow field immediately surrounding the innovator himself. Hence his masterpiece, the VW Beetle, and the rear engined sporting cars bearing his name and derived from that same humble mass transport vehicle have such idiosyncratic individuality that they are loved or loathed. Enzo Ferrari, although not in any sense a formal designer, exerted immense influence on the course of *pur sang* automotive design by encouraging and directing the work of others including Colombo and Lampredi, developing them and sending them out into the world to spread the Ferrari approach and influence.

One can continue to catalogue the work of individuals such as Bugatti, 229

Bertarione, Jano, Bentley and Lyons who, without being innovators, to a greater or lesser extent and over shorter or longer periods have advanced the course of automotive design or developed it to great levels of refinement and perfection in specific areas.

Colin Chapman does not fall wholly into any one of these categories, but has a claim for inclusion in all. Although far less of a true innovator than popularly regarded Chapman has exerted major influence on the course of overall automotive design, not purely in the field of high performance and racing. The key to this influence lies in the personality of the man himself. His method was very similar to that of Enzo Ferrari and it is no coincidence that the "Old Man" was one of the very few figures in the world of motor racing respected by Chapman. They formed a rather exclusive mutual admiration society.

To Chapman's deep seated "corner cutting" racing driver's character traits was allied irresistible personal charm. He possessed immense self-confidence rooted in

The introduction of the Mk.8 launched Lotus on to the International sports racing scene and by the time the Eleven appeared in 1956 top drivers were clamouring to drive Chapman's remarkable cars. At the Whit Monday Goodwood meeting in 1956 a monumental duel took place between Mike Hawthorn and Chapman (Hawthorn driving an FWB 1460 cc Eleven against Chapman's 1100 cc car). Chapman won after a bumping-and-boring episode which damaged the "Farnham Flyer's" car and here they are after the race in mighty good humour being interviewed by a youthful Raymond Baxter. Hawthorn drove the Eleven several times during that season as a respite from his normally much "hairier" mounts – Ferrari and Jaguar. For a driver of truly international standing such as Hawthorn to show admiration for the Lotus gave Chapman the greatest pleasure (as later when Moss turned to the Eighteen and gave Cheshunt its first Grande Epreuve victory).

the heady years of the mid-Fifties when Lotus carried all before it in small capacity sports car racing. So strong was Chapman's innate confidence that even the disastrous experience of the early Formula racing cars, the bitter disappointment of the Seventeen and the relentless discouragement of the Elite development programme could not permanently undermine his belief in his own talent – nay genius – and ultimate enduring success. There would be moments of depression and disillusionment, of wailing and gnashing of teeth, even tears of rage, but soon he would bounce back and achieve a miracle or two to show us all that he was master of his destiny. The personal charm, the self confidence and willingness to break rules in the pursuit of his goals had made him a powerful force by 1959 when we met.

The personal charm enabled him to assemble a remarkable group of collaborators in all fields, from finance through commerce and of course most importantly in design. The role of full-time technical associates such as Hickman, Mike Costin and Len Terry although essential to the Lotus success story, was frequently either unknown, ignored or perhaps even positively suppressed if it might detract from the Chapman legend. One example of this phenomenon can be found in John Bolster's book *The Lotus Elan and Europa* describing three cars in which the influence of Ron Hickman in varying degrees was of paramount importance. Hickman's name appears absolutely nowhere in 128 pages! In recognition of their pro-Lotus stance and discretion certain influential journalists were provided with "authorised" information which has bedevilled the unravelling of the Lotus story and in particular the thread of design development and responsibility since the first great bromide – Ian Smith's *Lotus – the Story of the Marque* was published in 1958. Apart from Bolster the approved list included David Phipps whose early reputation was enhanced by his "special relationship" status and his position as propagandist for the Marque during the very difficult years at the beginning of the Sixties while he occupied the post of Lotus Editor of *Sports Car and Lotus Owner* magazine. "Jabby" Crombac provides another example of a media man firmly under the Chapman (man and family) influence and therefore dedicated to the preservation of the Great Tradition.

Having been honoured with the prestigious Ferodo Trophy in 1956, 1965 and 1978 and having played a vital role in the success of the Vanwall Grand Prix World Championship victory, Chapman was accepted in the Automotive Industry Corridors of Power. He used this prestige to obtain support and access to material supplies in a way unmatched by others (including Cooper). His influence with the Ford Motor Company (engines) Renault (transmissions for

By the time that track testing of the Twelve single seater began in March 1957 the de Dion rear axle arrangements had been subtly modified to include longer radius arms and coil spring/damper suspension units with exposed springs. Nevertheless the car presented intractable problems of rear wheel adhesion as a result possibly of the unacceptably high unsprung/sprung weight ratio of the original rear suspension of this light, high powered little car. Early in 1957 Chapman had attended one of the 750 MC routine gatherings at the Abbey Hotel on London's North Circular Road, where the hard core of 750/1172 Formula racers met for serious drinking and note comparison at regular intervals. The leading 750 driver of the year, Roy Lee, used a Goggomobil T300 car as regular transport and alternate tow car with an Austin Ruby saloon for the LRM racer. Chapman was observed by Colin Peck (then Secretary of the 750 MC) crawling under the Lee Goggo to study the simplistic rear suspension of this German microcar of which, in the best Chapman tradition, all elements are required to perform multiple functions where possible. The Goggo rear suspension was pure swing axle in the best Teutonic tradition but it is suggested by those present that the Lee Goggo was the inspiration which led within a week or so to the creation of the Chapman Strut which solved the otherwise insuperable rear suspension problems of the Twelve. The Goggomobil system differs from the eventual Chapman Strut in that there is only one (inner) universal joint on the driveshaft, and the lower end of the coil spring/damper suspension unit is pivoted at the hub. Nevertheless the radius arm is, as in the first manifestation of the Chapman Strut, integral with the hub casting. Chapman's fertile imagination would have easily made the necessary forward leap in developing the Goggo precedent to his pressing need on the Formula Two car. With minimal alteration to the existing car he could graft what now became the "Chapman Strut" to the Twelve chassis and avoid missing out on the 1957 racing season.

Formula Junior cars) BMC (transmissions) Lucas (electrical equipment), and the German company ZF (transmissions) was of crucial importance. He used his aura of success to woo (some would say seduce) gifted designers and technicians including Mundy, Ansdale, Costin, Duckworth, Hickman, Frayling and Terry, whose stimulus to Chapman personally and creative input to the Lotus endeavour as a whole was of massive importance to the company's success. No other small motor manufacturer of the day could count on anything like this pool of commercial and technical influence and domestic design talent in the measure available to Chapman.

It is possible to accurately pinpoint Chapman's own design work in the overall Lotus picture. His work has a highly characteristic but evolutionary quality and to judge him as a pure designer we must identify and concentrate on such indisputable offerings from his drawing board. The following are particularly free from the Lotus-employed design input of others:

All Types up to and including the Mk. 6
The Twelve single seater Formula car
The Eighteen Series Formula cars
The Twentyfive Grand Prix Car

I single them out as examples of the purest Chapman design activity up to and including the time covered by this book. These types exhibit certain clearly defined characteristics: they are frequently ugly with (the Twentyfive excepted) scant conscious attention to aerodynamics or aesthetics beyond a studied reduction of frontal area. They are very simple, sometimes crude in concept – basic, "minimalist" designs ideally suited to the purpose in hand.

Consider how Chapman used Frank Costin to design the skin of his early full width sports racing cars from Mk. 8 onwards without restricting Costin's scope up to and including the original Eleven, but Chapman then continued to rely on Costin's ideas after the aerodynamicist's direct involvement had ended. Chapman could be overawed by older and experienced men and he would obviously regard Frank Costin with respect just as long as there were lessons to be learned and advantages to be gained. The Twentyfive was influenced by lessons learned from Costin but unlike any other strong Chapman-only design it was outstandingly beautiful, the most elegant of all Lotus single seater racing deisgns.

Just as Chapman was happy to draw on the talent of others, using that part of their ability which he needed or respected to complement his own gifts, he was able to root out and apply to his own schemes components and concepts from other cars. He also demonstrated a remarkable ability to rapidly absorb new technology and almost immediately to create at the highest level in that new field. His absorption (and creation) of plastic moulding techniques with which to achieve the Elite and his immediate grasp of the demands of working in steel sheet (the Elan backbone chassis) are good examples of this. It is an old adage that there is nothing new in automotive design and it is true that none of Chapman's concepts with the exception of the daring all-fibreglass structure of the Elite – had *never* been seen before in one form or the other. A small manufacturer is rarely able to consider the production of car details such as door handles, light fittings and other electrical equipment. It therefore becomes essential to adapt and incorporate existing components without making them look awkward or out of place. In this process Chapman was assisted by the able John Standen who spent much of his time seeking out bits and pieces which could be fitted to Lotus products at modest cost and without incurring high tooling charges. An excellent example of this is the neat application to the Elite of the Hillman Husky door handle which in fact is so appropriate that it could have been Chapman's own!

In my view his best adaptation of an engineering feature used elsewhere was

Although later replaced by a forging, the lower link of Ford's 100E family car front suspension (MacPherson Strut) was formed by a heavy steel tube, linked by a massive anti-roll bar passing round the front of the engine sump. So much did this arrangement appeal to Chapman that he lifted it to form the upper link (suitably inverted, shortened and painted Lotus Grey) on the Twelve Formula Two car of 1956. Lotus continued to modify humble Ford components in this manner until 1958 when in order to contain costs they substituted a specially designed upper link forging at about the same time that Ford did away with the tubular lower member on their car. This is a very typical Chapman adaptation in the best tradition of Special Building.

Chapman's "lifting" of the 100E Ford front suspension design detail in which the anti-roll bar passes through an eye in a tubular *lower* locating link between the MacPherson Strut and the front cross member. Chapman borrowed this feature for the new *upper* wishbone seen on the early Twelve Formula cars, the Eleven Series Two, Seven Series One and Elite where it is cut and welded to take a Silentbloc bush. Later the idea was "formalised" by the use of a compass section forging in this position (to reduce the cost of going the modified Ford component route) and made standard equipment. This neat use as a wishbone of a roll bar and single link to perform two functions is typical of Chapman's original thought but it is an even better example of his brilliant digestion and regurgitation of the ideas of others.

The singular success of Lotus in the period up to 1958 had switched Chapman from the earlier position of the underdog taking on and beating the established giants in his field to a reversal of role. So long as standardised power units and transmission systems were available to others a clever "special builder" could tilt at the established competition.

The comet-like arrival on the scene of Chapman at the beginning of the decade was followed by a lengthy period of uninterrupted Lotus superiority. However, a rival flashed across the sky in 1958 when the Broadley's Lola Mk. 2 arrived and Chapman's response to the threat of this Lotus-inspired but yet more advanced 1100 cc sports racing car at once revealed his strengths and weaknesses as a designer.

Lola was a creation of the brothers Broadley who like Chapman founded a motoring dynasty and are still creating successful competition cars today. The Broadleys often very cleverly entered areas of new endeavour and opportunity such as those available in the American market where their design work led to such classics as the Ford GT40 and the Lola T70 cars as well as a family of highly successful Indianapolis winners, but in the Fifties the Broadleys began by

The "déjà-vu" Ford suspension link as it appeared on the Twelve initially and Elite prototypes, Seven Series One, Eleven Series Two etc., until replaced during 1958 by Lotus' own forging.

This photograph at the SCCA New York Show reveals the front suspension system of the Seven; the definitive version of the characteristic Lotus IFS of the late Fifties first seen on the Twelve Formula Two car of 1956. Note the clever adaptation of the Ford 100E concept using the anti-roll bar (now rigidly aligned in aluminium blocks) as part of the upper wishbone arrangement, coupled with fabricated steel tubular lower wishbones. Although simple, this was a relatively expensive suspension system and was replaced by a cheaper but equally effective arrangement on the Elan.

constructing a successful 1172 Formula car that prophetically won the Chapman Trophy in 1957. For 1958 they decided that they would attempt the impossible by designing a car to compete with the Lotus Eleven on its own ground. It could be argued that the Eleven had things its own way for so long that apart from the change of front suspension it had been allowed to atrophy and become an over-familiar part of the racing scene. Just as the Cooper 500 cc car had killed Formula 3 racing with the boring monotony of its success there was a real danger that the overwhelming success of the Eleven might result in a declining interest in small capacity Club racing. The cheeky choice of "Lola" as a name made it abundantly clear that the Broadleys had Lotus in their sights and had allowed a little humour to enter the scene. "What Lola wants, Lola gets" goes the song and the impact of the new car which relied on precisely the same motive power – FWA Climax – as its illustrious and established competitor was devastating to the pride of Lotus. The new Lola was immediately virtually invincible in its class and frequently all Lolas present headed the entire Lotus and other opposition past the winning post.

Chapman was momentarily nonplussed by the advent of the Lola Mk. 2. Here was a car that was demonstrably superior to his own design work in most areas. Its weight and overall bulk were substantially less than that of the Eleven. The aerodynamics of the car were not studied in the way that they were on the Costin-influenced Eleven but nevertheless it was a very attractive car and slippery enough for the purpose. The Lola spaceframe was if anything more scientifically stressed, triangulated and constructed than contemporary Lotus offerings. It did

not suffer frame tube fractures to the same extent as Lotus. The braking system was perhaps a little archaic in that it relied on aluminium finned drums rather than discs, but Lola was so light that braking imposed relatively small demands on the system and the new car was never overtaken into corners.

The Lola front suspension was conventionally done by unequal length welded tubular steel wishbones, but they looked much more efficient than the composite type used on the Eleven. In fact shortly after the advent of Lola Chapman altered the upper wishbones of the Sixteen Series Formula cars to a Lola-like arrangement in the search for increased rigidity under heavy cornering and braking stresses, but it was in the rear suspension department that Lola broke new ground and exerted the greatest influence on future design tends. Since 1957 Chapman had himself used fixed length drive shafts in conjunction with Chapman Struts to transmit power and braking force to the rear wheels and as a means of lateral location. The Broadleys used a similar fixed length articulated drive shaft but their hub casting instead of continuing upwards to embrace the spring/damper unit, extended below the wheel centre line and was further located laterally a few inches above ground level by tubular links to the chassis frame. Fore and aft location was by parallel tubular radius arms extending forward to the space frame. Conventional pivoted combined coil spring/damper units provided the suspension medium. At one blow the Lola incorporated and extended the benefits of the Chapman Strut while overcoming its inherent disadvantages. Chapman had been beaten by the Broadleys in the pursuit of the natural way forward from his Strut concept.

Although it was as presented in the Lola Mk. 2 that this new form of rear suspension incorporating the use of fixed length drive shafts as the upper member of a "double-link' suspension system impressed the competition, the first

Faced with the Chapman Strut (for which Chapman had taken out a provisional patent) the competition devised a similar rear suspension system to replace the then commonly used de Dion rear axle which became progressively unsuited to ultra-light high-powered sports racing cars. Elva, not generally regarded as great innovators, constructed a prototype car which eventually became their Mark IV in the last months of 1957 and the photograph shown here appeared in January 1958. Previous state-of-the-art Elva sports racing cars had used de Dion rear suspension but now fixed-length "Lotus" driveshafts are matched with a parallel lower wishbone, rather flimsy radius arms extending towards the centreline of the car and suspension units pivoted at both ends above the hub assemblies. This same system was adopted in 1958 and used with devastating effect in 1959 by Lola on their 1100 cc car which wiped the floor with the Eleven and its successor the Lotus Seventeen. Chapman recognised an improvement on his own idea when he saw it and made the Elva/Lola "parallel link" suspension system his own by mounting the suspension units lower to pick up at the bottom of the hub castings.

manifestation of the layout has to be credited to another Lotus competitor, Elva. Although successful in the US as a result of the efforts of their importer Carl Haas, Elva were hardly in the Lotus class on the European circuits. Frank Nicholls of Elva (literally "elle va' – "she goes") built Mk. 2 and Mk. 3 Elvas with de Dion rear axles before deciding to go to IRS with his Mk. 4 which was on the drawing board towards the end of 1957. By January 1958 at least one photograph had been published of his new rear suspension layout in prototype form which – yes – was in all but detail as we saw the system used on the Mk. 2 Lola. The Broadleys must have been aware of the Elva layout and realised its potential value to their Lotus-beater. Chapman of course was even less impressed by Elva than he was by the "antics" of Cooper, but would undoubtedly have seen and studied the new Elva IRS system. However, the Broadleys were uninhibited by having a strut bearing their name and prestige and snapped up Elva's idea without delay.

Chapman's immediate action following the advent of the Lola was to conceive the Seventeen for 1959. The Seventeen is famed as the first disastrous Chapman sports racing car design and it pointedly ignored the lessons of the Elva/Lola rear suspension system although bearing an uncanny resemblance in size and overall appearance to the Broadley car. Under the skin however, appeared the ultimate, desperate manifestation of the strut theme – struts for both front and rear suspension. Although Lotus precedent had established this system as a workable arrangement at the rear, Chapman came massively unstuck in the way that he used it to provide front wheel suspension. At the front of the Seventeen a shortened MacPherson Strut abutted on a conventional lower wishbone and the whole thing looked impressively neat and logical, the front of the spaceframe being reminiscent of the simple Eleven Series One arrangement. However, on the circuit the car was found to be almost unmanageable as a result of binding of the front suspension under cornering loads, unnerving the driver in the process. This was the same affliction that had caused such crashing headaches with the BRM P25 car on which Chapman had earlier worked his magic as consultant. How ironical it was that the same cause – bowing and locking between bushes of the central damper rod – caused a repetition of the effect at the front of Chapman's own car. As had been the case at BRM, Chapman the designer could not see the wood for the trees in his own back yard.

After a season of humiliation at the hands of Lola and by late 1959 Chapman had overcome any residual reluctance to copy the Lola rear suspension arrangement. For the Eighteen Series Formula Cars, and their immediate successors he adopted rear suspension which was essentially identical to the Lola model and not long afterwards the same example was copied by none other than the illustrious Jaguar company for the E-type and sister cars!

Historic Formula Junior racing thrives and in this category the Lotus Twentytwo is hard to beat, particularly when endowed with modern tyres. This immaculately turned out specimen has a "modern" roll-over bar arrangement, fully adjustable dampers and a Hewland gearbox in place of the Renault-based transmission with which it left Cheshunt as an F3 car in 1963. The adjustable rose-jointed suspension arrangements are clearly visible and were largely the same as the layout used on the Lotus Grand Prix cars of the period.

Having at last been forced from the Chapman Strut into a line of development inspired by it, Chapman characteristically made the new IRS system his own. The next phase of development for the Elva/Lola system of rear suspension was to dispense with the dual purpose use of the drive shaft and switch to lateral location by single-purpose upper and lower links with the geometrically perfectly aligned unsplined drive shaft between the two but now again acting purely as a means of power and braking transmission. For the first time there appeared the Lotus (Rotoflex manufactured) rubber "doughnut" universal joint at the inboard end of the shaft to signal that the shaft no longer performed a lateral locating function. Simultaneously Chapman for the Twentyone Grand Prix car engaged in an extensive rethink of front suspension design philosophy motivated mainly by aerodynamic drag-reducing considerations at a time when the motive power of the 1961 $1\frac{1}{2}$-litre Formula was to be for Lotus the modest Climax FPF, already in its fifth season. In this model and its direct descendants the Twentyfour and Twentyfive the fabricated steel upper suspension arm was continued inboard of its pivot point and used to act upon a coil spring/damper unit in compression and pivoted near the floor of the car. By this step the considerable drag of the previously exposed spring and shock absorber was abolished and airflow around the nose of the car improved but as a result the upper wishbone and its pivot now carried the entire suspension loading of the front of the car and had to be stiffened substantially to cope. The "wishbone" instead of being fabricated from steel tube was now welded from stainless steel sheet and was reminiscent of aircraft practice in the manner in which it was executed. Chapman was now beginning to further extend his interest in aeronautical engineering and this tendency was increasingly apparent in his design "handwriting". Inspired by the Lotus example, in succeeding years Formula cars of all types began more and more to conform to aircraft practice in the manufacture of engineering structures and components.

In the period under review Chapman's evolving design philosophy may be summarised and illustrated by the following observations:

The spaceframe was already established (having been well and truly put on the map by Giacosa and Savonuzzi's design for Dusio's 1946 Cisitalia D46 1100 cc Monoposto) before Chapman first used it in the Mk. 6. But Chapman brought the concept – beginning with the complex structure of the Mk. 8 – to the highest level of perfection before suddenly abandoning the space frame with his pivotal Twentyfive monocoque. It was largely due to the success of Lotus space frame cars and most notably the Eleven that virtually all high performance sports racing cars in the period 1955 – 65 were so constructed. Eventually Chapman tired of devising ever more ingenious ways of compensating for the interruption to perfect triangulation by the necessary openings (doors, engine compartment etc.) with detachable tubes or local reinforcement – or even towards the end, by borrowing Len Terry's bulkhead hoops – before changing allegiance to the superficially simpler and structurally superior aluminium alloy sheet monocoque in 1962.

We accept Chapman not only as the master of chassis structure during the period up to the mid-Sixties but also as the undisputed overall leader in the field of vehicle suspension design. Chapman's work on suspension is evolutionary, not revolutionary. His suspension designs begin where Leslie M. Ballamy left off. Ballamy having innovated stuck too long with the same concept; beyond the point where his designs (particularly the LMB swing-axle IFS) were ultimately only considered suitable as low-cost conversions for the antiquated "English Perpendicular" small Fords of 1932–59, despite constant refinement and improvement.

The LMB swing axle IFS system appealed naturally to Chapman because of its simplicity, light weight and ease of attachment to the chassis frame (requiring

COLIN CHAPMAN'S LOTUS

If the Ford engineers at Dagenham could have seen what was done by Colin Chapman to the forged axle of their humble sidevalve 10 hp saloon car for the 1955 Le Mans race they would have been incredulous. Here we see the Ford axle on Colin's Mk.9, divided and converted into swing axle independent front suspension; fitted with an up-to-the-minute coil spring/damper unit and – almost beyond belief – disc brakes in place of the humble mechanical drum units of the standard Ford car. The use of a Ford axle beam naturally implies retention of the old fashioned kingpin steering swivels shown clearly here. The loads of cornering under racing conditions using tyres with good adhesion placed great stress on the humble kingpin which required regular replacement for safety.

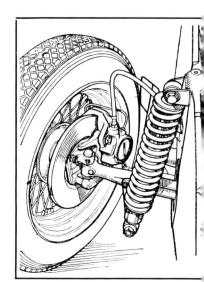

only a central mounting point each for the axle halves and radius arms together with simple upper mount(s) for the suspension medium). Chapman's first wishbone IFS system was intended to lead on geometrically from the swing axle while at the same time overcoming its inherent disadvantages, now emphasised by the more powerful versions of the Eleven Series One.

Chapman's de Dion rear suspension system was the most exquisite example of the type yet seen, displaying all the brilliant economy and elegance of the man at his best, refining an idea first seen at the dawn of the century, revived by Mercedes-Benz in 1936 for their 750 kg Formula cars and subsequently used in most high performance applications to the end of the Fifties, occasionally appearing later in such improbable settings as the Rover 2000 and Alfetta passenger cars. It was not until the Chapman Strut appeared in 1957 that he began to move away from strictly conventional suspension systems. The Chapman Strut was seen as a means of retaining stable handling characteristics under the wide load variation resulting from the need to carry large quantities of fuel at the rear of his new Lotus Twelve Formula car. Chapman loved the Strut and everything about it suited his approach. It was simple, light, fully employed in performing its duties (all components combining at least two functions) and relatively inexpensive to produce. No other constructor was able to borrow the design because of the provisional patent that protected it. Had they pirated the Strut there is a distinct possibility that they may have found as Chapman himself did that it had severe limitations; these emphasised by the imperfect geometry of the initial version with simple radius arm. The swansong of the Chapman Strut three years after its introduction on the Twelve was as the rear suspension (with wide based lower link) of the Elite Series Two road car.

Characteristically when Lola led the way ahead Chapman was quick to follow with a perfect imitation of the rival car's rear suspension. Just as in the case of his development away from the simple LMB swing axle IFS system, Chapman was able to move on from the basic Lola idea applied to the Eighteen Series and refined in his subsequent single seater designs.

In the field of front suspension Chapman resurrected (with the Twentyone) the inboard springing arrangements used earlier by others – most notably by Maserati on the 4CLT/48 San Remo – and as in the case of Maserati he would undoubtedly have been motivated by the benefits offered by this spring location in terms of aerodynamic efficiency and the concentration of suspension loads within the chassis structure.

It is interesting therefore to conclude that throughout this entire period the only wheel suspension innovation from Chapman's drawing board was his Strut (forced on him by the débâcle of the de Dion installation in the prototype Twelve Formula Two car) and even he was prepared to abandon it without hesitation when he saw a better way of achieving the same end.

In my view the greatest single automotive engineer of all time is Vittorio Jano, creator of the P3 Alfa Romeo and the later large 750 kg. Formula cars of this marque before joining Lancia to design the Aurelia, D50 and contemporary Lancia sports racing cars. I judge Jano to be the greatest because he created the entire car; every part of the chassis and engine layout was his and bore the

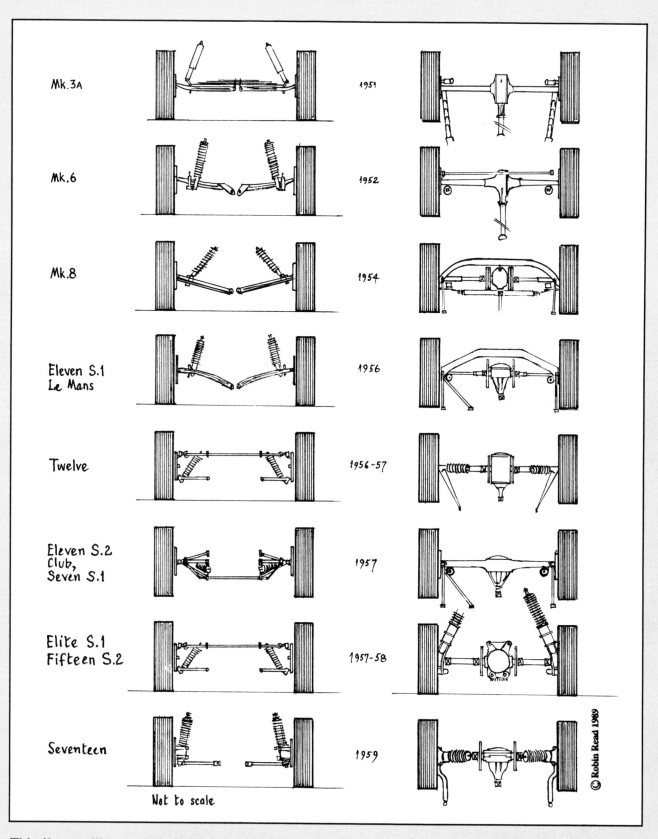

Mk.3A		1951
Mk.6		1952
Mk.8		1954
Eleven S.1 Le Mans		1956
Twelve		1956-57
Eleven S.2 Club, Seven S.1		1957
Elite S.1 Fifteen S.2		1957-58
Seventeen		1959

Not to scale

© Robin Read 1989

This diagram illustrates the development of Chapman's suspension systems from the Mk.3A to the combination of the Strut philosophy in the disastrous Seventeen. Chapman moved slowly in evolving his ideas and waited until 1956 before introducing wishbone front suspension (albeit with geometry closely derived from the wheel movement of the swing axle system that preceded it). He only abandoned his highly developed de Dion rear suspension when it at last failed to "deliver the goods" on the ultra-lightweight Twelve single seater. The hastily conceived Chapman Strut ultimately fitted to this car was then developed systematically to the end of the decade and oblivion.

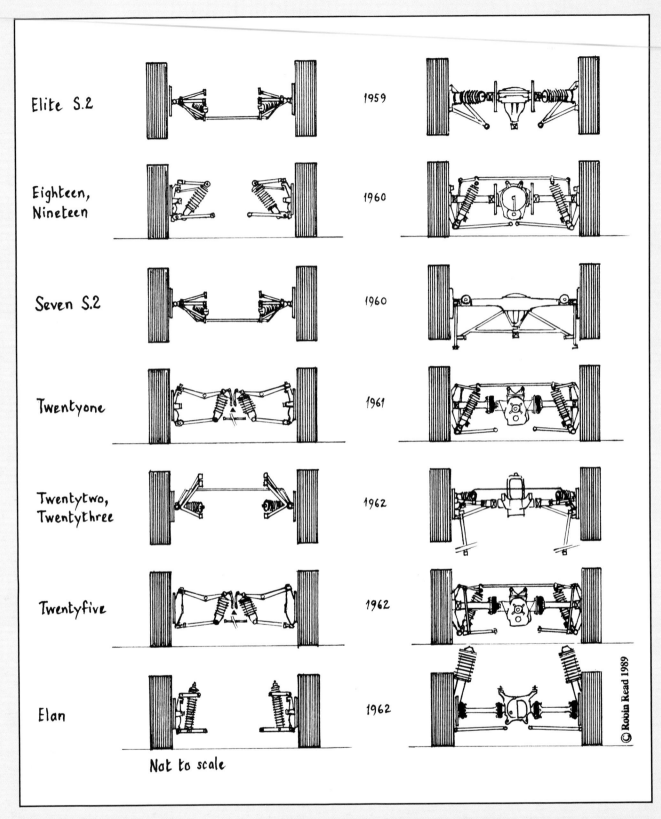

Elite S.2		1959
Eighteen, Nineteen		1960
Seven S.2		1960
Twentyone		1961
Twentytwo, Twentythree		1962
Twentyfive		1962
Elan		1962

Not to scale

© Robin Read 1989

Chapman was able to regain the initiative in the competitive world of vehicle suspension design when he swallowed his pride and followed the lead of Elva and Lola with their fixed length driveshaft rear suspension systems. The low line of the rear-engined Eighteen obliged Chapman to relocate the suspension unit to pick up at the lowest point of the hub casting – in so doing substantially improving the performance of this "new suspension". In a 1960 interview Chapman demonstrated that he had already adopted the Lola system as his own and in reference to the Eighteen stated "the only really new feature is the double-transverse-link rear suspension". The switch, for the Twentyone, to inboard mounted front suspension springing was also a "new" departure for Lotus although a system well tried elsewhere in earlier years.

unmistakable stamp of one great engineer-artist. But Jano was obliged to work for others and when his masters felt his powers to be on the wane (as was the case in 1938 at Alfa Romeo) they withdrew their support. Jano subsequently demonstrated to the world after the war that he had lost none of his brilliance and went on to design more distinctive and successful models for Lancia. When Lancia abandoned racing in 1955 it was the end of the road for Jano too and he moved with the team cars to Ferrari where he created the immortal Dino engine.

Chapman, by contrast, made absolutely sure that he was in control. With Fred Bushell at his side keeping the ship afloat under frequently difficult conditions Chapman was able to continue along his self-appointed path. He owned the company and was not about to lose confidence in his ability. His strong self-control enabled him when necessary to avoid wasteful self indulgence. He allowed the research and development effort of others to provide him with power and transmission components to which he would add the least expensive element of the "package"; the connecting structure of the vehicle with a Chapman suspension system to create a highly individual, characteristic whole. Chapman began his career as a special builder and he was certainly still that – albeit at a very elevated level – in 1962. Whereas it would not be correct to describe him as in the same class of designer as Jano and Porsche, he had infinitely more influence on the work of others. Chapman's daring and irreverent approach to established patterns of design showed the way ahead and more than any other single influence shaped the course of modern high performance car design. So we must hail Chapman as the great debunker: the master of the short cut and the simple solution. He had a developed disregard for convention (unless it might sell a few more cars – see the retention of wire spoked wheels for the sake of appearance on the Elite). Chapman was not interested to create a lasting memorial to his talent by the design and production of durable works of art. The "bombed-site" salesman lurking within propelled him to ever-newer, equally unenduring cars which have spawned an industry providing replacement parts to recreate the flimsy or rusted structures that issued from the Lotus Works. With the exception of the Elite which was a very special case, it was possible for a skilful welder and fitter to maintain or even replace part or all of a Lotus car and close examination of the survivors from the Fifties and early Sixties confirms that Chapman designed and created for the moment rather than for all time.

(ii)   Chapman's Early Influence

It is fascinating to contemplate the cross fertilisation of design trends arising from the appearance of the Lotus Mk. 3A in 1951 followed by the reverse direction of influence in 1958 from Lola and again the mid-engined revolution arising from the Cooper phenomenon which led both BRM and Ferrari to produce prototype racing cars of this configuration in 1959. Chapman was distinctly reluctant to follow the Cooper lead for reasons of personal pride. Although thoroughly friendly with John Cooper there was intense rivalry between them on the race track and the fact that Cooper generally were more successful toward the end of the Fifties with cars designed in accordance with risible (by Chapman's standards) principles, must have dented his pride considerably. The decision to reposition the power unit of the Lotus Formula cars was taken almost impulsively and there is evidence that Chapman frequently achieved his best results under such conditions. As recounted earlier the conception of the Chapman Strut was forced

I was delighted to discover that, a quarter of a century on, little had changed in Colin Chapman's private Design Department, which is exactly as remembered and occasionally used by me. In this compact facility, opening off his office, Colin would relax with the latest aviation magazine or ponder a knotty problem before taking a weight off his mind in the warmth and seclusion of the scene of many of his greatest conceptual triumphs. This smallest of rooms performed the additional function of affording a refuge to our hero in moments of stress or calamity.

upon him by the failure of de Dion suspension to work satisfactorily on the Twelve and with virtually no time in hand he had quickly to evolve a successful alternative suspension system which could simply be grafted on to the existing main structure of the car.

Knowing that both Ferrari and BRM were toying with the idea of a "rear engined" car Chapman realised that he would be left behind and would probably miss out in the competitive field of raising sponsorship and start money if he did not follow the trend with a thoroughly modern model. He would also have to continue to face the humiliation of receiving second best engines from Coventry Climax while Cooper enjoyed the finest that they could produce. It is undoubtedly the case that whereas BRM and Ferrari were only toying with the idea of rearranging the disposition of the main components of their cars, Chapman characteristically embraced the new philosophy wholeheartedly. He continued to run the odd front engined car alongside the Eighteen while replacements were under construction, but for racing he had forever turned his back on the configuration that had served him so well and at one swoop leaped ahead of his rivals. Suddenly from being the eternal also-ran of the Grand Prix world Chapman became the pace setter.

Ferrari persisted with front engined Grand Prix cars during 1960 and were generally outclassed because of it. They lacked the Chapman ability to so quickly change direction and the nevertheless successful Ferrari 1961 rear engined cars were a strange mishmash of old and new, retaining wire spoked wheels and knock-off hubs at a stage when most other contenders had switched to cast aluminium wheels and the acceptance that wheel changes during the course of a Grand Prix would no longer be required with the vastly improved suspension and road holding of the new wave cars.

After the first year or so however all competitors stepped into line behind Chapman's lead and closely followed his example in chassis and suspension. Ferrari as usual regained the advantage by having anticipated the inevitability of the $1\frac{1}{2}$-litre formula so that whereas British constructors had hoped for a stay of execution and a continuation of the use of $2\frac{1}{2}$-litre engines Ferrari had produced a high output purpose built V6 which was fast enough in a straight line to annihilate anything that could be put on the road by the competition before the arrival of the new V8 Climax and BRM power units. So unprepared were the British contingent that even BRM were forced to use antiquated Coventry Climax FPF $1\frac{1}{2}$-litre engines in the early part of the 1961 season.

(iii) Chapman the Consultant

Beginning with the Vanwall Grand Prix car in 1956 Chapman paved the way for the creation of the present day Lotus consultancy and external design division, the most notorious product of which was the DeLorean car. Tony Vandervell, who had been slowly and without much success developing a British Grand Prix car by conventional methods and with ideas borrowed from Ferrari and Norton racing motorcycles, spotted Chapman's talent at work and called him in together with Frank Costin to see what could be done to improve the mediocre

performance of his expensive venture.

A precondition of the exercise was that the existing engine, transmission (including the carbon copy Ferrari type transaxle) and the equally derivative front suspension using fully machined forged wishbones should be retained unaltered. Chapman rejected the original Ferrari-style heavy chassis and replaced it with a typical Lotus multi-tubular space frame coupling all the existing mechanical bits and pieces so neatly that it appeared that it had been ever thus. The most extraordinary contribution to this exercise was Costin's new bodywork which resulted in one of the most distinctive racing cars of all time. The Vanwall driver sat very high in the car above the mandatory transaxle and Costin created a rear body section extending to the top of the driver's helmet. As well as being one of the tallest racing cars it was also in its most common form (a short nose was used at Monaco) one of the longest and sleekest cars of all time. The substantial ground clearance meant that the underside of the car could be streamlined as effectively as the upper surfaces and the fine penetration and low drag of the bodywork conferred upon the car in its new form remarkable straight line speed.

Because he was obliged to retain the basic suspension system of the old car Chapman's contribution was confined to improving the structural strength of the whole and by making adjustments to spring rates and introducing characteristic Chapman touches such as negative camber on the rear wheels. Nevertheless the car's roadholding was transformed to match the new speed.

There were few people to whom Colin deferred. Enzo Ferrari was one and the other was certainly Tony Vandervell, whom he always called "Sir". There were one or two Lotus employees who addressed Chapman in this manner for the same reason that he in his turn showed courtesy to the millionaire industrialist who had put Britain firmly back on the map as a force in modern Grand Prix motor racing. Sadly, after winning the World Championship in 1958 and putting away his successful team of cars, for which Chapman and Costin must take so much credit, "The Old Man" – as Vandervell was known – had obvious difficulty in tearing himself away from the exciting world of motor racing that had occupied him since the early days of the V16 BRM project with which he was also associated before breaking away to do his own thing in 1952. After the official retirement of the team a lower and lighter version of the car was built and raced by Brooks in the 1959 British Grand Prix without success. Later parts from this car were built into a "low line" version of the front engined Vanwall incorporating independent rear suspension and new gearbox by Colotti. This car was driven by Brooks at the 1960 French GP, only to retire after nine laps.

In 1960 after the arrival on the scene of the new Lotus Eighteen mid-engined car, Vandervell commissioned a chassis from Chapman after visiting the Works at Cheshunt to see for himself what was going on in the Racing Department and into this a Vanwall engine was fitted. This car was never raced and subsequently sold as a rolling chassis less engine. In 1961 a completely new mid-engined car appeared fitted with a 2.6-litre Vanwall engine for Inter-Continental Formula racing. In this form it was raced by Surtees and Brabham and subsequently developed into a version of the car which survives. Failing health and the realisation that the Old Order was changing at a dramatic rate combined to allow the once-magnificent Vanwall racing effort to fade away for ever. The thought processes of Chapman and Costin inspired by the 1956 commission to develop the Vanwall led directly to the 1958-9 Lotus Sixteen Formula cars. In plan and elevation these were remarkably similar to the profile of the Vanwall, but arranged much nearer terra firma and provided with totally different suspension systems. Successful as the Vanwall was with Chapman/Costin structure and aerodynamics combined with italianate suspension and the highly original Rolls-Royce/Norton derived power unit, the same broad structure and shape in the Sixteen was a massive disappointment, to some extent due to the performance of the Chapman designed parts substituted for the original Vanwall suspension elements. The disposition of the engine and the non-availability of the desired constant velocity joint to cope with the extreme angularity of the propeller shaft furthermore resulted in severe power loss. Sixteens in their original form were disliked by the drivers (particularly in 1958 when the exhaust system was amazingly ducted within the bodywork) and their fragility and excessive tendency to understeer contributed to a poor reputation. Dedicated development in historic racing circles during the last thirty years has largely eradicated these early failings.

Although the Vanwall exercise was the most glamorous of Chapman's consultancy commissions in the Fifties he (acting alone without Costin) also made a significant contribution to the ultimate success of the P25 front engined BRM. This machine, which appeared in 1955, was initially as unsuccessful as its V16 forbear and in addition to bouts of brake failure its road holding and handling characteristics left much to be desired. For a long period during 1956 and 1957 P25 designer Peter Berthon and his team struggled in vain to pinpoint the cause of this problem. It took Chapman a few hours in mid 1957 to spot that the difficulty arose from binding of the oleo-pneumatic strut "springs" causing a virtual locking of the suspension under conditions of maximum cornering stress, coupled with sporadic locking of the driveshaft pot joints. The effects of this condition were frequently horrific and after the Chapman medicine (a comprehensive suspension redesign with the adoption of conventional coil springs) had been administered, the BRM from 1958 gained a reputation for being one of the better handling front engined Grand Prix cars. It is ironical that a similar fault (bowing and locking of the front suspension unit central shaft) contributed to the problems of the ill-fated Lotus Seventeen sports racing car in 1959. In mitigation however it must be said that at this stage Chapman was so preoccupied with developments in both design and commercial fields that it is not surprising that he overlooked the obvious in his own situation.

The close connection between the design of the Jaguar E-type rear suspension and the Lola-Lotus arrangement used on the Eighteen Formula cars so successfully during the year immediately preceding the introduction of the E-type have long intrigued me. Chapman was in very close contact with "Lofty" England of Jaguar in this period and may well have been consulted in connection with the design and development of the E-type suspension system. Was Chapman's own Mk. 2 Jaguar part of the remuneration package for such a commission?

Chapter Eight
Parting of the Ways

All good things must come to an end and I have to admit that by the time that I finally left Colin Chapman's employ, I was ready for a change. Working for the man could be exhilarating and draining – often simultaneously.

Because mine was probably the first formally-achieved dismissal in the history of Lotus I have gone to some length to quote from the correspondence involved in order to give an insight into the manner in which the Chapman-Bushell team operated. Fred had a remarkably civilising influence on Colin and tempered some of the worst excesses of those early years. Whether my case established a precedent I doubt, and suspect that some of my successors parted company under much less cordial circumstances.

Of all the United Kingdom Elite distributors among the most successful in terms of numbers sold was the ebullient David Buxton of London Road, Derby. David came from a local family of bakers but showed no sign of following that sober tradition. Instead he achieved the dubious distinction of becoming the first questionable Chapman business associate in the select sequence of such partners who joined forces with Colin over the years. He ran the sales side of the Derby business himself with at his right hand solicitor Bill Allen who preferred racing high performance cars to conveyancing. Bill was later a useful administrator/driver member of Team Elite although David regarded him as best qualified to keep him out of the trouble into which he frequently tended to fall.

David Buxton had a disarmingly friendly manner and a cheerful line of patter. An important element in his character was the same devil-may-care attitude found in Chapman's make-up. This reckless mood would alternate with periods when, with lowered voice and serious mien David could arouse great confidence in the listener by his apparently mature sophistication.

Nothing was impossible for David. If we had a surplus of cars David was our man. He saw the attraction of running a factory racing team with the joy of large sums of start and prize money in cash available in countries far from the Inland Revenue. Although Team Elite called regularly on the services of accomplished drivers such as John Wagstaff and David Piper for the more important events, Buxton and Allen were themselves capable of putting up a good performance. David was a competent organiser both of his own business and the racing team, supported by Bill Allen with responsibility for the day-to-day administration of Team Elite.

The relationship between Lotus and Buxton went well from the beginning. 245

Having achieved a rapport with Colin who enjoyed his braggadocio, Buxton followed the general trend and during 1961 launched himself as a newly-qualified pilot and dealer in light aircraft based at Derby Airport (now East Midlands). David would always put on a good show for the visitor and understood the importance of studying individual preferences. He worked on his relationship with me as the day-to-day link with Chapman and the company on which he depended so much. Aware of my predilection for Italian sporting cars, on one occasion he drove me to Derby Airport in a beautiful new red Alfa Romeo 2000 Superleggera Touring Spider – rather a tank in comparison with the Elite but nevertheless a desirable motor car. He insisted on driving me to his private plane and taking me for a couple of circuits, his newly awakening skills in the air leading me to the conclusion that I preferred David on terra firma.

If (at 26) I had been more sophisticated I would have asked myself how it were possible to develop a business so rapidly on the flimsy basis of a handful of Elite sales and a few "trades". Certainly my curiosity should have been aroused by his apparent ability to launch into the difficult world of aircraft sales with such lack of experience and resources. But David was always in good spirits and exuded confidence. Things were wonderful and we all loved him because he was so helpful to us when we needed assistance. We should however have been more influenced by the frequent warnings (interpreted then as envious resentment) and mature approach of the better established Lotus Centres such as the Chequered Flag where Alan Foster with the utmost politeness but firmness made it clear when they considered that they had sufficient of our rather risky products in stock.

David Buxton operated on the principle that anything good for Colin was good enough for him. The first ripples on the hitherto calm waters of our business relationship with David broke towards the end of 1961 when rumours began to fly that the finance companies supporting his floor plan (stocking) arrangements and hire purchase sales of cars to retail customers, were unhappy with certain aspects of their association with him. Later it transpired that the records of David Buxton Limited were somewhat unclear in detail and this could have resulted in certain cases in a car being the subject of more than one hire purchase finance agreement with highly profitable results for the company but a drastic reduction in security to the lender. Knowing David, I am sure that he was able, by talking louder and longer, to stave off the onset of disaster but the roof caved in early in 1962 and his finance company appointed a liquidator.

At Cheshunt we were preparing for the 1961 Racing Car Show at the Royal Horticultural Halls when I began to suspect that Colin had made the astonishing decision to introduce David Buxton into Lotus to take over the responsibility for Home Market Sales, now 100% direct to the customer. Most of us could not believe that this was true but when pressed, Chapman acknowledged that this was his intention on the basis that David was a super salesman who would help us to clear the increasingly excessive stocks of cars and kits. Colin assured me that my position was secure but I expressed misgivings.

One evening David arrived at Cheshunt after dark while I was working alone in the office. He was on his way to see Colin and carrying a rather scruffy brown suitcase. "Would you hang on to this for a week or so for me?" asked David. By now I was on the defensive and turned him down. We engaged in a rather uneasy conversation during which David characteristically assured me that all was well and that the little bit of trouble he had had with his business would soon be forgotten as he again helped us to resolve our problems in the domestic market.

I went for another conversation with Colin and stated my view that it would be disastrous to bring Buxton into the company at a time when there were irate Elite customers in circulation who had paid deposits to David Buxton Limited only to find that the liquidator had locked the company's doors. I reminded Colin of the painstaking work done by all in the Sales Organisation to remedy Lotus' poor past reputation in commercial matters. The absorption of Buxton would negate all our achievements in improving goodwill with the trade and retail public and under the circumstances I made it clear that I could not continue.

I had prepared a comprehensive commercial plan in November 1961 under the title "Proposed World Marketing Programme for 1962" and this was due to be discussed at a Board Meeting immediately before Colin's departure for the races in South Africa during December. I attended to present my paper and naturally David Buxton's rumoured appointment came up. Mike Costin took the same view as me and was obviously opposed to the idea. Nobby Clark who had grown accustomed over the years to accepting Colin's headstrong behaviour sat on the fence while Fred Bushell followed the usual pattern of events and his master's bidding. Peter Kirwan-Taylor kept his counsel. Colin was always, like the politician he was, aware of the importance of today rather than tomorrow and hastened to assure me that there was no immediate intention to proceed with the appointment of Buxton.

Almost immediately the rumours strengthened and it became increasingly obvious that discussions were proceeding between Buxton, Chapman and Bushell, which if as reported, would lead to my replacement as Group Sales Manager. I made my position very clear, stating that if Buxton came I would go, but I can only assume that Colin felt me to be bluffing. Very few senior people had resigned from Lotus; Colin considered it his prerogative to apply the boot.

Colin went to and returned from South Africa while Fred Bushell's negotiations with Buxton continued. Irate would-be Buxton customers of the past were besieging us with demands for their money to be returned and some of them, anxious to become Elite owners regardless of the cost, bought kits from Cheshunt. I found the situation increasingly embarrassing and unacceptable. I went home, pulled out my faithful Olivetti Lettera 22 and composed a letter to Colin dated 19th December 1961:

"Dear Colin,
I must ask you to accept my resignation as Group Sales Manager with effect from midnight, 31st December 1961.
From reliable sources I understand that the Board has decided to appoint Mr. David Buxton as Home Sales Manager of the Group ("On the basis that a probationary period of six months duration would be followed by a Directorship" – DGSB (Buxton)). This information is in the possession of at least four of my colleagues: Messrs. Lewis, Richardson, Warr, and Woolhead, although I as the person most affected by the appointment have not yet been officially advised of the Board's decision which of course completely contradicts your statement to me prior to your departure to South Africa . . ."

My letter went on to state that I had no objection in principle to a division of Home and Export Sales functions provided that the candidate for the post of Home Sales Manager would enhance the role.

The crunch came during the run up to the Racing Car Show. We had made a huge effort to present the new Twentytwo Formula Junior and matching Twentythree sports racing cars. Buxton arrived full of confidence and bonhomie. That was it as far as I was concerned and I gave myself an unofficial holiday over the New Year.

After a couple of days the telephone rang and a pained Colin spoke to me to remind me of the existence of my Service Contract and to insist that I immediately come to Cheshunt to discuss the situation. The meeting took place on 2nd January in Colin's office and he was able inevitably to persuade me to acquiesce by giving personal assurances which I accepted. Fred Bushell, aware of the delicacy of the situation drafted a letter to me for Colin's signature which read as follows:

"Dear Mr. Reid, (sic)
I would like to take the opportunity of confirming to you the basis of our discussions yesterday. I discussed fully with you the Board's desire to separate Export and Home Sales responsibilities and that it was their intention to engage Mr. David Buxton in the capacity of Homes Sales Manager for a probationary period of six months during which time he will be given the opportunity of dispelling all doubts concerning his methods of operating. You maintain your personal opinion that you cannot consider this to be an ideal choice but nevertheless assure me of your fullest co-operation in executing this company policy.

Regarding your own position you have my assurance that this division of the sales function will in no way prejudice your own position with the company and that there will be no question of Mr. Buxton being offered a Directorship in advance of consideration being given to your own position under the terms of your existing contract.

I think that the title of Group Sales Manager should now be discontinued and that you should assume the title of Export Sales Manager for Lotus Cars Limited and Lotus Components Limited."

The wily Fred then made a proposal in the sure knowledge that it would be turned down:

"Regarding the question of commission which is currently at the rate of 0.1% of all sales, since Export Sales are expected to be at least one half of the total of the sales I suggest this rate to be revised to 0.2% of all Export Sales, however the 0.1% of all sales arrangement will stand if you prefer."

At this point Colin departed abroad on Team Lotus business and it was not until 14th February that I confirmed my acceptance of the situation and formally withdrew my resignation. I also ended my letter with the statement:

"Since it was my contract and its spirit which kept me here I would like to leave the terms of the commission payment in accordance with the original conditions."

At least I got that part of the revised arrangement right.

It was vitally important to Chapman's strategy of bolstering David Buxton's reputation that I should be seen to be still around and thereby condoning the situation. My naivety and personal loyalty to Chapman won the day for him. Colin was now Master again as far as I was concerned and at some point during the Spring he must have decided that the time was fast approaching to be rid of me. We had some rather loose ideas about budgeting and I was conducting a modest advertising campaign aimed at the US market in the pages of *Sports Cars Illustrated*. Colin professed to be unaware of this activity and took strong exception to the programme, positively forbidding me to continue it. For some reason another advertisement slipped through the net and when the invoice arrived he called me to his office, waved the offending advertisement showing a rather blurred John Bolster cornering hard in Lotus Super Seven 8843AR (one of our more successful advertisements) and delivered the *coup de grâce,* with obvious enjoyment.

Poor Fred Bushell was left to clear up the mess but this time he signed his letter personally. It read as follows:

"Dear Robin.
I have to confirm the discussions at the Board Meeting today when it was decided that since

there are severe differences of opinion concerning the operation of your department, that it would be better in everbody's interest if your appointment with the company was terminated.

Therefore as was discussed between us following the meeting you will continue to receive your remuneration until such time as you have arranged an alternative position which you anticipate will take you not more than two months.

In conclusion I would remind you that the Board expressed regret that this difference had arisen but feel that in the circumstances there was no other alternative."

I was grateful to Fred for having cushioned my departure both spiritually and materially and soon I was back in the mainstream of industry, not returning to the automotive world until 1978, by which time all had changed.

I suspect that my departure, its means and the events surrounding it severely upset Mike Costin who was not a happy man during the time that I knew him at Lotus. He decided to leave in the same year and went at last to Cosworth where he continues to flourish.

From time to time I heard reports of the strange progress of David Buxton and his association with Lotus. I believe he popped up in Belgium shortly after my departure operating a joint venture with Chapman which ended somewhat disastrously for Lotus. The unrelenting finance companies might have had something to do with the disappearance of David for a couple of years, but he bobbed up later in the Moonraker boatbuilding partnership with Colin. Their mutual appeal was irresistible and understood by those of us who knew them well. David did not have the star quality of a DeLorean but he was without question cast in the same mould. Fortunately the results of his partnership with Chapman were less catastrophic.

Copy of letter forwarded to Mr F R Bushell, Directory/Secretary

'Longmynd'
Mountwood Road
Prenton
BIRKENHEAD

29 MAY 1962

Dear Sir
I thank you for your letter of the 25th instant, and have noted your comments. I have in fact already contacted the liquidator of David Buxton Limited, and as you well know the position here is completely useless and the possibilities of me claiming my deposit are nil. I should like to clarify one point, in that I do not obviously hold your Company liable for what has happened between myself and David Buxton Limited. It was however, promised by your Company, admittedly verbally that something would be done to see that part, if not all of the £170.0.0d would be passed back to myself.

I am now both disappointed and disgusted at your Company's attitude, and apparent lack of interest. I can now only assume that this is because I have now purchased a new Elite from you and have paid for it. At this point I should like to mention something which was amusing at the time, but nevertheless is indicative of the general attitude at Cheshunt. Upon taking delivery of my new Elite in February of this year I found that there was a bird's nest neatly built into one corner of the boot. When one pays as much as £1600.0.0d for a car one does not expect this type of thing.

Unless a little more interest can be shown by yourselves, I am afraid that my next purchase for racing will certainly not be a Lotus, especially if Mr Buxton is still in your employ.

Please look into this matter a little more seriously and let me have your observations in due course.

Yours faithfully
B J Smallthwaite

Appendices

To avoid unduly breaking up the narrative but to provide more information on certain aspects I have included a series of appendices. Apart from drawing on my own archive I have been greatly assisted by Ron Hickman and Ian McLeod, who like me have allowed the horrid fascination of Lotus to make it difficult to throw away some of the tastier morsels from our store of memorabilia.

Appendix One

Colin Chapman
and The Ferodo Trophy

The Ferodo Trophy is awarded by the company of that name (part of the Valeo Group) for outstanding achievements. It is not awarded automatically each year and was last held in 1984 by Maclaren. Colin Chapman was the recipient on no fewer than three occasions and the citations were as follows:

1956 "Awarded to Mr. A.C.B. Chapman who is responsible for the design and construction of Lotus Sports cars and made an important design contribution to the advancement in design of British Grand Prix cars."

1965 "To Mr. A.C.B. Chapman whose Lotus Coventry Climax and Lotus Ford Cars have dominated the motor racing scene throughout the 1965 season."

1978 "To Mr. A.C.B. Chapman CBE for his design, construction and team direction of the cars which have dominated Grand Prix racing in 1978."

Appendix Two

Lotus Specifications 1951 – 62

	MK.3A	**MK.6**
Type	750 Formula	Club Racing
Dimensions		
Wheelbase	81″ (2055 mm)	88″ (2235 mm)
Track front	48″ (1220 mm)	49″ (1345 mm)
Track Rear	46″ (1170 mm)	45″ (1145 mm)
Length	110″ (2795 mm)	121″ (3075 mm)
Weight	335 kg	435 kg
Engine	Austin 747 cc	Ford sv 1172/Ford Consul 1500/MG 1250/1500 or Climax 1100 cc
Chassis	Austin Seven, boxed and stiffened by front and rear tubular superstructure	Steel tube space frame
Body	Aluminium panels	Aluminium panels (Williams & Pritchard)
Transmission	Austin Seven 4-speed	Ford 3sp/MG 4-speed
Brakes	Hydraulic drum	Hydraulic drum/Girling mechanical drum
Steering gear	Modified A7	Modified Ford 10
Wheels	West London Repair 15″ rim Wire Type	Modified Ford pressed steel or Wire centrelock type 15″ rim
Suspension		
Front	Swing axle IFS (Ford) with transverse leaf spring/telescopic dampers	Swing axle IFS (Ford) with combined coil spring/telescopic dampers
Rear	Quarter-elliptic leaf springs/telescopic dampers	Ford torque tube/BMC axle/Panhard rod/coil spring/telescopic dampers
Production		
Years	1951	1953–1955
Number manufactured	1 (+ 2)	100
Price	–	from £425

	MK.8	**MK.9**
Type	Sports Racing	Sports Racing
Dimensions		
Wheelbase	88″ (2235 mm)	88″ (2235 mm)
Track front	49″ (1245 mm)	49″ (1245 mm)
Track Rear	48″ (1220 mm)	48″ (1220 mm)
Length	132″ (3355 mm)	140″ (3556 mm)
Weight	525 kg	460 kg
Engine	MG 1500/Connaught 1500/Climax 1100 cc	Climax 1100/MG 1500 cc
Chassis	Steel tube spaceframe	Steel tube spaceframe
Body	Aluminium panels (W & P)	Aluminium panels (W & P)
Transmission	MG 4-speed/chassis-mounted differential	BMC 4-speed/chassis-mounted differential
Brakes	Hydraulic drum; inboard at rear	Disc; inboard at rear
Steering gear	Rack & pinion	Rack & pinion
Wheels	Wire type 15″, stud or centrelock fitting	Wire centrelock type; 15″ rim
Suspension		
Front	Swing axle IFS (Ford) with combined coil spring/telescopic dampers	Swing axle IFS (Ford) with combined coil spring/telescopic dampers
Rear	De Dion type/bell crank actuated tranverse tension spring/lever dampers	De Dion type with combined coil spring/telescopic dampers
Production Years	1954–1955	1955
Number manufactured	5	23
Price	£1150 (Climax)	£850 less engine/gearbox

	Mk.10	**Eleven S.1**
Type	Sports Racing	Sports Racing
Dimensions		
Wheelbase	88″ (2235 mm)	85″ (2160 mm)
Track front	49″ (1245 mm)	46½″ (1181 mm)
Track Rear	48″ (1220 mm)	47″ (1194 mm)
Length	132″ (3355 mm)	134″ (3404 mm)
Weight	560 kg	436 kg
Engine	Bristol 2 litre Connaught 2 litre	Climax 1100/1460 cc (Le Mans/Club). Ford 100E
Chassis	Steel tube spaceframe	Steel tube spaceframe
Body	Aluminium panels (W & P)	Aluminium panels (W & P)
Transmission	Bristol 4-speed/chassis-mounted differential	BMC 4-speed/Ford 3-speed
Brakes	Disc; inboard at rear	Disc; inboard at rear (Club/Sports; Drum)
Steering gear	Rack & pinion	Rack & pinion
Wheels	Wire centrelock type; 15″ rim	Wire centrelock type; 15″ rim
Suspension		
Front	Swing axle IFS (Ford) with combined coil spring/telescopic dampers	Swing axle IFS (Ford) with combined coil spring/telescopic dampers

Rear	De Dion type with combined coil spring/telescopic dampers	De Dion type with combined coil spring/telescopic dampers (Le Mans). BMC "Live" axle (Club/Sports)
Production		
Years	1955	1956
Number manufactured	6	150
Price	£925 less engine/gearbox	£1437 nett (Le Mans)

	Eleven S.2 Le Mans 85/ Club/Sports	**Twelve**
Type	Sports-Racing	Formula 2 (& F.1 later)
Dimensions		
Wheelbase	88″ (2235 mm)	88″ (2235 mm)
Track front	45″ (1143 mm)	48″ (1220 mm)
Track Rear	47″ (1194 mm)	48″ (1220 mm)
Length	139″ (3530 mm)	131″ (3227 mm)
Weight	439 kg	300 kg
Engine	Climax 1100/1460 cc (Le Mans/Club). Ford 100E sv 1172 cc (Sports)	Climax FPF 1475 cc (F2), 2270 cc (F.1)
Chassis	Steel tube spaceframe	Steel tube spaceframe
Body	Aluminium panels (W & P)	Aluminium panels (W & P)
Transmission	BMC 4-speed/Ford 3 speed	Lotus 5-speed transaxle
Brakes	Disc; inboard at rear. (Club/Sports Drum)	Disc; inboard at rear
Steering gear	Rack & pinion	Rack & pinion
Wheels	Wire centrelock type; 15″ rim	Cast magnesium "Wobbly" type, 15″ rim
Suspension		
Front	Le Mans only – Wishbone/ IFS/integral anti-roll bar/combined coil spring/ telescopic dampers (Club/Sports swing-axle IFS)	Wishbone IFS/integral anti-roll bar/combined coil spring/telescopic dampers
Rear	De Dion type with combined coil spring/telescopic dampers (Le Mans). BMC "Live axle" (Club/Sports)	Initially De Dion type; then Chapman Strut with single radius arm
Production		
Years	1957–59	1956–57
Number manufactured	120	11
Price	£1690 nett (Le Mans) £1490 nett (Club)	Negotiable

	Elite (T.14)	**Seven S.1 Basic/ Super/America/'A'**
Type	Fixed head coupé 2-seat	Sports-Racing
Dimensions		
Wheelbase	88″ (2235 mm)	88″ (2235 mm)

Track front	47″ (1190 mm)	47″ (1190 mm)
Track Rear	47″ (1190 mm)	46″ (1168 mm)
Length	150″ (3810 mm)	129″ (3277 mm)
Weight	572 kg	420 kg
Engine	Climax FWE 1216 cc	Ford 100E sv 1172 cc (Super: Climax 1100 cc) (America: A-H Sprite) ('A'; Morris minor)
Chassis	Steel reinforced fibreglass monocoque chassis/body unit	Steel tube spaceframe
Body		Aluminium panels (W & P)
Transmission	MG or ZF 4-speed BMC CWP in Lotus diff. housing	Ford 3-speed/Basic BMC 4-speed
Brakes	Girling discs; inboard at rear	Drum
Steering gear	Rack & pinion	Rack & pinion
Wheels	15″ (x 4.80 tyre) Dunlop centrelock wire type	Pressed steel/wire centrelock type; 15″ rim
Suspension		
Front	Wishbone IFS/integral anti-roll bar Coil spring/damper suspension units	Wishbone IFS/integral anti-roll bar/combined coil spring/telescopic dampers
Rear	Chapman strut with single tube (S1) or triangulated (S2) radius arm	BMC "Live" axle/combined coil spring/telescopic dampers
Production Years	1958–63	1957–60
Number manufactured	ca.1000	100
Price	1960 £1387 nett 1961 £1299 gross (Kit)	from £526 (Kit)

	Fifteen Series 1&2	Sixteen
Type	Sports-Racing	Formula 2 (& F.1 later)
Dimensions		
Wheelbase	88″ (2235 mm)	88″ (2235 mm)
Track front	47″ (1190 mm)	47″ (1190 mm)
Track Rear	48″ (1220 mm)	48″ (1220 mm)
Length	137″ (3480 mm)	140″ (3556 mm)
Weight	445 kg	490 kg
Engine	Climax FPF 1475, 1960, 2495 cc	Climax FPF 1475, 1960, 2207, 2495 cc
Chassis	Steel tube spaceframe	Steel tube spaceframe (with "Terry" scuttle hoop in 1959)
Body	Aluminium panels (W & P)	Aluminium panels (W & P)
Transmission	Lotus 5-speed transaxle (S.1) BMC 4-speed (S.2)	Lotus 5-speed transaxle
Brakes	Disc; inboard at rear	Disc; inboard at rear
Steering gear	Rack & pinion	Rack & pinion
Wheels	Wire centrelock or cast magnesium "Wobbly" type; 15″ rim	Cast magnesium "Wobbly" type; 15″ rim

Suspension

Front	Wishbone IFS/integral anti-roll bar/combined coil spring telescopic dampers	i) Wishbone IFS/integral front mounted anti-roll bar (ii) As (i) but anti-roll bar behind upper link iii) All-tubular wishbones with separate anti-roll bar
Rear	Chapman strut with single tube radius arm	Chapman strut with single tube radius arm (1958) or lower wishbone/radius arm (1959)

Production

Years	1958–59	1958–59
Number manufactured	30	8
Price	Negotiable	Negotiable

	Seventeen	**Eighteen**
Type	Sports Racing	Formula Junior
Dimensions		
Wheelbase	82″ (2083 mm)	90″ (2286 mm)
Track front	42″ (1067 mm)	49″ (1245 mm)
Track Rear	45″ (1143 mm)	47″ (1194 mm)
Length	136″ (3454 mm)	140″ (3556 mm)
Weight	340 kg	365 kg
Engine	Climax 1100 cc (FWMA 745 cc optional)	Cosworth Ford 105E 997 cc (alt. Downton BMC 948 cc)
Chassis	Steel tube spaceframe	Steel tube spaceframe with "Terry" scuttle hoop
Body	Aluminium (lower) and fibreglass (upper)	Fibreglass panels
Transmission	BMC 4-speed	Inverted Renault 4-speed
Brakes	Disc; inboard at rear	Drums; outboard at rear
Steering gear	Rack & pinion	Rack & pinion
Wheels	Cast magnesium "Wobbly" type; 15″ rim	Cast magnesium "Wobbly" type 15″ rim
Suspension		
Front	a) MacPherson strut with lower wishbone (b) Double wishbone conversion fitted f.o.c. inc. combined coil spring/separate anti-roll bar	Double wishbone with combined coil spring/ telescopic dampers and separate anti-roll bar
Rear	Chapman strut with single tube radius arm	Fixed length drive shafts with lower "reversed" wishbone, anti-roll bar and soil spring/damper units. Parallel radius arms
Production		
Years	1959	1960
Number manufactured	ca. 20	125
Price	ca. £1600	£1275 (tax free)

	Eighteen (F1-F2)	Seven S.2 'F', 'A' types & Super
Type	Formula 1 & F.2	Sports
Dimensions		
Wheelbase	90″ (2286 mm)	87″ (2210 mm)
Track front	52″ (1321 mm)	46″ (1168 mm)
Track Rear	53″ (1346 mm)	48″ (1220 mm)
Length	140″ (3556 mm)	130″ (3302 mm)
Weight	445 kg	433 kg ('F')
Engine	Climax FPF 1475 or 2495 cc	'F': 100E; later 105E 997 cc. 'A': BMC 948 cc. Super: 109E Cosworth Ford 1340 cc
Chassis	Steel tube spaceframe with "Terry" scuttle and rear hoops	Steel tube spaceframe
Body	Fibreglass panels	Aluminium and fibreglass
Transmission	Lotus 5-speed transaxle	'F' 100E 3-s/105E 4-speed 'A': BMC 4-speed. Super: 109E 4-speed
Brakes	Disc; inboard at rear	Drum
Steering gear	Rack & pinion	Rack & pinion
Wheels	Cast magnesium "Wobbly" type	Pressed steel; 13″ rim
Suspension		
Front	Double wishbone with combined coil spring/ telescopic dampers and separate anti-roll bar	Wishbone IFS/integral anti-roll bar/combined coil spring/telescopic
Rear	Fixed length drive shafts with lower "reversed" wishbone, anti-roll bar and coil spring/damper units, Parallel radius arm	Standard Ten/combined coil spring/telescopic dampers
Production Years	1960	1960–68
Number manufactured	c.25	c.500 to 31.12.61
Price	Negotiable	from £499 (Kit)

	Nineteen ("Monte Carlo")	Twenty
Type	Sports Racing	Formula Junior
Dimensions		
Wheelbase	90″ (2286 mm)	90″ (2286 mm)
Track front	52″ (1321 mm)	49½″ (1245 mm)
Track Rear	53″ (1346 mm)	47″ (1194 mm)
Length	141″ (3581 mm)	139″ (3531 mm)
Weight	509 kg	366 kg (997 cc) or 401 kg (1098 cc)
Engine	Climax FPF 1960 or 2495 cc	Cosworth Ford 105E MkIII 997 cc or Mk. IV 1098 cc
Chassis	Steel tube spaceframe with "Terry" scuttle and rear hoops	Steel tube spaceframe with "Terry" scuttle hoop

Body	Aluminium and fibreglass	Fibreglass panels
Transmission	Lotus 5-speed transaxle	Inverted Renault or VW 4-speed
Brakes	Disc; outboard at rear	Disc; inboard at rear
Steering gear	Rack & pinion	Rack & pinion
Wheels	Cast magnesium "Wobbly" or Wire centrelock type	Cast magnesium "Wobbly" type; F 13", R 15" rim
Suspension		
Front	Double wishbone with combined coil spring/ telescopic dampers and separate anti-roll bar	Double wishbone with combined coil spring/ telescopic dampers and separate anti-roll bar
Rear	Fixed length driveshafts with lower "reversed" wishbone, anti-roll bar and coil spring/ damper units. Parallel radius arms	Fixed length driveshafts with lower "reversed" wishbone anti-roll bar and coil spring/ damper units. Parallel radius arms
Production		
Years	1960–61	1961
Number manufactured	13	100
Price	Negotiable	£1450 (tax free)

	TwentyOne	**TwentyTwo**
Type	Formula One	Formula Junior
Dimensions		
Wheelbase	90" (2286 mm)	90" (2286 mm)
Track front	53" (1345 mm)	49" (1245 mm)
Track Rear	54" (1372 mm)	47" (1194 mm)
Length	141" (3581 mm)	139" (3531 mm)
Weight	425 kg	403 kg
Engine	Climax FPF 4-cyl 1498 cc	Cosworth Ford 105E Mk IV 1098 cc
Chassis	Steel tube spaceframe with "Terry" scuttle and rear hoops	Steel tube spaceframe with "Terry" scuttle hoop
Body	Fibreglass panels	Fibreglass panels
Transmission	ZF 5-speed transaxle	Renault or VW (Hewland)
Brakes	Disc; outboard at rear.	Disc; outboard at rear
Steering gear	Rack & pinion	Rack & pinion
Wheels	Cast magnesium "Wobbly" type	Cast magnesium "Wobbly" type 15" rear/13" front rim
Suspension		
Front	Fabricated sheet steel upper suspension arms actuating inboard coil spring/damper units. Lower triangular wishbone	Double wishbone with combined coil spring/ telescopic dampers and separate anti-roll bar
Rear	Single-tube Upper lateral link; lower reversed wishbone with splined (early cars) inboard "doughnut" jointed (later) driveshafts. Coil spring/ damper units.	Single-tube Upper lateral link; lower reversed wishbone fixed length driveshaft with Hook outer; "doughnut" inner U/J (orig. sliding spline type)

Production		
Years	1961	
Number		
manufactured	10	77
Price	Negotiable	£1550

	TwentyThree	**TwentyFour**
Type	Sports Racing	Formula One
Dimensions		
Wheelbase	90″ (2286 mm)	90″ (2235 mm)
Track front	49″ (1245 mm)	53″ (1190 mm)
Track Rear	47″ (1194 mm)	54″ (1168 mm)
Length	140″ (3556 mm)	142″ (3607 mm)
Weight	400 kg	454 kg
Engine	Cosworth Ford 105/109/116E based 997 – 1498 cc	Climax FWMV V-8 cyl. 1½ litre
Chassis	Steel tube spaceframe with "Terry" scuttle hoop	Steel tube spaceframe with "Terry" scuttle and rear hoops
Body	Fibreglass panels	Fibreglass panels
Transmission	Renault or VW (Hewland) 4-speed transaxle	ZF 5-speed transaxle
Brakes	Disc; outboard at rear	Disc; outboard at rear
Steering gear	Rack & pinion	Rack & pinion
Wheels	Cast magnesium "Wobbly" type 15″ rear/13″ front rim	Cast magnesium "Wobbly" type
Suspension		
Front	Double wishbone with combined coil spring/ telescopic dampers and separate anti-roll bar	Fabricated sheet steel upper suspension arms actuating inboard coil spring/damper units. Lower triangular wishbone.
Rear	Single tube upper lateral link lower reversed wishbone; fixed length driveshaft with Hook outer "doughnut" inner U/J (orig. sliding spline type)	Single tube upper lateral link; lower reversed wishbone with inboard "doughnut" and outboard Hook U/J coil spring/damper units
Production		
Years	1962–66	1962
Number		
manufactured	c.75	12
Price	C. £1650	Negotiable

	Twentyfive	**Elan (T.26)**
Type	Formula One	Sports
Dimensions		
Wheelbase	90″ (2286 mm)	84″ (2134 mm)
Track front	53″ (1346 mm)	47″ (1194 mm)
Track Rear	54″ (1372 mm)	48″ (1219 mm)
Length	142″ (3607 mm)	145″ (3683 mm)

259

Weight	452 kg	713 kg
Engine	Climax FWMV V-8 cyl 1½ litre	(1962) Lotus Twin Cam 1498 cc – Later 1558 cc
Chassis	Fabricated aluminium with local steel reinforcement	Fabricated sheet steel backbone with forked extensions front and rear
Body	Fibreglass panels	One-piece Fibreglass body with local steel reinforcement
Transmission	ZF 5-speed transaxle	Ford 4-speed
Brakes	Disc; outboard at rear	Disc; outboard at rear
Steering gear	Rack & pinion	Rack & pinion
Wheels	Cast magnesium "Wobbly" type	Pressed steel
Suspension		
Front	Fabricated sheet steel upper suspension arms actuating inboard coil spring/damper units. Lower triangular wishbone	Upper and lower pressed steel wishbones with coil spring/damper units
Rear	Single tube upper lateral link; lower reversed wishbone with inboard "doughnut" and outboard hook U/J coil spring/damper units	MacPherson strut rear suspension with lower triangulated wishbone. Fixed length driveshaft with inner and outer "doughnuts" U/J
Production		
Years	1962 – 63	1962 – on
Number manufactured	7	(S.1) 330 to end 1963
Price	Team Lotus only	£1095 (kit) £1312 (Factory assembled)

Appendix Three

The 1172 Formula
of the 750MC (1959)

Chapman's assault on the newly created 750 Formula category with the Mk. 3A Lotus of 1951 is described elsewhere in these pages. By the end of the decade Lotus superiority in Club Racing was such that it became necessary for the 750MC to revise their 1172 Formula (for competition cars with four cylinder Ford sidevalve engines) to specifically exclude the more exotic Lotuses which had swamped a Formula intended to encourage racing by the Impecunious Enthusiast (or IE) so beloved of the 750MC and for whom to this day they continue to perform a wonderful service.

There is a slightly hysterical note in the 1959 Formula regulations and one can imagine the Committee burning the midnight oil as they seek to close every possible gap against the wily Lotus owners who nevertheless continued to dominate the Formula without too much interruption before it was replaced by Formula 1200 in 1963.

The Seven Fifty Motor Club Ltd
1172 Formula for 1959

The 750 and 1172 Formulae have been devised to make equitable bases for scratch racing for those with limited resources . . .

1172 Formula
(For competition cars with Ford Eight and Ten engines)

1(a) The car must comply with the Road Traffic Act as regards construction and must be capable of being driven to the Meeting under its own power.
(b) It must also comply with the RAC Regulations for cars taking part in competitions, i.e. Paragraphs 1 and 3 including 3j (Races) or 4 (Special Events) as appropriate, as published in the RAC Motor Sport Year Book and Fixture List, so far as these regulations are not inconsistent with the regulations following.
2. The internal width of the cockpit must be at least 32 in. Passenger seats should normally be positioned for a two-seater sports car and suitable for an average-sized adult. There must be a windscreen at least equivalent to one normal aero screen. Hoods, passenger seats and spare wheels need not be carried when racing.

3.   The car must carry full electrical equipment including side and tail lamps and at least one headlamp, starter, battery, and a production car dynamo, effectively mounted and driven and capable of maintaining a battery charge, with lights on, including at least one 36 watt bulb.

4.   The power unit is to be based on a standard side valve Ford 933 cc or 1,172 cc engine casing of any type (ie Eight, Ten, Popular or Anglia or Prefect of either earlier type or 1954 or later). Modifications must not include supercharging, conversion to ohv, reversal in function of the inlet and exhaust ports or the dividing of the siamesed inlet ports. The standard stroke of 92.5 mm must not be exceeded, and the bore must be no greater than 63.5 mm plus 0.060 in rebore allowance. Standard timing, camshafts and cam-follower profiles must be used unaltered in any way except for the advance or retard of the camshaft complete.

5.   There is no minimum weight restriction.

6.   When racing, one of the standard or premium grade fuels as supplied by roadside pumps must be used.

7   This formula is devised for the benefit of the amateur constructor-tuner with limited resources. The 750 MC Board reserves the right at all times to reject any car which it considers represents an attempt to defeat the spirit of the regulations, even though it complies with the letter of them. This also refers to expensive production cars, or cars developed with a high percentage of costly proprietary components, and those cars which are professionally maintained.

In order that existing and intending competitors should fully appreciate the intentions of these regulations the following **Notes of Explanation** will no doubt clarify the position:

(a)   The Formula envisaged "sports cars" of a type for daily use and occasional competitions, constructed by Club Members, and not costly proprietary production cars and sports-racing machines having no other use between races.

(b)   For the 1959 Racing Season the Lotus Mark VI and the Lotus Seven will be accepted **if built to the basic standard specification,** with, of course, the normal 1172 Formula engine modifications, and the fitting of modified gears to the standard Ford gearbox casing if desired. These cars will be ineligible if fitted with De Dion rear axles, disc brakes, wire wheels, or similar modifications involving costly proprietary components. The Lotus Mark VIII, Mark IX and the Lotus Eleven will not be acceptable in the 1959 season.

The Lotus Mark VIII, Mark IX and the Lotus Eleven are excluded solely on the grounds of their basic cost. The Lotus Mark VI, to standard specification, has always been regarded as a car for home building and racing by an amateur and the Lotus Seven in this respect is its logical successor. Any production car should be kept in its original form, i.e. Mark VI and Lotus Seven and Dellow Mark V, etc, to retain a non all-enveloping body with exposed front wheels. Buckler 90, Tornado, Convair and other similar low priced all-enveloping bodied cars being acceptable.

(c)   With the banning of the Lotus Mark IX and XI for the 1959 season it will not be in order to fit Mark XI bodywork to a Mark VI or Seven chassis or similar.

(d)   Genuine "one-off" Specials of the all-enveloping type will be acceptable, but in order to avoid misunderstandings and possible exclusion on a later date, intending competitors are requested to obtain individual rulings, by written application, as to the eligibility of cars either proprietary or Specials. If a Special, in the opinion of the Club Scrutineer, represents outlay substantially greater than a Lotus VII in kit form, plus amateur assembly, it is not considered to be in the spirit of the formula.

(e)   Whilst it is of course appreciated that machine work is necessary to modify engines, and build up chassis, etc, the term "professionally maintained" refers to complete and regular preparation by other than the competitor and this is not acceptable.

(f)   If was never intended that the Formula should provide a direct advertising medium for commercial interests. Therefore in future it is required that:

(i)   There shall be no trade names emblazoned on the side of cars. (The manufacturer's insignia or emblem affixed on the front is acceptable if normal size.)

(ii)   All entries for competitors events shall be from individuals and not trading establishments or equipes bearing the name of a trading concern.

It is appreciated that some club members are directly connected with garage businesses and there is no objection to their owning and personally competing. However, they should not enter cars for others to drive which may be interpreted as "works" entries in the professional sense.

(g)   Competitors in races under either Formula must realize that they are carrying the banner of the 750 MC before the public. A high standard of preparation and turn-out is therefore essential and will be insisted on.

(h)   If the control exercised by the Board is considered inadequate, complaints concerning any possible infringements should be made in writing to the Board of Directors, when matters will be investigated and action taken if deemed necessary.

The attention of competitors is drawn to the fact that the standard Ford Ten steering arms, of any type, are liable to fracture without warning under racing conditions when used without reinforcement. The standard cast flywheel is liable to burst if appreciably lightened.

(Reproduced by permission of The Seven Fifty Motor Club Ltd)

Appendix Four

Formula Junior

Regulations for the new International Formula, from the English translation supplied by the FIA.

1. **Definition** Cars of the Junior formula are one-seater racing cars, whereof the fundamental elements are derived from a touring car recognized as such by the FIA (minimum production 1,000 units in twelve consecutive months).

2. **General characteristics**

(a) Minimum wheelbase: 200 cm, (6 ft 7³/₄ in)

(b) Minimum track: 110 cm (3 ft 7⁵/₁₆ in)

(c) Maximum width of body: (measured outside) 95 cm (3 ft 1¹/₂ in)

(d) Maximum engine cylinder capacity: 1,000 cc

(e) Minimum weight: 400 kg (881.8 lb)

The latter weight limit however, is reduced to 793 lb for cars with a cylinder-capacity of 1,000 cc or less. The above-mentioned weight shall be measured with the car "in running order", viz with all accessories required by these regulations but with dry fuel tank(s).

3. **Mechanical elements**

(a) The cylinder-block, including the cylinder-head and cylinders (if the latter are removable) must be those of the engine belonging to a car classed by the FIA in the Touring category.

(b) The gearbox must be that of an FIA recognized touring car. Complete freedom is left with regard to the number and staging of gear ratios.

(c) The braking system and principle (viz. drum-brakes or disc-brakes) must remain the same as on the car from which is taken the engine.

(d) The system and principle of feeding (by carburettors or by injection) must be the same as on the car from which is taken the engine.

(e) The cylinder-capacities specified in the present regulations may be achieved by modifying the original bore (increase or reduction). No modification of the stroke is permitted.

(f) The car must have an automatic starter.

4. **Body** The body, open and offering only one seat, shall comprise around the pilot's seat, an anti-roll bar, protecting him from being crushed should the car turn over. There shall also be a protective device against fire as required by the International Sporting Code (Art. 125).

5. Silencer The supplementary regulations of the events may provide that an efficient silencer is compulsory.

6. Prohibitions It is not permitted:

(a) To use an engine with one or more overhead camshafts.

(b) To use a self-locking differential.

(c) To change the number of crankshaft bearings.

(d) To change the location of the camshaft.

7. Fuel Only commercial fuel, as defined by the FIA shall be used.

8. Certificate of origin Every car of the Junior Formula, when arriving at the beginning of an event, shall be equipped with a certificate issued by the national sports authority concerned and stating the origin of its fundamental elements.

Appendix Five

The Elite and its Racing Competitors – Specifications

Although the Elite faced a relatively broad range of commercial competition in road going form including cars with larger capacity engines such as the Porsche 356 family, on the racing track the situation was more favourable.

The Elite began to race seriously in 1958, principally in British short circuit events where it achieved immediate dominance in the 1300 cc category (and frequently overall). In the long distance races of the continent it had to deal initially with the Alfa Romeo Giulietta SZ (and SZT) which although at a serious weight disadvantage and without power superiority, proved outstandingly durable and formed serious competition.

Later the advent of the Abarth-Simca 1300 posed a major problem. The Abarth-Simca had only a modest weight disadvantage but real power superiority sufficient to overcome the shortcomings of its crude suspension and outlandish weight distribution resulting from the overhung rear engine.

The two continental rivals are shown overleaf compared with the later Elite Super 105 car; the hottest "over the counter" Elite version, although many earlier cars were privately developed with highly modified (usually by Cosworth) engines of the same general power output as the Super 105.

Lotus Elite Super 105 (1962)

Dimensions:	Wheelbase 88.2″, (2440 mm), track front and rear 46.8″ (1189 mm), length 150″ (3810 mm)
Dry Weight:	1261 lbs (572 kg)
Engine:	Coventry Climax FWE, 4 cylinders in line, all aluminium, single overhead camshaft, 1216 cc, bore, 76.2 mm, stroke 66.6 mm, maximum power 105 (DIN) at 7000 rpm, two Weber 40DCOE carburettors, water-cooled, cast-iron wet cylinder liners
Body/chassis:	Fibreglass monocoque 2-seat coupé with local steel reinforcement of chassis/body unit
Transmission:	ZF 4 synchromesh and reverse, dry single plate clutch, rear drive

Brakes:	Girling discs on all four wheels, inboard mounted at the rear
Steering gear:	Rack and pinion
Wheels:	15 x 4″ Dunlop centre-lock wire type
Suspension:	All-independent by coil springs and tubular shock absorbers, front double wishbones and anti-roll bar, rear Chapman Strut with triangulated radius arm and fixed length drive shafts
Maximum Speed:	130 mph (209 km/h)
Production Years:	1958–63 (all versions)
Number manufactured:	approximately 1000 (all versions)

Alfa Romeo Giulietta SZ [SZT]

Dimensions:	Wheelbase 88.6″, (2250 mm), front track 50.9″ (1292 mm), rear track 50.0″ (1270 mm); length 152″ (3920 mm) [158in (4070 mm)]
Dry Weight:	1687 lbs (765 kg) [1731 lbs (785 kg)]
Engine:	Alfa Romeo Tipo 120 Veloce, 4 cylinders in line, cast aluminium block and head, twin overhead camshafts, 1290 cc, bore 74 mm, stroke 75 mm, maximum power 100 (DIN) at 6500 rpm*, two Weber 40DCOE carburettors, water cooled, cast iron wet cylinder liners. * Standard Factory Tune.
Body/chassis:	Zagato light alloy 2-seat coupé body with tubular supporting structure on Alfa Romeo steel platform
Transmission:	5 synchromesh and reverse, dry single plate clutch, rear drive
Brakes:	Girling outboard mounted drums on all four wheels [Girling front discs on last 25 cars]
Steering gear:	ZF worm and roller
Wheels:	15 x 4¹/₂″ light alloy rim, steel centre
Suspension:	Independent front double wishbones with coil springs and anti-roll bar; rear live axle located by lower longitudinal trailing arms and upper A-bracket, coil springs, tubular shock absorbers front and rear.
Maximum Speed:	125 mph (200 km/h)
Production Years:	1960–62
Number manufactured:	213

Abarth-Simca 1300 GT

Dimensions:	Wheelbase 82.2″, (2088 mm), track front and rear 49.6″ (1260 mm), length 139.6″ (3546 mm)
Dry Weight:	1390 lbs (631 kg)
Engine:	Abarth, rear-mounted, 4 cylinders in line, cast iron block, aluminium head, twin overhead camshafts, 1288 cc, bore 76 mm, stroke 71 mm, maximum power 125 (DIN) at 7200 rpm, two Weber 45DCOE carburettors, water cooled

Body/chassis:	Abarth light alloy 2-seat coupé body on Simca steel platform
Transmission:	4 synchromesh and reverse, dry single plate clutch, rear drive
Brakes:	Discs on all four wheels, outboard mounted
Steering gear:	Worm and sector
Wheels:	13 x 4½″ cast light alloy
Suspension:	All independent, front wishbones and transverse leaf spring, rear semi-trailing arms and coil springs, anti-roll bars front and rear
Maximum Speed:	143 mph (230 km/h)
Production Years:	1962–63
Number manufactured:	approximately 100

Appendix Six

The Bristol
Contract and Specification

We were lucky that Ron Hickman had not only been intimately concerned with the development of the Elite into production but had also trained as a lawyer. When the time came to agree terms with the Bristol Aircraft Company for the Series Two Elite manufacturing contract in September 1959, Ron was therefore charged with drafting the contract for signature by Fred Bushell. He was also responsible for finalisation of the specification for the car and indeed (assisted by Albert Adams) the manufacture of an "absolutely standard" Elite chassis body unit to serve as an acceptance standard for the manufacturer.

A copy of the draft exists and is reproduced here in full. The original agreed price was £200 per complete chassis/body unit and at a total of 1000 units represented a value to Bristol of £200,000. When later, Bristol asked for a price increase to £250 per unit, thus increasing the value of the contract to £250,000, they claimed that the cost of production of their (one-off) masters and jigs had exceeded budget by £25,000 or £25 per car. The remaining £25 per car represented by their claim resulted from increased material costs, they stated.

Responding to the challenge, Chapman asked them if they were interested to build 1500 cars to which their reply was an eager affirmative. Colin then pointed out that the additional £50 per car claimed by Bristol for the 1000 unit contract if applied to 1500 cars would unfairly over-recover.

I was not around to see how the Bristol contract eventually ran out but I suspect that round one of the contest was fairly won by Chapman. When he had to go back to Bristol cap in hand at the time of the early production difficulties of the Elan in order to secure further supplies of the Elite CBU I can imagine that Bristol took a modest revenge . . .

Bristol Aircraft Ltd
Filton House
BRISTOL

18 September 1959

Contract for the manufacture of 1000 Lotus Elite Chassis/Body Units in accordance with our standard Conditions and as augmented or modified by the special terms and conditions set out below.

Price per assembled Chassis/Body Unit (Two Hundred Pounds) £200.

SPECIAL TERMS AND CONDITIONS

1 – GENERAL This order covers the manufacture and supply by you of Chassis/Body Units for Lotus Elite Cars in Resin Bonded Glass Fibre to the specification attached. Master patterns supplied and generally in accordance with the specimen Chassis/Body Unit inspected by you (replica of which to be left at your works during the period of the Order). Chassis/Body Unit to be supplied painted, trimmed and with all components, including free issue items, assembled as called for in the specification.

2 – MANUFACTURING STANDARD AND FINISH Laminates will be made of Glass Fibre of the weight specified in the specification. All details parts shall be fitted and located in accordance with the general arrangements shown therein. In order to control the shape and surface contours of the laminates and panels we will supply free of charge a set of master casts from which you will manufacture Epoxy Resin Moulds to a standard approved by our Representative.

3 – MATERIALS Laminates are to be made from 'E' Glass Fibre Chopped Strand Mat, and resin to be supplied by Mitchell & Smith or other supplier approved by us. No filler is to be used in the manufacture of laminates.

Apart from the Free Issue Items listed all other materials to be supplied in accordance with our specification and summarised in our Schedules 1, 2 and 3.

4 – MOULDS Sufficient Epoxy Resin Moulds will be supplied by you and maintained in good order as may be required to produce 15 Units per week.

5 – DESIGN STANDARD AND FINISH This to be based on the design standard and exterior finish of the units seen and inspected by your representatives and a replica of which is to be supplied by us.

Modifications to and variations and/or alteration in this standard or in the moulding specification will be the subject of a price adjustment to be negotiated in accordance with the increase/decrease in the work or materials resulting from these modifications etc. In the event of such modifications etc. resulting in the scrapping of existing moulds, then the appropriate price revision will be deemed to include the cost of the premature withdrawal of the scrapped mould from service; Should minor modifications to moulds be called for by us these to be carried out at our expense and in such a way not to interfere with your delivery programme.

6 – DELIVERY PROGRAMME This order is based on a delivery programme building up rapidly to fifteen units per week in accordance with the attached schedule.

Delivery of satisfactory Chassis/Body Units in accordance with the programme agreed is the essence of the contract.

7 – DELIVERY The Chassis/Body Units to be delivered by your own transport and at own risk to our factory at Cheshunt.

8 – REPAIR WORK Provision to be made to set aside productive capacity to undertake repair work and replacement of damaged Lotus Elite Chassis/Body Units or loose or sectional panels in addition to maintaining the Delivery Programme of new units. Such repair work to be undertaken or replacement panels to be supplied at an agreed schedule of rates to be negotiated but to be generally on a price basis commensurate with the main order.

9 – INSPECTION In addition to such Inspection as will be carried out by yourselves reasonable facilities are to be given for Lotus Inspectors to visit your works to observe the standard of workmanship during manufacture with particular regard to the quality of bonding.

10 – MASTER PATTERNS These to remain our property and will be insured by us while in your keeping but they are to be returned to us in original condition as supplied.

11 – GUARANTEES These to be as stated in the attached specification on sheets 3, 4 and 5.

12 – TECHNICAL ASSISTANCE We will render such reasonable technical assistance during the pre-production and initial manufacturing periods as may be mutually deemed desirable without charge.

13 – TERMS Nett cash payable 31st of month following date of delivery.

14 – FURTHER ORDERS Subject to your having fulfilled this order as regards quantity, quality, delivery schedule and prices we confirm our willingness to continue to take further supplies from you. In consideration of this you will undertake not to manufacture or supply to any other customer any monocoque car bodies or chassis/body units of a type substantially similar to or making use of the same principles and technique of construction as those called for in this order.

15 – PATENTS As the goods, the subject of Contract, are of our (i.e. Lotus) design we agree to indemnify you (i.e. Bristol) against all actions for actual or alleged infringements of UK or foreign Letters Patent by reason of the use of the articles hereby ordered.

p.p. LOTUS CARS LTD

Secretary (F.R. Bushell)

SPECIFICATION FOR PRODUCTION OF LOTUS ELITE CHASSIS BODY UNIT

The wording reproduced here is of the definitive (Issue 2) Specification dated 6th April 1960.

We require our Sub-Contractor to supply us with what we term a finished chassis body unit in accordance with the following specification.

ITEM 1 GLASS FIBRE CHASSIS BODY UNIT

Make and maintain sufficient epoxy and metal moulds from patterns supplied by Lotus Cars to produce exact replicas of the panels required, to the satisfaction of our Inspector and to the required tolerances; to produce adequate quantities as called for in our delivery schedule, and to provide complete or sectional panels for repair and replacement purposes when required. The said master patterns are to be returned in original condition. Epoxy, wood and/or metal applied pieces are to be made to patterns or drawings supplied by Lotus Cars.

Supply all glass, resin and hardener materials required for the production of the chassis body unit, and these materials to be of a type and quality approved by Lotus Cars.

The lay-up pattern to be determined by Lotus Cars basically as in the Schedule of Laminates, the complete unit to contain approximately 211 lbs. of polyester laminate, 20 lbs. of epoxy laminate, 17 lbs. of polyester and 11 lbs. of epoxy bonding material and 18 lbs. fillers, giving a final weight (excluding free issue items) of approximately 277 lbs., this to be held to plus or minus 5%. These weights to be subject to any changes or modifications to the lay-up patterns.

All laminates which are dry-bonded, and specifically excluding only the battery box which is to be pigmented black and parcel shelves, which are to be pigmented grey, are to be clear in order to enable inspection of bonding during assembly. No substantial quantities of filler are to be used.

During the laminating various free issue metal and wood components e.g. front suspension frame, gear box mounts, various bobbins and castings, as set out in Schedule 1, are to be bonded into the laminates in the manner prescribed by Lotus Cars.

Local metal Match-moulds are to be provided as specified in the Schedule of Laminates and to the specified dimensions to facilitate assembly and production.

The laminated panels are then to be trimmed to a high standard of finish, and also to close tolerances where necessary to ensure accurate fitting, notably of doors, windscreens etc. into apertures.

The relevant laminated panels are then to be locally roughed up (with a minimum of 90% roughing on all highly stressed flanges and 70% on the remainder) and thoroughly bonded together as specified in the Bonding Schedule with epoxy and polyester bonding material, the latter to be used only where the resultant distortion of body panels e.g. the undertray, is unimportant. In order to form a complete and sturdy structure bonding of all highly stressed flanges and at the periphery of bonded areas is to be at least 90% and generally at least 70%, and facilities are to be provided for the accurate control and regular inspection of bonding prior to painting and trimming.

The bonding of doors, boot and bonnet lids is to be effected in the manner prescribed in the Schedule of Laminates and in the Bonding Schedule so as to ensure accurate and consistent results and a distortion free surface.

Various free issue items as specified in Schedule 1 e.g. body jacking hoop, battery bolts, jack locating cone, and plenum chamber drain, are to be bonded in during the assembly process as specified in the Bonding Schedule.

Adequate jigging and clamping shall be provided to satisfactorily control and locate the panels and/or free issue items during laminating and assembly to ensure satisfactory and consistent results, although pop-rivets may be used as a temporary clamping means in certain specified areas provided that these are water-proofed as specified in the Water/dust proofing Schedule.

All mould flash lines and all open joints which will not be concealed by trim etc. and which will be normally visible, are to be faired in to a normal smooth surface.

Un-flanged or butt-joints between laminates e.g. inner mould to upper body through engine bay, and gaps under the wheel arches and between the nearside rear wheel arch and toolbox, are to be taped as specified in the Bonding Schedule, where necessary in accordance with the Water/dust-proofing Schedule.

The front sub-frame is to be thoroughly taped onto the inner mould, and the horizontal bar of the body jacking hoop is to be taped or laminated onto the lower edge of the instrument panel, as specified in the Bonding Schedule.

All joints between the engine compartment or transmission tunnel and the passenger compartment are to be sealed off so as to be gas-tight.

Approximately 40 shaped holes and 400 round holes of various sizes for access, attachment and drainage are to be cut and/or drilled as prescribed, in the holes list, drilling jigs being used where necessary to ensure accuracy e.g. door locks.

FREE ISSUE MATERIALS

These will be supplied f.o.c. by Lotus Cars, but steps must be taken to ensure that adequate stocks are on hand, and two weeks notice will be required on all requisitions.

Free issue materials as specified in the Schedule 2 Parts List are to be fitted to allow the doors, boot and bonnet lids to be hung, all door furniture, side windows, locks etc. to be fitted.

Certain loose panels, as per the Schedule of Laminates, are to be included and fitted, such as left and right hand parcel shelves (with heater flaps attached) spare wheel cover, conduit cover, door hinge covers and battery box.

All the above are to be prepared for painting and trimming, prior to which they are to be inspected and approved.

In order to ensure stability of finished paint surfaces after painting, all components of the chassis body unit should have been post-cured, at room temperatures for a minimum of two weeks after laminating, and at least one week after bonding, to allow laminates and bonds to cure to a reasonable degree.

GUARANTEE

Each one of these chassis body units must be guaranteed that the mouldings are completely air-free and of the highest quality; free of panel distortion or any other surface defects, and that all excess bonding material or droppings have been removed from critical areas or attachment points.

Individual pin-holes (i.e. of pin prick size) may be permitted, but clusters should be avoided.

All doors, window frames, lids and other loose components are to be correctly and accurately fitted and adjusted.

Each chassis body unit is to be guaranteed for faulty workmanship either of laminating, bonding or of any other kind, for a period of twelve months. Providing the vehicle is being used for the purposes intended.

ITEM 2 PAINTING

All wax and parting agents to be removed, and surface to be cleaned with a fine abrasive prior to commencement of painting.

The Chassis Body Unit is to be completely painted on upper body, underside, in the wheel arches, inside the doors, boot and bonnet lids, on the instrument panel, in the engine bay, front air intake and in untrimmed parts of the boot with 1 coat of self-etching primer ('Aristocrat', or I.C.I. approved type).

Three coats of I.C.I. Primer surfacer or other approved filler are then to be applied to the whole of the outside body surface (including doors and lids etc.) and one coat of same to the inside of boot and bonnet lids and the instrument panel.

The whole is then to be rubbed down, and sprayed with one coat of I.C.I. sealer.

Two coats of body colour as specified in the Annexure hereto are then to be applied to the underside, in the wheel arches, untrimmed parts of the boot locker, insides of the boot and bonnet lids and doors, on the door hinge covers and on the whole of the outside body surface normally visible. The latter is then to be rubbed down, and is to receive two further finishing coats of body colour, and is finally to be polished with a suitable compound and polish.

The instrument panel is to be sprayed with two coats of I.C.I. or other approved matt-black cellulose.

The engine compartment and frontal intake are to be sprayed with two coats of I.C.I. or other approved oil and petrol resistant paint.

The headliner area and rear suspension strut housings are to be flock-sprayed with 'Spraytex' flock in either of the two standard colours specified by Lotus Cars.

SUMMARY OF COLOURS

Body colours in any of the following colours, as determined by Lotus Cars.

Signal Red	I.C.I. type P030–437
Moonstone	I.C.I. type P030–3197
Light Blue	I.C.I. type P030–TW–14266

GUARANTEE

All upper body surfaces to be free of pin holes, blisters, paint runs, orange-peel and other blemishes. This finish to be continued out of line of normal vision onto the body underside and wheel arch flanges.

The paint on the instrument panel is to be of sufficient density to withstand penetration of a flash-light beam.

The headliner flock spray is to be neat and clean and of sufficient density.

Each unit is to be inspected as detailed in Stage II of the Inspection Schedule and the finish to be guaranteed against faulty workmanship for a period of six months.

ITEM 3 TRIMMING

To trim the body chassis unit generally, and the interiors of the passenger compartment and boot locker to the specification of Lotus Cars, with the following free issue materials as per Schedule 2 and 3, parts lists.

Fit bumpers (with PVC beading), radiator grille, door kick plates, side-window drip rails (as per Water/dust-proofing Schedule), interior light, and courtesy light switches, interior mirror, exterior badge and heater inlet mesh (with PVC beading) in the manner prescribed by Lotus Cars.

Fit front and rear windscreens in accordance with the Water/dust-proofing Schedule.

Fit under-felting and sound-proofing in passenger compartment, doors and boot locker, using materials and own adhesives, as specified in the Adhesives Schedules.

Fit carpet and trim to floor and interior up to waist height, trim excess as necessary, fit with press-studs, screws and own adhesives as specified in the Adhesives Schedules.

Fit gear-lever gaiter, trim and fit door trim-panels, trim and fit front and rear parcel shelves, trim top flanges of doors with leather-cloth.

Fit push on draught excluder around door aperture, and rubber water seals to doors, boot and bonnet lids (or apertures) and door hinge covers as specified in the Water/dust-proofing Schedule, and Adhesives Schedule.

Fit Armacord carpet in boot, trim wheel arches, tool-box, side-walls as specified in the Adhesives Schedules.

GUARANTEE

The fitting of the above free issue parts is to be of the highest standards, as specified by Lotus Cars, and is to be firmly adhered, clean and free of surplus adhesive etc.

ITEM 4 DELIVERY

Delivery to Lotus Cars, Cheshunt by Sub-Contractors' own transport and at own risk, and in sufficient quantities as detailed on the agreed Delivery Schedule.

BONDING SCHEDULE

1 – In order to ensure the strength of the following highly-stressed bonds, the surfaces to be bonded must be at least 90% roughed up using a sander or other suitable abrader:

a   –   Front bulk-head to upper body.
b   –   Front bulk-head to inner mould (all joints).
c   –   Rear bulk-head to upper body.
d   –   Front windscreen aperture flanges.
e   –   Rear windscreen aperture flanges.
f   –   Both door aperture flanges.
g   –   Headlamp aperture flanges.
h   –   Rear of boot aperture flanges.
i   –   Upper to lower body joint all round.
j   –   Where inner mould is taped to upper body in engine bay.
k   –   Top of Diff. box mating surfaces.
l   –   Perimeter flanges of boot lid.
m   –   Perimeter flanges of bonnet lid.
n   –   Bootliner flange joint onto spare wheel recess.
o   –   Bootliner flange joint onto disc brake housings.
p   –   Headliner to inner mould joint at rear.
q   –   Inner to undertray near rear suspension top-struts.
r   –   Inner to undertray near rear suspension front pick-ups.
s   –   Undertray, where body jacking hoop passes through.

2 – The remainder of the bonded surfaces, as listed below, are to be at least 70% roughed up using a sander or other suitable abrader.

a   –   Upper body to undertray at front fenders.
b   –   Inner mould to undertray at front fenders.
c   –   Upper body to undertray at rear fenders.
d   –   Inner mould to undertray at rear tenders.
e   –   Upper body to headliner (central area).
f   –   Upper body to bootliner.
g   –   Undertray to bootliner (also disc brake housings).
h   –   Upper body and inner mould around body jacking hoop.
i   –   Inner mould to undertray – seat floors and tunnel area.
j   –   Inner mould to undertray – engine bay and front air intake.
k   –   Inner mould to undertray – front of diff. box.
l   –   Demisters to headliner/instrument panel.

3 – All highly-stressed bonds as listed in Paragraph 1 above as well as the perimeter areas of bonds listed in Paragraph 2 above are to be at least 90% firmly bonded, with the remainder at least 70%.

4 – Care to be taken in the handling of abraded laminates to avoid the deposition of grease and dirt. All dust deposited during the abrading process to be removed by dusting off or solvent washing. The laminates are then to be bonded together in the following order, being jigged as necessary for location and control. Approximate quantities of bonding material necessary for adequate bonding are shown in brackets.

a – Inner mould to undertray		14 lbs Polyester
		14 lbs Slate
b – Bootliner to undertray		3 lbs Polyester
		2 lbs Slate
c – Bulkhead to inner		2 lbs Polyester
		1 ½ lbs Slate
d – Plenum chamber to bulkhead	}	
e – Radiator cowl to inner		1 lb Polyester
f – Headliner to upper body excluding body jacking hoop		2 lbs Epoxy
		2 lbs Versimid

Appendix Seven

"Thoughts on the Elite's successor" – Ron Hickman

Ron Hickman and I were among the earliest Lotus personnel to extensively use the written word to communicate with colleagues. In late 1959 Ron produced the following paper in which he assessed experience with the Elite and examined the alternative structural methods available for the S2/M2/Elan project. Being Ron, he took the opportunity to put over his propaganda for plastic and foam bumpers of the type which eventually appeared on the Elan. Chapman would probably have read the paper but it would then be necessary to argue with him over a period of time to gain acceptance of any proposals made. The Chapman method was to produce small clear sketches to illustrate conversation and the carefully considered Hickman alternative may have been somewhat premature in the Lotus environment of the day.

Ron had been very much involved in developing repair techniques for the Elite and the heavy emphasis in this paper on the need to design future cars to allow efficient repair results from this activity.

The 'Elite' form of construction brings unique problems in the matter of repairs, and by the time its successor is due more reaction will have been felt regarding repair costs and insurance premia, which will very likely show urgent need for more careful consideration of this problem in future models. To date all repairs have been effected by the manufacturers, who naturally have not only the moulds, but also very specialised knowledge concerning the construction and assembly of the bodies.

Damage to Elite bodies can probably be categorised as follows:-

Minor Damage:
a – Front upper body/headlamp/fender. Non-structural, hence easily repaired, but for tricky areas around headlamps particularly advantageous to have local lay-up to graft on.

b – Front lower body/flasher/intake. Becomes complicated when (as is very usual) both this *and* upper body are damaged, as extra attention is required around the joggle joint which is very vulnerable and apt to split from end to end.

c – Complete length of body side or part thereof. With the side body joint tucked well under, damage is likely to be confined to upper body and door only. It is difficult to graft new sections on the front fender, other than above the wheel arch, owing to the inaccessibility of the inside. Laminating of the grafted section could of course be done through a hole cut in the wheel arch bulkhead and later

refilled. Door repair should be a fairly clear-cut case of patching or replacement (manufacturing price of a new one – excluding frame etc. approx £9), although agents likely to undertake repair should be instructed to use epoxide resin only.
d – Rear door pillar and fender. All accessible from behind, but difficult to ensure correct location of rear quarter to line up with boot-lid. Underside not very vulnerable, and fairly easy to repair. Owing to lack of other protection, boot lid is usually damaged.

Major Damage:
a – Large frontal area on both upper and lower panels, inner mould, bonnet lid and *front suspension frame*. Extremely difficult to locate accurately new frame or straighten distorted one *in situ;* also very difficult to line new upper body correctly to ensure good fit of replacement bonnet lid. Considerable instruction should be given regarding overlapping of joints between the three main mouldings. Difficult to ensure good fit and bond of joggle across front of car; also fitting replacement bumpers.
b – Body side and door. If sill of door and lower box section are badly damaged, reinforcement from behind is difficult owing to inaccessibility. Up to front of door accessible through hole cut in wheel arch bulk-head, otherwise probably advisable to remove complete outer panel from lower joggle joint to flange around door opening.
c – Rear end and undertray, where suspension or diff. pick-up points are damaged. This area comprises largely flat surfaces, so that repair of actual laminates is simplified. Main difficulty is ensuring satisfactory repair standards and accurate location.
d – Body jacking hoop. This may be damaged at the lower end by curb-fouling at speed, by impact on the door hinge brackets, or at the windscreen pillars by under-riding a truck or roll over. Some practical method should be found to prevent such localised damage from amounting to a total write-off.

A useful comparison can be made with conventional bodies and their methods of repair and replacement.
1 – Monocoque metal bodies: Although extensive damage may necessitate replacement of large pressings, or sometimes even the complete body shell apart from usable doors etc., skill and experience in welding is widely available. Replacement panels are generally available from overseas spares depots. An inherent disadvantage of these bodies is the wide spread of impact damage and the accurate detection and rectification of distortion in surrounding panels.
2 – Classic type: If the chassis and suspension is intact, repair and replacement of panels is quite easy, although accurate rectification of distortion in large panels can be very difficult. Evidence of this can be seen in a very high proportion of repaired bodies.
3 – Chassis or space-frame construction with fibreglass bodies: If the chassis is basically sound, body repair is probably not very critical, being non-structural in most instances. Damage will probably be confined to the impact area, although distortion may be spread by the metal frame. Generally speaking access to the panels will be easy in the absence of integral bulkheads, undertray etc. The repair of the chassis or frame to any accurate standard is probably rare.
4 – Aluminium or alloy bodies: Same as applies to items 1 and 2, except that they are probably not quite as readily reparable.

In order to compete favourably with other types of construction on a time and cost basis, the following suggestions are made regarding future sales and service

policies.

a – Agents should be capable of effecting even major repairs, and this requires that they should be trained in the use of fibreglass and moulding techniques. In most cases involving moderate damage best results will probably be obtained by grafting in new sections, so that finishing of the final surface will be confined to the fairing in of joint lines rather than attempting to model large areas and then have the almost impossible task of achieving the original lines, sufficient structural strength, or good surface finish. To do this, agents will either have a full set of actual *moulds* in which they can do local lay-ups as required, or be able to order up sections from a central depot. In order to facilitate this and avoid the requisitioning of vastly extravagant areas, a chart or source of reference should be devised. With one or two exceptions it will probably not be worth the agents' while to stock replacement sections, as there are no distinctive panels, and those in stock will be either too large or too small for the job in hand.

b – Agents will have to have access to locating jigs for accurately positioning the new mouldings. Although perhaps *structurally* accurate location is only essential when suspension or other mechanical pick-up points are involved, it is equally essential to ensure good fitting of such standard replacement items as doors, boot and bonnet lids, bumpers, windows, lights etc.

c – These jigs would probably take the form of sectional female moulds, suitably reinforced, and flanged all around for attachment to each other. A standard size e.g. 20″ square, split accurately on 'ten' lines, would enable accurate ordering from the 'depot' on a simple chart. These mould forms could pick up onto existing bobbins, or by clamping onto prominent local points, and a permutation of such moulds should provide accurate location *of* any body section *on* any other, to cater for any possible damage. In some instances, it might be wise to provide metal jigs for the checking or spacing of suspension pickup points etc. In some instances it may also be simpler to use the mould form for doing a lay-up *in situ,* and in any event it may be as well to charge a hire fee on these moulds to encourage their careful usage and speedy return to the depot. For both production and repair work it may be advisable to have a flat bottom on the car and on the major areas of wheel arches and inner moulding, and to have them scribed (on the mould) lightly with 'ten' lines for easy reference and checking.

d – Although many panels can be replaced by bonding in from the outside, i.e. by first bordering the perimeter of the hole with strips of laminate to prevent the grafted section from falling inside and then securing it in place with epoxy slate-mix, it will probably be advisable wherever possible to avoid double-skinning and large 'boxed-in' areas which are inaccessible from behind.

e – Bonding in of large metal components should be avoided, owing to the impossibility of repairing, welding or straightening them in close proximity to the fibreglass.

f – Body joint lines at front, side and rear should be so placed as to confine damage in average impacts to a minimum number of panels, and should be designed for maximum shear strength so as to avoid splitting on impact. From the assembly and finishing viewpoint, the visible joggle as used at front and rear of the Elite or on the Stirling and Frisky requires less attention than the flush lap joint, which invites laborious fairing-in when slightly mis-aligned. Both types are inferior to the open flange joint when it comes to jigging or clamping for assembly, and provided the latter type can satisfactorily be hidden, they are more desirable. The most common method of disguising similar conditions in metal bodies is to conceal them with bumpers, chrome strips etc., but in the light of the aforegoing suggestions concerning body repairs, there seems to be much to recommend the use of *fibreglass bumper panels* at both front and rear.

Both the potency of the vehicle and the absence of head-lamp peaks or tail-fins to indicate the extremities make minor damage in traffic or parking very easy. It would be impossible to fit heavy chrome bumpers at front or rear which would cope adequately with any American car bumper, and still maintain proportionate good looks. There is also the ever present problem of manufacture and tooling costs, and the use of standard chrome or stainless steel bumpers will undoubtedly considerably limit the styling.

A Brief Analysis of Bumpers

Function:
1 – Protection of body panels from minor impacts, usually against other bumpers, lamp-posts etc.
2 – Absorption of moderate impact pressure, then spreading it gradually to the main body shell.
3 – Towing: particularly where no starting handle is provided.
4 – Lifting (with jacks). Slinging usually done by wheels.
5 – Concealment of body joints, and brightening effect.

Drawbacks of Existing Type:
1 – Being only 2″ – 3″ deep they seldom meet others, owing to lack of standard design height, effects of loading, braking etc. Hence, over-riders.
2 – They show damage easily, and kinks are extremely difficult to repair.
3 – Tooling for limited quantities is expensive, and average cost is therefore fairly high.
4 – Quality of chrome usually poor.
5 – With sports cars, difficult to use standard sections which are generally heavier in proportion. Tubular over-riding bars are often used to supplement the bumper bar.
6 – With Elite-type construction, satisfactory attachment could become a real problem, as the traditional type of stays would have to be removable for replacement, and in any event would probably transmit shock to the immediate vicinity of the front assembly.

An Ideal Type Should:
1 – Be resilient enough not to distort widely with slight impact.
2* – Actually *absorb* minor shocks, so that up to 2″ movement or several hundred pounds of pressure would affect neither the attachment points nor the main body panels.
3* – Give the deepest possible protection, preferably 12″+.
4* – With unitary construction, abide by the principle and spread the load (or shock) to the body as widely as possible.
5* – Be reasonably cheap and easy to remove, repair or replace.

Materials suggested are rubber, plastic, or fibreglass, and a variety of approaches to the problem can be found by studying the Bristol 403 (rubber and metal strips); Peerless (fibreglass replicas of metal bumpers – very cheap in appearance); the rubber 'pods' on Cadillacs, Simca Vedette etc.; the body panel bumpers and outsize over-riders of the Triumph Herald; and numerous attempts by Italian coachbuilders to design suitable bumpers for sports cars e.g. Ferrari Spyder, Fiat 1100 TV Sport, which have rubber 'over-riders' only.

Using a plastic foam and fibreglass sandwich construction a satisfactory solution to all the above requirements may be found. Here are some of the more apparent advantages and disadvantages:-

Advantages
1 – This is an ideal and practical application for foam, using even present day types. A section 3″ deep would give considerable shock-absorption, and

combined with a heavy fibreglass lay-up would have good resilience.

2 – Having the body of foam throughout, local gashes could easily be rebuilt and faired-in. Characteristically, damage in minor impacts would be localised and distortion of the panel as a whole would be nil.

3 – Suitable sculptured recesses could be provided for the air intake, and to fully protect lamps, number plate etc.

4 – Actual damage in moderate front or rear impacts would be mainly confined to *one removable panel;* a great boon to repair work.

5 – By mounting the bumper panel on sponge rubber strips or strong springs over the whole frontal area, requirements (2) to (5) marked * could all be met.

Disadvantages

1 – It would be difficult to use self-coloured panels, which would have the best scratch-resistance, and unless the actual leading edge was protected by a rubber or metal rubbing strip the owner would have to retouch scratches from time to time.

2 – The car could not be lifted by the bumpers, but in any event if they are styled as part of the body form no one would instinctively use them for this purpose. (Where are the jacking points anyway?)

3 – Some other arrangement e.g. an A–bracket from the front suspension pickups would have to be provided if towing was to be catered for.

4 – Customer acceptance of an unconventional idea.

With regard to the latter, I feel that this could in fact be played up on its merits as a very good sales feature. It would have the advantage over any other sports car, and over most production saloons, by having deeper protection; and could certainly have the advantage over Italian and other metal-bodied sports cars from the styling view-point. At the expense of a $1/8''$ joint-line styled in across the front and rear of the body, this car could have the nose of a Vanwall or a Ferrari (or even a Lotus), without any excrescences. Eye-catching brightwork to replace bumpers could be extremely tasteful and delicate, and if necessary could be placed well back from the leading edge e.g. chrome air-intake, head-lamp surrounds etc.

I would like to suggest that some serious styling exercises should be done to investigate the possibilities of the bumper panel, and that one of the Development Elites (1003?) should be converted for experimental work. I would also like to suggest that from the earliest design stages full consideration should be given to the matter of repair moulds, jigs and procedure.

Appendix Eight
Elite: Technical Problems

Elite owners and all of us associated with the car can at the drop of a hat (bonnet or boot lid – if the wind is blowing) recall a string of problems ranging from simple irritations to serious potential disasters. Following a session when Ron Hickman and I were remembering the time when the Elite was a daily affliction, Ron listed as many problems as he could recall from intimate association with the car. He managed a grand total of 26 at the first pass:

1.   Perpetual paint blisters and bubbles.
2.   Distortion of external body panels at the point where inner box sections, bulkheads etc., meet.
3.   Bad fits of individual panels caused by the original dry bond technique (but subsequently cured by wet bonding).
4.   The notorious paint discoloration problem – particularly serious in California.
5.   Body noises caused by flexing, dried bonding resin, etc.
6.   Prodigious oil consumption by the FWE Climax engine. We took up with "Wally" Hassan of Coventry Climax, joint designer of the FW series of engines, the question of excessive oil consumption. He attributed this to failure by the average owner to observe the need to very carefully "run in" the Climax engine. Eventually Hassan stipulated that for up to 500 miles the car must be alternately accelerated and allowed to slow even when driving on the motorway when one would normally cruise at a constant speed (there was no overall speed limit in Britain at the time). We therefore religiously instructed new owners to observe this policy which was handed to them initially in note form. They may well have followed the Hassan recommendations but in fact it seemed to make no difference to the oil drinking habits of the FWE.
7.   The detachable diff. box problem (temporary but overwhelmingly serious at the time).
8.   Excessive engine noise. An aluminium engine, particularly if designed to power a fire pump – tends to be far noisier than one with iron block. The Elite engine was particularly noisy and also had a tendency to excessive vibration. The very direct mounting of the engine in the Elite conducted noise and vibration into the resonant structure of the car where it was in effect magnified.

9.   "Grumbling" differentials. This problem was exacerbated by the tendency of

the oil seals in the Lotus-designed final drive unit to leak. The Elite arrangement was adapted from that of the Eleven where racing practice dictated regular changing of these vital components. Oil would trickle steadily from the diff. and the alert owner could spot telltale traces on the under surface of the bodywork. Failure to do this caused a rapidly rising growling crescendo from the differential unit accompanied by hot smells and eventual disaster.

10. Exceptionally noisy gearboxes – particularly the MG variety of the earlier cars was another perennial problem. Even the ZF was noisy and suffered from the additional irritation of a buzzing lever.

11. Rear wheel bearings. The rear hubs in the Chapman Strut were mounted in a pair of RIV taper rolling bearings requiring regular lubrication. Any deficiency in the fits of the bearings or excessive cornering loads could in a relatively short period of time loosen the outer race of the bearings in the Strut casting resulting in rumbling, and ultimately, premature bearing failure.

12. Rear radius arm cup wear. This was particularly bad on Series One cars in which the radius arm cups were more heavily loaded than the later Series Two version. However both types used radius arm cups derived from the pre-war Ford 8 hp family car in which the hard rubber bearing material would quickly be pulped and allow the spherical end of the radius arm to rattle infuriatingly within the unprotected metal cups.

13. The Chapman dogma that wherever possible, no opportunity should be given to the owner to adjust his car was very effectively applied to the rear suspension of the Elite. If the factory made a mess of setting wheel alignment or if any of the usual problems (11 and 12 above) developed, the handling of the car was immediately affected.

14. It was a fact that the headlamp height of the car was illegal and this created problems in the United States market where it became necessary to shim the suspension on cars submitted for approval by Highway Authorities.

15. Left-hand drive Elites listed seriously as a result of re-distribution of loads about the centre line of the car. It was necessary to pack the suspension to maintain an even keel.

16. Untrimming. Even the later Royalite trimmed cars were not immune from the tendency to shed trim from all points as inadequate gluing came to light.

17. Warping and buckling of the so called "bumpers". These although beautifully made by Miles Aircraft, were little more than flimsy trims and customers would frequently object to the clearly visible weld marks and distortions resulting from the hand-made process of manufacture.

18. Roof interior finish. Because the complex internal shape of the roof area made it impossible to apply a head lining, this section of the car was finished with paint "spattered" in dark tones over a light grey base. This was splendid as long as it lasted but it was physically impossible to successfully touch up after damage or soiling.

19. Generally unreliable electrics.

20. Door fits. The doors frequently sagged and were excruciatingly difficult to set up initially or to subsequently adjust.

21. Shrinkage and leaking of the Claylastic windscreen filler strips. The Claylastic strip was chromium plated and originally developed for the Mini (launched in 1959). Leakage resulted from capillary action caused by shrinkage and a further major problem was the unacceptable discoloration that quickly set in.

22. The difficulty of making satisfactory arrangements for body repairs. Initially all Elites were repaired by Maximar at Pulborough and then partially at Cheshunt. It was impossible of course to continue for ever on this basis and when the time came to pass on information about repair of the highly unusual Elite structure many difficulties resulted. One benefit of the situation was the need to

produce a particularly comprehensive workshop manual in order to convey as much information as possible about the problem.

23. Windscreen fits. The double skinned technique and the presence in the pillars of the Elite of the steel body jacking hoop frequently caused distortion of the structure making it difficult to achieve an acceptable fit for the windscreen. Apart from grinding away the fibreglass windscreen surround there was no easy solution to this problem.

24. General water leaks. Most of these were solved during the production life of the car.

25. Pedal mounting problems. The brake and clutch pedals were mounted on an aluminium casting fitted directly to the fibreglass structure of the car. This arrangement was somewhat lacking in rigidity and frequently required repair.

26. Valve burning. This problem could be aggravated by inaccurate valve clearances preventing the valve from seating correctly, general abuse by the driver or inferior petrol. It must not be forgotten that the FWE was never properly developed by Coventry Climax as a road car engine and many of its characteristics – unacceptable in a touring car – were perfectly understood and accepted by the racing fraternity (and fire pump operators).

Many of the above points were not apparent to a potential customer showing interest in the Elite. From the point of view of those of us engaged in the sale of the car the main problem that we faced was the generally high "NVH" factor of the Elite. We didn't use such a buzz (pun unintentional) phrase at the time but Noise, Vibration and Harshness were frequently the main problems intruding at demonstration time. Elite NVH levels were unacceptable when compared with the Porsche 356 and Alfa Romeo Giulietta. We could overcome the problem to some extent by making the demonstration so "busy" that the potential customer was overwhelmed by the road holding, handling and general agility of the car and not able to appraise it at the relatively constant speed levels of high speed touring when NVH really intruded.

A combination of rapid demonstration and incessant conversation could usually mask this serious problem. We very carefully checked the demonstrators on a daily basis and took every precaution to ensure that the doors closed properly (or at least just closed) and that everything that could add to the general hurly-burly such as worn radius arm cups, hub bearings etc., was maintained correctly.

Appendix Nine
Body assembly methods for the Elite and Elan

While Ron Hickman and John Frayling were buried in the heart of rural Sussex at Maximar Mouldings developing the Elite to production form, they considered and rejected several alternative basic methods of assembly. There were very few precedents for the tasks before them and therefore with considerable lack of inhibition they toyed with the following sequence of alternative means of joining the many separate panels that together form the complete Elite car.

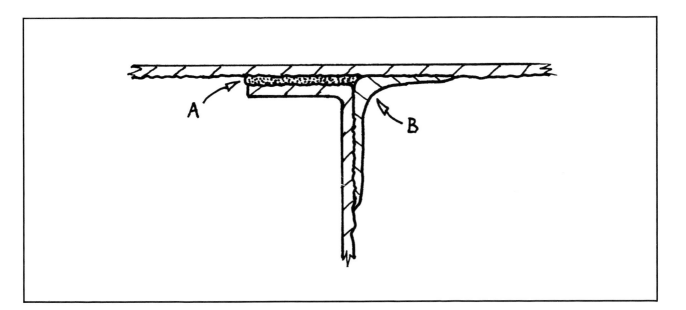

Method No. 1

This system was considered for the joining of panels meeting at right angles. Separate panels were joined with Bondix glue (A) and where necessary reinforced with an additional lay-up of laminate (B).

At this very early stage of creative thought the use of honeycomb materials and foam injected sections was also considered as a means of reinforcement of the structure before the final choice of local reinforcement by steel fabrications alone. The foam injection method reached prototype form but it was discovered that the chemical reaction of the foam was so unbridled as to cause distortion and sometimes even bursting of hollow sections into which it was injected. Although modern technology would probably have gone along that particular route, in 1958 the idea had to be abandoned.

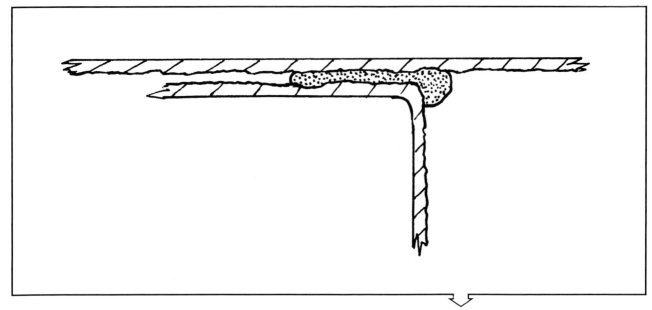

Method No. 2

The ideal for production had it ever been possible to achieve the necessary degree of quality control, would have involved the application of adhesive between fully cured laminate panels separated by a theoretically even gap. In practice it was never possible to achieve consistent thickness of mouldings because of the inevitable "handmade" nature of fibreglass technology of that era. This meant that it was never possible to accurately control the depth to which adhesive penetrated between panels with consequent wide variation in bond strength. This sketch reveals the actual discrepancy in laminate thickness not visible from study of the exterior of the double skinned structure.

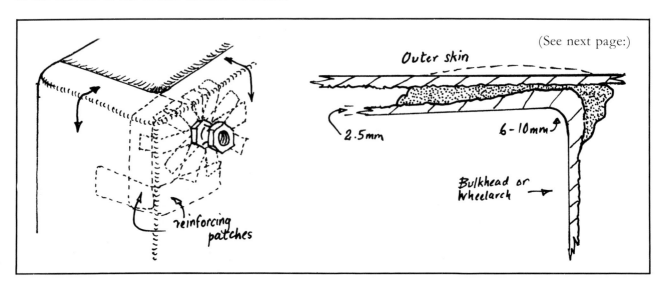

(See next page:)

The Horrible Truth

In practice, massive compromise was necessary at all times. This sketch illustrates the laminating arrangements at a junction, particularly if complicated by the installation at that point of a bobbin. In this extreme case it will be seen that up to six layers of laminate could occur at one point with consequent wide variation in panel thickness.

Where sections turned at right angles local reinforcement could get completely out of hand so that a panel in its horizontal section could be as little as 2.5 mm thick but reach anything up to four times that thickness as a laminate "turned the bend". The effect on the surface as adhesive cured would be to cause considerable distortion (easily visible to the eye) while the wide variation in inter-skin volume from car to car in a given location could leave excrescent glue to add to the complication of production.

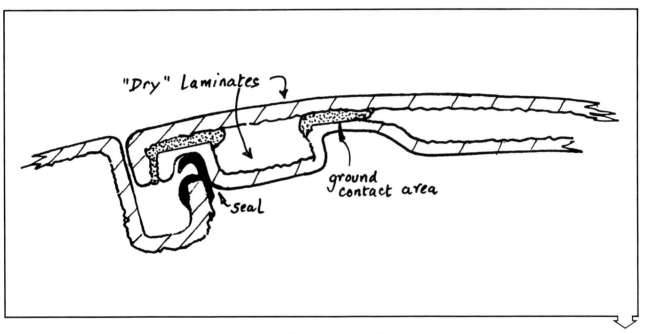

Dry Assembly Method

The original method chosen for the assembly of delicate double skinned components such as the boot and bonnet lid was as shown here. Completely cured "dry" laminates were bonded subject to haphazard variation in the gap between panels despite grinding to ensure the best possible contact.

Small, neat seals were used but the precision of these meant that there was very little tolerance for error and distortion in the mating components.

"Wet" Assembly Method (over page)

After considerable frustration caused by the distortions of the dry assembly method, experiments were carried out which led to the method ultimately adopted for "sensitive" elements of the structure such as the boot and bonnet lids which were to be assembled by the so called "wet" method. Here the surfaces of the laminate which would mate in the final component were laid up last and with slower "mixes". They were then pressed together and clamped in this position

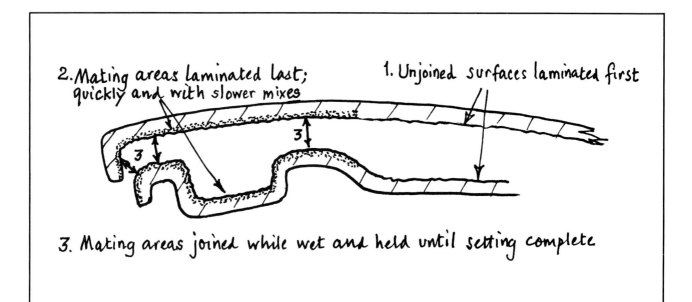

while still wet to ensure that the joining surfaces were perfectly matched. It would then theoretically be possible to apply adhesive to the subsequently cured panels knowing that the adhesive was spreading evenly at all points.

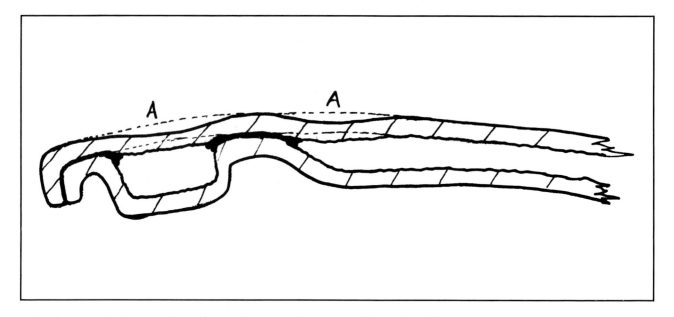

Unfortunately the use of standard polyester resins resulted in serious distortion at the points marked A above. This problem was only solved by the use for boot lid, bonnet and doors of laminates made up with epoxy resin. Epoxy resin has the great disadvantage of being three times as expensive as the polyester alternative but in compensation it is ten times less subject to shrinkage. It is also very unpleasant in use and liable to cause dermatitis. Previously its use had been confined to the aircraft industry. As related elsewhere it was the epoxy resin based panels which continued to cure in the California sunshine and cause so much trouble during 1960 and 1961.

The Elan production method

So thoroughly fed up were Chapman and Hickman by the experience of assembling the Elite by the haphazard dry assembly method that they evolved a completely new system for the Elan based on technology already in existence at Maximar and used for the production of high performance yachts. Chapman called it the "Monolithic" method – a term based on his experience in the construction industry – but Ron Hickman refers to it as the "Unimould" system. This method was highly successful on the Elan and was continued for the Plus Two that followed it.

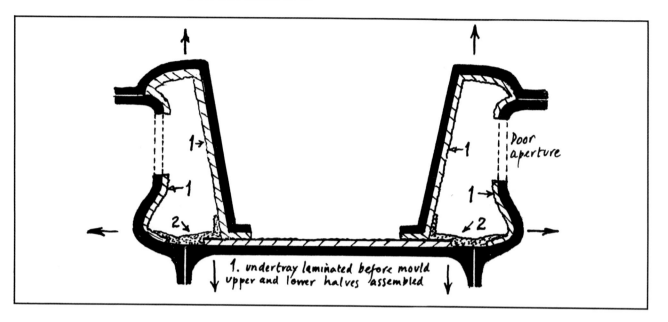

Expressed simply the Unimould system involves the gradual building up of a complete chassis body unit within a multi-section mould. After curing the mould is dismantled leaving a one-piece structure ready for attachment to the mechanical elements of the car. The method is illustrated diagramatically here showing a notional cross section of the car; assembled in the following sequence:

Stage 1 – Laminating internal panels and undertray
Stage 2 – At this point the upper and lower halves of the structure are brought together and the bridging laminates performed.
Stage 3 – Remove external moulds as shown by arrows revealing complete Unimoulded, assembled chassis body unit.

Appendix Ten

Sales Office Meetings 27 July – 8 December 1961 (Extracts)

After returning in mid 1961 I had to face a collapsing home market for the Elite matching the débâcle of our performance in the United States. Something had to be done quickly. In my absence the sales force (Ron Richardson, Export; Peter Warr, Competition Cars and Ian McLeod, Home Market) had performed magnificently under great difficulties and with strictly limited management from above. It was necessary in the first instance to co-ordinate our efforts. In order to monitor progress I instituted a series of Sales Department meetings (originally intended to take place weekly) which were run on formal lines with detailed minutes of the proceedings (usually issued by me) and with copies sent "upstairs" to Fred Bushell for information. By a quirk of fate Ian McLeod has kept his copies of the minutes from which I have selected excerpts with relevance to my story. I have deleted the usual "committee dross" about repainting the offices and moving the desks to a different angle (our equivalent of re-arranging deck chairs on the Titanic).

Meeting of 27 July 1961

It was resolved:
"That the Sales Department should strive to achieve as rapidly as possible a position where it would provide the impetus for the improvement of the Company's financial position. All members of the department appreciated that there was a unique opportunity amounting to a duty to take initiative to pull the Company from its present position of low morale and efficiency."

"A notice would be fixed to the entrance of the Sales Department composed by Mr. Richardson and signed by the Sales Manager, to the effect, that entry of unauthorised personnel on other than business matters or for the purpose of clocking-in or out would be prohibited. The Sales Department is currently regarded as a happy meeting place by outside members of the staff, with consequent reduction in efficiency."

Meeting of 4 August 1961

"The Sales Manager described progress which had been made on the various topics discussed at the previous meeting and mentioned that the important points

290

had all been discussed with Mr. Bushell with a view to securing his approval of our intended action. Mr. Bushell welcomed the general resolve of the Department to take initiative in improving the financial position of the Company and promised every support reasonably requested. The Sales Manager was authorised to hire a Secretary (mine having vanished during my absence abroad)"

"Members were then called upon to describe the outline of their activities during the preceding period and it was seen that morale and actual achievements were definitely on an upward trend. Members felt a definite sense of purpose and felt that this would continue."

"The Sales Manager then outlined the basic plan for the remainder of 1961 during which time concentration would be made on penetrating virgin export markets, and also touched on the future of the Seven in the United States during 1962 with reference to the discussions taking place with the Schapiro Group. It was felt that there were still opportunities to improve the Elite position without taking any drastic measures beyond an endeavour to reduce our world export price to the lowest economical level. The Board would be requested by the Sales Manager to consider a proposal for reduction in ex factory prices of this car to overall discount of $22^{1}/_{2}\%$ to enable us to penetrate high tariff markets."

"Advertising programme for the remainder of the year was briefly discussed and it was resolved that consideration would be given to making special announcements of the Super Seven (Cosworth 1340 cc) model in the following magazines: *Autosport, Motor Sport, Car Mechanics* and continuing a series in *Motor Sport* only. An advertising programme for the American market for publication in *Car and Driver* was also to be evolved. It was noted that the Press List was being kept up-to-date and Mr. Warr in his new work as PRO would make use of this to the best advantage."

(Note: At this time *Motor Sport* magazine dominated the UK field with a circulation approaching six figures and we were concentrating our advertising efforts on this journal)

"The question of weekly production delivery programming was discussed and it was learned that a high standard of accuracy in maintenance of delivery promised was achieved by Lotus Components Ltd., but that difficulties in obtaining accurate forecasts were alleged to be received from Lotus Cars Ltd. This allegation would be carefully watched by the Sales Manager during the next two week period and Mr. Richardson would be responsible to advise the Sales Manager of any shortcomings in this respect."

"Mr. Warr proposed three new schemes involving simplification of Stores Orders, Invoice Requisitions and paying in of cash received procedures, which were considered by all to represent a definite improvement in efficiency and reduction in time wasted in normal day-to-day work. Mr. Warr was requested to produce forms in accordance with his proposed measures."

"The Showroom has now been brought to a level of respectability and steps have been taken to avoid abuse of the telephone and use of the Showroom as a store. The Showroom should be used for informal business discussions with clients wherever possible. Three cars only will be on show at any one time of which one would be an Elite and one a Seven."

"Great satisfaction was expressed by all concerned with the performance of Lotus Components Ltd., in enabling the difficult Letter of Credit requirements from Western Distributors to be maintained. Mr. Warr proposed that the Directors should recognise this by an informal celebration at a local Public House on Tuesday evening 8th August, the cost of which will be borne out of petty cash . . . A total of 33 cars passed through the factory doors during a five day period."

Meeting of 17 August 1961

"Orders entered since the last meeting
  Elite 4   Seven 5   Junior 0

"Mr. Read proposed that Mr. Charles Fox be employed to tackle the improvement of our PR and advertising with a view to ultimately tackling other duties as well. Members felt this move to be a good one since Mr. Warr was heavily committed to sales and after sales service matters. Mr. Bushell and Mr. Chapman would be approached for approval."

"Shortages in both Companies were delaying deliveries. This was understood to be a temporary measure but anxiety was felt lest the Fuyo Trading Co. order should be badly handled in particular as a new Distributorship."

"Mr. Warr reported that his new forms were at the printers and was able to show one proof."

"Mr. Read queried whether Mrs. Tucker's Invoice Record Book was efficiently compiled. Members hastened to assure him that they could provide full particulars of any car sold in a matter of seconds. Mr. McLeod's Central Record Book would in any case provide information in the absence of any member."

"Mr. Read called for a report on the CKD requirements for Eire (local assembly). Mr. Richardson would provide these and the question of supply of Elites to Armstrong would be taken up with Mr. Lewis."

"Mr. Richardson would set up a wall map of UK Elite Distributors for the guidance of members, bearing in mind difficulties in finalising territory due to broken undertakings by Chequered Flag and D. Buxton Ltd., this would incorporate an easily altered boundary indication."

"Mr. Richardson stated that he had ordered keys for the Showroom to prevent continued abuse."

Meeting of 25 August 1961

"Orders entered since last meeting
  Elite 1 (Export)   Seven Super 3 (Home   Junior 1 (Export)
                       Seven 105E   3 Market)

"Mr. Read stated that no further developments had taken place in the US Letter of Credit position but that representatives of Western Distributors were expected next week and the resultant discussions would obviously have a bearing on the matter."

"The question of improvements to the Showroom with a view to increasing

Retail Sales efficiency was discussed. This would be thrashed out in detail during the next week and proposals put up for approval."

"Mr. Richardson stated that an accurate check was kept on the distribution of Elite Workshop Manuals, in the form of records maintained by him and Mr. Shann. (These are the beautiful James Allington books, which were individually numbered for security and which are now a collectors item)."

"The forthcoming intensification of Seven and Elite retailing plans was discussed in basic terms. Detail work-out would follow according to instructions from the Board, and members were asked to reflect on associated problems for discussion at the next meeting. Particular reference was made to the part to be played in this programme by Messrs. Warr and McLeod."

Note: At this time a final decision had not been taken to proceed with the Elite kit car programme. The idea was certainly present in Chapman's mind, but resisted by me. Hence the next item:

"Arrangements for Earls Court were in suspension pending clarification by the Board"

"Plans for a race success congratulatory service would be evolved by Messrs. Warr and Fox." (This would send telegrams to successful entrants and drivers of our products).

"The Seven Demonstrator would be painted BRG (British Racing Green) and attempts made to sell to Weathermatic Corporation (Sy Kaback) to enable it to be replaced by a Super Seven."

Meeting of 31 August 1961

"Orders entered since last meeting:
    Elite Nil   Seven 105E Kit   1 (Home)
                                                   1 (Export)
    Junior 1 (Export)

Note: Although this was right in the middle of the holiday season and right at the end of the racing season sales at this level with the productive capacity at our disposal were terrifying to say the least.

"Mr. Warr stated that his Stores order forms and Sales Department paying in slip systems were now in operation and that his invoice forms would be in use by Tuesday 9 September."

"With reference to the Super Seven marketing scheme and project "Jumbo" (the code name for the Elite kit project). It was decided that a series of sub-committees would be established to deal with the varying aspects."

"Mr. McLeod was advised that he was personally responsible for the rapid preparation of the Downton Seven demonstrator for immediate use painted BRG and to be tuned by Downton's Janosz. He would advise the Sales Department at the next meeting that this car was now in use."

Note: Janosz Odor, a refugee from the Hungarian uprising of 1957 had been employed by Daniel and Bunty Richmond of Downton on arrival in the United Kingdom. He subsequently left Downton and established the hugely successful Janspeed Company.

"Mr. Bushell will be asked via this minute what plans he had for repairing the car park entry road before the onset of the monsoon made this impracticable."

"The question of new overseas distributors was occupying the Sales Manager's attention on a 95% basis and the new programme would start within seven days' time."

"Mr. Richardson was asked to investigate in conjunction with Mr. Fox the correct use of the Brochure Stand in the Hall which apparently has become a receptacle for visiting sales representatives' unwanted literature. It will be used solely for holding Lotus publicity material and copies of Sports Car and Lotus Owner."

"The Stand equipment for Earls Court was presently being cared for by Mr. Shann, and Mr. Richardson was requested to find alternative storage for recommendation at the next meeting."

Meeting of 8 September 1961

Orders entered since last meeting:

Elite	Nil	Seven 105E Kit	3 (Home)
Super Seven Kit			2 (Home)

"Members had been considerably occupied during the week with a series of sub-committees to discuss the various aspects of the forthcoming intensified home market sales programme. The decisions reached at these meetings were being forwarded to the Board for approval so that instructions could be issued to members."

"Mr. Read reported that the situation in the US contemplated the early supply of a further 12 assembled Seven America Sprites to the Weathermatic Corporation (Kaback) and a temporary cessation of Junior (Twenty) deliveries to them in view of the fact that they are at present holding three examples of this type in their stock and a further five are awaiting collection at Idlewild, (now JFK Airport). Western Distributors were still in a state of flux and we do not know at the present time exactly what their future requirements will be. It was explained at the same time that the Posselius situation had revived and a contract had been sent to him for discussion leading to possible signature. However, Mr. Warr pointed out that Production were interested in no less than 25 Formula Juniors to be firm orders before they would extend their build authorisation from 100 units."

"Mr. Read stated that the Seven America 1962 programme had been put back one week in view of the uncertainty surrounding Mr. Hessler's activities with his two potential distributors."

"Mr. Warr was requested to make himself responsible for designing suitable invoices and Works Orders on Lotus Components for the Elite Kit project."

Note: This is the first "open" mention of the decision to market the Elite as a kit.

"Mr. McLeod was requested to prepare a recommendation in memo form as to the best method of providing customers for component cars with information in cases of difficulty. Mr. Warr stated that he had in his possession a wealth of rare technical information concerning earlier Lotus marks and that he would use this information in conjunction with Mr. McLeod's recommendations to provide a dossier for vital statistics for members of the Department."

"Mr. McLeod said that he had received a certain amount of co-operation from Southern Industrial Trust concerning hire purchase facilities for cars in component form but not enough encouragement to make it possible for a "blanket scheme" to be put into operation."

Note: There was then a gap in the series of meetings while I flew to the USA to follow up negotiations. At the end of September Colin flew over to join me for a visit to Detroit where we met John Posselius and Ray White. The onset of the preparations for Earls Court where the Elite was exhibited in "exploded" form to demonstrate how easy it was to assemble prevented us from sitting down until November.

Meeting of 6 November 1961

"The Sales Manager congratulated members on their excellent performance at Earls Court and the subsequent week and all members agreed that no effort would be spared to ensure that the momentum generated during the Show would be continued. At 31 October 1961 orders had been taken for a total of 58 cars in component form, of which 22 had been delivered. The week ending 3 November had seen a further 19 orders for the Elite and a definite upswing in the trend of orders for the Seven series, with the Super leading by a long margin."

"Mr. Fox outlined his programme of road tests for the Super Seven and Elite. The Super Seven was presently passing through the hands of the *Autocar* and the *Motor,* and the Elite was being road tested by John Bolster. We should try and "jam in" a number of short road tests for the cars before the onset of the winter season to avoid unfavourable comments on weather protection."

"Mr. Warr described progress and his thoughts for the Racing Car Show and it was decided that a sub-committee meeting should be immediately arranged to finalise matters for Board approval. It is suggested that this should take place at 6 p.m. on Wednesday 8 November. It is essential that Messrs. Read, Warr and Fox attend, although other members are welcome if free. We shall be showing a Seven, a Twentytwo, a Twentythree and possibly an Elite, although this latter has not yet been fixed."

"Mr. Read mentioned that the question of sales commission was under active re-consideration by the Board and that he expected to let them have further details by the middle of the current week after further consultation with the Managing Director (Chapman) and the Company Secretary (Bushell).

"Messrs. Warr and McLeod stated that they had evolved satisfactory arrangements to cover attendance on Saturday."

Note: Bland statements like the above (intended for the eyes of the Senior

Management above) often hid acrimonious discussion and disagreement. I had been under pressure for some time to introduce a form of sales commission to encourage effort but Colin inevitably considered that we were all overpaid in any case. There was no question of extra pay for Saturday attendance but of course this was prime selling time now that we had become largely a retail operation.

"The question of part exchange was discussed by all concerned and members were depressed by the low prices quoted by Cliff Davis Cars Ltd. The Sales Manager said that in certain cases it would be possible for the factory to subsidise such sales from the margin of £150 available in the car, but this was to be discouraged, since as soon as Cliff Davis learnt that this was our practice, they would possibly automatically under quote. Members were urged to persist in this practice as long as possible before turning over "impossible" cases to the Chequered Flag or other Trade contacts."

Note: Now that we had effectively gone "downmarket" with the Elite we had to offer part exchange facilities for cars presently owned by Elite customers. Cliff Davis (famed for his exploits in Cooper and Tojeiro cars JOY 500 and LOY 500 and a well known "bombed site" dealer), was approached by Chapman to handle used cars offered to us in part exchange. Naturally the prices that Cliff offered were abysmally low and with the tiny margin of profit (£150) available in the new £1299 price for the Elite kit we could not afford to give away much at Cheshunt. The alternative was to hand over the entire transaction to the Chequered Flag and hope that they with their long experience of such situations could wring something out of the deal and make do with the 10% commission available to them."

"Members were discouraged by the unsatisfactory number of Elite deliveries available compared with the forecast totals. It was understood that the Production Department was experiencing considerable difficulties at the present time but it was seriously hoped that no short deliveries would be made due to our long experience with the difficulties involved."

Note: Revenge is sweet! Now after a long period when Graham Lewis had done all within his power to embarrass the Sales Department by lining up new unsold cars in Chapman's path we have managed to reverse the position.

Meeting of 16/28 November 1961

"The meeting was held in two stages on Thursday 16 November and Tuesday 28 November. The reason for this division of sessions was as a result of endeavours by the Sales Manager to resolve the commission question with Mr. Chapman. These endeavours were unsuccessful and he (Chapman) has now agreed to meet Messrs. McLeod and Warr to discuss the matter fully."

Note: I would have enjoyed being a fly on Colin's office wall.

"There was a definite downward trend in orders received for both the Elite and Seven models. As a result of this members were questioned by the Sales Manager on the follow-up techniques being used . . ."

"Attempts to maintain the value of order income would be made by endeavouring to improve the follow-up resources of the Sales Department to capitalise wherever possible on the advertising programme. However, it is very likely that by the end of December we shall have received the initial order income from people who were "sold" on the idea of the Elite at its higher price, but unable until recently to purchase this car . . . Members were not in any way complacent nor would they accept the fact that orders might decline to anywhere near the level of the assembled car with Purchase Tax".

"Mr. Warr stated that the Saturday rota system with Mr. McLeod was working satisfactorily, although demonstrations recently given on Saturday had proved fruitless".

Meeting of Friday 8 December 1961

"Mr. McLeod reported that this week showed a decline in Elite sales, there being only six new cars to report since the last routine Sales Department meeting. Members were very concerned by the increase in number of customers threatening cancellation due to extended delivery. During this same period only three cars had been delivered against a promise by Mr. Lewis of 15 units and although the Sales Department was making every effort to work in close co-operation with Production its task was made most difficult in view of the heavy pressure being brought to bear by customers. Each member reported that he expected two or three telephone calls per day from dissatisfied customers with cars on order and since we are in this instance dealing in an impulse market, the matter was of grave concern to all."

"The question of the remaining Twenty Formula Junior cars was discussed. Mr. Read stated that these would be offered in *Autosport* and also directly to potential customers by means of a device to show them as two cars built expressly for Team Lotus in the hope that this would heighten interest and achieve sales."

Note: The Chapman technique was beginning to rub off on me by this stage.

"Mr. McLeod to arrange for the installation of a mechanical rev. counter in the demonstration Super Seven. A strict rev limit of 6000 rpm would be observed by all drivers."

Appendix Eleven
Elite sales

January 1960 – May 1962

The factory records for Elite sales are reproduced in Dennis Ortenburger's 1977 book "The Original Lotus Elite – Racing Car for the Road". However, certain parts of the text have been rewritten as cars shipped speculatively to the USA were re-allocated, thus confusing the original date of shipment. The figures in my table are based on the succeeding appendix showing sales by value.

Clearly illustrated is the build-up of export sales (principally to the USA) during 1960 reaching a peak in October of that year and rapidly falling off as the Chamberlain business collapsed. Export sales of the Elite never recovered and we were forced to look to the domestic market for salvation.

From the London Earls Court Motor Show of October 1961 we marketed the Elite as a kit car with the dramatic change of fortune visible from the home market sales figures.

Whereas the scene in the first five months of 1962 is dominated by the impact of Elite kit car sales, the Twentytwo and Twentythree Formula Junior/Sports Racing Cars were again available at the right time; having been launched at the Racing Car Show at the turn of the year.

It is remarkable how just as one element of the Company's commercial activity collapsed another product range would "leap to the rescue". This is very much to Chapman's personal credit. It was he who decided on the original Formula Junior programme despite continual considerable internal opposition. It was also his idea to convert the Elite to a kit car during the disastrous second half of 1961 when unsold cars and components were piling up around us.

Note: The identical figures for February and March 1961 result from the fact that only combined results for those two months exist.

YEAR/MONTH		HOME	EXPORT	TOTAL
1960	January	3	9	12
	February	3	14	17

	March	6	30	36
	April	4	13	17
	May	15	16	31
	June	7	17	24
	July	8	41	49
	August	1	35	36
	September	3	20	23
	October	4	48	52
	November	6	12	18
	December	3	5	8
TOTAL 1960		63	260	323
1961	January	6	18*	24
	February	4	11*	15
	March	4	11*	15
	April	3	8	11
	May	3	6	9
	June	3	12	15
	July	2	3	5
	August	1	5	6
	September	3	7	10
	October	21	1	22
	November	19	2	21
	December	25	10	35
TOTAL 1961		94	94	188
1962	January	27	2	29
	February	28	5	33
	March	42	5	47
	April	25	3	28
	May	36	1	37
TOTAL JAN – MAY 1962		158	16	174

* These were speculative US shipments not covered by a Letter of Credit. 30 cars remained unsold at 31st May 1962.

Appendix Twelve

Lotus Group
Sales by value (£/Sterling)
October 1959 – May 1962

In order to compute commission payments due to me under the terms of my contract of employment it was necessary for the Accounts Department to produce monthly figures. This information was not analysed for the last three months of 1959 but from January 1960 onwards to the end of May 1962 the value of sales (net of British Purchase Tax) are analysed in some detail and shown on the attached table which includes parts and service transactions.

Whereas the Elite figures are straightforward (and used to compute the volume data shown in Appendix Eleven), the picture on the Lotus Components/Racing Engines Limited side covering all other types is less clear. There is a steady flow of Seven sales at low unit values (down to as low as £399 on the home market) but the impact in April to September 1960 of the Eighteen Formula Junior sales programme can be clearly seen. The home market was slow to recognise the superiority of the Eighteen Formula Junior car in view of the disappointing performance of the prototype on 26th December 1959 at Brands Hatch. However, as soon as the season got under way Team Lotus cars dominated the scene and the fickle racing fraternity rushed to buy, many of them waiting until mid season for delivery. This meant that Juniors were not available for export until the end of 1960, most of them going to the States as bribes to take Sevens, Elites etc.

As soon as the Eighteen began to arrive in export markets at the turn of the 1960 – 61 the Twenty flooded on to the home market at the correct time (February 1961 onwards). This was possible because the Twenty was largely a face-lifted Eighteen requiring minimal development work and reaching peak domestic sales in April just as the season really got into its stride. By June 1961 shipments of Juniors to the United States were well under way as the figures show.

Year/Month	Elite Home	Elite Export	Seven/Racing Cars Home	Seven/Racing Cars Export	Total Cars Home	Total Cars Export	Parts	Service	Grand Total
1959 Oct – Dec	—	—	—	—	—	—	—	—	43100
1960 January	3300	9900	400	2700	3700	13600	900	100	18300
February	3300	16000	7500	3800	10800	19800	1100	100	31800
March	6700	34700	7500	600	14200	35300	4100	900	54500
April	4400	14900	15900	1400	20300	16300	2200	800	39600
May	16600	18800	14800	3000	31400	21800	6600	600	60400
June	7800	19400	26000	7300	33800	26700	3900	500	64900
July	9100	45300	13500	8300	22600	53600	3300	500	80000
August	1100	38600	9300	—	10400	38600	3700	1200	53900
September	3400	22700	23700	10300	27100	33000	4800	1500	66400
October	4300	52900	4100	13900	8400	66800	3100	2600	80900
November	6800	13900	8500	43900	15300	57800	1400	2800	77300
December	3400	6300	11400	31200	14800	37500	1900	900	55100
Total 1960	£70200	293400	142600	126400	212800	420800	37000	12500	683100
1961 January	7100	20200	5100	6300	12200	26500	4600	700	44000
February	4750	13050	25250	10550	30000	23600	3350	1150	58100
March	4750	13050	25250	10550	30000	23600	3350	1150	58100
April	3400	9400	44200	5500	47600	14900	3200	700	66400
May	3700	6600	17800	13500	21500	20100	4900	1100	47600
June	3500	13200	11500	55100	15000	68300	6600	400	90300
July	2200	3300	10800	5700	13000	9000	4500	900	90300
August	1100	5500	7900	39500	9000	45000	4500	900	59400
September	3300	7700	7700	5300	11000	13000	4500	900	29400
October	25200	1100	5800	7900	31000	9000	4500	900	45400
November	22800	2200	9200	2800	32000	5000	4500	900	42400
December	30000	11000	6000	2000	36000	13000	4500	900	54400
Total 1961	£111800	106300	176500	164700	288300	271000	53000	10600	622900
1962 January	35100	2900	7300	10300	42400	13200	—	—	55600
February	36600	5600	19700	5400	56300	11000	—	—	67300
March	54800	6100	14500	17700	69300	23800	—	—	93100
April	33500	3800	26500	6000	60000	9800	—	—	69800
May	46900	1600	18900	24400	65800	26000	—	—	91800
Total Jan – May 1962	£206900	20000	86900	63800	293800	83800			377600

Appendix —

(Deleted in Accordance
with Lotus tradition)

Appendix Fourteen

"Proposed World Marketing Programme for 1962"

In the autumn of 1961 our commercial fortunes were at an extremely low ebb. It was a time for reappraisal and drastic action. We introduced the Elite in kit form for October 1961, thus reviving its seriously flagging performance and having prepared the sales department for the anticipated increase in retail sales activity I sat down to prepare a marketing programme for the following year intended to avoid earlier pitfalls.

We knew that we had to regard the entire world as our potential market place and we were always geared to exploit any opportunities abroad that came our way. Available for all potential overseas distributors was a comprehensive document describing the product range, the terms on which the appointment of a distributor was made, draft agreement etc. Later following the initial success of the kit Elite on the home market we devised a direct selling operation for the USA (yes!) in which an airmail weight sales letter signed by Chapman and incorporating an order form enabled the potential buyer on the other side of the Atlantic to order an Elite in a box. One or two did go this way but it was not a repeat of the domestic success story.

In addition to our various schemes to promote sales of the existing product range we knew that we had to make preparations for the launch of the Elan (M2). At the time that I drafted my "World Marketing Programme" in November 1961 Colin had persuaded the Ford Motor Company that they should be intimately involved with the Elan marketing programme and had even talked them into considering allowing us access to the domestic network. Reference to this is made in my plan which is largely reproduced in its entirety and which was circulated to Chapman, Bushell, Clark, Costin and Kirwan-Taylor.

1 Introduction

The proposals contained in the following pages are submitted for Board approval in accordance with instructions given at the last Board Meeting when a time limit extending to the end of December was set for the preparation of a forward plan for marketing operations to the end of 1962.

Before proceeding to the particular, I would like briefly to explore the general aim of the Board in its long term policy since the worth of any proposal such as this must be assessed in the light of its possible contribution to the achievement

303

of general aims of company policy. My assumption is that it is the aim of the Board to develop the Lotus Group of Companies to a point where annual production rises to, but does not exceed the level of approximately seven thousand five hundred units. This might be regarded as a workable target over a period of five years from now or in other words, approximately seven and a half years from the time when production began at the Cheshunt Factory. I don't think that I am being unjust in stating that the period to now has been completely wasted in terms of achieving the long term aim of the Board, and my reasons for stating this are as follows:-

The Elite was intended to represent the first step up the ladder towards our goal, but for a variety of reasons, which, it might be argued were beyond our control, has degenerated into a "bailing out" operation, conducted under circumstances of acute embarrassment. As originally conceived, the Elite would have enjoyed a reasonable market, but during the period leading to production, the price of the machine rose and it became almost impossible to adhere to the basic necessity for success of giving good value to the customer.

The Seven never was a production car and probably never will be. The outstanding and invaluable contribution to our business made by the type Eighteen and Twenty Juniors, serves to underline the failure of the Elite as our staple product.

On the credit side, we are still here after two and a half years, and have learned a great deal collectively and are as ready as ever to proceed profitably, but with the M2 now rapidly approaching reality, representing as it does our first genuine hope for expanded production, and market penetration, it is vitally important that we run at full pressure from the opening of next year to ensure that our seed does not fall on barren ground.

Now, more than ever, it is essential to formulate a long term sales policy which must be adhered to with unfailing consistency. Due to circumstances beyond our control, it has proved prudent in the past to adapt our marketing methods almost on a month by month basis to the demands of maintaining sales at any price, but study of month by month sales figures over the 1961 period, for instance will indicate how incompatible is such an operating method, with a desire to ensure a regular, economical flow of production, leading to the gathering of nett profit. The only way to achieve this simple aim is to create stability of both marketing and production, so that efforts can be made to develop manufacture and sales hand in hand. I cannot remember a single week in my time with this company that both aspects of our activity have run at the same speed.

Despite boisterous sharpening of wits in the Board Room, I feel that all interested parties are fundamentally in agreement on the methods necessary to achieve our long term aims. The time is now ripe for us to formulate positively.

The proposals covered by the following pages are intended to smooth the path towards the effective operation of a long term marketing policy. 1962 will see the transition from the "Hornsey spirit", to a small industrial unit. This transition must start within the Sales Department and the adoption of a simple plan by that sector of our activity, will enable other Departments to develop in step with an increase in turnover.

The proposal contains the essential elements of a plan to bring our 1962 turnover much nearer the one million pound mark. However, this ultimate aim cannot be guaranteed without the fullest support of the Board to all aspects of the overall programme on which the forecast is based. In other words the existing sales force and the mental attitudes which govern the activities of that sales force cannot miraculously be developed to yield an increase in turnover. The staff of the Sales Department has to be increased; operating budgets have to be set at higher levels than are now acceptable, but what is most important is that if the

Board really wants to achieve the targets covered by this proposal, it must provide the Department with clearly written terms of reference, accepting that if we change our policies, with the frequency that has been necessary during the course of this year, when we were operating without the benefit of a long range plan, disaster will be inevitable.

If you are prepared to accept these proposals largely as they stand, you will get the organisation and the results promised.

2 Condensed sales review of 1961

My full report on the trading activities of 1961 will be presented to you in January of next year, but it is essential to have available certain basic information in light of which to judge the value of the proposals made for 1962.

A table is attached indicating deliveries throughout the year, in which the December figures are estimated, together with Group turnover at Home and Abroad for the period.

Home Market

At the beginning of the year the Board took the only possible step apparent at the time and revised the Home Marketing methods for the Seven, with the result that sales have continued through 1961 at more or less the same level as for 1960. Once taken, it is almost impossible to convert the step of marketing direct from the Factory into any other form, and proposals for 1962 recognize this inescapable fact. The lesson that is to be learned from our experience at the beginning of this year, is quite clear; marketing "conventionally" is in the long run the only possible method by which to increase volume to a really high level, but the process requires special skills and organisation which were not available to us at the time when the policy change was made. As a component form car, the Seven was available at an acceptable retail price when sold through the Trade, but I feel that no amount of skill or organisation could have saved the Elite, which with the Purchase Tax was grossly overpriced for the market. Trade participation in the marketing scheme now in operation for the Elite has shown (at a two to one sales ratio), the valuable part played by retail outlets of more or less conventional type, even in the context of our fundamentally unconventional marketing methods.

The Junior programme, intended as a make weight, has again played an invaluable part in subsidising other production models.

A positive and reasonably well organised sales effort in the last months of this year has enabled us to maintain sales at an unusually high level for the time of year and although the existing Sales Department is working very near its optimum efficiency, with available man power, the advantage gained will be lost unless the proposals made here are adopted. Since my return from the United States, I have pursued a policy of improving the efficiency of the available resources, which has led to a satisfying improvement in business, but this favourable trend cannot be maintained without expansion.

Export Market

1961 has been a doubly disastrous year for export, largely due to the collapse of the American market following the Chamberlain liquidation. The United States is more or less lost to us as a volume outlet if sales are to be made on a conventional basis and the proposals made for your consideration concerning the possibility of direct marketing, will have to be adopted if we are to sell noticeably during the first half of 1962 in what is undoubtedly our largest potential export field.

1961 Ex-factory deliveries

(*Estimated)
(Turnover figures as supplied by Accounts where not estimated)

a) Home Market

Type	Jan	Feb	Mar	Apl	May	Jun	Jul	Aug	Sep	Oct	Nov	Dec	Total
7	6	4	17	16	8	12	17	12	11	10	21	15*	149
Elite	4	6	8	3	11	7	2	1	3	21	19*	25*	110
18	1		12	24	11	1	1	1	1	1			53
20		2											2
19													
Nett £1000	12	10	46	48	22	15	11	9	11*	31*	32*	36*	283*

b) Export Market

Type	Jan	Feb	Mar	Apl	May	Jun	Jul	Aug	Sep	Oct	Nov	Dec	Total
7	2	3	3	5	2	22	8	20	1	3	2	7	78
Elite	2	2	8	4	3	4	3	5	7	1	2	10*	51
18	4	2	6	1	5	13	6	17	3	1	1		59
20			1	1	1	3	1			1			8
19													
Nett £1000	27	17	29	15	20	68	9	45	13*	9*	5*	13*	270*

c) Combined Monthly TO in £1000

	Jan	Feb	Mar	Apl	May	Jun	Jul	Aug	Sep	Oct	Nov	Dec	Total
Nett £1000	39	27	75	63	42	83	20	54	24*	40*	37*	49*	553*

Machinery is even now being established to enable us to forge ahead abroad in all territories and this is covered in greater detail in Section 4 of this proposal. 1961 has seen no real trend in any direction in our export fortunes, largely the result of diversion in other directions and the lack of sufficient staff to adequately handle even the administration of existing distributorships.

Home Market Sales Strategy

1962 will see us phase gradually from the existing production models into the era of the M2. I feel that there will always be a place for the Seven or a car of similar type, and sales will tend to increase throughout the year. The Board may wish to artificially terminate the life of the Elite, but we would expect to sell all the cars at present on hand, together with a further 100. It then might be logical for the Elite to be elevated to a higher price category with a suitably improved specification to form a prestige model that would in no way affect or be affected by the M2. Combined Twentytwo/Twentythree sales will continue at very nearly the level established by the Twenty this year and sales of the M2 at a retail before tax figure, of £900 will largely depend on availability.

Sales methods to be employed for each of the models under review are examined in closer detail below:-

Seven Range

Should the verbal approval given by the Ford Motor Company to our desire to use the Home Market Ford dealer network for distribution of the M2, be confirmed, the effect on our Seven marketing programme at home will be minimal, since the price structure of this model precludes more than a passing association with Trade outlets. The programme of development that has been applied to the Seven range since its inception, has been thoroughly justified and the Sales Department now has a highly attractive proposition available for greater exploitation in 1962. The popular image of the Seven in the minds of the general public is of a rather primitive, under-powered car that handles extremely well. Our advertising and public relations programme will endeavour to inform the public as effectively as possible that the Seven is now far more acceptable as a road-going car and is now handsomely powered. The value for money and easy assembly themes will be heavily stressed and we know from our own direct experience of selling the Super Seven, that although considerable effort is required, it is possible to positively sell this model to an otherwise doubting prospect. Our task will become progressively easier as more and more Super Sevens are seen on the roads, and tried both at the Factory and privately by our clientele. Since the physical sales force available to directly sell the car is limited, great emphasis must be laid on a carefully chosen advertising and promotional campaign to achieve our ends.

As with all retail operations, it will be essential for us to further refine the efficiency of our machinery for the processing of enquiries and although the theoretical basis for this has been established for some weeks, the process of putting it into operation is still in its infancy and needs considerable improvement. All these aspects will be attended to as the 1962 programme goes forward.

Elite Range

Remarks concerning the Ford Motor Company collaboration covered by the above section apply equally to the Elite. Here, however, I would again direct the attention of the Board to my memorandum of the 16 October, 1961, under the heading of Marketing Techniques for the Elite, in which I clearly laid down my feelings that maintenance of the initial interest in the Elite arising from its lower price, would have to be maintained by further enlisting Trade co-operation. Fortunately, available margins of profit in this car would make such a plan possible and in 1962 we shall have to take positive steps to interest the Trade in the car rather than as at the present time, rather grudgingly permitting them to share in the pie. The Trade in this context is not of course the Ford network but the coterie of dealers with whom we are currently or have been in the past associated. I am frankly, however, more interested in using the Elite as a "foot in the door" on the export market, to provide distributors with merchandise in the major period of 1962 before the advent of the M2. This proposal is framed with such an aim in mind. Home Market advertising for the Elite will continue at approximately the current pressure and the overall Home Market situation for the Elite will be re-evaluated in January to decide whether the sales volume should be maintained by investment in advertising, or increased and/or wider spread Trade Discount.

Competition Cars

In this field we know of course that the sales potential for the racing car is largely governed by its competition successes and the picture of 1960/1961 will lend a great deal of momentum to the programme for the new models in 1962. The sales programme for this type of car is also influenced by the individual efforts of Messrs. Chapman, Costin and Warr, but although I am personally optimistic about our chances with the new models, I have deliberately kept a very conservative set of figures in the planned ex Factory delivery programme covered by Section 5.

This year, I would like to feel that we were making greater efforts to increase the profitability of each sale by avoiding wherever possible the granting of discounts on the almost automatic basis used in 1961.

M2

Whether we are fortunate to secure the formal approval of the Ford Motor Company to enable us to approach their dealer network to handle this model or not, it will be handled via the Trade in a conventional manner.

Our two previous efforts in launching a Trade scheme similar to the one that we shall undertake for the M2, both enjoyed an initial success which later turned to disappointment as it proved impossible to effectively administer and develop the initial arrangements. I think there can be no doubt however that we have effectively demonstrated that we have sufficient know-how to enable us to adequately plan such a programme, provided that we have the necessary resources with which to maintain the effort. Selling to the Trade is utterly different from the retail operation and specialist knowledge of the techniques involved is essential to success. Briefly speaking, the most important aspect of the representative's task is to sell the company that he serves to the prospective dealer, who has probably already made up his mind as to whether he likes the product or not. The dealer is interested in:-
a) Profit
b) Consistent support from the manufacturer (by this I mean an indefinable feeling that the two are working on the same wavelength)
c) Reliable and ethical warranty programme
d) A little security in the form of formal territory.

If he can enjoy all these points above, the dealer can do a valuable job for the manufacturer. He only fails if one or more of the above points are being adversely affected.

Your present Sales Department is well equipped with the basic skills necessary to carry out the programme of introduction of the M2 to the Trade, whether it be through Ford or other outlets.

Sales turnover on the Home Market will very nearly equal results abroad, but the advent of the M2 will mark the point where the Export Market begins to assume the conventionally much superior position.

Export Market Sales Strategy

Although we have a total of 16 overseas distributors, most of whom are potentially highly efficient, we have never been able to really develop this most important aspect of our operation. 1962 will see a concentrated effort to improve the situation, much of the groundwork for the 1962 programme having already been carried out and discussed informally with the members of the Board. There are two sides to our 1962 export programme: the improvement of existing outlets available to us and the creation and development of new export distributorships, many of whom will only become available to us as a result of our unique ability (among small series car manufacturers), to supply cars for local semi-skilled assembly. Preferential tariffs for CKD cars instituted by the Governments of small countries in the forlorn hope that they would encourage the development of a local industry, can and will bring us sales in some surprisingly remote corners of the world.

The 1962 export expansion programme is intended to at least double the number of distributorships at present available to us and to vastly improve the performance of existing connections. If we are able to produce a thousand units of the M2 in the first twelve months of production, seven hundred of them will be destined for export.

Model by model breakdowns appear below:-

Seven Range

Export prospects for the Seven are patchy inasmuch that we can expect a substantially rewarding market in the United States and in one or two other spheres, while the majority of our Distributors will only be in a position to take one or two examples of the car throughout the year. This is entirely due to the specialised nature of the car, which can only appeal to the rabid anglophile abroad.

The estimates for the export market for the Seven in 1962 include a 75% allocation for the United States market, which is valid no matter what means of distribution we finally adopt for that market. Whether we sell in the United States direct from the Factory, or through distributors, my minimum figure will hold good.

The Elite

As mentioned in the appropriate paragraph of Section 3, the Elite will be used to build up our Export markets abroad, since this is the only car of our range which has a truly universal appeal. We may only be able to deliver the 32 examples at present in the United States in that sector of our export field, and I plan to deliver the remaining projected quantities in other markets. Success with this particular model is of course tied to the question of our nett price and you have before you my recommendations for the basis on which we offer the car. We have to compete with extremely strong competition from Alfa Romeo and Porsche and with export, as in any other volume market it is price, price, price all the way, since import tariffs are almost invariably based on invoice value and the only market where we might have made an "easy killing" – the United States – is barred to us for other reasons.

Competition Cars

Fifty percent of our export competition car allocation will go to the United States. The remainder will be scattered rather thinly in the same way that has been the case with previous models of this type sold abroad. Target figures here are conservative.

M2

As with the Home Market, sales will be largely governed by availability and the spade work conducted in the first six months of 1962 with existing models, will create immediate outlets for the M2 in quantity abroad. Personally, I would like to see the Ford approval extended to overseas markets and the Board might be interested to note that we do have one distributor at the present time also handling Ford (Portugal), so we do have a precedent to support our argument. The Ford Motor Company raised no objection to this particular appointment.

Although the foregoing would tend to give the impression that selling the M2 is an extremely easy job, I will not gloss over the considerable preparation that is necessary to do correctly an overseas selling operation. Sales packs must be produced to assist overseas Distributors who are not in a position regularly to consult the Factory for advice; warranty matters have to be thoroughly organised; documentation has to be available if necessary in foreign languages and the Factory has to be prepared to regularly visit its overseas Distributors on the spot. It is no exaggeration to say that one visit per annum to an overseas distributor would double his offtake of cars against his purchases if he were just left to his own devices and contacted merely on paper.

The great majority of the organisation and planning for export onslaught has already been completed. However, an extension of our staff resources is essential if the machinery is to be put into operation.

Ex-factory delivery programme

Some notes of explanation are necessary and I shall be pleased to elaborate on individual aspects of the attached delivery programme should they seem confusing.

Home Market

a) Seven

The monotonous target of 15 units per month is based on a natural "peak" of approximately 15 units per month, which can be achieved by good retail selling during the season. I feel that this figure can be maintained initially by the impetus given by the Racing Car Show and towards the end of the season by a combination of the Earls Court effect and the gradually improving acceptance of the car.

b) Elite

Sales of the car in component form will rise to 125 units by the end of 1961 and this will be tailed off as the year advances and export demand increases. However, the Board may decide to continue the car beyond the extra 100 units at present envisaged if the market seems to warrant it. We shall not be fully aware of the long term situation until the Chancellor of the Exchequer introduces his new budget. For the time being however, we should concentrate on pumping as many units of this model into the Home Market as possible while the going is good.

c) Competition Cars

It is very difficult to accurately pinpoint deliveries of the Twentytwo and Twentythree, since there are so many variable factors involved. However, I feel that the Board will agree that my tentative suggestions are fairly accurate.

d) M2

The situation is entirely governed by production.

Export Market

a) Seven

This market will be more seasonal than the Home Market due to the United States fluctuation, which begins to have effect in April as the Northwest, Midwest and East Coast racing programmes get into their stride.

b) Competition Cars

Again mainly governed by United States considerations.

c) M2

See detailed notes in Section 4.

d) Elite

As mentioned earlier, the Elite will be used to provide merchandise for the expansion of our Export Distributorships as the Home Market demand tails off towards the middle of the year. The Board will appreciate the necessity of this artificial manoeuvre since we will be unable to approach potential distributors unless we are able to offer them automobiles for sale. The last 100 of the total of 160 planned for sale next year, would best be the 100 new cars contemplated to provide turnover in the period between the rundown of the Elite and the runup of the M2. It is possible that a proportion of the cars listed for sale towards the middle of the year will enter the United States market in Super 100 form.

An explanation of the basis on which turnover is calculated will be necessary. The figures suggested are very approximate:

	Seven	Elite	Twentytwo/ Twentythree	M2
Home Market	£500	£1100	£1550	£700
Export Market	£550	£1100	£1550	£700

I live in the hope that in the very near future efforts will be made to rationalise the relationship between the Sales Department and Production. At the present time chaos reigns for reasons that we are perfectly prepared to accept, but sooner or later the interests of both sections of the company will have to be drawn closer together.

Our Export programme will then enable Production to build on a 90 days ahead schedule and retail deliveries will probably be at least 30 days to enable a certain amount of planning to be put into effect. The opportunity is available right now for instance for Elite Production to be put on this basis with a considerable reduction in heartache for all concerned.

Sales Promotional Programme

I have suggested that advertising and public relations expenditure should be tied at $1\frac{1}{2}\%$ of turnover, calculated quarterly on the basis that the next quarter's promotion should be $1\frac{1}{2}\%$ of the preceding quarter's turnover. In this manner we shall have a degree of control to ensure that expenditure on advertising is being properly exploited by the organisation behind it.

Four advertising programmes will be prepared to cover the 1962 season and the first of these is now in process for presentation to you in early December. A great proportion of the expenditure will be in the Home Market, since $2\frac{1}{2}\%$ per car allocation is made to overseas distributors for their independent programme. A direct retail organisation in the United States will of course involve expenditure in that field again on a results basis. By normal standards our advertising budget is extremely modest and in actual fact as you will see later, we intend to operate the entire Sales Department including all advertising on a turnover percentage basis substantially less than most manufacturers expend on advertising alone.

We are particularly fortunate in having the services of BDMW Associates to assist us in the design of our advertising material and we shall concentrate on simple but striking presentation of our range in photographic form with sensible but provocative wording intended to whet the curiosity of the reader. Greater efforts will be made to exploit the potential of free editorial matter to supplement that which we already receive from the activities of Team Lotus.

Our paid advertising in the United Kingdom is solely intended to bring the prospect to the door of the Factory or dealer.

The programme of road tests for the Elite and Super Seven allocated to us for this purpose will continue ad infinitum; the benefit being very noticeable in terms of sales realised and the costs reasonable in the extreme.

1962 Sales Department Operating Costs – estimated budget requirement

a) Salaries and Commissions	£
Group Sales Manager	2362
Home Sales Executive	1250
Export Sales Representative	1250
Competition Car Sales Executive	1250
Retail Salesman 1	1000
Retail Salesman 2	1000
PR/Advertising Officer	750
Export Assistant (Admin)	750
Sales Clerk	550
Combined Secretarial Staff	3000
	13162

b) **Home/Export PR/Advertising/Exhibition Allocation**
(Allocated Quarterly Ahead as $1\frac{1}{2}\%$ of
previous 90 days turnover)   12925

c) General Operating Costs
including depreciation and operation
of Demonstration cars, materials used,
conversion and maintenance of offices etc.   2000

d) Travelling and Entertainment Expenses   2000

Group Sales Department Overhead Charge   £30,087

Expressed as a percentage of Group Turnover   3.48%

Suggested 1962 World Price Structure (Ex Factory)

Model	Home			Export		
	Retail	Discount	Net	Retail	Discount	Net
Elite GT Coupe Regular Model	£1299	£150 (£25)	£1149 (1124)	£1393	22½%*	£1080
Elite GT Coupe Special Equipment	£1425	£175 (£25)	£1250 (1225)	£1495	22½%*	£1159
Elite GT Coupe Super 100 Model	£1825	£250 (£25)	£1575 (1550)	£1895	20%'	£1516
Seven Regular (Seven Classic Export)	£499 plus	£25	£474	£798	22½%*	£618
Super Seven (Seven Super Classic Export)	£599	£35	£564	£900	22½%*	£708
Twentytwo	£1550	12½%	£1356	£1625	12%'	£1431
Twentythree	£1650	12½%	£1444	£1725	12%'	£1519
M2	£895	20%	£716	£895	22½%*	£694

* Includes 2½% Export Warranty Allowance
' Racing car; no warranty

1962 Planned ex-Factory Delivery Programme

a) Home Market

Type	Jan	Feb	Mar	Apl	May	Jun	Jul	Aug	Sep	Oct	Nov	Dec	Total
7	15	15	15	15	15	15	15	15	15	15	15	15	180
Elite	25	20	15	15	10	10	10						115
22 & 23			15	15	10	5							45
M2							5	15	20	30	40	50	160
Nett													
£1000	36	31	48	48	35	27	23	30	22	29	36	42	407

b) Export Market

Type	Jan	Feb	Mar	Apl	May	Jun	Jul	Aug	Sep	Oct	Nov	Dec	Total
7	10	10	15	20	25	30	35	30	25	20	15	10	245
Elite	10	12	15	18	20	20	20	20	15	10	15	30	160
22 & 23		15			10	5	5	5	5				45
M2							5	10	15	20	25	30	105
Nett													
£1000	17	42	25	31	51	46	52	53	49	36	26	27	455

c) Combined Monthly TO in £1000

	Jan	Feb	Mar	Apl	May	Jun	Jul	Aug	Sep	Oct	Nov	Dec	Total
Nett													
£1000	53	73	73	79	86	73	75	83	71	65	62	69	862

Appendix Fifteen
Contemporary Road Tests

The pressure to allow a road test of the Elite built up to an almost intolerable level by 1959 when production began at Cheshunt. Chapman successfully resisted the approaches of journals at home and abroad, knowing that the car was nowhere near ready for a thorough road test. But by early 1960 he was no longer able to hold back the interest and at this time the first road tests were conducted in America and Britain.

I have chosen the *Motor* road test of the Elite, John Bolster's *Autosport* road test of the Super Seven Series Two with Cosworth 1340 cc engine (delivered from Cheshunt to Praed Street London by Ian McLeod to Bolster in what Ian claims was record time) and David Phipps' excellent track test of the Eighteen Formula Junior car as representative of the period.

Colin always enjoyed great support from the motoring press and one has the feeling on reading contemporary road tests that far greater tolerance of shortcomings was available to Lotus than others. In many ways this was helpful, but it frequently caused serious disappointment to owners of "commercial" versions of road test cars which had been scrupulously prepared up to the last minute, very frequently performing well ahead of standard because of it.

The Motor Road Test No. 17/60

Make: Lotus **Type:** Elite

Makers: Lotus Cars Ltd., Delamare Road, Cheshunt, Herts.

Test Data

World copyright reserved; no unauthorized reproduction in whole or in part.

CONDITIONS: *Weather: Mild and fine, with light wind. (Temperature 55°-70°F., Barometer 29.9 in. Hg.) Surface: Dry tarred macadam and concrete. Fuel: Super-premium grade pump petrol (approx. 101 Research Method Octane Rating).*

INSTRUMENTS

Speedometer at 30 m.p.h.	6% fast
Speedometer at 60 m.p.h.	6% fast
Speedometer at 90 m.p.h.	6% fast
Distance recorder	2% fast

WEIGHT

Kerb weight, (unladen, but with oil, coolant, and fuel for approx. 50 miles)	13¼ cwt.
Front/rear distribution of kerb weight	46/54
Weight laden as tested	16¾ cwt.

MAXIMUM SPEEDS

Flying Mile.

Mean of four opposite runs	111.8 m.p.h.
Best one-way time equals	113.2 m.p.h.

"Maximile" speed. (Timed quarter mile after one mile accelerating from rest.)

Mean of four opposite runs	102.3 m.p.h.
Best one-way time equals	104.7 m.p.h.

Speed in gears (at 6,500 r.p.m.)

Max. speed in 3rd gear	83 m.p.h.
Max. speed in 2nd gear	50 m.p.h.
Max. speed in 1st gear	30 m.p.h.

FUEL CONSUMPTION

51.0 m.p.g. at constant 30 m.p.h. on level.
54.0 m.p.g. at constant 40 m.p.h. on level.
52.5 m.p.g. at constant 50 m.p.h. on level.
48.5 m.p.g. at constant 60 m.p.h. on level.
43.0 m.p.g. at constant 70 m.p.h. on level.
37.0 m.p.g. at constant 80 m.p.h. on level.
33.0 m.p.g. at constant 90 m.p.h. on level.
29.5 m.p.g. at constant 100 m.p.h. on level.

Overall Fuel Consumption for 2,025 miles, 59.4 gallons, equals 34.1 m.p.g. (8.3 litres/100 km.)

Touring Fuel Consumption (m.p.g. at steady speed midway between 30 m.p.h. and maximum, less 5% allowance for acceleration). 40.5 m.p.g.

Fuel tank capacity (maker's figure) 6½ gallons.

STEERING

Turning circle between kerbs:

Left	35 ft.
Right	33¾ ft.
Turns of steering wheel from lock to lock	2½

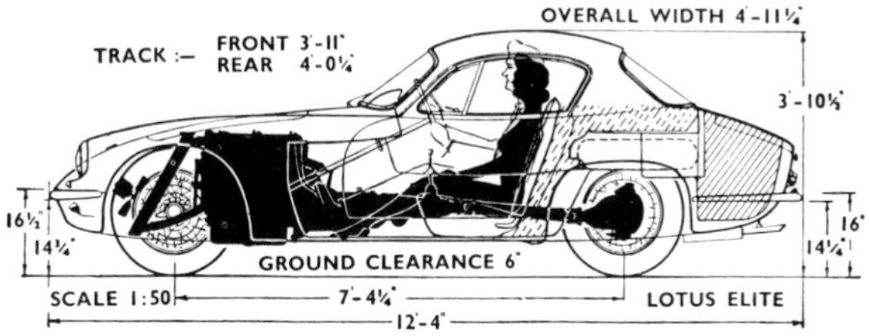
OVERALL WIDTH 4'-11¼"
TRACK :— FRONT 3'-11" REAR 4'-0¼"
3'-10½"
16½"
14¼"
GROUND CLEARANCE 6"
16"
14¼"
SCALE 1:50
7'-4¼"
LOTUS ELITE
12'-4"

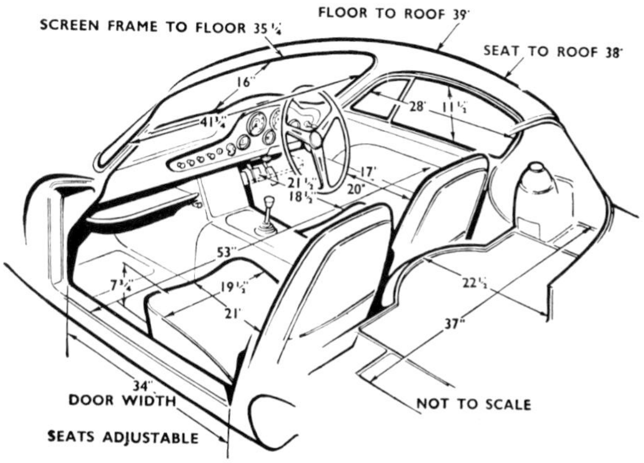
SCREEN FRAME TO FLOOR 35¼
FLOOR TO ROOF 39
SEAT TO ROOF 38
16"
41¼
28"
11½
17"
21½
18½
20"
53"
7¼"
19½"
21"
22½
37"
34"
DOOR WIDTH
NOT TO SCALE
SEATS ADJUSTABLE

ACCELERATION TIMES from Standstill

0-30 m.p.h.	3.8 sec.
0-40 m.p.h.	5.8 sec.
0-50 m.p.h.	8.0 sec.
0-60 m.p.h.	11.4 sec.
0-70 m.p.h.	15.5 sec.
0-80 m.p.h.	20.4 sec.
0-90 m.p.h.	28.3 sec.
0-100 m.p.h.	41.1 sec.
Standing quarter mile	18.4 sec.

ACCELERATION TIMES on Upper Ratios

	Top gear	3rd gear
10-30 m.p.h.	12.3 sec.	8.3 sec.
20-40 m.p.h.	10.3 sec.	7.4 sec.
30-50 m.p.h.	10.1 sec.	6.7 sec.
40-60 m.p.h.	11.3 sec.	6.5 sec.
50-70 m.p.h.	10.8 sec.	7.8 sec.
60-80 m.p.h.	10.7 sec.	9.0 sec.
70-90 m.p.h.	13.1 sec.	—
80-100 m.p.h.	20.1 sec.	—

BRAKES from 30 m.p.h.

0.99 g retardation (equivalent to 30½ ft. stopping distance) with 130 lb. pedal pressure.
0.90 g retardation (equivalent to 33½ ft. stopping distance) with 100 lb. pedal pressure.
0.65 g retardation (equivalent to 46 ft. stopping distance) with 75 lb. pedal pressure.
0.47 g retardation (equivalent to 64 ft. stopping distance) with 50 lb. pedal pressure.
0.27 g retardation (equivalent to 111 ft. stopping distance) with 25 lb. pedal pressure.

HILL CLIMBING at sustained steady speeds

Max. gradient on top gear	1 in 9.7 (Tapley 230 lb./ton)
Max. gradient on 3rd gear	1 in 6.2 (Tapley 355 lb./ton)
Max. gradient on 2nd gear	1 in 3.9 (Tapley 560 lb./ton)

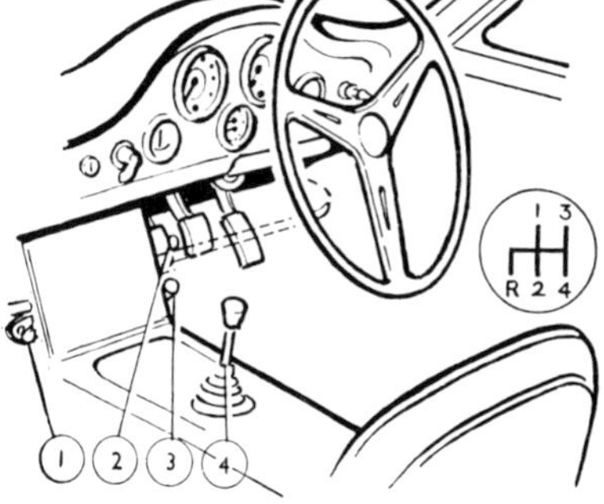
1 3
R 2 4
1
2
3
4

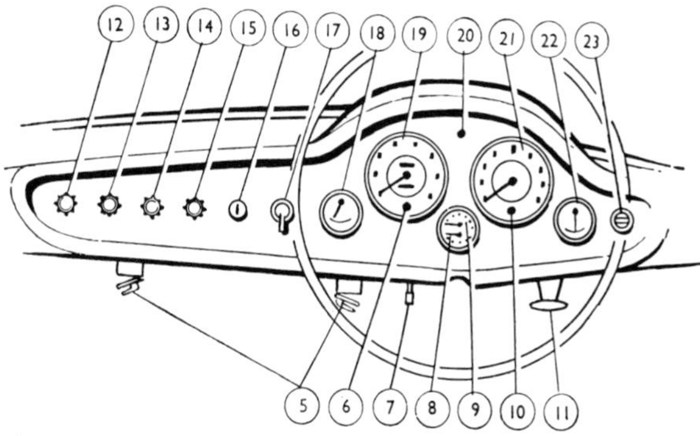
12 13 14 15 16 17 18 19 20 21 22 23
5 6 7 8 9 10 11

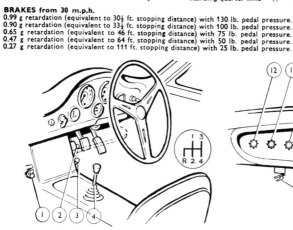

1. Heater temperature control. 2. Windscreen washer button. 3. Headlamp dipswitch. 4. Gear lever. 5. Heater air outlet shutters. 6. High beam indicator lamp. 7. Trip re-setting knob. 8. Water thermometer. 9. Oil pressure gauge. 10. Dynamo charge warning lamp. 11. Handbrake. 12. Choke control. 13. Heater fan switch. 14. Windscreen wipers switch. 15. Lights, panel and interior lights switch. 16. Ignition and starter switch. 17. Direction indicator switch. 18. Fuel contents gauge. 19. Speedometer. 20. Direction indicator warning light. 21. Rev. counter. 22. Ammeter. 23. Horn switch and headlamp flasher.

The Lotus Elite

A Very Small Car Offering Speed, Comfort and Controllability

WHEREAS a great many manufacturers of touring cars have also built racing models, the Lotus organization is altogether unusual in having concentrated upon racing and other forms of competitive motoring for many years before ever attempting to build cars for everyday road use. Even this first "utilitarian" Lotus model, which made its début at Earls Court as a prototype in October, 1957, has been tested-out with tuned engines in a wide variety of races before being put into production as a fully equipped and silenced car for daily business or pleasure motoring. This racing background has produced a car which is right out of the ordinary and, although expensive, a most attractive vehicle.

Throughout the history of the Lotus organization, Colin Chapman has concentrated on producing cars of low weight and wind resistance which had high standards of controllability, so that quite a moderate amount of engine power would provide very high speeds around a racing circuit or from point to point. Without pretending to be very quiet or very weatherproof, many Lotus two-seaters which were built for sports car racing during the past five years proved surprisingly comfortable, and the Elite has not needed to differ appreciably from them in dimensions, suspension layout or power unit type. One big innovation on the coupé model is that, instead of using a multi-tube chassis clothed in metal body panels, it has a chassisless "hull" of polyester resin plastics and glass fibre which combines strength with lightness, smooth contours and quiet, weatherproof comfort.

Fundamental to appreciation of the Lotus Elite is the concept that, although many people require their cars to be fast, comfortable and safe, bigness is no virtue and can, in fact, be a serious disadvantage. The Elite is no larger than its designers have thought necessary for the transportation of two people and their luggage at speeds up to 110 m.p.h. or so, with uncramped elbow room and with racing car standards of road holding. It is a technical tour-de-force to have produced a comfortable, fully equipped car which does this very well indeed for a kerb weight of 13¼ cwt., using a single-carburetter 1,216 c.c. Coventry Climax engine which is working very well within its known limits.

Economy of fuel cannot be regarded as of prime importance for a car costing over £1,900, but the features which have given the Elite its performance have also produced such outstanding petrol consumption figures as 52½ m.p.g. at a steady 50 m.p.h. and 29½ m.p.g. at a steady 100 m.p.h., the light

and compact 6½-gallon fuel tank giving a reasonably wide cruising range at 34.1 m.p.g. overall consumption.

Easier to enter than most other very low-built cars, the Elite is certainly a very comfortable two-seater. Individual seats upholstered in leathercloth of high quality have high backrests shaped to provide a reasonable amount of lateral support without making them hard to enter, and sponge rubber cushioning is supported on elastic webbing cross straps. There is plenty of room for long legs and for a straight-arm driving position, quite sufficient headroom, and as much elbow room as could be wished above the central transmission tunnel and in the hollowed-out doors.

Among the few points at which metal is used invisibly to reinforce the body structure is around the windscreen, so that the roof pillars are not so thick as to arouse serious criticism, but the steeply raked windscreen is rather shallow and, whilst a 6-foot-tall driver was exactly satisfied with the seat height, those of greater stature found that upward and forward vision was limited, whereas short drivers would prefer a raised seat to improve vision over the steering wheel rim and the hooded instrument panel.

Early examples of this model which have been seen in races were rather austerely furnished, but the interior trim of current production Elites (the hull of our test car was one which had been moulded by the Plastics Division of Bristol Aircraft) was of very pleasing quality. Inside and out, a discreet touch from the hands of professional stylists has combined neat appearance with honest functional merit. Racing ancestry is recalled by the lightweight wood-rim steering wheel and by the full set of clear, circular-dial instruments, but the touring motorist finds deep and well-fitting pile

carpets with rubber inserts, an interior lamp with door-operated switches, variable-brightness instrument lighting, twin windscreen wipers, capacious door pockets, parcel shelves and turn indicators with a time switch to cancel them. Optional extras which were built into our test model comprised a heater and screen demister taking fresh air from an intake on top of the scuttle, and a toe-operated pair of windscreen washing sprays.

Docile Power

Developing 75 b.h.p. in this single-carburetter form as compared with 98-100 b.h.p. when tuned for competitions (with higher compression ratio, twin carburetters, different camshaft and other modifications) the Coventry Climax engine is a potent performer yet very docile. Prompt in starting from cold, it is perfectly happy down to 20 m.p.h. or less in top gear (recording acceleration times from 10 m.p.h. in this ratio seemed no more than mildly cruel) yet gave a timed maximum speed of 111.8 m.p.h. (as the mean of runs in opposite directions) after a rather limited amount of running-in. As the top gear acceleration times recorded on the data page make clear, this engine pulls well at speeds as low as 1,000 r.p.m., but its best torque is not felt until 3,500 r.p.m. is approached, the peak of the power curve is at 6,100 r.p.m., and the red sector on the rev. counter dial starts at a speed of 6,500 r.p.m. which was only just reached in top gear during our timed runs on level road. This is not a silent engine mechanically when the bonnet is open, but a lot of felt and foamed plastic keeps the car interior reasonably quiet, and twin silencers subdue the exhaust note with a completeness which permits unhesitating use of full power on the road at almost any time and place.

Our test car was equipped with a

In Brief

Price with 4.22 axle £1,387 plus purchase tax £579 0s. 10d. equals £1,966 0s. 10d.
Price with 4.55 axle ratio (including purchase tax) £1,949 0s. 10d.

Capacity	..	1,216 c.c.
Unladen kerb weight	..	13¼ cwt.

Acceleration:
20-40 m.p.h. in top gear..   10.3 sec.
0-50 m.p.h. through gears   8.0 sec.
Maximum direct top gear gradient:
  1 in 9.7
Maximum speed   ..   111.8 m.p.h.
"Maximile" speed   ..   102.3 m.p.h.
Touring fuel consumption .. 40.5 m.p.g.
Gearing: 16.85 m.p.h. in top gear at 1,000 r.p.m.: 38.6 m.p.h. at 1,000 ft./min. piston speed.

The low, sleek Elite has no cooling apertures to mar its frontal streamlining, even the radiator air intake being used to house the number plate. A hinged panel gives access to the engine bay in which almost every item is easy to reach.

The Lotus Elite

4.22/1 rear axle ratio which is listed as one of several extra-cost alternatives to 4.55/1 gearing. Whilst the latter may be suitable for rallies or for races on slow circuits, the easy and economical speed provided by higher gearing on our test car was something which we would not have wished to sacrifice in order to gain even livelier acceleration in top gear. The four-speed gearbox with central remote control was by no means the car's best feature, third being a good ratio with its maximum of just over 80 m.p.h. but second (in which maximum r.p.m. represented a bare 50 m.p.h.) low enough to be used as a starting-from-rest gear on many occasions: extra running-in would no doubt loosen up a gear-change which was rather stiff, first gear being distinctly awkward to find with the car at rest.

Even with its stiff gearbox and an engine which had enjoyed little running-in, the Lotus Elite can produce very rapid acceleration indeed, from a stand-still or for overtaking from any speed in the range. On a car as light as this our usual test load of two men and their

test instruments is a substantial burden, but such figures as 0 to 60 m.p.h. in 11.4 sec., 0 to 100 m.p.h. in 41.1 sec., and 60 m.p.h. to 80 m.p.h. in 10.7 sec., using top gear or 9.0 sec. using third gear, are outstandingly good for so compact and comfortable a closed car.

Silence cannot be claimed for the body interior, there being various resonances from power unit, transmission and road surface which still escape the silencing and sound insulating measures, but the noise which is heard is neither persistent nor ever unduly loud. With the Chapman strut-type independent rear-wheel suspension there are no splined driving shafts to cause transmission snatch, but a vague thud was heard from the hull-mounted final drive unit as the clutch was engaged after changes of gear. Subconsciously, a driver slightly adjusts the throttle opening one way or the other and avoids cruising at the more audible combinations of speed and load, a critical member of our staff who drove and rode more than 800 miles in the Lotus Elite within a 48-hour period being less tired than he would have expected after similarly

intensive motoring in almost any other car. The body is well ventilated, with a fresh air heater and screen demister, hinged ventilator flaps of safety glass which really do their intended job, and framed side windows of transparent plastic which lift out completely when a catch is released and can be stowed safely in pockets behind the seats. Thanks to quite exceptionally smooth air flow around the bodywork, removal of the side windows does not result in great noise, draughtiness or appreciable entry of rain during fast driving.

Smooth Riding

Moderately firm springing has been combined with very low unsprung weights to make this car ride exceptionally well over almost any surface. Farm tracks do not worry it (there is reasonable ground clearance despite very low overall height) and the irregularities of fast main roads are ironed out excellently, the shock-free and completely flat ride being very pleasing to passengers. Occasional "bottoming" of the rear springs did, however, raise doubts as to whether the range of spring travel would prove entirely adequate for fast Continental

Two comfortable seats are divided by a high transmission tunnel from which projects the central gear lever. Instruments and fittings are to a keen driver's liking. The seats can be tipped forward to give access to the detachable moulding concealing the spare wheel, above which is a useful shelf between the suspension mounting "domes."

The neat lines of the Elite are evident from any viewpoint; broad but shallow bumpers surround the tail. Although spare wheel and petrol tank protrude into the boot there is reasonably good luggage room.

motoring with the sensibly shaped rear locker really full of luggage.

Extreme sensitivity of the steering and outstandingly good wheel adhesion are the key to the Elite's handling qualities. Collecting it from the factory with incorrectly set tyre pressures, it was brought home to us how sensitive it is to having the correct amount of air in each Firestone 4.80-15 Nylon Sport tyre, and some experiment led to us going somewhat beyond the recommended 20% front/rear pressure difference to use 19 lb. and 25 lb. pressure at front and rear respectively for most motoring. Too soft rear tyres can make the car hesitant directionally when it is being put into a corner or straightened out, although even then it is stable on the straight or when actually cornering. Given the right balance of tyre pressures, it becomes a car which, when tested on the circular steering pad, turns at the same radius for any given steering wheel deflection regardless of car speed, showing neither under- nor over-steer. On the road, rack and pinion steering which feels utterly positive (in spite of a rubber-cushioned universal joint in the steering column which prevents excessive kick-back on rough going) lets the car be steered precisely with incredibly little movement or effort, and even on slippery wet roads remarkably high cornering speeds are needed to provoke a gradual loss of adhesion.

Very smooth control of the car's speed is provided by Girling disc brakes, those at the rear being mounted inboard to save unsprung weight. No brake servo has been thought necessary on such a light car, and these brakes ask for high enough pedal pressures before the wheels will lock to ensure virtual immunity from skidding, but the driver soon becomes supremely confident of their performance on either wet or dry roads, from high speeds or around town. The convenient pull-out handbrake is reasonably powerful, although it would not be safe to leave the car parked on a gradient steeper than 1 in 5.

When a car as unusual as the Lotus Elite comes for test, there is far more which could be said than can be squeezed into four pages. Speed, controllability in all conditions and comfort in all its aspects make this compact two-seat coupé an immensely desirable property for anyone who wants to enjoy covering big daily mileages: expensive in relation to its size and weight, although realistically priced in relation to what it will do and how it does it, the Elite is a perfectly docile runabout for shopping errands and its buyer has no need to budget for a hack "second car" as well as this mettlesome thoroughbred.

The World Copyright of this article and illustrations is strictly reserved.
© Temple Press Limited, 1960

Specification

Engine
Cylinders	4
Bore	76.2 mm.
Stroke	66.6 mm.
Cubic capacity	1,216 c.c.
Piston area	28.2 sq. in.
Valves	Single chain-driven overhead camshaft
Compression ratio	10/1
	(Optional 11/1 in stage 3 tune)
Carburetter	One S.U. type H4 horizontal
Fuel pump	AC mechanical
Ignition timing control	Centrifugal
Oil filter	Full-flow
Max. power (gross)	80 b.h.p. (75 b.h.p. net)
at	6,100 r.p.m.
Piston speed at max. b.h.p.	2,660 ft./min.

Transmission (as tested)
Clutch	Borg & Beck 8-in. s.d.p.
Top gear (s/m)	4.22
3rd gear (s/m)	5.57
2nd gear (s/m)	9.28
1st gear	15.49
Reverse	15.49

(Standard final drive ratio is 4.55, with options of 3.7, 4.22 as on test model, or 4.875.)
Propeller shaft	Hardy Spicer open shaft to sprung final drive unit.
Final drive	Hypoid bevel
Top gear m.p.h. at 1,000 r.p.m.	16.85
Top gear m.p.h. at 1,000 ft./min. piston speed	38.6

Chassis
Brakes	Girling hydraulic disc type, inboard mounted at rear.
Brake/disc diameters	9¼ in.
Friction areas	26.88 sq. in. of lining working on approx. 320 sq. in. rubbed area of discs.

Suspension:
Front: i.f.s. by transverse wishbones, anti-roll torsion bar, and coil springs mounted on Armstrong telescopic dampers.
Rear: Chapman strut-type i.r.s. (Coil springs on Armstrong telescopic damper struts, unsplined double-jointed driving shafts and trailing radius arms.)
Steering gear	Alford & Alder rack and pinion.

Tyres: Firestone nylon high-performance 4.80-15 tubed 4-ply.

Coachwork and Equipment

Starting handle	None
Battery mounting	In boot
Jack	Lazy-tongs type
Jacking points	2 points, one under each side of body
Standard Tool kit:	Jack and handle, 3 spanners, adjustable spanner, sparking plug spanner, pliers, screwdriver, copper wheel nut hammer.
Exterior lights:	2 headlamps (Lucas 7-in. "Le Mans"), 2 sidelamps, 2 stop/tail lamps. 2 number plate lamps.
Number of electrical fuses	1 plus 1 circuit breaker in lighting switch.
Direction indicators	Amber flashers with self-cancelling time switch
Windscreen wipers	Lucas two-speed self parking, with twin blades.
Windscreen washers	Optional extra (Tudor toe-operated)
Sun visors	None
Instruments:	Speedometer with total and decimal trip distance recorders, rev. counter, oil pressure gauge, coolant thermometer, ammeter, fuel contents gauge.
Warning lights	Dynamo charge, headlamp main beam, turn indicators

Locks:	
With ignition key	Ignition/starter switch, driver's door, luggage locker
With other keys	None
Glove lockers	None
Map pockets	Two inside doors
Parcel shelves	One behind seats, shelves below facia integral with ducts for optional heater
Ashtrays	None
Cigar lighters	None
Interior lights	One in roof with courtesy switches
Interior heater	Optional extra Smiths
Car radio	None offered
Extras available:	Interior heater, windscreen washers, special colours, seat belts, Lotus stage 2 or stage 3 engine tuning modifications, close-ratio gears, and other racing equipment.
Upholstery material	Leathercloth
Floor covering	Carpet
Exterior colours standardized	3 (Any other colour at £35 extra)
Alternative body styles	None

Maintenance

Sump	8 pints, S.A.E. 20 winter, S.A.E. 30 summer
Gearbox	4½ pints, S.A.E. 40 winter, S.A.E. 50 summer
Rear axle	1¾ pints, S.A.E. 90 hypoid gear oil
Steering gear lubricant	grease
Cooling system capacity	12 pints (1 drain plug)
Chassis lubrication	By grease gun every 1,500 miles to 14 points
Ignition timing	2°-3° before t.d.c. static
Contact-breaker gap	0.014-0.016 in.
Sparking plug type	Champion N3
Sparking plug gap	0.018 in.

Valve timing	Inlet opens 12° before t.d.c. and closes 56° after b.d.c.; Exhaust opens 56° before b.d.c. and closes 12° after t.d.c.
Tappet clearances (Cold)	Inlet 0.006 in. Exhaust 0.008 in.
Front wheel toe-in	$\frac{1}{16}$ in. to $\frac{1}{8}$ in.
Camber angle	1¼° to 1½°
Castor angle	7°
Steering swivel pin inclination	9°
Tyre pressures	Front 19 lb. Rear 23 lb. (see text) Raise pressures by 7 lb. for very fast driving.
Brake fluid	Girling crimson
Battery type and capacity	12 volt, 57 amp. hr.
Miscellaneous	Car should be jacked up ONLY by jacking points provided.

THE LOTUS SUPER SEVEN

WITH COSWORTH-FORD CLASSIC ENGINE

THERE is a very real demand for a sports car which can be used on the road all the week and compete with success in club races at week-ends. The typical sports car of commerce is too heavy and too expensive and it generally has too much comfort and not enough roadholding. Now, I have discovered a really "hairy" sports car which meets all the requirements, and I have just spent

middle ranges, with 62 b.h.p. at 4,000 r.p.m. and 77 b.h.p. at 5,000 r.p.m.

This Cosworth-Ford unit costs only £182 complete. The tubular chassis and aluminium body assembly works out at £260 and the remaining components required total £157. Thus, the cost of assembling a Lotus Super Seven is £599. Provided that certain conditions are complied with, and that a genuine amateur

ing is employed. At the rear, cost considerations have dictated the use of a proprietary hypoid rear axle. It is located by tubular trailing arms at the top on either side, and a single "A" bracket beneath the differential, which also gives lateral location. The springs are helical, and the dampers are telescopic all round.

Drum-type brakes and bolt-on wheels have been chosen for reasons of cost,

a most exciting week of Le Mans motoring.

The Lotus Super Seven is descended from the Seven which all enthusiasts know so well, but it has been absolutely transformed by a new and much more powerful engine. Briefly, the unit is a Cosworth-tuned version of the 1,340 c.c. Ford Classic 109E. Fitted with two twin-choke Weber carburetters, this engine develops 83 b.h.p. at 6,000 r.p.m. and is still producing 82 b.h.p. at 6,500 r.p.m., which is the safe limit as at present developed. Much more important, however, is its immense "punch" in the

puts the car together himself, H.M. Customs and Excise, by a special concession, will levy no purchase tax.

A tubular space frame is the basis of the car, the floor panels and prop-shaft tunnel being also stressed members. The other body panels are secured by Dzus fasteners, rendering accessibility first class. The driver and passenger really sit "on the deck" with a minimum of seat padding.

The front suspension is by wishbones and helical springs, the anti-roll torsion bar also acting as the forward halves of the top members. Rack and pinion steer-

but are entirely adequate. A spare wheel and petrol tank behind the rear axle serve to balance the engine which is well forward, thus giving a high polar moment of inertia. The test car had close-ratio gears in its Ford box, which would cost £35 extra.

No attempt has been made to streamline the car. The screen is uncompromisingly flat and the lamps project. Some rather pleasant flared front mudguards do keep the mud off the screen, which the previous cycle-types did not, but they add a little more to the wind resistance. By stripping the screen, lamps

64

and mudguards off the car, another 12 m.p.h. or so might be available, but on the short British circuits where club races are run, this is not of great importance.

The Super Seven is so low that one sometimes trips over it in the dark. It is easy to enter though slightly harder to leave, and the weather protection is adequate for driving without goggles. There were no sidescreens on the test car and I did not use the hood, though it seemed practical if a little "blind".

On moving off, it is at once obvious that the acceleration is phenomenally good. If you keep away from M1 you can beat any sports car short of the "E"-Type category. Acceleration from 0 to 60 m.p.h. in 7.6 secs. or a standing quarter-mile in 16.1 secs. are indications of the really immense performance of this red hot little machine.

With a weight of only 8¼ cwt. and an 83 b.h.p. engine with tremendous torque, the car fairly shoots forward on any gear. Even on top gear, the Lotus will leap away up quite a steep hill and will soon be travelling at over 90 m.p.h.

I was able to achieve a timed 100 m.p.h., which is equivalent to 6,200 r.p.m. on the rev. counter. This speed can be obtained after quite a short run, but even on a long straight it seems about the limit. One imagines that the air is really piling up at this speed, so I did not bother to make numerous runs over the timed stretch as the ultimate maximum is not of prime importance.

Roadholding presents quite a problem with so light a car, for the back axle forms a large lump of unsprung weight. Let me say, straight away, that the cornering power is phenomenally high on a smooth surface, and much better than would be expected over bumps. The axle does hop on occasion, of course, but the effect on the line which the driver is following is remarkably little. After some practice, one can do almost anything with the car, and there is enough power for a lot of fun on the bends.

The natural characteristic is an understeering one but a full drift can be

As an ordinary road car, the Super Seven is the greatest possible fun. Of course, one takes a mackintosh along in case it rains, but the mud-in-your-eye of the old cycle guards has been avoided. The driver and passenger are in fact quite well protected and there is ample luggage space for a week-end for two. An

". . . enough power for a lot of fun on the bends"

electric fan may be turned on to keep the radiator cool in traffic and the sparking plugs do not soot or oil up in London. This machine is fairly stark, but it is quite practicable as an everyday business hack.

I covered a large mileage during my

test, driving the Lotus really hard and enjoying it to the full. One or two small parts needed securing from time to time, but absolutely nothing went wrong with any of the major components. I formed the opinion that this is a tough, sturdy little car, and that if it were conscientiously assembled by a careful amateur,

using plenty of lock nuts, split pins and so forth, it would be exceptionally reliable. Modern short cuts in assembly are wonderful, but for a "hairy" sports car there is still a lot to be said for the old engineering methods of keeping things secure.

There is little that one can criticize in this car, for it achieves so much more than one would believe possible. For touring, the petrol tank is too small and one needs a gauge. For racing, I would be happier with a safety catch or a strap on the bonnet as the clips sometimes rattle loose. In general, though, this is a thoroughly practical car that has improved steadily, as a result of competition experience, with successive models.

The Lotus Seven is not all that comfortable and it definitely is not quiet. Furthermore, you need an extra pullover or two when the nights are cold. If you mind about this sort of thing, this car is too good for you, and you had better buy the dreary conveyance which you deserve. If you want shattering acceleration, the right sort of handling and a jolly good chance of passing the chequered flag while it is waving, the Lotus is your car. The Seven has always been fun, but with this new Cosworth-Ford engine it is a real ball of fire. I wish I could think of a good excuse to borrow it again! For further details, apply to Lotus Components, Ltd., Delamere Road, Cheshunt, Herts.

INSTRUMENTS *include (left to right) ammeter, speedometer, oil-pressure gauge, 8,000 r.p.m. rev. counter and water temperature gauge. There is no fuel gauge, but there is plenty of room to fit one if required for, say, touring purposes.*

achieved by the application of maximum engine power. On wet roads, the tail does become more lively, and care must be taken not to lock the front wheels when braking. On dry roads, the brakes can cope well with the performance of the car.

SPECIFICATION AND PERFORMANCE DATA

Car Tested: Lotus Super Seven sports two-seater. Price in component form, £599; close-ratio gears £35 extra (see text).

Engine: Four-cylinders, 80.96 mm. x 65.07 mm. (1,340 c.c.). Pushrod-operated overhead valves. Compression ratio, 9.5 to 1; 83 b.h.p. at 6,000 r.p.m. Two twin-choke Weber carburetters. Coil and distributor ignition.

Transmission: Single dry-plate clutch. Four-speed gearbox with central remote control; ratios. 4.1, 5.248, 6.953 and 11.959 to 1. Open propeller shaft. Hypoid rear axle.

Chassis: Tubular space frame. Independent front suspension by wishbones and helical springs with anti-roll bar. Rack and pinion steering. Rear axle on helical springs with trailing arms and central "A" bracket. Hydraulic brakes in 8 ins. x 1¼ ins. drums (front) and 7 ins. x 1¼ ins. drums (rear). Bolt-on disc wheels fitted 5.20-13 ins tyres.

Equipment: Twelve-volt lighting and starting. Speedometer, rev. counter, oil pressure and temperature gauges. Ammeter. Windscreen wipers.

Dimensions: Wheelbase, 7 ft. 4 ins. Track, 4 ft. ½ in. Overall length, 11 ft. Width, 4 ft. 10½ ins. Turning circle, 28 ft. Weight, 8 cwt. 64 lbs.

Performance: Maximum speed, 100 m.p.h. Speeds in gears: 3rd, 80 m.p.h.; 2nd, 61 m.p.h.; 1st, 37 m.p.h. Standing quarter-mile, 16.1 secs. Acceleration, 0-30 m.p.h., 2.8 secs.; 0-50 m.p.h., 5.8 secs.; 0-60 m.p.h., 7.6 secs.; 0-80 m.p.h., 14.4 secs.

Fuel Consumption: 28 m.p.g.

The Author wishes to thank Haymarket Magazines Ltd. (The Motor), Autosport and the proprietors of Sports Cars Illustrated for permission to reproduce these original Road Test Reports

by David Phipps

▶ After building technically-advanced front-engined cars for more than ten years, Colin Chapman has at last gone over to a rear-engined layout on his Formula Junior Lotus. There is nothing particularly novel about the design — which suggests that this car could be a winner right from the start, with no need for the painful development period which innovations often require — and it is in fact one of the simplest and neatest inspired by the new formula.

Lotus's reasons for adopting the rear-engine scheme are explored in detail in the Formula 1 car review on the next two pages, so suffice it to say that the changeover has been made without substantially changing either weight distribution or roadholding. This I discovered when Colin Chapman invited me to Goodwood to try the prototype during a testing session.

Colin himself, Development Director Mike Costin and Team Lotus driver Alan Stacey all tried the car during the morning, experimenting with a variety of anti-roll bars, shock absorber settings and tire pressures, and when all three seemed fairly satisfied I was allowed to do a few laps to see how the first rear-engined Lotus behaved.

The chief purpose of the outing to Goodwood was to

for Lavant, going through the first part of the corner at about 4000 rpm and reaching 6000 rpm soon after the left-hand kink on the straight. Only very gentle braking was needed for Woodcote, where a large puddle on the exit was a little disconcerting, and after the shift down into third for the Chicane the power could be put on very early, with the tail sliding only a little toward the barricade and needing very little correction.

6000 rpm came up in third by the beginning of the pits, and just under 6000 in top matched my cutoff point for Madgwick. The car was very little affected by the bump in the middle of this two-part corner and was soon up to 5000 rpm again on the exit from the second part. It reached 6000 just before Fordwater and stayed above 5000 rpm all the way to St. Marys, where it seemed as steady as a rock despite the adverse camber, emerging from the left-hander at about 4000 rpm and accelerating hard down the dip toward Lavant.

The roadholding can only be described as extremely good. When the tail slides out, in the dry at least, there doesn't seem to be any need for sudden correction, and it's possible to go through sharper corners pretending to be "doing a

TRACK REPORT LOTUS FORMULA

test roadholding and handling characteristics rather than to set up lap records, so a limit of 6000 rpm was set for the moderately-tuned Ford 105E engine. As a "Brands Hatch" axle ratio (4.7 to 1) was fitted I was warned that this would mean backing off slightly on Lavant Straight and perhaps at Fordwater.

With a total length of 133 inches and an overall height of only 34½ inches the Lotus is one of the smallest Formula Junior cars, but one of the advantages of mounting the engine at the rear is that ample space is left for the driver. My 6 feet 4 inches fitted in quite easily fore and aft, with plenty of room both at shoulder level and around the pedals. As Colin Chapman and Alan Stacey also drove the car in exactly the same trim the seating position is obviously very versatile.

The control layout is conventional, with the small, leather-covered steering wheel almost at arm's length but well away from the instrument panel, the pedals well-spaced and the short, Renault Dauphine gear-lever conveniently placed on the left.

The ignition switch is on the right, with the starter button below it, but to save the battery I was push-started in second gear. The engine fired immediately and the car accelerated away briskly, with the needle of the Speedwell electronic tach swinging 'round extremely smoothly and dropping back with never a waver after the shift up into third, and then top.

The gearshift — with first and second on the right, third and top on the left — proved to be very pleasant, though after the first lap I was only changing down to third for Lavant Corner and the Chicane, and doing the rest in top. Later I found that it wasn't even necessary to shift down

Jack Brabham" without any fears of losing it altogether. Roll is scarcely apparent, except perhaps at the Chicane, though at Madgwick and Fordwater the scenery does seem to be leaning over somewhat. With a very low center of gravity and a fairly hefty anti-roll bar one would hardly expect body roll of sedan proportions, however.

As it has been "built heavy" to comply with the weight limit regulations, the Formula Junior Lotus looks and feels very strong. Just to prove this point Colin Chapman jumped up and down on the radiator. "It's not every car you can do that on", he said. But even though it's thus considerably heavier than is really necessary, from a design point of view, it accelerates very rapidly — particularly in the upper speed range where the small frontal area begins to pay dividends.

During my brief run the brakes seemed rather fierce, but the system is due for slight modification before a full production specification is drafted. Alan Stacey summed up the braking, when asked if he thought there was too much on the front or too much on the rear, by saying briefly, "Just too much". The occasion on which I needed the brakes most was when I came through Fordwater to see a vast, black, shapeless mass extending right across the track. As I slowed the mass suddenly dispersed, as hundreds of crows took off and wheeled away to the south.

Formula Junior is obviously going to have a big appeal for young — and not so young — drivers, and the Lotus will certainly be among the chief contenders for honors in this category. It's a most enjoyable car to drive, and with its quick, precise steering seems extremely controllable and free from any kind of vice. But the most surprising thing about my run is that I was never really aware that it was a rear-engined car.

—*D.P.*

JUNIOR

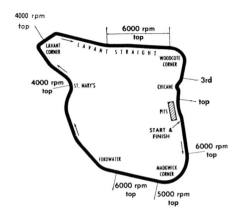

4000 rpm top

6000 rpm top

LAVANT CORNER

LAVANT STRAIGHT

WOODCOTE CORNER

3rd

4000 rpm top

ST. MARY'S

CHICANE

top

PITS

START & FINISH

6000 rpm top

FORDWATER

MADGWICK CORNER

6000 rpm top

5000 rpm top

In top gear, and traveling fairly fast, the Lotus F. Jr. goes through Woodcote corner on England's Goodwood circuit in a display of good handling.

The new Lotus is powered by a Ford 105E engine. Small, short stroke, Anglia power plant is ideally suited for F. Jr. with a strong lower end design.

35

Appreciation and thanks

In writing a book of this type, one is dependent on the goodwill and direct assistance of numerous authorities and friends. I have partially acknowledged my debt in the appropriate section at the beginning of the book, to which I would like to add special thanks for help with material to illustrate the text to:

Autosport Magazine
Mike Costin
Geoffrey Goddard
Ron Hickman
Rob Iles and Mike Pereira
of Haynes Publishing Group
Ian McLeod
David Phipps

Cyril Posthumus
Jon Pressnell and Haymarket Publishing Ltd.
Malcolm Ricketts
Eddie Sear
Alan Smith
Vito Witting da Prato

Photographs frequently come down over the years in a form which makes it difficult or impossible to accurately trace their origin. If there are within these pages any such unacknowledged illustrations, I extend my apologies and thanks to the photographer or artist concerned.

Author's note

COLIN CHAPMAN'S LOTUS is divided into smaller sections within each main Chapter. The Chapter and sub-divisions are listed in the Contents Section on pages 5 and 6 for general guidance. The Index provides detailed references to most personal names, car types and models, locations, etc. within the text.

The Section covering LOTUS indicates the precise location of information about each model within and without the appropriate "dedicated" section to supplement the main Contents.

For reasons which it is hoped will be understood by the reader the Index contains no references to either ACBC or the Author.

Index